Wasn't That a Time?

Wasn't That a Time?
Growing up Radical and Red in America

Robert Schrank

The MIT Press
Cambridge, Massachusetts
London, England

This book was set in Sabon by Northeastern Graphic Services, Inc.

Printed and bound in the United States of America.

Library of Congress Cataloging-in-Publication Data

Schrank, Robert.
    Wasn't that a time? : growing up radical and red in America / Robert Schrank.
        p.   cm.
    Includes bibliographical references and index.
    ISBN 0-262-19389-2 (hbk. : alk. paper)
    1. Schrank, Robert.   2. Socialists—United States—Biography.
3. Radicals—United States—Biography.   4. Labor movement—United States—History—20th century.   5. Working class—United States—Political activity.   I. Title.
HX84.S42A3   1998
335'.0092—dc21
    [B]   98-9714
                                                                    CIP

Many years ago as we sailed around in the Great South Bay of Long
Island Sound, Herb encouraged me to write about my childhood
among German socialists and anarchists and my work in politics and
the labor movement. Well, Herb, here it is. I wish you'd been around
to guide me through it.

Contents

Acknowledgments

I would prefer to says thanks in person to the various people who have encouraged me over the years to write this book—and to go on with it when the going got rough. As that is not feasible, I want, as the next best thing, to thank them here. Shoshana Zuboff assured me that it was a project worth undertaking, while Kate Abel and Bob Martin kindly looked at the earliest drafts. Leonard Wolf also read an early draft and made useful suggestions for tightening up the story. Bernard Lefkowitz kept me going when I hit that writer's time of questioning the worth of the endeavor, while Stanley Aronowitz urged me to continue because there wasn't another book like it. Last, but not at all least, my deepest gratitude goes to editor Roberta Clark, who not only made numerous valuable suggestions for improving the narrative structure but also kept a persistent cool when faced with my defense of certain "precious sentences."

I reserve a whole separate category of affectionate and loving thanks for my dear wife, Kathy Gunderson. From the time of my first ruminations about the book to the end, she not only listened patiently but repeatedly reminded me to "just write it down." Without her the book would never have been published.

Thank you all.

Introduction

I was born two weeks before the Bolshevik Revolution into a immigrant family that was part of New York's large German socialist community. The "Ten Days That Shook the World" that October of 1917 raised their hopes for humanity's future to levels of joy Moses and the Israelites must have felt when they first glimpsed the Promised Land.

The vision of a new world my family shared with our fellow true believers was forged out of the fierce struggles of nineteenth- and early-twentieth-century workers against a rapacious capitalist system. Marxists and other socialists saw themselves as at war against the bourgeois enemy—the owners of the financial and industrial institutions that employed them and controlled their lives. They did not see industrialization and capitalist development as a result of the "invisible hand" of the marketplace but as a concerted effort by one class to deprive another of the rewards justly earned by its labor. My father and his friends never doubted that all the problems of hunger, disease, slum living, and ignorance were solely the result of the economic order. In a socialist society, these problems, and the class distinctions that engendered them, would disappear; the workers would all live happily ever after, sharing equally in the goods they produced.

When I was six my mother died, and my father, my two older sisters, and I became part of an extended socialist family. My father encouraged us to scorn such patriotic rituals as saluting the flag or singing the "Star Spangled Banner." He sent us to the Modern Sunday School he had helped found on the model of the schools established by the Spanish anarchist Francisco Ferrer. By the time my twelfth birthday arrived, the great Wall Street crash of 1929 had sent the country into a deep economic depression, reinforcing the Marxists' prediction that the twilight of capitalism was at hand.

Four years later the Nazi seizure of power and the eruption of rampant German nationalism tore apart our German socialist community. Father, who was a leader in this band of brothers, was fiercely anti-Nazi, but others thought Hitler's National Socialism might be good for German workers. After the war, confronted with the reality of the Holocaust and disgusted with the Stalinism of the Soviet Union, my father retreated into a private world and painted pictures.

During those first decades of my life, I was part of a world of true believers. From the time we got out of bed in the morning until we left the last meeting at night, we ate, slept, worked for, and dreamt of a socialist future. The revolution was our reason for being and was never far from our thoughts. The vision of a world free of the economic insecurities of the existing system anticipated many of the changes brought about by FDR's New Deal. To us, however, the new measures seemed but very dilute socialism. We were deeply involved with the union movement, which we saw as the most important element of the working-class struggle against capitalism. In the 1930s, with our Marxist analysis of how the economic system functioned, communists and assorted other radicals became leaders in the unions, though we rarely revealed our party affiliations.

American Communists in the 1930s labor movement lived in two worlds. We were for peace when it coincided with the interests of the Soviet Union and expended much—if not all—of our credibility trying to justify the Nazi-Soviet Pact.* We sent some of our best comrades off to fight and die in the Spanish Civil War. But with each new report of Stalin's paranoid purges of his imagined opposition, the dream of our earthly paradise slowly but surely died a little more. When the Soviets became our allies during World War II, our hopes that a democratic socialist society might emerge from the ashes of war rose again. But it never happened.

During World War II, I was elected New York State president of the Machinists' union and served on the Democratic National Labor Committee for the 1944 presidential election. After the war, although the Ma-

---

*In August of 1939, with Hitler poised to invade Poland, Stalin concluded a nonaggression pact with Hitler in exchange for a "sphere of influence" in eastern Poland, Finland, Estonia, and other areas.

chinists expelled me three times for "supporting Communist causes," the courts—in a landmark case (Schrank *vs.* Brown, New York State Supreme Court, 1949)—twice reinstated me. In the early anticommunist 1950s I was an international representative of the Mine Mill & Smelter Workers Union, which had been expelled from the CIO for being "Communist-dominated." I spent several strange months in Butte, Montana, in an effort to save Mine Mill from being taken over by the Steelworkers' union. By then, my day-to-day dealings with the working class had made me increasingly doubtful of Marx's prediction that the workers would, or could, lead us to the promised land of socialism.

This memoir, then, is in part the story of how the communist movement affected all phases of our lives: whom we slept with, whom we married, our appreciation of the arts and sciences, our ability to think critically, and everything that makes up the stuff of everyday life. Those of us who were part of that movement represented a cross-section of America. We were naive in our hopes and gullible in the way we hung onto our utopian dreams, refusing to acknowledge that the rottenness of the Soviet system had eaten away the nobility of the original vision.

Part of this story is also the cat-and-mouse game we played over the decades with the FBI of J. Edgar Hoover. I have been forced to conclude that in his overzealous—if not obsessive—pursuit of communists under every bed, Hoover was not always wrong.* There undoubtedly were Soviet spies in the United States, as well as Moscow gold supporting the American Communist party. But, except on foreign policy questions, the views we espoused on behalf of the workers in our day-to-day party activities were not so different from those of many other American progressives and liberals. Finally, however, the truth of the hellish nightmare of the Soviets' reign of terror against their own people could no longer be denied. In shock and disbelief, those of us who had supported the Soviet Union—not unlike the Germans who went along with Hitler—fell into a deep silence of shame.

Hopelessly blacklisted and deeply depressed, I began 1955 working for my old enemy, Corporate America. To my great surprise, I found that the world was not so clearly black and white as I had believed. I have written

---

*Under the Freedom of Information Act I obtained a copy of my 750-page FBI file; I occasionally refer to it for reference purposes.

this book, in part, to reconcile my youthful ideals with my later perspective on American society. I needed both to understand the good things we—socialists and communists and labor organizers—contributed to America and to acknowledge belatedly responsibility for our wrongheaded support of an inhumane regime. This memoir is the story of a journey through a movement that affected many lives, and of a deep personal crisis that led me to see the world in an entirely new light.

Like Grandma's old photographs and lace in the attic, memories of times gone by fade and become musty. Reconstituting them may be at best a dubious undertaking; to jog the memory is to ask it to imagine a little in order to remember. Does it matter whether things happened exactly as I report them here? I would hope not. When all is said and done, this remains but one person's memoir of events long past.

Prologue

When a man has come to the turnstiles of Night, all the creeds in the world seem to him wonderfully alike and colorless.
Rudyard Kipling

The year was 1960. I was 43 years old and dogged by the question of how best to end my life.

The oncoming train in the subway station was a temptation to end it all then and there. I had to push myself against the wall away from the tracks to defy the inner voice saying "Do it! One leap and this misery will end." I dared not look out a window from any height, because I wasn't sure I could control my urge to jump. I had turned off the car engine running in a closed garage only after realizing that I could not let my sister Alice be the one to find me. I carried a shotgun in the trunk of my car; I just needed to find the right place to use it.

My depression had come on slowly. Bit by bit, it seemed, the things that had excited me and brought me joy—family, a wife, and especially two fun-loving kids, making and listening to music, art, friends, politics, reading, tinkering with machines—all had become fearful, gray, tiresome, devoid of interest. Unable to generate any energy, my whole being felt comatose. Slowly a dark emptiness canceled out any hope for future happiness. Despairing that this demon would ever leave me, I decided that continuing in this miserable state was not worth the daily effort required just to stay alive.

Fiercely ingrained habit got me up every morning to go to work, but I was as close to being a robot as is humanly possible. My clothes hung on me like a scarecrow's. All my interest in food, drink, and sex had vanished.

I had moved away from my family and was living in a room bare of everything but a bed and a dresser—a monastery cell.

Among my family and friends at that time were many steeped in psychology, including my sister Alice, who was a therapist. After a good deal of her coaxing and cajoling and comments like "What have you got to lose? Surely you can't be any worse off than you are now," I grudgingly agreed to try therapy: "Oh, what the hell! So people will know I'm crazy. Who cares?" Alice's advice was to find someone "you like and you feel empathizes with you and isn't hung up on running you through his pet theory."

Two weeks later I was seeing Ralph Gundlach. He turned out to be a good teacher and became a dear friend. A tall, graying man who wore steel-rimmed glasses, he had twinkling eyes, a wry midwestern smile, and a helluva sense of humor. He had begun his working life in a Utah coal mine, became a psychology professor at the University of Washington, and was now practicing therapy in New York. Through my tears, I told him about the desperation I felt, and he listened without saying much. When I was leaving, he said, his arm around my shoulder, "Let me promise you only one thing. The condition you are in is temporary. It came on, and it will go away. We just have to get all your ghosts out of the closet and into the open air. Try to remember that they can only survive in dark corners of the soul, not in the light of day."

"Doc, if only I could be sure this living death would end, maybe I could accept it and try to get on with my life."

"It will. It will," he said, handing me an article: "Here, take this. Read it. It will help you see that your misery is not unique. Your kind of depression is more common than you think. Here are my phone numbers." He looked hard at me: "Before you consider doing anything stupid, call me first. Okay? Have we got a deal?"

I hesitated. Could I go through with this? But I liked him and didn't want to disappoint him, so I said I would try.

Finally, still standing in the office doorway, he said, "Therapy is like going to school. Our curriculum will be your life. What we learn about it will help us deal with the present."

Twice a week after that I showed up at Ralph's office and began to talk. Before many sessions had gone by I was trying to explain—through a torrent of tears—what had happened on that spring day in May of 1924.

1

At Home in the Bronx

In my youth the Van Nest neighborhood of the Bronx was a predominantly Italian enclave of one- and two-family houses set between Bronx Park and the New Haven Railroad tracks. It is one of those places lost in time. When I visit it today, the only sign of change I see is the replacement of the trolleys by buses.

My life did not begin there, but, in some ways, it ended there. In a twenty-four-hour period of May in 1924 the sunny world of a curly-headed six-year-old boy turned into a screaming nightmare. Over and over again in the years since then I have heard the echoes of that scream.

My family—Papa, Mutter, Alice (the oldest by five years), Hattie (next oldest, by three years), and me—was happy there, although times were tough. Papa had once worked as a presser in a men's garment factory, but not now. He was blacklisted in the industry because of his participation in the founding of the Amalgamated Clothing Workers' Union. In our community of German socialists and freethinkers, being blacklisted for union organizing was a badge of great honor, but for our family it was a terrible burden. In an effort to reduce expenses, we had moved to a two-family house on the north side of the Bronx Zoo. In exchange for our rent, Mutter and Papa served as caretakers for a dentist's office, building, and garden.

Sunday, May 11, 1924, was a bright spring morning. As we often did on Sunday, we excitedly helped Mutter put together a picnic lunch. As we got off the subway at Pelham Bay Park, we were hailed by many of the other German radical and socialist families who had arrived before us. On any given Sunday there might be forty to sixty people gathered at the picnic site—about twenty of them children. The adults would get busy setting out the food and installing the beer barrel, cooler, and ice that were hauled to the park by subway on the backs of strong men who prided themselves on their physical prowess.

We kids immediately made for the beach, though, in the cold May waters of the bay, we did more leaping around and shrieking than swimming. It wasn't long before we headed back to the picnic grounds to play games, eat, and play more games. In spite our strong desire to be American and play baseball, we played soccer, because our immigrant parents considered baseball a "schtupit game." The German adults considered many unfamiliar American things "schtupit." A regular source of embarrassment for the boys was the insistence of one rotund German mama that we play "a nice circle game." This usually involved being blindfolded and walking around the outside of the circle of seated picnickers while everyone sang

Grünes grass frisch ich habe	I have fresh green grass
unter meinen füßer.	under my feet
Dies wie den besten sind,	The one who is the best,
Dieser mußt ich kussen.	This one must I kiss.

When the blindfold came off you had to kiss the person in front of you, then run around the circle until you could jump in next to someone you liked. Then that person ran around, and so forth. The object of the game was to end up next to the person you most wanted to kiss. All the boys, of course, griped about "all that kissin', sissy shit."

After the games, there was more beer drinking and an endless round of singing. The adults never tired of singing the same old German and worker songs over and over. But finally the evening was over, and we returned home, tired and happy.

The next day started like every other day. Meine Mutter was up in the dark, standing at the stove stirring the oatmeal, fussing over Papa's lunch, and getting my older sisters and me ready for school. Before I ran out the door she pressed my curly head against her ample bosom and told me she wouldn't be home at lunchtime. Our neighbor would give me something to eat. The school was only a few blocks from our home, making it a nice walk home for lunch. I remember feeling somehow uneasy about my hug that morning. It was so intense.

I was in the first grade at P.S. 34, which was close to the Bronx Zoo. The path I took to get there crossed several backyards and some vacant lots that served as the neighborhood's dumping ground for old cars, appliances, and things the garbage trucks didn't pick up. I skipped off, making a running stop at the back of the ice wagon, knowing the iceman would shake his fist at me and yell, "You steala my ice, I killa you" if I found just a little piece that had fallen off the big chunks he delivered for the iceboxes in our neighborhood.

In 1924 the streets were shared by automobiles, horse-drawn wagons, pushcarts, and trolley cars. Peddlers hawked produce from their wagons, calling out "Hey, we got potatoes, fresh strawberries," and—like an operatic tenor—"ice-cold watermelons—sweet ice-cold water—melon. Come and get it." On such bright spring days I took my time meandering through the streets and rubbish-strewn lots. Up ahead, P.S. 34 loomed like a prison. It took a lot of willpower and fear of retribution to get me through those school doors. I would much rather have roamed about, watching the peddlers and their horses, fooling around with the junked cars, or escaping into the magic of the Bronx Zoo, where I could fantasize about living in the wild with the lions, elephants, and wildebeest.

Instead, sitting in the classroom with its rows of little desks screwed to the floor between the lockers on one side and the windows on the other, I spent most of the day dreaming about the wondrous things going on outside. Like other school days, that one ended with the three o'clock bell, as all four hundred of us flew out of the building like a flock of birds released from a cage.

Sometimes, walking home through the backyards, past the pigeon coops and under wash lines, we kids would build "hideouts" of junk and roast "mickeys"—sweet potatoes—over fires in the vacant lots. But not that day. Nor for many days to come.

Mutter wasn't there to greet me when I got home. There was no one but our neighbor repeating over and over again, "Bobbie, everything is all right. It'll be all right" and trying valiantly to hide her tears. Before supper time I usually ran to meet my father at the subway station. Papa, a tall, strongly built man, carried his pride in his posture. He would swing me through the air, give me a big hug, and start the game of "can you guess what's in which pocket?" Excitedly, I would dig my small hands through the pockets of his jacket, vest, pants until, with a triumphant "I found it!," I discovered what Papa always called a "good piece of chocolate."

But on that day, supper time came and there was no Papa at the station and no sisters or Mutter at home. There was only the neighbor saying, "Come eat with us. You'll like it." Shy and frightened, I declined and instead munched on a staple in our home—a hunk of black pumpernickel bread spread with salted goose fat. It grew dark, and still there was no sign of my family and no explanation of what was happening. My fears kept growing and growing, and Mrs. Neighbor kept saying over and over "Don't worry, everything will be all right."

Finally, late that night, the wreckage of my once-proud Papa stumbled through the door, alone. What could possibly have happened? I froze in fear. He sat down and hugged me to his chest, sobbing and saying nothing. When he tried to speak he was overcome by tears. He would mutter something, turn his face away from me, blow his nose, wipe the tears, and try again. Time passed. Papa was a good storyteller. He finally began to speak, making Mutter's sudden departure into a story about a "long, long trip she is taking to a far-off place. We really don't know if she will ever come home."

Holding me closely in his arms, he spent the night in his favorite Morris chair, sleeping little and saying nothing. In the morning I learned that my sisters Alice and Hattie were not home. His eyes swimming in a renewed stream of tears, Papa explained that they were staying with friends. As the day wore on, his grief became so overwhelming that I felt I should leave him alone, and I retreated to my little hut in the backyard.

Behind our two-family house was a long narrow yard that ended abruptly at a railroad embankment. At the foot of the embankment was an old shed that had once been a chicken coop. The roosting shelves, now covered with the dust of time and laced with cobwebs, held old flower pots, lanterns, and garden tools. Over the years, the siding had shrunk, leaving wide spaces through which I could watch to see if anyone was coming. It was my own little house. I sometimes sneaked off there with my dog Kaiyoodle—meaning *mutt* in German—and pretended it was our home. Once before it had become a sanctuary from the world. Some neighbors had complained to the dogcatcher about Kaiyoodle's barking and told me the dog officer would come to take him away. On the appointed day, after securing food and water, I locked us in the hut. Holding Kaiyoodle tightly in my arms, I told him not to worry; if they tried to take him, we would escape over the railroad tracks into the park. For what seemed an eternity I peered through the cracks, clutching my little dog. Suddenly there they were. I was shaking with fright. I was sure the dog cops would seize Kaiyoodle and toss him into one of the little cages on their truck. Fearing that he would let out a bark and give us away, I clasped my hand around his snout and watched as the dog cops in their brown uniforms looked around the yard. Seeing nothing, they shrugged their shoulders and left. Kaiyoodle and I were saved. We emerged from our hideout feeling proud of having survived the attack.

But now, confused, afraid, and alone I sat in my little hut and cried. What could have happened to my mother? Through my lookout crack, I saw Papa emerge from the house and stand under the back porch; he pounded his body against the foundation wall repeating "No, no, no." Finally he fell to the ground exhausted and seemed to sleep. I don't know how long I stayed in the hut. I didn't dare come out until Papa had slowly risen, brushed himself off, and gone back in the house.

That evening brought visits from our many friends, expressing their grief over this terrible event. They would murmur their condolences to Papa, then glance at me, shake their heads in sympathy and say "das poor kindt." My sisters Alice and Hattie were staying with friends who were part of our German anarcho-syndicalist community. Somehow their absence added to my fears about my mother, though I couldn't understand why and nobody explained anything to me. For the next few days Papa seemed torn between killing himself and the need to take care of his children. In the end, he had no choice but to go back to his factory job.

On the first day I returned to school, Papa came with me to talk to the teacher. We walked in silence until we reached the classroom. Embarrassed by Papa's presence, I ran to my little desk at the back of the room as my teacher hastened to meet him at the classroom door. All the time that Papa spoke she looked at me, shaking her head and wiping her eyes. Everyone in the room was looking at me, and I wanted to run and hide in the coat closet.

Periodically our neighbor would tell me that my father would be getting home late, and she would give me supper. One night after supper she tucked me in and left. I lay watching the shadows on the ceiling and listening to the clank of the trolley bell and the occasional clip clop of horses' hooves. Was it an hour, two hours, or four hours later? I don't know. I was awakened by the unmerciful sound of screaming in a language I did not understand. In abject terror and guided only by the light from the street, I leapt up and ran to the front of the house where the screaming seemed to be coming from.

I stood trembling on my tiptoes as I sought to peer over the top of the window sill. In an apartment in the building opposite I could see a huge redheaded man framed in a window with all its panes knocked out. Bathed in the police searchlights, he was screaming at the sky and flailing his arms wildly. He appeared to be on fire, and I was sure he was about to explode. As I watched, terrorized, it seemed in some strange way that this horrible scene had something to do with Mutter's disappearance. The redhaired man seemed to want to jump out the window, and the cops were wrestling with him, trying to pull him back in. They finally got a rope around his waist. God knows how many men it took to pull him in. By now the street was full of police cars, ambulances, and onlookers. The whole neighborhood had turned out to watch the spectacle of the "Mad Russian gone loony." I could hear people talking. "Oh yeah," one man said, "it's that Red, the Mad Russian. It'll take the whole force to bring him in." The street was completely blocked, and the trolleys were backed up in both directions. The Russian was still screaming his defiance to the heavens as they brought him out the front door, tied into a straitjacket. After a moment, except for the fire in his eyes, he became quiet. I wondered if this is what had happened to Mutter. I stood with my chin on the sill as though frozen until Papa found me. He wanted to know how long I had been there. When I asked him about the Mad Russian, he said, "Sometimes life is unbearable, and we go crazy. Let's go to bed now."

After some time—how long I don't know—life seemed to resume some sort of normality, though it was never the same as it was before Mutter died. Before those nights of terror, our family life was a most loving world. The earliest home I remember was a walk-up in a five-story building on 181st Street near the entrance to the Bronx Zoo.

Sunday was the day we went to Sunday School, came back home for dinner, and then, often, went to the zoo. Our Sunday School was not of the traditional religious variety. It was part of the Modern School movement started in Spain by the anarchist Francisco Ferrer. Ferrer agreed with Ignatius Loyola that what you teach children from zero to six—whether Roman Catholicism or anarchism—will stay with them forever. My father, an ardent follower of Ferrer and a philosophical anarchist who didn't believe in violent means, was one of the founders of our local Modern Sunday School. At its peak, the school had three branches, in the Bronx, Brooklyn, and Queens.

Mutter did her best to dress us nicely for Sunday School so as not to disgrace the family. For a nickel we would all ride the trolley to the borough headquarters of the Socialist party on McKinley Square in the Bronx. The headquarters was a series of meeting rooms on the second floor of a local furniture store. All over the city there were countless meeting rooms like these for the various ethnic, political, and singing societies. Of the thirty or forty kids who showed up for Sunday School there were always a few boys my own age. We would quickly organize some kind of game that involved running around, peeking into other meetings in progress, making weird noises, and then giggling and dashing away to hide. Eventually one of the adults would corral us and insist firmly that we sit quietly with the older kids at the Sunday School meeting.

At the Sunday School we called each other "comrade," because we considered forms of address like "Mr." or "Mrs." or "Ladies and Gentlemen" meaningless bourgeois formalities. Like their religious namesakes, the Sunday School sessions opened with hymns of praise—praise of the working class.

Who digs the gold,
Who picks the coal,
Down in the dangerous mines?
Who drudges from the early morn
Till all tired out at night?
We know it is the workers,
The proletariat!
We know it is the workers,
The proletariat!

There was a whole book of songs devoted to praising the workers and portraying our devils—the capitalists, bosses, landlords, and military—as greedy, selfish, evil people who exploited us. We saw white-collar workers as, mostly, flunkies in the service of the capitalist masters. Only the workers, the creators of all wealth, were the chosen people. And, because unions represented the workers, they came in for their fair share of hallelujahs in such songs as "Hold the Fort."

Hold the fort
For we are coming,
Union men be strong.
Side by side
We battle onward
Till victory is won!

Several of the songs described how the capitalists used religion to keep the masses passive and docile. We sang,

Long-haired preachers
Came out every night,
Try to tell you
What's wrong and what's right.
Till they get all your coins on the drum,
Then they'll tell you
That you're on the bum.

And then the chances were that we'd really boom out with

You will eat bye and bye
In that glorious land above the sky.
Work and pray,
Live on hay.
You'll get pie in the sky
When you die.
THAT'S A LIE!!!

Papa was the Sunday School teacher. I admired the way he stood in front of the class, tall and straight in his suit and tie. Papa taught in what he liked to call his Socratic style, questioning students in depth and letting them come to their own conclusions. He often started with a newspaper article, a picture, or a cartoon. Holding it up, he would ask for comments. A headline article from *Hearst's Journal American* might read "U.S. to Send Marines to Nicaragua," and the article was often about a threat to some American business interest. The older kids would be eager to explain how the United Fruit Company was exploiting the peoples of Central American "banana republics." He might ask them how much of the best growing acreage in Central America was owned by United Fruit? How much were the fruit pickers paid? How much profit did the company make last year?

At the end of the session, after a lot of discussion, Papa would summarize, perhaps closing with questions like "Do you think this is fair?" or "Do you think these people who were the owners of United Fruit and went to church every Sunday were living their Christian beliefs?" To send us out thinking, he would read a pertinent quote from Karl Marx, Goethe, Rosa Luxemburg, or Thomas Paine. We would then sing another song and take the trolley back home for Sunday dinner.

It was a special treat on a summer Sunday to make the exciting trip to Coney Island. Even now the smell of hard-boiled eggs throws me back to the wonder of those days. As usual, Mutter would be up early packing the lunch basket. As we boarded the subway at 181st Street, I would beg Papa to ride with me in the first car so I could watch the tracks, bridges, tunnels, switches, and signals as they swept by. At the end of the line the train would click slowly across the last switch and pull into the Coney Island station.

We would meet other Sunday School families at an appointed place—usually one end of the beach away from the crowd—before heading for the locker rooms. Papa would buy a locker for his and my clothes, and we would wander through acres of lockers yelling "locker boy, locker boy" until he brought the key to open it. I remember having a proud sense of being a part of the "men's stuff" in that crowded locker room with Papa and the other men.

We spent the morning and early afternoon running in and out of the surf with the papas and devouring picnic baskets full of Mutter's good German food—potato salad, black bread, bologna, and, always, a few pieces of marzipan cherries, strawberries, and peaches. Mostly I recall eating hard-boiled eggs gritty with sand. Late afternoon was the time to go the amusement parks, after making a stop for hot dogs and cotton candy, which guaranteed that I would throw up on the ride home. If Papa had steady work, we could buy combination tickets for all the rides in the park.

I remember that there was a hidden wind tunnel in the broad entryway to Steeplechase Park. As the women walked over it, a sudden burst of wind would blow their dresses up over their heads, and they would scream hysterically as they tried unsuccessfully to push down the billowing skirts. Hidden from the unsuspecting females was a gallery of men and boys who watched and roared with laughter. I thought the fun was watching the women's frantic efforts to cover themselves. But the way the men slapped each other on the back grinning and snickering as they pointed at some of the women gave me my first clue that hidden under their skirts women had something mysterious and forbidden that men wanted to see. It wouldn't be long before I wanted to see too. "The Tunnel of Love," a boat ride through a darkened tunnel painted with erotic scenes, also aroused my interest—primarily because of the way the adults chortled and giggled over it. The women seemed embarrassed, the older girls screamed, and people of both sexes were obviously excited over this sight of forbidden fruit. Though I hadn't the slightest idea what it was, the seeds of sexual mystery had been sown.

We rode on the roller coaster, Ferris wheel, bumper cars, and the carousel with the gold ring that Papa was particularly good at snatching. On the subway home, with Papa hanging on to me, I threw up between the moving cars, then fell asleep for the rest of the journey.

Papa always spoke of Coney Island as a miracle for working people. In Europe, he said, such places were reserved for the rich. "Where else in the world can people who work in sweatshops all week go to a beautiful ocean beach and the world's greatest amusement park and spend the day for a few cents? Nowhere but America!" Soon after the Coney Island amusement parks opened in the late nineteenth century, a Boston preacher had described them as the handiwork of Lucifer himself; he was sure that people who enjoyed the pleasures of Coney Island on Sunday would never be ready for work on Monday morning.

We spent other Sundays closer to home. It hardly mattered what time of year it was for our trips to the Bronx Zoo, where we arrived carrying a bag of stale bread for the animals. There Papa—always the teacher—took the opportunity to explain human behavior. "Now watch what happens when we throw a piece of bread over the monkey fence," he would say. "The male boss monkey decides who gets some and who doesn't—just like in our world." Then he would add, "But aren't we supposed to be more civilized, cultured, religious, and concerned for our fellow man than monkeys are? Here in the zoo, life is more honest, because there's no pretense." For the radicals of the Modern Sunday Schools, hypocrisy was the cardinal sin. Never being a hypocrite meant practicing a socialist philosophy based firmly on the brotherhood and sisterhood of man.

Papa also loved to use the monkey house for a lesson on Darwinian evolution. "Look at that orangutan," he would say. "Isn't he our grandfather? See? He holds the banana and peels it just the way we do. The mother holds her baby like your mother held you, and her hands curve inward just as ours do. You may not like it, but these are our very own grandparents. It's better to understand that than to believe in some nonsense about a god making us." I felt proud when Papa talked about things like evolution and the need to strive constantly for the truth to achieve freedom from superstition and fear. At the time, I was only four, five, or six years old, and often I didn't understand what Papa was talking about—and I never thought to wonder how a poor immigrant worker who never went to college had gained all this knowledge. Many years later—as Loyola had predicted—I caught myself saying things Papa had said without knowing where I'd learned them.

On the walk home from the zoo I would inevitably plead, "Please carry me, Papa, I tired," and he would hoist me up to his shoulders. My head nodding to the rhythm of his slow, sure-footed walk, I would fall fast asleep. It was a place to be forever on a Sunday evening.

On weekday mornings at 181st Street, just as on her last day, Mutter would be the first one up to make the oatmeal we ate for breakfast with a slice of "real" bread (black pumpernickel). At that time Papa was working in a sweatshop—a men's garment factory that the Amalgamated Clothing Workers' Union were trying to organize. Because Papa was deeply involved in the union effort, his job was always in jeopardy, and he was eventually fired. Believing in socialism meant a firm commitment to the rights of workers to organize unions. People like Papa had to put their livelihood—and sometimes their lives—on the line for what they believed in.

Across the hall from us on the fourth floor of our tenement lived a man I called Miter Howe. As a field supervisor for the Sheffield Farms Milk Company, his job was to ride around with a little horse and wagon checking up on the milkmen. Miter Howe was a short, rotund, Scotsman with a jolly round face topped with a derby hat. Rubbing his hand over my curly head, he would remark to my puzzlement that "the good Lord put those curls on the wrong head." Sometimes in the early dawn I would plead and cajole until Miter Howe agreed to let me join him on his rounds. Standing in the dimly lit hallway, he would announce, "Well, now boy, get your lunch, 'cause we're going to work." I would rush to Mutter who, after confirming the arrangement with Miter Howe, would hurriedly make me a black-bread sandwich. With a jubilant "Good-bye, Mutter," I would stride proudly out to meet Miter Howe and be lifted into his wagon.

Driving a horse and wagon in the Bronx in 1922 required extraordinary care, because the automobile was becoming a menace. Miter Howe would keep up a steady stream of commentary. "Got to watch your corners. Never know when some damn fool in one of those cars will come tearing right into you." In Miter Howe's world there were lots of "damn fools"—including most of the car drivers and those teamsters (wagon drivers) who galloped their horses on city streets. He had nothing but scorn for policemen who did not grant a horse-drawn wagon the right of way and for "damn fool cars that backfire with an earsplitting bang and scare the devil out of a poor horse."

Our first stop of the morning was the Sheffield Farms' two-story dairy, which covered half a square block. The refrigeration, bottling plant, and wagon storage were on the first level, while row after row of horse stalls filled the second floor. The wagons were being loaded as the milkmen arrived; they would go up to the barn, harness their horses, and lead them down the ramp to hitch them to the wagons. After signing a slip for the milk, eggs, and cheese received, they took off on their assigned routes.

Miter Howe and I would then ride around the different routes, where he would record how many bottles were left on the porches or at the door inside apartment buildings. When he got down to check on some delivery, he would hand me the reins and instruct me to "take care of her." If the horse so much as stomped a foot, I'd say, fearful but bursting with pride, "Whoa, whoa there." If I held the reins too tight, the horse would snap its head forward, and Miter Howe, coming into view, would say, "Give her her head boy. Don't muzzle her. She ain't a goin' nowheres."

Sometimes on the way back to the barn he would let me drive. The horse knew the way; I just had to watch out for the "damn fools" coming around the corners. Holding the stiff wide reins and having the horse obey my commands to turn left or right or stop made me feel like a giant. The creak of the wagon and the leather harness, the swish of the tail, the pungency of the wheel grease and the horse shit—those sensations from my first adventure as a teamster have never left me.

When I strutted into our apartment, a puffed-up four-year-old, my sisters would laugh and hold their noses, pointing at me and saying "Gott in Himmel! Du stinkst von horse manure. Mutter, here comes your little liebchen. Beware, er stinken." I paid no heed to their mockery but went straight to Mutter to tell her about my adventure. She listened, smiling in delight, to my stories but insisted that I bathe in the kitchen tub right away, before "dein Vater kommt." Papa was always the major threat for discipline in times of wrongdoing, and when Mutter wanted to move things along she would exclaim, "pass auf für dein Vater!"

Although later in life mass meetings became a commonplace experience, I will never forget my very first one. It was in the summer of 1922, and I was almost five years old. Papa announced that we were going to welcome one of America's great men—Comrade Eugene Victor Debs—on his release from prison. Who was he and why was he in prison? I wondered. Papa explained that he was the leader of the Socialist party and had devoted his entire life to supporting the workers in their efforts to create a better world. He had organized unions, led a bitter strike against the Pullman Sleeping Car Company, run for president of the United States on the Socialist party ticket in 1912, and opposed American entry into the Great War (World War I). For all these reasons, Papa said, "the bosses put him in prison." But, he emphasized, "nothing shook his certainty that socialism was the only way working people would ever achieve peace and justice."

The Debs celebration was held at the Hunts Point Palace on Southern Boulevard in the Bronx, one of the many all-purpose meeting halls that dotted New York. Every inch of space in the hall was packed with Debs's thousands of enthusiastic supporters. When we entered the hall, Papa had to stop every few steps for a bout of vigorous handshaking and mutual expressions of great joy. He seemed to know everybody.

The meeting began with speeches by various leaders of the Socialist party. My only clear recollection is of Ludwig Laura, the editor of the New York *Völkerzeitung* (the New York People's Paper), who looked like Germany's late Chancellor Bismarck. Speaking in German, he was by far the most dramatic orator there and received frequent enthusiastic shouts of "*ganz richtig*" (completely right) from the audience. As a small boy, I had little or no understanding of what he was talking about, but I could experience the thrill with which thousands of true believers heard his message of hope.

Finally, after many more speakers, there was a sudden hush and a simultaneous murmur of "He is here" ran through the packed hall. A tall, thin, bald, gentle-looking man came onto the stage and stood waving and smiling and waiting patiently for the cheering to end. All I remember of his speech is the anguish he expressed for the people kept behind bars, locked up like animals. On the way home I asked Papa if Debs was talking about the animals in the zoo. "No, he was talking about men," Papa explained.

"But why," I asked, completely puzzled, "Why is it all right to keep animals behind bars but not people?" I never heard Papa's answer, for I had fallen asleep on his shoulder.

Two years after this meeting, our family moved to the house in Van Nest. A short time later Mutter disappeared, and those of us who were left had to try to put the pieces of our lives back together.

2

The Troubled Twenties

For the first year or so after Mutter died, Papa tried hard to provide us with a stable independent family life. He did not always succeed, and my behavior probably didn't help much. I was confused and prone to angry outbursts without knowing why. After school I wandered aimlessly around the neighborhood streets and vacant lots or shut myself up in the hut by the railroad embankment.

Around this time I found a wondrous new place of escape. Our local movie theater was a converted meeting room that sat about fifty people. On rainy afternoons in the darkness of that stuffy little room I first experienced the joys of retreating into a land of fantasy. I was introduced, among others, to Fatty Arbuckle, Rudolph Valentino, and the Keystone Cops.

The theater probably had another name, but I remember it as the Garlic Opera House. The Italian people from the neighborhood who came to watch the silent films also used it as a picnic ground. Being mostly from Naples, their food was heavily flavored with garlic—hence the name. When people in the audience thought the piano player's improvisations didn't fit the action, they pelted him with bits of fruit or garlic bread. When they didn't approve of the way the story was going, they would holler, threaten, and noisily condemn the heroes and villains—mostly in Italian

I don't remember what Papa thought of the Garlic Opera House, or even whether he knew I was sneaking off there whenever I had a few pennies. I suspect he wouldn't have approved. Like everyone else in our German socialist community, he believed fervently in the health benefits of the great outdoors, especially for children. In 1925, the first summer after

Mutter left, Papa announced that my sisters and I were going to camp for a month. The news frightened me. I had never slept away from home and I had developed a terrible fear of being sent to an orphan asylum. The unsettling news that we would be moving to a new apartment at the end of the summer added to my apprehension.

The Manumit School Camp in Pawling, New York, run by a group of the most progressive educators of the time, turned out to be nothing like the ill-famed orphan's home. When we arrived, Hattie and Alice went off to the girls' section and I was assigned a cot in a large circus-type tent and told to stow my trunk under it. I was scared stiff.

For a city kid, camp was a whole new world. I had been on picnics at many parks, but this was the real country—with its deep woods, immense trees, wide fields, and strange night sounds. On a warm July day soon after we arrived a counselor took us to the camp farm. There were cows, two fierce-looking bulls with nose rings, several massive draft horses, and some pigs and chickens. I was greatly impressed by the huge barn with its cavernous hayloft, stanchions for sixty to eighty cows, stalls for the horses and bulls, feed rooms, and milking machines. An extended family of cats and kittens had free rein to keep the mice population under control.

Scattered about the barnyard were mysterious pieces of farm machinery—plows, hay cutters, rakes, silage choppers, and a manure spreader. These implements were mounted on wheels and were pulled by the horses. The animals and the machines fascinated me, and I wanted to learn everything about them.

The farm was run by a family of three brothers who had quite recently immigrated from Italy. One of them was married and had a thirteen-year-old daughter who helped her mother cook and keep house for the family. They were very good-natured, friendly people who appeared eternally happy just to be there. They spoke a minimum of English. When Mike, the oldest, was introduced as the boss farmer, he bowed slightly and said something in Italian. His broad shoulders made him appear even bigger than he was, and he had huge hands and twinkly eyes. One of the brothers, Luigi, spoke no English at all and communicated almost exclusively through his varied ways of laughing.

After I saw the farm, the camp's regular activities—the usual assortment of sports, swimming, games, rest period, and cookies and milk—

held no interest for me. I would run off to the farm, hoping to help with milking, barn-cleaning, or whatever else was going on. The Italian farm family and I easily adapted to each other. After walking barefoot around the barns and fields all day I smelled like a cowpat. When I walked into the tent in the evening the kids would hold their noses and make jabbing motions at me until the counselor sent me off to the showers.

The big Belgian workhorses became my favorite animals. They obeyed a small boy almost as well as they did the farmers. Not so the pigs. One day Mike directed me to clean the pen of a pair of large fat sows; I should first move them into another pen, he said. I had no idea how to do this, and the meager instructions he gave me in his broken English didn't help much. I opened the gates between the pens and invited the big sows to move over, but nothing happened. I tried coaxing them with oats, bran, and carrots, but they just looked at me and set up this terrible, high-pitched squealing. I still don't know why that sound sent me into such a rage. I ran to the barn, grabbed a whip, went back into the pen and in a blind temper tantrum began to beat those huge pigs. In a panic, they ran about the pen, splashing me with mud and excrement until I was covered from head to foot. I cried, pleaded, and screamed at them to get out of the damn pen. It was all in vain. Their frenzied squealing finally brought Mike and his brother running.

Mike reached into the pen, grabbed me, and lifted me out. He held me close to his face, my clothes dripping with stinking pigpen slop. "Hey, what the hell you do? You lucky pigs no knock you down, bite, kill, eat you live. Musta be crazy! Go back camp, stay there." Overcome with shame and remorse, I crept back to my tent, showered, dressed in clean clothes, and tried unsuccessfully to join in camp activities.

The next day I was summoned to the camp director's office, sure that they would send me home. Farmer Mike was there. Over and over they asked me, "Why did you do it? Why did you whip the pigs?" Fighting to hold back the tears, I finally whimpered almost inaudibly, "They wouldn't go in the pen." The director asked if I wanted to go home. Stricken with fear, I was unable to speak. Papa would be so angry! The director asked Mike if he would take me back on the farm—since I hadn't shown any interest in camp life. "Yes," he answered, "if he no hit animals. Next time they kill him maybe!" God, I was relieved.

The director added, aside, to Mike: "Sunday is visiting day. I think his father is coming. You know, his mother died a short time ago." I was thunderstruck. Mutter was dead? Even though I had thought it must be true, this was the first time I had actually heard anyone say so. Still unable to understand what it all meant, I was overcome with grief all over again.

That night was campfire night. All the kids and counselors gathered in an open meadow where an eight-foot pile of logs was burning. As darkness descended, the flames went shooting straight up to the stars, forcing us to back away. As the fire burned down and the night engulfed us, we roasted marshmallows and sang traditional camp songs—"I've Been Working on the Railroad," "Froggy Went a Courting," "Bingo Was His Name." Then the camp director gave a talk about freedom and responsibility. He described a camper who was trusted to work on the farm until one day, without any reason, he was found beating pigs with a horsewhip. Like all progressive educators of that era, he hoped that children could learn from discussing each other's mistakes. I was asked to come forward and explain my behavior. I sat there in the dark, too scared to move. "Where is he?" the director asked, and the kids began to yell, "He's back here." Several of them were telling me, "Bobbie, you better get up and say something." Somehow I made my way to where the director was standing. He put his arm around my shaking shoulders. "Tell us, what happened?" I tried to speak, but nothing came out. I just shrugged helplessly. After a long silence, I began to weep. The director took my tears as a sign that I was sorry, and I was allowed to walk back into the darkness to hide my shame.

The next morning I skipped breakfast and went straight to the farm. As I passed the farmhouse the wife called "Robishe, you eata breakfast?" When I shook my head, she led me into the kitchen by the arm and fed me the best breakfast I ever ate. She talked to me earnestly in Italian, and I nodded in agreement, not understanding a word. Then she packed me a lunch, walked me out to the barn, and yelled something to Mike in Italian. He tapped me on the head and gave me a friendly slap on the behind. I felt so good. For the rest of the summer I enjoyed breakfast on the farm every morning. At least temporarily, I had found a family. Dinner was the only meal I ate at the camp cafeteria. The other kids said they were glad to be rid of me, because I smelled so bad. Their ribbing supported my pride in being a working farmboy—stink and all.

That Sunday Papa was supposed to visit me and my sisters. Though I had only been at camp three weeks, it seemed like forever. That morning I went to the farm as usual and managed to go off to a distant field with Luigi to fix fences. When I returned after lunch, Mike told me a camp counselor had come looking for me. I was overcome with a strange feeling. I just didn't want to see Papa. I took the horse we'd been using to the barn, fed him bran and oats, and climbed up to the hayloft to drop him some hay. I curled up in a secluded corner of the loft, sure that no one could find me. I don't know how long I stayed up there. It must have been late in the afternoon when I began to worry about how Papa would feel if I were lost. I walked down to the camp office. There was my big Papa. His arms hung at his sides, his eyes were filled with sadness, and a cigarette was dangling from the corner of his mouth. He tried hard to smile.

"Where were you?"

"I was working at the farm."

"Are you all right?"

"I'm fine."

"Here are some chocolate bars and clean clothes. Hurry, let's go to your bunk so I can pick up your dirty ones." We walked to the tent in silence. Finally he asked, "Why did you beat the pigs? Why aren't you in camp like the other kids?"

"I don't like camp. They don't let you do what you want. I like the farm. I can do different things, and I like the animals, mostly the horses and cows." Papa was trying hard to understand, but my failure to show up for visitors' day had clearly confused and hurt him.

When he opened my camp trunk, he backed away from the reek and looked at me in consternation. "How can you let your clothes get in this condition? Ask the farmers for a pail and some soap and start washing these things regularly. You hear? You must learn to do these things for yourself. Do you understand?" I nodded yes, glad that we had to hurry back to the office so he could catch the bus. There would be no more time for scolding.

I was greatly relieved that my meeting with Papa was over. Camp life settled into a pleasant pattern; I went to the farm daily and was part of that kindhearted working family. Toward the end of the summer I helped with the haying. The crew would cut, rake, bale, and load the hay into the wagon, bringing it to the barn to be hoisted into the hayloft.

In the heat of August, Mike's wife sometimes surprised us with a bucket of lemonade and I was sent to fetch ice to cool it. Inside the little icehouse, sheltered from the summer sun, it was cool and sweetly scented with heaps of sawdust that covered large blocks of ice cut from the local pond the winter before. As I took my turn to drink from a dipper out of that bucket of ice-cold lemonade, the men made comments about me in Italian. I could not understand what made them look at me and laugh, but it felt good to be part of this band of cheerful workers.

As the summer wore on, I became the exclusive driver of the manure wagon. Because the cows were fed and milked in the barn, they left a lot—I mean a lot—of manure there. I would rush to clean the barn so I could get the wagon out to the fields. Often just as I was leaving Luigi would yell to me in Italian from the opposite end of the barn; then he would say "flip flop, flip flop, flip flop." That meant there was more manure to shovel. Damn cows! I was sure they produced more shit than milk.

When the wagon was full, one of the big Belgians would be harnessed up, and Mike, laughing, would admonish me to "deliver a nice load to pasture, yes?" Not minding the smell, I would climb up to the seat, snag the rein, say "giddyup," and off we would go on our delivery. While I got down to open and close the gates to the fields, the Belgian stood and waited patiently for me to give him his orders. Back and forth across the field we went; at each turn I had to open and close the rear gate of the spreader as well as start the conveyor belt on the wagon bed. Back at the barn I would take off the harness, find one of the brothers to remove the bridle (it was too heavy and I was too short), and lead the Belgian first to the water trough and then to his stall for oats and bran. While the horse' s big soft lips nibbled bran from my palm, I would try eating bran the same way from my other hand. It was a great love affair between a small boy and a big workhorse.

That summer, the smells of freshly mown hay, warm cow's milk, horses, manure, pungent silage, and the sweet breath of cows—all became a part of of my very being that endures to this day. At the farm I learned for the first time that the way people work together determines the kind of community they create. Since then I have looked at every workplace primarily from that point of view: What kind of a community has it constructed?

At the end of the summer, we took the train back to New York. Papa met us at Grand Central Station, and we all kissed him dutifully on the cheek. He explained that we were going to our new home, not far from where we had lived before. He repeated several times that we would be on our own and would have to learn to take care of ourselves.

Our new two-bedroom apartment was on White Plains Road across from a firehouse. Alice—who was thirteen and five years older than I was—tried very hard to assume the mother role, but I would have none of it. Instead, she became the target of my anger. I have no recollection of why my sisters and I ended up having such terrible fights. I recall throwing a piano stool at Alice once. Luckily, it missed her, but it made a big hole in the living room wall. Papa was distraught by the chaos in his family and didn't know what to do about it. At P.S. 34 my interest in school was declining steadily, and I was rapidly being tagged "a behavior problem." Within a year he decided to move us again, this time to live with the Prince family.

The Prince family—Mr. Prince a mailman, his wife, a son George, and a daughter Martha—were members of the Modern Sunday School and part of the socialist world that tried hard to live their philosophy of caring for fellow humans. Ours was a family in distress, so they came to our rescue.

For me, the high point of our brief stay with the Prince family was a Model T Ford that belonged to two of their friends, who were both on crutches from the effects of polio. That Model T was the start of my lifelong love affair with the car. When one of the men lifted the hood to check the oil and water, a world full of wonders was spread out before me in a puzzling tangle of wires, hoses, and metal parts. I was hungry to know how it all worked. How could a liquid (gasoline) poured into a tank make the wheels of an automobile turn and move the car? No one seemed to know—or care—how the automobile worked. My mechanical education would have to wait.

The car's owners often showed up on a Sunday to take us for a ride. As soon as they went into the house I would run out, sit in the parked car, and make believe I was driving—pretending to start it up, steer, back up, and shout "damn fool" at other drivers. Excitedly, I would run into the house to tell everyone where I had been. Then, invariably, Alice, Hattie, or George Prince—who was six years older than I—would belittle me and accuse me of lying: "You never left the front of the house. You just sat in the car going vroom, vroom, vroom, vroom." Everyone would laugh and I would feel thoroughly humiliated.

The Prince house was a few blocks from the top of the longest hill in Van Nest. A snowstorm had a magical effect on this Italian community. As long as the ice and snow stayed on the road, the hill would be thronged around the clock with sleds of every description. Bonfires roasting mickeys lit up the night as we went barreling down the hill on several sleds tied together for ten to fifteen kids to ride and on homemade bobsleds made of twelve-foot-long two-inch planks fitted with runners on both ends.

At night, the boy-and-girl stuff was all over the hill. I would hear the big guys talking about getting Mary or Louise to sit in the front of the sled so "you can feel them up from behind" or how to catch her belly-whopping (lying flat on the sled). "Then as soon as she takes off, run and jump on top of her and just rub it in on the way down." It was all mysterious and exciting—like the skirts blowing up at Steeplechase Park—but I didn't have a clue about why they were all laughing so hard.

At the bottom of the hill there was a main intersection. When it turned icy and fast, the sleds would sometimes cross right over it. One night I was riding down the icy hill at a really fast clip and there was no way I was going to stop at that intersection. As I crossed the road I heard the screams of a lot of kids. I wasn't at all sure what had happened until my sister Alice came running with an appalled look on her face. "Didn't you see that truck? You shot right under it between the front and rear wheels. You could have been killed." For at least that one night, the kid who rode his sled under a moving truck was the talk of the hill. The Catholics on the hill were saying, "He gotta have a guardian angel." It was a totally new idea to me, and it felt pretty good.

Except for the regular Sunday visits of the Model T, life at the Prince house was uneventful. I don't think Mr. Prince and Papa got along well.

Mrs. Prince seemed impressed with Papa's intellectual capacity. Her husband's limited abilities to converse on subjects of importance must have made him feel inadequate with Papa around. After less than a year with the Princes, we moved on once again.

In 1927 we moved in with the Tanzers—Siegfried, Tanta Belle, and their two daughters—another socialist Sunday School family. Alice and Papa remained at the Prince's for a few months. The Tanzers' house was only a short distance from where we had lived with Mutter and, like most of the houses in Van Nest, it was a two-story frame structure with a basement. A large sign hung over the front porch proclaiming "Real Estate." The office was in the front room of the house and was complete with oak roll-top desks, file cabinets, and a mimeograph machine. The small fenced-in backyards of the neighborhood were crisscrossed with wash lines, and each one had its own small garden plot. Many of the Italian families in the neighborhood had grape arbors to supply the annual winemaking ritual.

Papa was still blacklisted because of his union activity and only able to hold a job for short periods of time. The prosperity of the roaring twenties was passing us by. Like some slow-growing dark fog, Papa's sadness continued to engulf him. I remembered how much he had enjoyed spending an evening at one of the many German singing societies that dotted the city. Now he no longer laughed or sang. Later his laughter returned, but his songs never did.

At the Tanzers, Hattie and I slept in a room in the basement. From my bed at night I could see the glow of the fire through the open furnace door and the flickering shadows it cast on the walls. Shaking with fear, I would try to block out the howls of the neighborhood cats as their shadows passed across the small cellar windows. When I was not in school or out on the streets the basement became my retreat. There was a large pile of old bricks in one corner, and I spent endless hours piling them into neat, orderly stacks.

One day as I was re-piling my bricks, an alley cat emerged out of the coal pile. It stared at me malevolently—or so I thought. Without thinking I grabbed a coal shovel and began to pursue the cat. Many years later I tried to exorcise my child's fear and rage by writing a poem about the night I killed the cat.

In the beginning there was smells of old musty earth,
A mausoleum of life's junk.
On cold winter nights the open furnace door
Crackled in the darkness.
Ghostly ballerinas danced on the whitewashed walls.
Against the little windows,
Drawn by the fire's glow or in want of a mate,
Huddled the screaming alley cats.

It leaped through a broken pane.
My blood ran cold,
My spear or club a shovel.
Stalked, it hissed—leaped over broken pots, empty jars,
Black dust rolled across the firelight,
Eyes peered from jungle depths,
Flames whirled on the walls.

The shovel went whack
Blood spurted over old ball jars
I grew eager for the kill,
H-O-W-L H-O-W-L H-O-W-L
Dirty black blood under pretty rooms.
It jerked its head again,
Twitched bloody bleeding mouth.
No heat screech now.
Dirge for the ballerinas on my cellar wall.

Not long after this incident, Papa and Alice came to join us at the Tanzers, and our household was complete. There was Papa, Siegfried, Mama Tanta Bella, Alice and Hattie, and the Tanzers' two daughters—Matilda, ten, and Pansy, twelve. This extended family of eight would be together for the next eight years.

The second-floor apartment was occupied by an elderly couple—the Ruhs, who gave up two of their rooms for us. Hattie and Alice shared one room, and Papa and I slept together in the other one on a sofa bed. When I awakened in the night from a bad dream, the warm touch of Papa's big healing hand was there to reassure me. During the day our bedroom was a living room and was furnished with Papa's many books, prints of great paintings, and a bust of Beethoven.

Papa was still having no luck in his search for a job, while Siegfried, whom we called Uncle, was doing well with his real estate business. Papa finally decided to join Siegfried to help run a second office in the North Bronx. It was Papa's first desk job. A car being essential, he had to learn to drive and, with money borrowed from Uncle Siegfried, buy a car. He showed up at the house one day asking proudly, "Who wants to come for a ride in my new Chevrolet?" My sisters and I couldn't believe it. Here was our working-class Papa in the real estate business, and with a car! Alice, Hattie, and I were ecstatic as we ran out to see the 1927 four-door, green Chevrolet and fight over the front seat. In those days, cars were considered men's stuff, so boys usually got to ride in the front. That day Papa decided in my favor, as he always did thereafter. Even in his politically progressive circle, women and girls were still thought of primarily as wives and mothers.

For us kids, a Saturday visit to Papa's real estate office could be a bit confusing. There sat Papa with a couple of strange men sitting around a desk playing pinochle. In Sunday School Papa said that the only people who mattered in society were those who worked with their hands to produce useful things. All others were "leeches, bloodsuckers, landlords, bookkeepers," and, worst of all, "bosses." I didn't see Papa and Uncle Siegfried producing anything in their real estate office. One day I got up the nerve to ask, "Papa, what do you make in real estate?"

For a second a silly little grin colored his otherwise sad demeanor. "Why do you ask?"

"Well," I said, "I remember you said only people who make something are the ones we care about."

He was embarrassed but tried to explain. "People want to buy a house," he said, "but they don't know where or how. We help them understand whether they can afford it and show them how to borrow money for a mortgage. If they buy a house, the seller gives us a commission for selling his house." Still not comfortable with his explanation, he stressed that he helped people who might otherwise buy a house they couldn't afford.

Some time later, I believe, Papa's social conscience got the best of him, and he told Siegfried that a family who wanted to buy a certain house couldn't afford it. Siegfried, an impatient man by nature, snapped, "We're not in business to decide what people can afford. That's their problem, not ours." It was the first of many similar arguments between Papa and Siegfried. To me and my sisters it was all very confusing. Children do not easily understand that the behavior of otherwise good people is sometimes inconsistent with their beliefs.

The good times did not last for long, but Papa did get to enjoy some of the high life of the 1920s—in spite of feeling uneasy about his bourgeois job. After his first sale as a broker, he arranged a surprise celebration. Off we all went in Papa's Chevy and Uncle Siegfried's Studebaker to see Franz Lehar's *The Merry Widow*. For me, it was the first of many, many memorable theater evenings.

Tanta Bella did the cooking for all eight of us, with help with the shopping from Siegfried and the girls. At dinner she would set the big pots of potatoes, goulash, lamb stew, tripe, fresh ham, noodles, or vegetables in the middle of the table and people would help themselves—adults first then, though it was never said explicitly, children in order of their age. This put me last. As I watched food disappear, I often became fearful there would be none left for me. But Papa, who sat next to me, would grin and assure me "not to worry, you won't go hungry. And there's always good rye bread and butter." After a while I saw that people learned to regulate how much they took in consideration of others.

Every evening, dinner was the occasion for discussions about the events of the day. Charles Lindbergh was about to be the first person to fly an airplane across the Atlantic. As the son of a good socialist father, he was almost like one of our own and we liked him. The Sacco-Vanzetti case was a regular subject of debate too. At every opportunity, Papa would explain how these two Italian anarchists accused of robbing the Brinks payroll had been framed by capitalist exploiters in Massachusetts. As anarchists, they believed in a world without private property, exploitation, greed, and profit. They were being tried, he asserted, not for a robbery or murder but for their ideas; the power of those ideas made them a threat to the authority of the ruling class. Impatient with this argument, Siegfried would sometimes ask, "But what about the laws they broke?" The laws, Papa said, were passed primarily to protect property, not people. Then Tanta Bella, troubled by any hint of conflict between the two men, would ask Siegfried, "You don't think they're guilty, do you?" Siegfried was trapped. There was a long silence. He never did answer.

I was becoming friends with a lot of kids in our new neighborhood. In the mornings I would often rush out early to play handball in the schoolyard. As I hurried out of the house one of the girls would sometimes point out an unbuttoned fly, a torn shirt, or unlaced shoes. I would reply that there weren't any buttons, the lace was broken, or I had no other shirt. One day Papa, overhearing one of these excuses, grasped me firmly by the arm as I ran out. His viselike grip was always a signal that a serious talk was at hand. He led me to a small alcove off the hall and closed the door, emphasizing the importance of what he would say. Seating himself squarely in front of me, his eyes focused straight into mine, he said in his stern Germanic voice, "You must learn to take care of yourself. You hear? There is no one else. I will teach you to sew on buttons and patches. You must become a little man we can all be proud of." When he said things like that he often became teary-eyed and turned away from me. I did not understand, but I wanted so badly to reassure my poor sad Papa. As often as he would say, "You've got to take care of yourself," I would repeat, "Yes, of course I will." And I did learn to sew on buttons and wash my own clothes.

At P.S. 34, though, I was not such an exemplary citizen. I became the ringleader of all the mischievous boys in the class. We spent most of our time thinking up new ways to distract our classmates from their lessons. My learning energy went into creating diversions like a device to produce a "Bronx cheer." It was made by cutting a slit a few inches into the end of a long enema hose picked up on the way to school. The cut end was handed to my buddies, who passed it under their desks, finally placing it beneath some nice girl's desk. Blowing oh-so lightly into the hose made a nice farting sound. The boys then held their noses and pointed at the girl. The girls were furious, and we loved it. At other times a stray kitten we found on the way to school somehow made its way into the coat closet just before the morning bell. Inevitably it would begin to meow, and the students would giggle until one of the "goody" girls would stand up, point at me, and say, "Mrs. Dorm, I saw who brought that kitten into school." Once again I was in trouble.

There may have been a connection in my mind between defying the school's authority by playing pranks and the conviction of my family's anarcho-syndicalist community that it was heroic not to conform to the everyday cultural norms of the bourgeois world. We were atheists. We did not salute the flag, pledge allegiance, sing the "Star Spangled Banner," or in any way express support for what we saw as patriotic jingoism. It was our way of resisting the capitalist system, with its evil warmakers, munitions merchants, and imperialist colonial exploiters of the poor.

Each day on May first (May Day) my sisters and I were kept out of school to participate in the parade and celebrations of the workers' holiday. When the teacher asked for an explanation of my unexcused absence I would proudly declare, "It's a workers' holiday, that's why." Papa would have to come to school and quietly but firmly explain to my teacher why May Day was the most important holiday of the year. "After all," he said, "where would we be without the working class to build our cities, dig the coal to heat our homes, and run the trains?" Looking over the class at me, her face said it all: "No wonder this boy is a problem!"

Embarrassed to stand all alone against the authority of the school, I organized a little gang of boys to join in the fooling around. All in all, P.S. 34 was quite tolerant of my little gang of troublemakers. The school tried shifting us around so as to break-up the clique, and Papa had to make regular trips to the school to see what could be done with his unruly child. These visits always left me feeling that I had let Papa down, for I knew he wanted me to be as interested in things of the mind as he was. I would resolve to try harder, but my good intentions would last only a few days. The results were more visits to the principal's office and report cards lined with Ds that led Papa to refer to me as Señor DD. Then, from time to time, he ran out of patience and gave me a good whack on the side of the head.

Finally, the principal, I think, had the bright idea that putting me in charge of the cookie sale might make me into a responsible citizen. During the milk period each day I would go from room to room selling Oreos for two cents apiece. I knew he was daring me not to eat any, but out of a big box of a thousand, how could I resist a few cookies for myself and my friends? I was sure they'd never be missed. Unfortunately, I wasn't able to figure out a way to balance the account to make up for the missing cookies. Now, in addition to everything else, I was branded a thief.

Again Papa was summoned. He paid the $3.00 for the unaccounted-for Oreos and was told that the school had "had it with Robert Schrank." Poor Papa! Like all immigrants, even the radical ones, he tended to get nervous around officious petty bureaucrats. On this occasion, he managed to protest lamely, "So he took a few Oreo cookies. Is that so bad?" The principal gave him a horrified look that said, "Now I know how this kid went wrong."

Siegfried, unlike Papa, was an ardent fan of technology. He was determined to enjoy all the new gadgets America produced. The house had a piano, a wind-up Victrola, an automatic coal furnace, and, shortly after we arrived, a radio. Because my job was to wind up the Victrola, I heard such celebrities as opera singers Caruso, McCormack, Galli-Curci, and Schumann-Heink, and vaudevillians like Gallagher and Shean. Of course, among my contemporaries, I could not admit that I liked music or I would have been branded a sissy.

There was one helluva lot of excitement when the Atwater Kent radio— one of the first in the neighborhood—arrived at our house. It consisted of a receiver about the size of a wooden fruit box, an amplifier with a bunch of radio tubes that looked like black light bulbs, and a huge tuba-horn speaker. The whole business was powered by a six-volt automobile-type battery and a half-dozen B-batteries each about the size of a round salt box. The radio also required a fifty- to hundred-foot aerial that had to be strung outside. Tuning the radio was a tricky business. The big numbered dials were tuned first to pull in the station, often with strange squeals; then finetuning was done with the various subsidiary dials.

Before the radio, we spent a lot of time reading, sewing, and playing with toys. Our entertainment was to gather round the piano to sing or listen to a four-hand piece played by two of the girls. We sang songs of love, adventure, sad times, and good ones. Though I seldom participated in the singing, I never failed to experience the inner warmth and glow that comes from people who sing for the sheer joy of it. Once the radio came, things began to change. Little by little the Happiness Boys, the "Telephone Hour," "The Shadow," "Amos and Andy," and the newscaster H. V. Kaltenborn captured our full attention. During our evenings at home we usually ended up sitting around the loudspeaker. Singing and piano-playing continued for a time, primarily for parties or for Sunday evenings when people dropped in for a kaffeeklatsch.

Although I enjoyed listening to Siegfried's radio, and riding around in Papa's car was fun, I really wanted to know what made everything run.

I would beg Papa to open the hood of the Chevy so he could tell me the names of all the parts. He was patient, but his knowledge of machinery was skimpy and his interest was limited. The social and economic problems of the masses had a much higher priority for him than the operation of the internal combustion engine. Like many intellectuals at that time, he admired people who worked with their hands but reserved his real respect for what he called "the great thinkers."

I had an equally fierce curiosity about how the gadgets in our household worked. An old alarm clock I could take apart and try to put back together again was a perfect gift. "How does the Victrola make the sound come out of the record?" I would ask Papa, Siegfried, or the girls. They didn't know, or very much care

It was our upstairs neighbor, Mr. Ruh, who became my first teacher about things mechanical. He was an inveterate tinkerer who had set up a small workshop in his bathroom. One day not long after we moved to the Tanzers I saw him carrying a metal part. "Hey, what's that?" I asked.

He was a tall, thin gray-haired man in his sixties; he wore frameless glasses and gave the impression of being very precise and correct. Startled, he drew back a little, then smiled and scrubbed his hand across my head. "What is your name?" he asked.

"Bob," I replied.

"And what else? Is that all the name you have?"

"Schrank," I answered

"Let me introduce myself," he said. "My name is Mr. Ruh, and my wife is Mrs. Ruh, and that is how to address us—not as 'Hey.' Hay is for horses." Holding up the part, he said, "You want to know what this is? It's a carburetor from the Dodge parked in front of the house, and I am going to clean it out. If you want to watch, you can, but do not get in the way."

In his workshop, Mr. Ruh proceeded to disassemble the carburetor. I was about to begin learning what makes an automobile run. He gave a running commentary on intake, ports, needle valves, venturis, and float valves. He told me how the carburetor converted the liquid gasoline into a mist that was then injected into the cylinders. I understood only part of what he said but was fascinated with the magic of the automobile and intent on learning all about it. From then on, Mr. Ruh was my highly respected friend and teacher.

Later, although I don't remember asking him, Mr. Ruh answered my questions about sound recording and reproduction. Sketching them on his shop blackboard and using a magnifying glass, he showed me the little mountains and valleys that were the sound vibrations pressed into the phonograph record. He placed my finger on the little mica diaphragm of the Victrola to let me feel the vibration when the needle passed over the revolving record. He said it vibrated at exactly the same speed as the original sound and sent the sound waves into the horn, which then amplified them. Mr. Ruh went on to explain the motor, which was driven by a wind-up spring, and the little three-ball governor that kept the record spinning at the critical speed of seventy-eight revolutions a minute. If the speed was too slow or too fast the sound sounded like long-drawn-out moaning or fast talking in Chinese. After explaining a mechanical process like this one, Mr. Ruh would ask me to tell him how it worked and would listen, slowly nodding his head in satisfaction. When I got it right, he would pat my head and say, "That's enough for now. Run along."

I would then run to Papa, eager to tell him how the Victrola—or some other gadget—worked. He was not impressed. By Papa's standards, Mr. Ruh was not a politically or intellectually interesting person. Like so many of his fellow radical intellectuals, Papa looked upon technology as a tool used by capitalists to increase the exploitation of the working classes or to rob hand craftsmen of their traditional skills. Papa had little or no curiosity about how things worked.

Sometime later the Atwater Kent suffered from a severe case of the squealees that Siegfried's scant knowledge could not repair. Mr. Ruh came to the rescue, with me tagging along behind. Siegfried kept admonishing me not to get in the way, but Mr. Ruh just looked over his glasses and said in his usual clipped manner, "Let him watch. That's how he learns." Encouraged, I ventured to ask, "Why can't you hear the sound when it's going through the air but you can hear it when comes out through the radio and the speaker?" Looking a little distressed, he said, "Soon as we get the squeal out of here, you and I will go upstairs and we'll figure it out."

Again using his trusty blackboard, Mr. Ruh showed me how the radio transmitters turned the very same sound vibrations we saw on the phonograph record into electrical impulses or waves and discharged them into the atmosphere. They were then picked up by the radio aerial, converted back into sound vibrations by the radio, and amplified by the speaker. When I fed back to him what I had learned he said, "That's good. As soon as you save the two dollars needed for the parts, you can build your own radio with earphones that will let you listen to whatever stations you want to."

Thereafter I saved my allowance, ran errands for nickels and dimes, and collected deposit bottles to redeem at the store. In a short time, I had my radio kit—earphones and all. Step by step, with Mr. Ruh's guidance, I wound the wires into coils, soldered connections, plugged in the single tube, and added the batteries and aerial. It was finished. With both of us glued to one earphone, he told me to switch it on. In my excitement I clicked the shoebox-sized radio on and then off. He laughed and clicked it on again. The squeal that came out was the most magnificent sound I had ever heard. Mr. Ruh, aware of my excitement, stuck with the tuning dial. My God, there was a voice, a human voice, coming over the radio *I* had built. Bursting with pride and unable to contain it, I ran to tell everyone in the house. Their matter-of-fact approval or casual "that's nice" were deflating, but when Papa said, "Did Mr. Ruh make that for you?" and "If you're so smart, why do you get nothing but Ds on your report cards?" I was crushed.

I was not fulfilling Papa's ideal of a scholarly young boy studying the classics and learning the wonders of Plato and Goethe.

When I was about eleven years old, Mrs. Ruh fell ill, and the couple decided to move back to Ohio. Before they left, Mr. Ruh offered to ride with me on the subway to show me how it worked. Standing at the front window of the first car, he explained that eight hundred volts of direct current of electricity run through the third, "hot" rail and power the electric motors that turn the wheels. He also described how the air brakes press steel plates against the wheels to slow and stop the train. After knocking on the engineer's door, he asked politely, "Can the boy here watch you start and stop the train?" Pleased by our interest, the engineer replied in a broad Irish brogue, "Certainly! Come on in here son, and we'll be letting you run her. What do you say to that?" The next thing I knew I was on his lap, my hands on the controls with his on top of mine, running the subway train. He explained about the air brake pressure gauge, the red-yellow-green light system, the automatic brakes that tripped if he went through a light, the switching system, and how the control towers knew where to send the train.

Well into my adolescence, I continued to ride in the front subway car to observe the tracks, the variety of tunnels and elevated structures, and the ever-changing signal system. As an adult with my own son riding in the first car to watch the signal lights flashing by, I remembered that wondrous trip on the motorman's lap and heard again that Irish voice say, "Come on in here son, and we'll be letting you run her." Years later, my early romance with technology helped me understand what went on in all kinds of workplaces and quickly grasp what was involved in individual jobs—a helpful attribute for a union organizer.

3

Our Socialist Utopia

In the spring of 1927 a new subject of dinner table conversation was the planning of a summer camp for workers' children. Our community of German socialists glorified nature and saw it as the source of all good health, mental healing, sound thinking, and beauty. Papa thought such a camp would both build strong minds and bodies and help create good socialist citizens. By removing children from the turmoil of the city streets and liberating their minds and spirits, he believed camp would provide a living socialist experience of learning to care for each other as true comrades.

The Modern Sunday Schools purchased land for a camp in Lincoln Park, New Jersey, just west of Paterson. Bruno, a big, blond, muscular toolmaker at the Singer Sewing Machine Company, was head of the camp committee. His trademark was the Hohner harmonica he carried in his shirt pocket always ready for a sing-along. A group of twenty or thirty men, mostly craftsmen like Bruno, spent their weekends building the camp.

On the road up the hill from the village to the camp a number of individual Sunday School families also bought lots and built their own little summer cottages. Most of these folks were skilled factory workers—glassblowers, bakers, plumbers, toolmakers, tailors, and machinists. The exception was Fred, a short husky man with a Hindenburg mustache who owned a small metal heat-treating plant on Spring Street (now SoHo) in Manhattan. Back in Switzerland, Fred had been a blacksmith. His tough manner, muscular arms, and broad shoulders fit our image of the village smithy standing at the anvil pounding a red-hot iron bar into a horseshoe.

At the top of the hill the male comrades built the children's camp. It consisted of two girls' and boys' barrack-style dormitories for about forty kids each and a dining room and kitchen building that doubled as a social hall. There were also two six-seater outhouses and the wash-up shed—a long series of sinks with cold-water taps and an extended umbrellalike roof. The first couple of years, our water came from a shallow well and was pumped by hand to an elevated tank from which it flowed by gravity.

Although the camp cost only three dollars a week per child, for most working-class families that was a lot of money. Costs were held down by having the kids help run the place. Before camp started, we all sat around sewing name tags into sheets, pillow cases, towels, underwear, and pants. At camp we spent part of each day removing trees, rocks, stumps, and debris or working at special projects like building a shower house.

It was late in June that first year when Papa, Alice, Hattie, me, and the Tanzers left for Lincoln Park on the Lackawanna Railroad out of Jersey City. There, to my delight, stretched a huge shed filled with trains, their steam locomotives puffing away up ahead. As I looked at the huge engines releasing their unused steam a burst at a time, I wished Mr. Ruh were there to tell me how they worked. After we boarded, I kept my head out the window trying to see the engine and listening to the rush of steam as the train pulled out of the station and, to the steadily accelerating choo-choo-choo-choo, rolled through the countryside.

Except for the work detail, our schedule was much like that of other camps: up at 7:00 A.M., calisthenics at 7:30, breakfast at 8:00, then back to the dorms for bedmaking and inspection. After work detail, we would repair to the ballfield for games. There was a real conflict about whether to play soccer or American baseball. We played both.

At lunch—usually baloney sandwiches, cookies, and milk—pictures of the same two whiskered men I had encountered so many times in socialist meeting rooms looked down from the dining room wall. Marx and Engels had the distinction of looking like the Smith Brothers, so we called them the cough drop twins.

For swimming the whole camp of sixty or seventy kids would walk a couple of miles along the Lackawanna tracks to the Housatonic River. The trip down was okay, and so was the cool swim in the hot July sun. But the return hike along the heat-radiating tracks was like a Foreign Legion desert march. The only way to avoid that miserable trek was to hitch a ride.

Some of the parents saw the daily hike to the swimming hole as a healthy challenge to overcome adversity and build character as well as muscle. Bruno and some of the others, however, believed we were in danger on the long march to and from the river, because of the high-speed trains and the temptation of hitchhiking with strangers. Moreover, after a heavy rainfall the river current generated powerful whirlpools that necessitated several lifeguard rescues. They decided to build a swimming pool—a project that exposed us children to the process of socialist decision making.

One Sunday afternoon under the big oak—amid much beer drinking, wurst eating, and singing—there was a loud argument about where to build the pool. Charlie's voice was the loudest. He was a big powerful man who worked as a boilermaker and told wonderful stories about his days as a Shanghai fireman (stories Papa dismissed as "sailor's tales"). Charlie insisted that the pool should be built at the bottom of the hill: "Any jackass knows vater flows down, not up. So if vee don't want to be forever pumping, put it down there," he said, indicating a point on the map someone had scratched in the ground. But Fred objected: "No, that's all solid rock. Put it up here—where it's just dirt. We dig it out in a few days." And so it went, until, one day, there they were at the bottom of the hill with star drills and hammers, drilling and blasting through what was, Charlie conceded, "the toughest blue rock in the vorld."

The image of that group of resolute craftsmen hammering and drilling to cut blasting holes in the hard blue rock will stay with me always. To me, there has never been a greater determination to build a socialist utopia in capitalist America than was displayed by those men stubbornly pounding through a rocky outcrop in Lincoln Park, New Jersey. The chipping, cutting, and blasting seemed to go on forever, but eventually, "by Gott," there was a nice little sixty-foot-square pool. A natural spring left over from the last glacier slowly fed it with cold water. Swimming in its icy waters became a new test of toughness and character. Fortunately for us, by the middle of that summer the spring had dried up, and a fund drive had to be launched to raise money for an artesian well.

One of the unique features of our camp was the daily discussion period, which was carried on pretty much in the tradition of the Modern Sunday School. We talked about current events, but the primary concerns were issues related to the class struggle. Strikes, persecution of radicals by the government, and the progress or lack of it in building socialism in the Soviet Union were regular agenda items. I remember we once had a rather frank sex talk, which caused consternation among some camp families, who thought the younger children shouldn't have been exposed to such explicit descriptions of sexual intercourse. As one of the younger kids, I found it a most fascinating discussion.

For the people who had built our camp, these few acres were their very own socialist enclave. They felt free to come at any time. On weekends they would show up in droves, turning the whole place it into a huge picnic grove. They ate frankfurters and bratwurst, drank beer, played ball, swam, and argued. Sometimes I was ordered to serve the beer, always with the admonition, "Now Bobbie, not all foam! You understand, I don't vant to drink a lot of air. That just makes farts. No more than half inch of foam." Thus was launched my lifelong search for a glass of beer with a perfect half inch head of foam.

Fervent political arguments went on all the time. Slowly I began to understand a little of what the adults were talking about. Comrade Pellegrini, a glassblower by profession, wanted to go to Russia to help build socialism there, but Comrade Ritzen and others declared after Trotsky was expelled from the party that Stalin had betrayed the revolution. Bruno argued for giving the Soviet revolution time because, after all, it was surrounded by capitalist enemies.

Whatever else they disagreed about, the immigrants shared an intense pride in being German. As they listened to the horror stories of relatives and friends trying to survive the economic tragedy consuming the Vaterland in the 1920s, their pride was bruised. A few of the children in camp had recently arrived from Germany looking half-starved. But even worse was a strange frightened look in their eyes—as if they had seen the devil. We heard at firsthand stories about the nightmare of German inflation, wheelbarrows full of paper money that bought nothing but a piece of stale bread, and thousands dying of consumption (tuberculosis), weakened by the lack of the bare necessities.

During one afternoon discussion period, I remember hearing comrades explain that Germany's troubles were the result of rapacious firms like Krupp and Thyssen, which were growing ever richer and more powerful.

They agreed that only a socialist revolution could save Germany. Ritzen insisted that Lenin—in order to extricate Russia from World War I—had undercut the German revolutionary parties and strengthened conservative forces in 1918 by giving in to the Junkers' territorial demands in the Brest Litovsk treaty. The Trotskyites believed that socialism could only succeed if the revolution engulfed the whole of Europe. This same argument went on for several summers.

During that summer, a friendship developed between myself, Willy, and Heinrich, one of the recent German refugees from starvation. He had wondrous blue eyes that seemed fixed in a frightened stare. Though he spoke little or no English, he was clearly delighted to find himself in a threesome with Willy and me. Periodically we managed to sneak away from the camp to hide and smoke cigarettes we made from hand-crumbled cedar bark and toilet paper.

On one such outing we came upon a large concrete-block construction deep in the woods a couple of miles from camp. About the size of a three-car garage, it was a good eight to ten feet high and had a ladder conveniently attached to one side. When we climbed up to look inside we found that the structure was full right up to the top with cool, clear water. It was a hot July day, and for a while we just sat on the edge dangling our feet in the water. Little by little our clothes came off and before long the three of us were splashing and swimming about and having one helluva of a good time.

As we were swearing each other to absolute secrecy about our wondrous find, Willy started pointing frantically toward the ladder. We were struck dumb by the sight of a trooper perched at the top of the ladder and staring at us in outrage. "What the hell do you kids think you're doing in there? This is private property. You're under arrest for trespassing." Oh, my God! Besides being frightened half to death, we were balls-ass naked. The cop said, "Okay, come out of there now. Get your clothes on, we're going to the police station." With that, Willy and I began to cry. Heinrich, lucky fellow, didn't have a clue about what was happening; the rudimentary German Willy and I spoke didn't help our attempts to explain the situation to him.

Willy said, "Jesus, we're gonna be like Sacco and Vanzetti. They'll never let us out. What we gonna do?"

"Maybe once we get out of the pool we should make a run for it."

"We can't," Willy protested, "he's got our clothes. Shit, we can't run home naked. My father would kill me!"

The cop asked our names and where we were from. When we told him the Modern Sunday School Camp, he said, "What can you expect from that crowd? Okay, get your clothes on and come along." He ordered us into the back of the police car and drove to the Lincoln Park Police Station; the three of us were shivering from the combination of cold water and fright. At the station we were told to "sit on the bench until someone comes from that camp to pick you up." "At least this is better than jail," Willy whispered. Some time later Bruno walked in. He stopped, looked at the three of us sitting there with our feet dangling, and shook his head in disbelief. He was clearly irate. Even if we escaped jail, our troubles were far from over.

The cop told Bruno he had found us "absolutely naked" (he repeated "absolutely naked") swimming around in Mr. Maybe's cistern. "For God's sake, it's the man's drinking water, and these dumb kids think it's a swimming hole!" He said he always figured there was something funny about that camp on the hill. Bruno was still apologizing when Mr. Maybe himself showed up.

Dressed in a light summer suit and tie, he was a man of average height and above-average indignation. He would drain the cistern, he announced, and the camp (he emphasized the word *camp*) would pay to have it pumped full again. Bruno protested: "Oh come now, Mr. Maybe, they're just three small boys in thousands of gallons of water. How much harm could that do?"

Puffing himself up, Mr. Maybe demanded irascibly, "Suppose they peed in it? Do you expect me to drink that?"

Bruno looked over at us. "Now, boys, I want you to tell the truth. Willy, did you pee in the cistern?"

Willy looked Bruno straight in the eye and said, "No sir, not me."

Bruno then spoke to Heinrich in German. The cop said, "Oh, a foreign kid, eh. Great!" and Mr. Maybe objected, "By God, we don't know what you're telling him." Bruno insisted he was only translating "Did you pee in the cistern?" into German. That came out as "*Hast du——in das cistern?"* because Bruno wasn't sure of the German word for cistern. *"Nein, nein, nein!"* denied a tearful Heinrich.

I was last: "I'm absolutely sure I peed just before I went up the ladder. Honest!"

Not satisfied, Mr. Maybe wanted to know what about pollution from the dirt on our bodies. We had done our part, now Bruno did his. "As part of morning inspection these boys are showered and scrubbed, so I can assure you of their bodily cleanliness." Willy was choking back giggles over Bruno's declaration; there were no showers in the camp. We loved him for his loyalty.

Finally Mr. Maybe announced that he would have the water tested. "And if it comes up contaminated, the camp will have to pay." With that, Bruno asked, "Can we leave now?" and the cop nodded: "Yes, you can, but you better teach those kids some respect for private property."

On the ride back to camp the three of us sat in the back seat and were lectured on the need for "socialist discipline." "But," Willy tentatively objected, "if we don't believe in private property, what do we care about Mr. Maybe, who is just a capitalist landowner?"

Bruno thought for a moment. "That's true, Willy, but as long as we live under capitalism—with its golden calf of private property—we are forced to respect that law. Under socialism this would never happen, because all property would belong to everyone, and we would treat it with respect and know not to swim where we drink. Right?"

Heinrich, still frightened, sniffled, *"Ich kann nicht Englisch reden"* (I couldn't read the sign). Vill dey send me back to Deutschland?"

After reassuring Heinrich, Bruno said "There will be a camp meeting about this. We all need to learn more about how capitalism works." No matter what the problem—the "cistern affair," a miners strike, nudity, boys caught masturbating, U.S. Marines in Nicaragua, or a union organizing drive—it was always important to "hold a meeting" to analyze how capitalist society influences these things.

We got back to camp late in the afternoon when all the kids were hanging around the center waiting for the dinner bell. As we stepped out of the car there was a spontaneous outburst of cheers. Kids were shouting questions. "What was it like in jail?" "Were you fingerprinted?" Surprised by this heroes' reception, we were waving to our admirers when the dinner bell rang and someone yelled, "Hooray for our own victims of capitalist oppression." A loud cheer went up, and our fear and foreboding vanished. We had defied the capitalist landowners and emerged victorious!

Bruno was not so impressed. He took the three of us aside and instructed us not to talk about the incident. "We may still have a lawsuit on our hands. Understand? And besides, you're only victims of your own foolishness." Heinrich understood none of it and only wanted to know whether we were going to have dinner." To which Willy replied, "*Nein Heinrich, wir haben Mr. Maybe für schnitzel*" (No Heinrich, we'll have a cutlet of Mr. Maybe), which left poor Heinrich perplexed and contemplating a distant horror we could not understand.

That night at the campfire, one of the counselors explained the Marxist view of private property as the cornerstone of capitalist exploitation. Some of the older campers, including my sister Alice and Pansy Tanzer, got involved in a lengthy argument over the pros and cons of the swim in Mr. Maybe's cistern. After all, weren't the water, the cement, and the woods all objects of nature that belong to everyone? Then how could they belong exclusively to Mr. Maybe? Why aren't they everybody's property? Bruno agreed that these were the right questions to ask but reminded us that we still lived in a society in which private property is protected by the Constitution. "But," they protested stubbornly, "if we accept the capitalist definition of private property rights, aren't we just reinforcing the existing unjust system?"

Willy, Heinrich, and I were out of it. Much of the Marxist analysis was well beyond our understanding. For me, it had simply been a very hot July day, and the cistern seemed like a great place to cool off.

In that summer of 1927 the executions of Sacco and Vanzetti were drawing near. From a blackboard in front of the dining hall we all copied appeals to Massachusetts Governor Fuller, demanding a stay of execution for the "two innocent men." But neither our appeals nor the massive worldwide demonstrations had any effect, and on August 23 Sacco and Vanzetti were executed.

The following Sunday so many people showed up at camp for a memorial meeting that it had to be moved to the ballfield. After numerous speakers in both English and German, Bruno introduced Papa as "our beloved comrade and teacher." I had become accustomed to Papa's public speeches and often paid scant attention to what he said. This time, perhaps because of the drama surrounding the executions, I listened intently.

Papa spoke softly but with deep emotional conviction. I sat in awe as the audience gave him their absolute attention. He spoke of "the nature of class warfare and its martyrs—Sacco and Vanzetti, Mooney and Billings, the McNamara brothers, the Haymarket martyrs." All were victims of the war between the working class and the capitalists. There was a burst of applause and many fervent shouts of "*ganz richtig.*" "The rulers of the present system charged Sacco and Vanzetti with robbing a payroll," he said. "Were they concerned with a mere payroll robbery?" He paused. "Of course not. They were far more fearful of Sacco and Vanzetti's idea that there is an alternative to the hateful profit system of capitalism." He became more insistent as he went on. "It is private ownership of the factories, mills, and land that permits the bourgeoisie to exploit the working class. Sacco and Vanzetti understood this. That is why they were considered dangerous and had to be executed." In the most dramatic terms, he affirmed that these two innocent humans had died "simply for what they believed in. Nothing else!" At this, the people in the crowd rose to their feet, applauding and shouting agreement.

I was embarrassed as Papa sat down. His speech was followed by several memorial poems and many songs. At the end, the whole field of comrades burst spontaneously into "The Red Flag."*

The workers' flag is deepest red,
It shrouded oft our martyred dead;
And ere their limbs grew stiff and cold
Their hearts' blood dyed its ev'ry fold.
Chorus
Then raise the scarlet standard high!
Within its shade we'll live or die.
Though cowards flinch and traitors sneer,
We'll keep the red flag flying here.

*Though many associate "The Red Flag" only with the Communist party, it was a favorite of the Wobblies (I.W.W.) and American socialists and once served as the official anthem of the British Labour party. It is sung to the tune of "O, Tannenbaum."

Many of our comrades experienced these executions as a personal pain and wept as unashamedly as if a member of their own family had died. I will never forget that field of mourners. The meeting ended in a somber silence, and a much subdued band of true believers went off under the trees to their usual picnic of beer and knockwurst.

Poor Heinrich, upset by the sight of all these adults in tears, had to be reassured again that he would not be sent back to Germany.

When we returned to the Tanzer house, everything seemed surprisingly unchanged. At the dinner table that first night Tanta Bella, Uncle Siegfried, Papa, Pansy, Alice, Hattie, and Matilda seemed to pick up the conversation just where they had left off before we went to camp. The Sacco and Vanzetti case was still not over. The postmortem discussions centered on the failures of the defense committee and the differences among the diverse groups of radicals involved in it. Papa argued that the communists only worked for the defense to further the Party's interests and not because they were interested in saving the anarchists' lives. Pansy and Alice defended the Party as "the only aggressive militants in the fight to save Sacco and Vanzetti." From discussions like these, I early gained the impression that—except for their agreement about the absolute rottenness of the capitalist system—the various radical groups had a tough time agreeing on anything.

My Italian street pals in the neighborhood—Mario, Perry, John, Louis, Vinny, and Nicky—were glad to see me back in town. But Papa was becoming increasingly concerned about what he called "this attraction you have for those street bums." He suggested that I could more profitably spend the time working until school started (and on Saturdays) as a delivery boy for an acquaintance, Mr. Goldstein. Eager to earn some money, I agreed enthusiastically.

The shop was located under the El on Third Avenue near 33rd Street. It was a strange-looking place." Under a sign reading "Bottling Supplies" was a window full of wine and liquor labels—Hennessey, Calvert's, Gordon's, Black and White, and so on. There were displays of grape presses for winemaking, corks and corking machines, even tinfoil, wire, and an assortment of champagne labels and bottles. The store was long, narrow, and, because of the El, dark. When the train rattled by we had to holler to be heard.

Mr. Goldstein was a short, fat, middle-aged man who was evidently a friend of one of the Sunday School members. He wore wire-framed glasses and had an oily pockmarked face that he mopped constantly. He started by apologizing, in a heavy Jewish accent, for the condition of the store: "You see, Bob—that's your name, no? You see, vee have a few regular customers, mostly just phone orders, and your job is to deliver the stuff to them. But ven you're vaiting around you could clean up, sweep the sidewalk and get us coffee, okay Bob?" His soft-spoken manner conveyed the feeling that he was telling me in confidence things of very great importance.

While I was wondering about my pay but was too embarrassed to ask, the telephone rang. Goldstein answered. "Yes, of course vee got that, and vee vill deliver it right away." There was a silence as he listened. Covering the mouthpiece, he turned to me, "So vhat's your full name?"

"Robert Schrank. People call me Bob. The Italians call me Robishe."

"Okay." He went back to the caller. "He's a nice kid, his name is Robishe. No, don't vorry, he's a good kid. Okay?"

Leading the way with a flashlight, Goldstein motioned me to follow him down into the cellar. A bare light bulb hung in the middle of a room twice the size of the store and completely filled with barrels. I asked him if this was a wine cellar like I saw once in a picture. He explained that the barrels contained medicinal alcohol for sick people. "There's a law called Prohibition, so sick people couldn't get it, so vee help them to stay alive, see? If you talk about this, people could die. You understan'? You never, ever talk about this. You hear?"

Oh, my God, I thought; this must be like the Dutch Schultz gang over by Crotona Park. Some of the Van Nest kids who played baseball against the Bathgate Devils in the park told me that sometimes Dutch, the big man himself, showed up and bought soda and hot dogs for everyone. We kids thought he must be some great guy. Mr. Goldstein sure didn't look like Dutch Schultz!

I assured him I could be trusted as I already knew Dutch Schultz. He was surprised: "You know Dutch Schultz?"

"Well," I amended, "some of my friends play ball in Crotona Park. Sometimes he buys them hot dogs and soda."

"So this does not mean you know him. To say that is to lie. That's not nice. Don't do that, you hear?" He then proceeded to show me how to run "the medicine" into the bottles; then he would put in the flavors and corks and I would deliver them. We put the filled, labeled, and corked bottles into boxes marked "olive oil."

My first delivery was in the east fifties. Goldstein gave me carfare and told me how to get there. The doorman at the apartment house accosted me as I walked into the lobby: "Where do you think you're going?" It was my first encounter with a doorman. I handed him the paper with the name and address. He said, "Okay, this is a delivery. You get your little ass around to the service entrance and take the elevator to the 24th floor and they'll be waiting for you." A tall man in a velvet jacket met me at the elevator door and took the package. He gave me a conspiratorial wink and handed me a dollar bill. I stood staring at it, thinking he wanted change. He said reassuringly, "It's okay. It's yours. Just forget you were ever here. Go now." Could this be true? It was the easiest buck I ever made. Feeling like I had gone to heaven, I stopped for a couple of hot dogs and a soda pop and meandered along the streets, singing my way back to 33rd Street. By the time I reached the store I had calculated—based on a dollar for every delivery—that I'd soon be a millionaire.

When I got back to the shop Goldstein wanted to know what took me so long, and I told him they kept me waiting around until I could get on the service elevator. "So, how much did they give you?" When I told him, he said not to expect that much all the time: "Some people are cheap so you gotta take cheapies with the sports." A "sport," he explained, was "a fella who likes to show off how he made it big, even if he didn't, so he gives away big tips and that makes him feel big even if he ain't. Get it?"

There wasn't that much to do at the store between deliveries. Goldstein had a lot of girlie magazines around the place, with pictures of bare-breasted Ziegfeld Follies dancers. He also liked to talk sex, especially on a lazy summer afternoon. Encouraged by him to talk about "fooling around vitt girls," I would boast about "playing doctor" in the basement with Matilda. He was avid for titillating details, most of which came straight out of my imagination. After a while, he would excuse himself and retreat to the toilet for a few minutes.

One Saturday afternoon Goldstein began a very casual conversation about Papa and his woman friend Anita. He was curious about whether she and Papa traveled together and if, when I visited her house, she walked around in a "see-through nightgown." Stuff like that. There was a part of me that was angry at Anita for taking my Papa away from me, so I chimed in when Goldstein made sly suggestions about the kind of a woman she was. I found this man-to-man sex talk exciting, and I hastened to agree with whatever he said about Anita. Not quite ten at the time, how could I have foreseen the dreadful consequences of encouraging his sex fantasies?

Some time later Papa approached me a somber mood and demanded to know why I was saying "awful things" about him and Anita? Goldstein had told them how I talked about Anita, he said. It was no use lying. A terrible rush of shame swept over me. Hard as I tried I couldn't figure out how this had all come about. Why had Goldstein done this to me? Desperately searching for an answer, I became more confused and unable to respond. I liked Anita, and I idealized Papa. I was bewildered by the terrible wrong I had done them, but sure I was being unfairly condemned. I retreated to the cellar in tears and shame and stayed there until Alice coaxed me up for dinner.

For many weeks, Papa avoided looking at me or speaking to me. I knew that most of the people I lived with had already pegged me for a liar, because I exaggerated and sometimes made up things. More than anything else, I wanted Papa to believe that I did not say anything bad about him or Anita.

When Papa and I finally talked about the incident, I asked him if he realized that Goldstein was nothing but a lousy bootlegger and maybe he should not have listened to him. Anyway, why didn't he ask for my side of the story so I could tell him how Goldstein got me into this sex-talk shit and then went and blamed me for it? It did no good. I had been turned into a bad seed. No matter what I might say, it did not matter. Instead Papa defended Goldstein with a speech about why Prohibition was a dumb capitalist idea and what people chose to eat or drink was none of the government's business. That's why Prohibition would never work. "Papa," I protested, "what the hell has this got to do with Goldstein and his stories about me?" He did not respond. Why couldn't he hear what I was trying to say? With all my might I wished for him to forgive me, but he never did.

As I write about it now, I think that Papa—with his Wagnerian notion of loyalty to the dead—simply couldn't deal with his own shame, let alone mine. For me, the episode marked the beginning of a growing mistrust of adults, including Papa. Anita, who remained Papa's close friend for the rest of his life, never saw me or spoke to me again.

As a result of Goldstein's gossip, my job as a "rum runner" in the age of Prohibition came to an abrupt end. I had earned what I thought was big money, about $22 in six weeks of delivering booze—the easiest money I ever made. Decades later, it helped me understand ghetto kids who told me that selling dope was the simplest way to make a buck.

In the late years of the twenties, in spite of their criticisms of the economic system, the radical crowd was enjoying the prosperity along with everyone else. The real estate business was good, enabling us to go to concerts, musicals, plays, and a lot of dance recitals. On Sunday School mornings Papa still held forth on the decadence of the capitalist profit system, sometimes using metaphors from the arts to show how the evils of avarice, materialism, selfishness, and fear flowed from the capitalist system. Once, I remember, he played an excerpt from Wagner's Ring Cycle on the Victrola and told us the story of the Niebelungs; it demonstrated, he said, how the obsessive quest for gold destroys humanity. The same lust for gold is represented in our time, he said, by the munitions manufacturers—the "merchants of death"—and by the oppressors of colonial peoples as they seek to accumulate more wealth for the idle ruling class at the expense of the workers.

We would then sing "The International" and go home for a nice roast pork dinner. After dinner we might visit a museum or go to a play or a movie. The preaching about capitalist evil seemed somewhat hollow in the face of all the fun that was going on around us.

On Sunday evenings, friends might drop in for a kaffeeklatsch or a session of singing, poetry recitations, and talk—endless talk. On one occasion when ten or fifteen people were present, a tall, gaunt woman came to read her latest poetry. One of the adults whispered in my ear, "Greta is a nice lady but don't go near her, she is sick." Someone else whispered, "She has the consumption (TB) and only has a few months." It was very scary. In the midst of all the prosperity, many people were dying of TB, which Papa called "the working-class disease" because it resulted from overwork, overcrowded living and working conditions, and poor diet.

The people who gathered for these evenings of poetry, music, and talk represented the full spectrum of radicals: socialists, communists, anarchists, atheists, Nature Friends, nudists, and Wobblies.* It was like being back at camp: the arguments never stopped. Devoted supporters of the Russian revolution held that building the revolution took time because its leaders had to stand alone against a hostile capitalist world. The socialists and Wobblies asserted that the dictatorship of the proletariat was just another form of repression and that the withering away of the state prophesied by Marxist theory would never happen. Anarchists insisted that all governments were by nature oppressive; only by placing complete trust and responsibility in the individual could real freedom be achieved.

Papa leaned toward the Wobbly or anarcho-syndicalist position that the world ought to be run by workers' councils. As the workers produce the world's food, shelter, and clothing—all wealth as we know it—they should decide on its allocation. To the pure anarchists, though, the councils smelled of government, while the followers of Leon Trotsky agreed that there should ultimately be a government of the workers but thought it could not succeed while the rest of the world remained capitalist.

Opinions about politics often spilled over into the arts. There was a real split between modernists and traditionalists, who referred to cubism and abstract painting as "nothingism"—forms devoid of any meaning or idea and therefore not art. They wanted the arts to express philosophical ideas and send messages of concern for the oppressed.

But all agreed that religion was the "opiate of the people" and was, among other things, responsible for the sexual repression of the masses. The vision of a utopian future based on equality was another thread of

*Nature Friends was a German organization devoted to hiking, canoeing, and various outdoor activities; they believed that all wisdom was contained in nature.

the fabric that bound together these different radicals. In that new world, comrades would share all good things equally and act for the welfare of all. So, though arguments over the means of getting there or the details of its ultimate operation could be heated, we shared the great vision of a world dominated by brotherly love. And we all sang lustily of "the commonwealth of toil that is to be."

In the midst of all the talk there was a constant need to raise money for various causes. The Modern Sunday School camp had become a big financial burden and required a continuous round of fund-raising fairs, dances, and festivals. My memory of these events is of fun-loving, amiable people celebrating a good time for a good cause. One of my favorite fundraising entertainments—the ride to Bear Mountain Park on a Hudson River triple-decked side-wheeler—provided an opportunity to further my mechanical education. The river boat *Peter Stuyvesant* was powered by a huge steam engine whose rocker arms reached above the top deck as they moved up and down like giant seesaws. Once on board, I would invariably find my way to the top of the stairway looking down into the engine room. On one occasion the engineer, a brawny gray-haired Scotsman, saw me and asked, "Well boy, you want to see how it works, do you?" I nodded dumbly, and he invited me down into the sanctum sanctorum. He started with the coal-fired boilers. They were stoked by men the engineer called "Bohunks." "They can't speak a word of English, but they're good at shovelin' coal into those fires. The boiler heats the water into steam, and the steam engine drives those two paddle wheels alongside. The more steam we give her the faster she goes. You got that, son?"

"But," I wanted to know, "What happens inside the engine. What makes it go back and forth, and how does that make the paddle wheel go?" He explained about pistons, connecting rods, and the slide valves that let the steam in one end and then out the other to move the pistons back and forth. He compared the action of the crankshaft to the way pedaling a bicycle turns the wheels. I spent the rest of the trip trying to visualize what was happening inside that steam engine. If Mr. Ruh were there, I thought, he would draw me a diagram.

When the boat docked at Bear Mountain, we would spend the day in a picnic grove, playing the usual games and listening to the usual speeches about the evils of capitalism.

The evening fund-raiser I remember most clearly was held at Hunts Point Palace. It began with entertainment, including a baritone singing Wagner's "Sweet Evening Star," and a soprano who warbled the "Bell Song" from *Lakmé*. Whenever I hear Tchaikovsky's "Marche Slav" it brings back a mental image of a modern dance group performing an epic story of cruel oppression that leads to a revolt; as the working class breaks the chains of its bondage and triumphantly raises the red flag, the dancers leap off into nirvana to thunderous applause. There were also one-act plays performed by kids from the Modern Sunday School; these always featured evil bosses and good working people who emerged victorious no matter what the odds.

After the entertainment came several long fund-raising speeches. Finally, the chairs were cleared from the floor, dance wax was applied, and the band took its place on the stage. After eating our hot dogs and sauerkraut, the younger children would climb to the balcony to watch the dancing. Leaning over the balcony wall I would wait to catch the first notes of Strauss's "Southern Roses" waltz and watch as the huge ballroom burst into a tidal wave of joyous dance. A few minutes later the dance floor would be covered with couples whirling to the magic of the "Blue Danube." To this day, the opening passages of those glorious waltzes recall for me that wondrous moment when the whole ballroom seemed to explode into rapturous motion.

At around two or three in the morning, when Papa came to take me home, I would be fast asleep, the strains of that marvelous music still spinning through my brain.

4

The Great Depression

According to the screaming headlines and the frantic radio bulletins, the world was coming to an end in October of 1929. Over Thursday and Friday the 24th and 25th and into the following week, "extra" newspaper editions appeared on the streets every few hours chronicling the sickening drop in share values. The stock market crash and its aftermath stunned many optimistic Americans—some of them investors "on the margin"(that is, with borrowed capital)—who could not believe that the prosperity of the decade was not based on a sound economic system in which everything was possible.

I was just twelve years old when I heard the stories about the crash. Around our dinner table the talk was of companies going under and the many people who would lose their jobs. There were a lot of sensational newspaper stories about ruined investors and stockbrokers throwing themselves out of windows. My vision of Wall Street was of a place downtown where fat, selfish bankers sat in their skyscraper offices earning great sums of money at the expense of the poor. After reading the ticker tape telling them they had lost all their riches, I pictured them running to a window, throwing it open, and leaping to their deaths. I was sure it would be dangerous to walk in Wall Street, where one of them would almost certainly fall on your head. Whenever I heard one of these stories I would run out to tell my street buddies Mario and Perry. It was all very exciting.

As sensational as it was, the stock market collapse did not have an immediate impact on our world of socialists and radicals. Early on, there was even an element of rejoicing. In the heady days before the crash, people like Papa and Bruno were laughed out of the room when they predicted that the bull market would end in a big crisis as it had so many times before. They felt vindicated and overflowed with the smugness of "we told you so."

The Marxists were better prepared than most people to cope emotionally with Black Friday and its effects. They had never believed in the capitalist system in the first place and, like Marx himself, had foreseen its downfall. As Bruno said at a Sunday School meeting, "The system is collapsing from its own contradictions. This crisis will hasten the disintegration of capitalism and bring us closer to socialism." With capitalism in its death throes, he said, the Russian Revolution would take on a whole new significance. He called it our "model for the future."

For the first months after the crash, many skilled craftsmen in our radical community held onto their jobs. But when the banks began to fail they, like everyone else, lost their life savings. As the economic crisis grew and the number of unemployed kept increasing, a pall of despair settled over the country. The gatherings of the Sunday School radicals took on a new urgency and turned to discussions of "what now?" All of them saw the crash as an opportunity for fundamental change, but there was little agreement about to how to bring it about. The Italian anarchist Arturo Giovanetti, whom Papa had interested in the Sunday Schools, was certain that "the workers would rise up in protest and sweep away the whole system."

Bruno thought it would take time for the calamity to sink in. "More than ever now," he warned, "the world capitalists will seek to overthrow the Russian Revolution. We must make sure it is protected from capitalist intervention." Comrade Pellegrini too worried that the crash could offer the United States a good excuse to launch a war against the Russians, destroy the revolution, and crush dissent at home.

Radicals like Papa and Bruno had good reason to be worried, for they had seen, as Papa said, "the cowards suddenly turning into flag-waving patriots" during World War I. Hostility toward socialists and anarchists, who were outspokenly opposed to American intervention—and against all German-Americans—was rampant and encouraged by federal officials seeking to whip up support for the war. In the aftermath of the peace in 1919, fear of radicalism aroused by the Bolshevik Revolution and the creation of the Communist Third International resulted in the imprisonment and deportation of both genuine radicals like Alexander Berkman and union organizers seeking only a piece of the American pie in a time of high inflation.

While the radicals' debate went on forever, everyday life on the streets of Van Nest was changing, but ever so slowly. At first the crash had little or no effect on the activities of my gang: Perry, Louis, Vinny, Nicky, and, Mario, who was my best pal. We played stickball, kick-the-can, and ring-a-leavio—a sort of prisoner's base—and freely gave the "finger" to people who complained about our noise or our ball breaking their windows. The older guys in the neighborhood belonged to a gang called the Van Nest Steamrollers and referred to us as the "jerk-off kids." They were our role models, and we tried to act as tough as they were.

Our playgrounds were mostly the many empty lots used as dumps for discarded automobiles and broken household appliances. We took apart these objects to figure out how they worked and built huts with discarded cardboard boxes or pieces of scrap lumber. It was in those little hideaways that we smoked our first cigarettes and looked at girlie pictures of scantily clad dancing girls. We spent a lot of our time speculating and bragging about sex. Once after I caught my sister Hattie and Matilda Tanzer reading *What Every Young Girl Should Know* under a blanket with a flashlight, I searched out their hiding place and read it avidly.

Playing doctor with Matilda, who was a few years older than I, was both a challenge and treat. She was a pretty blonde, and her little breasts were just beginning to puff up. "Please," I would plead, "let's go down the cellar. Please, Matilda, just this once." She wouldn't go unless I promised to think up something new.

"You just want to do that same old stuff," she complained. Finally she would yield: "Okay, but that's it. This is the last time." Matilda was scared stiff we would get caught. "What would my mother say? She'd kill me!" I had to reassure her that we would hear as soon as anyone started down those creaky old wooden steps.

Down in the cellar, we would dress up in some dingy white shirts we found in an old trunk and—with a stethoscope made from an old enema-bag hose—play hospital. I would lift up her dress, and she would bend over just enough for me to see her backside. She had an uncanny way of protecting what she called, "my front." I kept talking doctor stuff. "Matilda, I think you need an operation on your dingpuss, so if you will lie over on your stomach I'll do it."

"No, you did that last time. Do something different."

"Okay. Matilda, you need your leg cut off 'cause it's rotten." I would take a saw from the tool rack and using the smooth edge make believe I was cutting off her leg.

"Ow! You're hurting me."

"Well, if you spread your legs out a little more, it wouldn't hurt," I urged. I was playing a sly game, rubbing on her behind and trying to feel around to the front.

When she felt me getting too close, she would yell, "Cut that out! I told you not around there," and I would promise to be more careful.

When it was my turn to be the patient, she would say something like, "I think you have the chicken diphtheria and need to be cleaned up." Wetting a small washcloth with warm water, she would rub my legs, stomach, and crotch. As soon as my excitement became evident, she would stop, saying "I'm going upstairs now. You better get dressed before my father comes to put coal in the furnace. You're a pig. Every time you promise we're just gonna do what real doctors and nurses do, and then you start with the sex stuff. I'm only gonna play if you promise to cut that out."

All during the period of the market crash, with desperate people jumping out of windows on Wall Street, we continued to play doctor.

Looking back, it seems that I and my pals thought of nothing but sex at this time. One time when a bunch of the gang were hanging around a neighborhood stoop, John, one of the big guy Steamrollers, came by. He told us they had discovered a new place to pick up girls—the monkey house of the Bronx Zoo. "See it's always crowded in the monkey house. An' the monkeys got nothin' to do all day, so they ends up jerkin' off. You just need to look for a girl who is watchin' the monkeys doin' it. If she keeps watchin the monkey, she's gonna get hot, get it?" The idea was to stand in the crowd behind the girl and try a little feel. "Just a little one, so if she gets mad, you can make out like it's an accident. If she doesn't tell you to scram, you whisper does she wanna go in the bushes with you."

I told him, "John, you're nuts. You could get arrested."

"No, you just gotta be careful, that's all."

John's idea was exciting, and scary. Perry, Mario and I, with an arousing mixture of anticipation and fear, set off for the zoo to give it a try. It was a cool, clear spring day, and there was a pretty good crowd at the monkey house. It was just past feeding time and the monkeys seemed in a very languid mood. Lying on their backs, the chimps were finishing some leftover pieces of banana, and a couple of rhesus monkeys were grooming each other. "God damn it, Perry," I griped, "nobody's jerkin' off. We came all this way for nothin'."

"Hey, guys, we just gotta hang around. Look, there's a nice girl right over there. Robishe, you go get her." She was kind of nice. A little homely, with glasses. The guys were urging me, and before I knew it I was standing in back of her. Slowly, ever so slowly, I let my hand touch her buttocks. Jesus Christ! I thought I would faint. My heart was pounding, but she didn't move. Her bottom was pleasingly soft, and I pressed it lightly and moved my hand up to her crack. I didn't dare move it away, and the crowd was dense enough to provide great cover. She was shorter than me, so I had to sort of scrunch down to keep my hand on her.

"Say, would you like to go in the bushes?" I said it! I said it! There was no answer. Nothing. She just stood there frozen—like me. What the hell! I tried again: "Say, would you like to take a walk in the bushes?" The girl never responded; nor did she give any sign that she felt my hand. Suddenly the crowd began to move in the direction of a loud screeching noise coming from the other end of the monkey house. Without so much as a look back, she walked away.

I told Mario and Perry.

"Did you ask her to go in the bushes?"

"I did, I did. She never answered."

"Where is she now?"

"I think she left."

"Oh, you're stupid. stupid! You shoulda followed her. I betcha she went to the bushes."

"Oh, my God! Listen, I'll go look. Maybe she's waitin' out there." I was off running, dodging my way through the crowd, spinning through the revolving door. Outside, I sized up the bushes. They were low but real thick. I jumped over a low iron-rail fence looking under a hedge. "Damn!" I thought. "If I blow this chance the Steamrollers are really gonna razz me. This is stupid. I'm looking under a bush where there might be just enough room for two squirrels to do it."

I was about to give it up when, all of a sudden, there's a big cop standing over me, tapping his club on his hand. "Now why in the name of the good Lord are you tearing up these bushes?" he demanded in a broad Irish brogue.

Scared, and feeling real stupid, I blurted out, "I lost my watch."

"Pray now, how could you possibly lose a watch in these bushes?"

"Well, a friend of mine threw it to me from the monkey house 'cause it was crowded, and I missed it and it went in here somewhere."

"Well now, I've heard it all. Just get yourself out of those bushes before you have to pay for the damage."

I didn't need any coaxing. I ran back to the monkey house where Mario and Perry were waiting. "No luck, fellas. Couldn't find her." I knew I had blown my big chance. When the big guys heard about it I was gonna get laughed at for being nothing but a "jerk-off kid."

But the story of the monkey house caper grew. By the time we finished our half-hour walk home, I had screwed Helen—somehow that became her name—from behind, right there in the crowded monkey house while Perry and Mario watched.

"I swear," said Perry, "I saw him do it. Jeez, fellas, that was really somethin'."

I have often wondered what I would have done if the girl in the monkey house had accepted my proposal. I believe I would have fainted.

Sex, it seemed was on everyone else's mind too. Even at the family dinner table the subject would periodically emerge, much to Tanta Bella's discomfort. I remember a small disagreement that erupted into a surprising argument. It all started with a discussion of whether or not the modern dancer Isadora Duncan should have danced naked in a London recital. (I had been taken, often dragged, to lots of dance recitals with the rest of the family, but, believe me, I saw no naked dancers. If I had, I would probably have become a keen dance fan.) Papa defended Isadora—a darling of the radicals who had died in a freak automobile accident in 1927—on the grounds that the human body is a thing of beauty.

Only dirty minds, he said, could fail to appreciate the beauty of the human form. "Then why do we wear clothes, Papa?" I asked him. He replied that we had no choice but to conform to the customs of the society we live in. Tanta Bella was very upset by this conversation; she feared that Matilda, who was studying to be a dancer, would suffer from the bad name Duncan had given modern dance.

Alice and Pansy seemed to be taking on Papa and Tanta Bella. Alice quoted Isadora as saying that the people who were critical of her dancing nude were as gray as the paint on the walls, and Pansy was certain Emma Goldman would support Duncan's right to dance nude. Goldman, a woman anarchist who had been imprisoned in World War I and deported during the Red Scare of 1919, believed in what was popularly known as "free love." She and Margaret Sanger had long been telling women on the left that they needed to be as free as men to determine their own way of life—whether to bear children or to marry or to live with a man on a basis of complete equality.

Alice was particularly disturbed by the issue of who controls a woman's body and asked defiantly, "Who, besides me, has a right to tell me what I can do with mine." Pansy pointed out that Goldman did not believe in marriage precisely because a woman gave up that right to the husband in the marriage contract. Papa demurred. Women needed to be careful, he suggested, or men would look down on them. Besides, he insisted, Goldman's years of living with Alexander Berkman were equivalent to being married. This was a side of Papa I had never seen before. I had always thought he was in favor of free-love relationships; now he seemed to be defending marriage.

The girls clearly admired Emma Goldman's independence, especially her challenge to women's marital status. Some years after being deported to Russia she wrote *My Disillusionment in Russia,* in which she described how the Soviets had persecuted noncommunist radicals like her anarchist mentor Peter Kropotkin and were suffocating the freedom of the Russian masses through forced industrialization and agricultural collectivization. Pansy, though, thought Goldman did not understand the need for order and discipline during the industrialization period and questioned how women were faring under the Soviet system. Alice considered Goldman's anarchist ideas splendid but too far ahead of their time to be workable.

I was more interested in her pal, Alexander Berkman. Papa explained that he was an anarchist who had tried to assassinate Henry Clay Frick, a "robber baron" and chairman of Carnegie Steel, during the Homestead steel strike in 1892. He was condemned to a twenty-two-year prison term and served for fourteen years. I wanted to know why he would try to kill someone? Papa went into a long explanation about Frick's responsibility for having families of striking workers evicted from company houses and for sending in Pinkerton strikebreakers who fired on workers, killing a number of them. The exploitation, he hinted, was so severe that there may have been no alternative but to take violent action. Alice, however, pointed out that Berkman was not a steel worker and said she wasn't at all sure the workers themselves supported his action. Was Papa in sympathy with Berkman's assassination attempt? she wanted to know. No, he wasn't, but he could understand the emotional desperation behind the effort to stop Frick's cruel exploitation.

I was confused and troubled. Until then I had only known about the frame-ups of innocent men like Sacco and Vanzetti. I had never heard of a radical who decided to kill an enemy of the working class and actually tried to do it. Did anarchists attempt to abolish capitalism by terror? How many others, I wondered, had tried, and maybe succeeded? These things were difficult to understand, and I was sorry I had heard about Berkman's attack on Frick.

I don't remember when people began to refer to the period following the crash as the depression, but it was at mealtimes that I first began to experience it. First the roasts, steaks, and chops diminished, and the stews, noodles, and organ dishes increased. Uncle Siegfried would proudly present the stews he made from lung, tripe (cow stomach), and kidneys. They all tasted pretty good, except for the kidney stew. No matter how much marinade or vinegar he poured over the kidneys, they always tasted pissy.

The regular Thursday night four- or five-man pinochle game at our house continued in spite of the depression. I liked hanging around and listening to all the tough man talk. When a tight hand was being played, it could get very tense. I just loved it when Papa whipped out a card and slammed it down on the table to win the hand, grinning as if he had won the Irish sweepstakes.

During the game I could usually pick up a dime or two doing little errands—buying cigarettes or beer for the players. As times got worse though, the dimes gradually reduced to a few pennies and I noticed some of the players rolling their own cigarettes, which they called Wings.

Uncle Siegfried kept a little pinochle cash box on a sideboard in the kitchen. When his winnings were up I would dip into it, as I explained to Matilda, to get some candy for our hospital meetings. Hands on her hips, head thrown back haughtily, and her mouth wide open, she would declare, "That's stealing."

"It's okay," I said "Soon as I turn in some deposit bottles or sell some junk I'm gonna pay it back."

Soon enough, as the depression reduced the pinochle box to a few pennies, Siegfried became suspicious. More than once, he grumbled at the dinner table about the twelve or fifteen cents missing from the box. Worried that Matilda would give me away, I once tried slinking down in my chair to give her a kick under the table. Instead I kicked my sister Hattie. "Baah-bee," (she always said Bobby like "ba ba black sheep"), "what are you kicking me for?"

Tanta Bella usually came to the rescue. "Siegfried," she said with the same haughtiness Matilda was acquiring, "You don't *think* (pause) for a moment that anyone in this house would take money from your pinochle box? You don't think that, I hope."

Siegfried's crossed leg would be jiggling back and forth nervously as he looked over his glasses at a corner of the ceiling. Blowing out a puff of cigar smoke, he would mutter exasperatedly: "Oh, I didn't say anyone here took it. All I'm saying is it's missing."

"Well, I'm glad you didn't think it was anyone in this house," Tanta Bella responded with great relief. I thought, Tanta Bella, I love you That innocent lady believed only in good things like May pole dances, butter cookies, and nice children who held hands, skipped, and never used a bad word.

The real estate business was dead as a doornail. It was degenerating into a full-time pinochle game. Naturally there was no more allowance for me, and the condition of my clothes began to show the effects of the depression. Shoes were worn until the toes came out at the fronts and displayed my oft-darned socks. My pants were continuously being repaired until the pockets were gone and the knees were worn right through. My pal Mario and I figured we could make a little money by finding some copper, tin, or zinc and selling it to the junk man. The hunt for scrap metal sent us on long bicycle trips around the Bronx. Near the present Bruckner Boulevard there was a big garbage dump we rode to on bikes we assembled from discarded parts.

By 1932 or so the depression was affecting our scavenging efforts. Before then there might be a few old derelicts picking around in the garbage for stuff they could sell to buy a bottle of Thunderbird. One day, standing at the edge of this great field of garbage, Mario looked around and said; "Christ, Robishe. Look at this crowd. There ain't nothing for us no more. Next thing you know these people will be collecting our deposit bottles."

We started looking anyway until Mario found a piece of copper cable and began to pull it out from under a load of freshly dumped garbage. Behind him was the usual flock of seagulls waiting to get at the garbage. On the other end of Mario's cable a little Italian man was pulling and yelling "Itsa my cable—I found it a first, you betta let go."

Watching this tug-of-war between my pal and the little man, I ran toward Mario yelling, "Police!" Mario looked stunned as he watched me hurdling over the garbage. The little man looked frightened and let go of the cable. "Run with it," I yelled. Mario began running to the bikes with the cable, with me pounding along behind him. We coiled the cable, jumped on our bikes, and pedaled off. Looking back, I saw the little Italian man shaking his fist at us.

Back at the house we cleaned off the insulation and figured we could get a quarter or thirty cents for it. Mario said, "I can't believe we had to fight some old fart over a lousy piece of copper cable."

Siegfried was getting restless. Papa was earning nothing from real estate and the debts were piling up. Early on, Papa had been pretty cocky; after all he understood the reasons for this capitalist crisis. But understanding the causes didn't ease the pinch of our increasing poverty, and soon Papa had to join the hordes of job hunters.

For many men during the depression, job hunting became a full-time occupation. It was still pitch dark when I would hear Papa leave the house, and he often didn't arrive back home until late in the afternoon. Shoulders slumped, his long arms dangling from his six-foot frame, he had something of the appearance of a human scarecrow. I'd yell "Hi, Pop," but there would be no response. I became overwhelmingly aware of his sense of failure. He would retreat to his room and lie down on the couch to sleep.

At supper time I would go to wake him. There was my Papa asleep on his side with his hands together under his cheek in a prayer position—like a little baby. I hated to disturb him. I knew he was reluctant to come to dinner and face Siegfried, who continued to collect rental income from houses he had bought during the boom years. These "landlord's" rents were now feeding us all. Tanta Bella, always perceptive about Papa's moods, would sense his humiliation and launch into one of her let's-all-cheer-up efforts, perhaps announcing enthusiastically "I've made butter cookies for dessert!"

Papa didn't cheer up, and, as the potatoes and lung stew were being passed, someone was sure to ask about his job hunt. Papa would answer in a slow, deliberate voice, as if he had trouble getting the words out. "I tried the old garment shops, but the bosses just laughed at me. 'What, are you kidding? We got nothing to do ourselves.'" He tried hospitals and told them he was an experienced orderly: "I can lift helpless people, mop floors, and fold bandages." He paused, then said "Yes, and I told them I was an experienced morgue assistant." In the old days I would have asked about the morgue job he'd had many years before, but not now. Usually he said he found dead people were the easiest to deal with.

Tanta Bella hated this conversation and wanted us to talk about something more cheerful: "For God's sake, aren't things bad enough?"

This might set Siegfried off. "What are we gonna do about money for coal?" he wanted to know. "It's gonna be cold again soon. We have about a ton left. That won't last more than a couple of months. Electricity costs money! How about keeping the lights turned out when we don't need them? Especially you, Matilda. You leave the bathroom, you leave the lights on."

"Well, it's dark in the hall, and it makes me feel scared."

Siegfried's nervous leg would start to go again and, the cigar end protruding from the corner of his lips, he would look up at the ceiling in a kind of cockeyed way. "Okay, when the electric company cuts the power off because we can't pay the bill, you'll see what dark is really like."

He was forever telling us kids "Turn out the lights!" "You're wasting hot water!" "Shut the door, the cold's coming in!" "You're wasting soap!" "Close the icebox. The ice is melting." "Who uses all the toilet paper? Don't waste it!" "The way you treat your shoes, you'd think money grew on trees." I think he really hated being the bad guy and was the only one who knew how poor we really were.

The neighborhood kids gathering on the stoops wondered what had gone wrong in their houses too. Why all of a sudden there was no money. One kid said, "Our parents got the money, they just hate kids."

Another one said, "I heard Perry's father tell his mother that if they didn't have all these kids it wouldn't be so bad. You see," he says, "we're the trouble. If we weren't around, everything would be okay."

"So maybe we should run away?"

"Where would we go, stupid?" I said.

I stopped asking my father for money, because I knew it made him feel bad. He hated to say that he was broke. Besides, he was likely to say something scornful like, "You should be rewarded for your great report card?"

Our parents' desperation was spilling over to us kids. In our stoop talks, we agreed that all the food we really liked was disappearing. There was no longer cream for the Jello, or cookies, or cake and ice cream. Forget it. It was all gone. One spring day, Mario, Perry, and I were hanging out in the cellar trying to think of something to do when the subject of the vanishing desserts came up.

I was thinking. "Listen, you guys, here's a great idea—why don't we steal desserts? This is how it works. When one of has to go to the store, he whistles a signal and the other guys come out and we go together. Let's say I'm getting milk. Old Pasquale is stirring up the milk with the dipper and lookin' in the can. That's your chance. You grab a can of peaches, plums, apricots, or a box of cookies, stick 'em inside your jacket and walk out like nothin' happened. We hide the stuff in the cellar. Then whenever we feel like dessert, we meet and have a feast. Whatta ya say?"

The next time I was sent for milk, I grabbed the two-quart can with the swinging handle and gave out the three-whistle signal at Mario's house. He came running out of the alley.

"Let's go. I gotta get milk." Then we went around the corner to Perry's and gave the whistle. He came out on the fly.

There wasn't a soul on the street, and we were feeling really nervous. Trying hard not to look suspicious, we walked along, fooling around, bouncing a ball, and telling our favorite shit jokes as we made our way to Pasquale's. I walked into the shop carrying my milk can and, according to plan, they came in right behind me. "Hi, Pasquale. Two quarts of milk." Pasquale wanted to know if we were together, and we said "Yeah." He and I walked back to the big milk can at the rear counter while the other guys were doing their stuff up front.

"And my aunt says make sure you mix it so we get some cream."

"Your aunt, your mother, they all wants cream. So why they no buy cream? You canna get cream when you buy milk, you unnerstan'?" He ran the long-handled dipper down into the twenty-five-gallon can, stirred it around a few times, and pulled it up with the milk splashing over its side. He tipped it into my milk can and dropped the dipper back in the big can while I dug around in my pants pocket for the dime, all the time keeping an eye peeled for Perry and Mario. They were on their way out of the store. I was so excited I almost dropped the dime. "So long, Pasquale."

I ran to catch up with them. "Whadya get, whadya get?" Perry showed his box of mixed cookies and Mario a can of cherries. We agreed to meet the next day after school for our first dessert feast. "Hey, you bring spoons, I'll get a can opener. We'll have a party."

The party was a great success, as were our future visits to local grocery stores. Other kids heard about our dessert parties and wanted to join, and we agreed, as long as they contributed to the menu. Things were going great. We had stashed a large variety of cookies, candies, and canned fruit in the cellar. As luck would have it, Uncle Siegfried came upon our hiding place. First he assumed that I had been stealing from our kitchen, but Tanta Bella—Bless her heart!—saved the day. She said, "Why I never bought anything like that, especially those cookies."

Uncle was stumped. "Well, where did you get it?" I wasn't afraid of Uncle. I knew I was the prime example of the kind of dishonest kid he detested. I thought he kept me at a distance so as not to be contaminated.

I told him we found the food. "When the trucks deliver stuff to the store, they always drop some boxes. We just hang around and pick them up. Not knowing how to continue this bizarre conversation, Uncle just shook his head in disbelief. But I was concerned, even though he had little or no conversation with Papa in those days, that he might tell him. This could result in Papa's squeezed-arm technique for extracting the truth. The trick was to keep going with Uncle until doubt combined with disgust made him drop the whole thing.

As the depression deepened, so did Papa's indebtedness to Siegfried. I knew that we had become really poor when even the rare occasions for real meat disappeared entirely. Besides potatoes we were now eating only animal organs—things that used to go to the cat.

People were trying all sorts of schemes to make a little money. Some sponsored cooking parties to sell "waterless Club Aluminum." They would invite friends and neighbors for lunch or dinner and after they had eaten try to sell them the pot the meal was cooked in. If there was one thing people didn't need during the depression, it was pots. Still, anything that killed time was helpful, and the pot parties required time for planning a menu and preparing as nice a meal as possible. A number of women—including Tanta Bella—also tried learning to be beauticians. She practiced by giving permanents, haircuts, marcel waves, and so on to the girls and their friends. Their polished nails and curly tresses at least brightened the increasingly drab atmosphere of our home. Predictably, neither the pot sales nor the hairdressing produced much if any income. They did keep people busy and engendered a bit of cheer to lift hopes that somehow things might get better some day.

Like millions of other unemployed, Papa decided to look for a job in a different field. The effort to develop a new marketable skill was becoming a national obsession. It was as if fifteen million people were trying to play musical chairs with their occupations. Out-of-work accountants hoped to become radio or appliance repairmen, while the latter sought work as bookkeepers and accountants. After Papa had given up hope for the real estate business I showed him a full-page ad in my favorite magazine, *Popular Mechanics*. In big bold letters, it said, "You Can Make It in Real Estate. We will train you in six weeks in your own home—no overhead—all you need is a phone and a business card, which we will supply as part of your tuition. Get in the six-figure income column." He just shook his head wearily. "Bobby, that's not like selling pots. You might have a friend or two who can buy a pot. That's very different from finding anyone who could even buy the coal to heat a house—no less buy it. What person in this country who is out of work could possibly have a friend that could buy a house?" Sometimes the ironies of the situation would get to Papa and he would forget his miserable burden of longing and guilt and start to laugh, slowly at first, until his whole body shook.

Everyone in the family got involved in what kind of job Papa could possibly get. Combing through the want ads, Hattie might say, "Oh, here's something, Pop. A counterman, how about that? That's easy, you just make sandwiches." Reading the ads and suggesting new career possibilities for Papa became a nightly routine. He would sit there expressionless, saying nothing, and I could feel his shame at the indignity being heaped on him. He seemed to grow smaller, like an inner tube with a slow leak gradually going limp. I hated to see him like this. My hero Papa seemed to wither and die.

To perk him up, I would sometimes ask how this economic situation had come about. In spite of his radical criticisms, Papa liked to refer to this country as, "the good old USA." Politically he was most in sympathy with the Wobblies' ideas, though by then they were a spent force in the labor movement. Still, for him they represented the "Good America," as against the Robber Barons of the "Evil America." Papa said it was "the rich—the Morgans, Rockefellers, Mellons, and Carnegies—who are reaping a fortune on the backs of the unemployed. That's what brought on the depression." As he railed against capitalist devils, I could see him coming back to life. I knew that when I asked a question and he got talking he would, at least for a short time, be distracted from his sadness.

Though I knew it by heart, I never got tired of listening to Papa's story of how he arrived in America on the Fourth of July 1907. Because of the holiday, the ship had to wait before unloading its immigrants at Ellis Island and was temporarily tied up to a Brooklyn pier. Papa and his friend Bruno, worried that they might be sent back to Germany and drafted into the Kaiser's army, decided to jump ship. With nothing in their pockets, they slid down the hawsers onto the dock. "We were two absolute strangers who spoke not a word of English." They walked the streets looking for someone who spoke German. Somehow—Papa did not remember exactly how—they found their way to Ridgewood, a little German community in Brooklyn.

From his very first day in the United States until he died, Papa never got over his "wonder of all these different nationalities living close to each other and actually getting along." The camaraderie between ethnic groups Papa saw on the streets and subways made him conclude that socialism could work in America. Europeans, he said, because of their long history of nationalism and overcrowding, ended up at war, killing each other for more living, working, and farming room. But in America there was plenty of room for everyone. He was convinced that America was living proof that left alone, even within the capitalist system, people of different nationalities, languages, and cultures could live peaceably together.

On the streets of Ridgewood Papa could speak German to his fellow countrymen. He sought out people from his home town (*Landsmänner*), Mannheim, and within a few days had found work at the German Hospital doing a variety of jobs, including morgue attendant. (During World War I, when everything German was anathema, the name was changed to the Wyckoff Heights Hospital.) Full of enthusiasm for his new-found homeland, this intelligent, self-educated man dedicated to bettering the lot of his fellow workers uncomplainingly worked at all kinds of unskilled jobs. The worst thing about the depression was not that it kept people like Papa from earning a living but that it deprived them of their most precious form of self-definition: a job.

When Papa's stories came to an end he was faced again with the inevitable question of how he and his family were going to survive. Increasingly, the newspapers carried pictures from all over the city of people living in encampments of cardboard and tin shacks called Hoovervilles, in honor of the president. As part of our education in the evils of capitalism, Papa sometimes took us to see the desperate conditions of the homeless unemployed. The thought of ending up in a cardboard shack scared me half to death.

I was very happy when—after several years of unemployment—Papa found "some work" as a painter's helper through a Wobbly friend. "Some work" might mean only a day or two a week and earning only enough for carfare, with a couple of bucks left over. But it was at least a job, and Tanta Bella cheerfully predicted that it might be a real opportunity: "Who knows? Maybe it will lead to membership in the painters' union and a regular job." It was an important occasion for all of us. I was excited and got up with Papa at 6:00 A.M. to see him in his new pair of white painter's overalls. Carrying a brown bag lunch of liverwurst on black pumpernickel and a milk bottle full of coffee, he left for his new job.

I believe Papa would have liked me to have a very different kind of life from his—to read serious books and grow up to be a scholar. But my performance at P.S. 34 continued to be a source of real tension between us. The printed word seemed lifeless compared to all the mysterious and exciting things going on in the streets. Unlike me, the four girls in our home all did very well in school. We lived in different worlds. I could not understand why they spent their out-of-school time reading, writing, and talking about what they read. They were also enthusiastically involved in the arts. Alice and Pansy played the piano, and Hattie and Matilda danced. In fact, Matilda was emerging as something of a star.

Every morning after my the usual breakfast of cocoa and a roll, I went off to school. The day Papa started his new painting job I wondered about how it would change things. Would there again be enough money for shoes or a new pair of pants? Maybe even an allowance ? Completely absorbed, I almost walked right passed Krause's Bakery, where the local milkmen stopped after completing their morning rounds. While their horses got a feedbag of oats, the milkmen would finish their paper work over coffee and cake. Years before, Miter Howe had shown me how to be the horses' pal by tipping up the feed bag so they could get at the oats on the bottom. After a time the horses learned to recognize me from a city block away, and all six or seven of them would start stomping and neighing when I turned the corner. As I held up the bag for those last delicious oats, a milkman usually came out of the bakery with a piece of coffee cake. "Here kid, thanks for feedin' the horses." Giving me a friendly scrub on the head, he would say, "You're all right, kid. These horses know you're their pal." With a warm happy feeling, the cake crumbs scattering from my mouth, I had to run to beat the last school bell.

I am not at all sure what triggered it, but in 1930, sometime near the beginning of the fall semester of seventh grade, a serious discussion about my future took place at P.S. 34. I was sent to the principal's office where, to my surprise, I found Papa, my homeroom teacher, a counselor, and the principal, all looking grim. I saw from their expressions that I was in deep, deep trouble. Many times I had been tagged an "incorrigible behavior problem" and been threatened with reform school. I understood "reform school" as a boys' prison like the Catholic Protectory, a huge walled-in place where "bad kids" were sent and where, according to neighborhood gossip, the priests "beat the shit out of the kids." As the counselor was about to speak, Mr. Finerty, the shop teacher, arrived. He looked at me, smiled, and even greeted me: "Hello Bobby."

On earlier occasions when I smelled the threat of reform school I had made immediate plans to run away—stashing food in a knapsack and pocketing enough carfare to get out of the city. Now I had no time to get away. As the committee of grim-faced school officials described my escapades—a sort of "can you top this one" presentation—I started to cry. They all just looked at me in wonder. Finally, lean, six-foot Mr. Finerty placed a reassuring hand on my shoulder and suggested that I work with him as a shop assistant. "I've noticed he's good with his hands. He can help other students who aren't as handy with shop tools." That day Mr. Finnerty perfectly fit my Catholic friends' definition of a guardian angel.

It was agreed. I would spend the seventh and eighth grades in Mr. Finerty's shop. He was friendly but firm as he laid out the rules. There was to be absolute punctuality. Any fooling around would mean the end of my shop career. I had daily assignments of things to read and had to solve arithmetic problems related to shop projects. If some other boy was having difficulty with his work, Mr. Finerty would suggest that I help him out. It was a new role for me. I was actually assisting someone who was less able than myself. Many years later I applied the same idea in the Mobilization for Youth work programs by getting ghetto youth to help the children of migrant laborers.

One morning Mr. Finerty called me to his desk. Looking at me over his rimless glasses, he said, "I want you to build something that will show the school what we can do here in the shop. He gave me a list of potential projects and told me to pick one. I was to research it—though I didn't have the foggiest notion what that meant—plan it, and build it. The list included a model sawmill, a doll house, a model airplane (not from a kit), and the one I chose, a working model of the Gatum Lock of the Panama Canal.

"Well," said Finerty, "you sure didn't pick an easy one! Okay. Now for the research. Go to the library and read all you can about the lock, make notes, and tomorrow you can tell me what you've learned and then we'll get started."

It was the first time I had ever been in a library. The librarian helped me find the Panama Canal in the encyclopedia, and I slowly read and made notes about the canal and the Gatum Lock. Proud of my new knowledge, I couldn't wait to tell Mr. Finerty how the French had started the Canal, got stuck because of yellow fever and lack of cement, and how Teddy Roosevelt had vowed to finish it. I explained how the Gatum Lake lock lifts the boats up or drops them down by filling or draining the lock with water. When I was finished, he rested his hand encouragingly on my shoulder and said with a satisfied smile, "I knew you could do this. Now go to work." He taught me how to draw a plan to scale and from that to figure out what materials I needed. At each step in the building process of the model, Finerty would insist on detailed and often written explanations of what I was doing. Sometimes I became impatient with his demands. He would suggest I take a part of the model, go back in the corner of the shop, and sit there and sandpaper it until I'd cooled down.

The completed working model consisted of pumps, electric trains, lights and ships. Many of the items were purchased, which meant that I had to work out a budget and adhere to it. There was no end to the things I had to learn. When I felt over my head and drowning, Finerty would be there with a calm reassurance: "We can do it."

My street pals knew I was working in the shop, but they didn't know what I was up to. I didn't want them to think I was going soft or becoming a "goodie two-shoes." At home I said nothing about the canal project for fear I would be laughed at.

I was in my last year at P.S. 34. I decided to avoid the absurdity of job hunting by trying to go to high school, but it proved to be too late. In my final year I managed a B+ average; but as I had achieved a straight-D record from first grade until then, the school simply never considered me for the academic track. Several times I had overheard adults saying things like, "You know he's good with his hands, but otherwise he's not very smart." It was generally considered best that I go to work. It was inevitable. I would have to resign myself to it.

The graduation photographs were taken for the yearbook and were offered for sale. About to leave it, I was beginning to feel sentimental about P. S. 34. Holding those little negatives and wishing I could buy the pictures, I knew what Papa would say: "What? Money for graduation pictures from a school you hated, when we need food?" I was too ashamed to ask. Papa had already laughed at my request for the required white flannel graduation pants.

It was June of 1932, the day of the graduation ceremony. I was hanging out backstage of the auditorium fooling around with my friends and waiting for our names to be called to receive our diplomas. During the awards ceremonies some of the kids started saying, "Hey Robishe, they're calling you for an award." Sure. Were they kidding? I laughed: "Oh yeah, they're gonna give me the pain-in-the-ass award." Finally Mr. Finerty walked up, took my hand and started leading me to the stage: "Let's go, you made it. I knew you would, and now you can stop being a clown."

With me in tow, Mr. Finerty arrived at the podium. The principal was holding a medal and reading a citation from Cooper Union: "For the best model produced in the city's public school workshops, the Haney Medal is awarded to Robert Schrank of our own P.S. 34." Mr. Finerty allowed that there were things about me that didn't make me the best student. "But look at what Robert Schrank can do once he puts his mind to it."

I had had no knowledge that Finerty had submitted the model for judging as "the best in the city." I was the most surprised kid in the world, and part of me was sure this had to be a mistake. All I could manage was a mumbled "thanks." But I had a new feeling, a feeling that maybe I could do something besides make trouble. Papa had had to go to work that day, and I was real sorry he couldn't be there. All my life I have tried to hang on to the knowledge that many of us need a Mr. Finerty to believe in us when we ourselves are full of self-doubt.

Some years later I was walking on Forty-second Street. At the corner of Lexington Avenue I saw a large group of people looking in the window of the Chrysler Building. They were watching a working model of the Gatum Lock of the Panama Canal labeled "winner of a city-wide public school contest sponsored by the Texaco Oil Company."

At dinner that graduation night, Tanta Bella was bubbling with joy, saying in her sweet voice, "You see, I always knew he wasn't so bad." Then, a little puffed up, she averred, "He can always get a job working with his hands. After all, there is nothing wrong with that, is there?" Everyone in the extended family—sisters, cousins, uncle, Papa—all agreed that I could get a job working with my hands. I was good for something. What bothered me underneath was the fact that the girls were going to high school and college and dancing school, while I was destined to go job-hunting.

Though he didn't show it much, Papa was happy I had managed to make it out of P.S. 34. If he was at all impressed with the Cooper Union medal, he never said so. I figured he probably thought Mr. Finerty built the canal model and gave me the credit. The following week, though, he suggested we take a trip down to Orchard Street on the Lower East Side. In spite of his Germanic sternness there was a pixie side hidden inside Papa, although it seldom surfaced after Mutter died. When it did, a silly grin would take over his usual somber face and his eyes would laugh. This time when I asked, "what are we going to get?" I glimpsed that old happy self for a fleeting moment.

"Oh, you'll see."

The Lower East Side was a replica of an Old World bazaar, with hundreds of pushcarts and street vendors selling almost everything short of automobiles. The primarily Jewish merchants had brought with them to America the tradition and atmosphere of an Eastern European market. As we walked around, Papa began to look in the windows of the men's and boys' clothing shops. Through that little sheepish grin, he asked, "Well, which suit do you like?"

I didn't believe I was about to get my first real man's suit, long pants and everything. It had been years since I had gotten even a new pair of the high socks and knickers that made me a target of my street pals' taunts: "Hey Robishe, you a golfer or you gonna yodel—Yoh da lo ho hee?"

But no, it was true. Papa wanted to know, "So which suit is it?" He had not been on the painting job that long, and I wondered about the money. (I still do.)

There was a light blue one with a fine white stripe. I pointed to it excitedly: "That's the one, Papa."

He thought it was a little light-colored. "But if it's what you want, let's see if we can get it."

We went into the store and were greeted by a smiling salesman. "Papa said, "I'd like to see the blue striped suit in the window for the boy."

The salesman nodded approvingly: "An excellent choice. That's a fine piece cloth, will last forever. You could give him also an extra pair pants." After a lengthy discussion about size, out of the racks came a jacket and—I still could not believe it—a vest and long pants! I was really excited.

I tried on the jacket in front of the mirror and saw myself transformed into a real grown-up person. Papa and the tailor pushed and pulled on the jacket until they finally agreed; then the salesman instructed the tailor to take up the sleeves two inches, the shoulder one inch, and the pants two inches. He said we could pick up the suit in a week. That's it, I thought. I have my first real man's suit. But not so fast.

Papa inquired, "So, how much you asking for it?"

The salesman considered: "Uhm, remember this is excellent material, the latest cut. With alterations should be twenty dollars, but for you a special—eighteen dollars."

Papa looked at him and shook his head, saying to me, "Come boy, this man is not serious." We started for the door.

The salesman came after us, stepping in front of Papa: "Look mister, I know the boy likes the suit. Look at him, he gonna cry. I tell you vhat, I'll cut our profit. Take it for sixteen dollars. Believe me, is a steal. No place here you could get such a bargain."

I was sure that was it, but Papa looked at me, grinned, shook his head no, and the next thing I knew we were on the street in the middle of the crowds of pushcarts. I was about to burst into tears when Papa said, "Just keep walking. Don't worry, we'll get it." I started to cry.

When we were a block away from the shop the salesman came running, the suit over his arm. "Look, I talked to the boss. He said 'Okay make a special deal for the boy. Give him the suit a present, fourteen dollars.'"

Papa looked at me: "You sure you like it?" I nodded, afraid to speak, and Papa acceded. "All right, I'll give you twelve dollars."

"You vant to rob me, get a gun! You don't know a bargain when you got it."

"Twelve dollars. Take it or leave it."

"Thirteen fifty."

"Thirteen."

"Well, you stole it. So pay fifty cents for alterations."

"All right, but make sure you do it right."

I had had my first lesson in the strategy of bargaining. I remembered it years later when I was negotiating for the wages of thousands of workers in union contract talks.

A week later I picked up the suit and wore it home, refusing to sit down on the subway so I could show it off. I was the proudest boy who ever rode the Lexington Avenue line.

It wasn't long afterward that I overheard Papa and Alice having one hell of an argument. She had been going full time to Hunter College, but the money problems at home kept getting worse and she was forced to drop out of school. She was working at a twenty-five-cents-an-hour job in an eyeglass frame factory and going to City College at night. She met a guy there and began staying out late.

I don't know what the argument was really about. Maybe Papa was just annoyed with her new-found independence and trying to exert his waning authority. Anyway, it was two o'clock in the morning on a Saturday night, and there was a very nasty quarrel. I heard Papa accuse Alice of behaving like a whore. I was astounded. The thought of my straitlaced sister acting like a whore was ludicrous.

A few weeks after this strange incident my two sisters found a one-room studio apartment and moved out of the house. I wanted so much to go with them but thought it would be disloyal to Papa. Besides, they never asked me to come.

5

Job Hunting

The despair brought by unemployment comes not only from the threat of destitution, but from the sudden view of vast nothingness ahead. The unemployed are more likely to follow the peddlers of hope than the handers-out of relief.

Milan Kundera

It was the winter of 1933—the pit of the depression. The renewed hopes that "Happy Days Are Here Again" excited by the election of FDR were not being fulfilled. Even the approaching repeal of Prohibition was being greeted with apathy. For me, and for the still-growing hordes of unemployed workers, job hunting offered no bright prospects.

Catching the subway at 6:00 A.M., I would curl up like a cat in a corner seat and sleep until the train pulled into the 42nd Street station half an hour later. I would start by walking through the garment and fur districts of the Lower East Side looking for "Help Wanted" signs. By 7:00 A.M. the streets were full of people—a few hurrying to a job, the rest looking for one. There *were* no "Help Wanted" signs. If someone had put one up, there probably would have been a riot. All over the city, an army of unemployed were asking bosses and foremen, "Any chance of some work? Can I leave my name just in case?" I would walk and look, walk and look, walk, walk, walk! Some days it felt as if I had walked from one end of the city to the other.

Months of job hunting went by, with no results. But walking in the city did have its rewards. Once the morning had been spent looking for nonexistent "Help Wanted" signs, I could tell myself that I had tried and seek out something else to do. Arriving home too early would leave me open to the accusation that I hadn't looked hard enough. One place to kill a meaningless hour was the medicine show on 14th Street. The be-draggled, downcast looks of the spectators clearly identified them as un-employed and miserable. The "theater" was an open storefront with a stage at the back end. On one side of the stage stood a table full of bot-tles; on the other was an old Chevy roadster. "The Mighty Adam," a very muscular man of medium height, posed himself between them. He had a huge head of hair that hung down to his rear. "Before you leave here," he would announce, "I'm gonna show you what a healthy body can do. See that car over there? Well, I'm gonna pull it across this stage with my hair!"

He would then hold up a small bottle of brownish liquid and go into a long spiel about all the things this tonic would do for our "poisoned" bod-ies. "Look at you! You're a pretty sight, with your ugly pimples, dandruff, bald heads, bunions, hemorrhoids, and bad backs!" He paused for a long second. "And, besides, you smell awful! For God's sake, do yourself—and hey, your friends—a favor. Clean the poisons out of your system!" By now the room would be rocking with laughter." It didn't phase him a bit. Pointing a finger at us, he would continue: "You're getting uglier just standing there. Why? It's the worst thing of all." Another dramatic pause. "You can't move your bowels!! You're sittin' there squeezin' your guts out, giving yourself a great bunch of piles, and nothin's comin' out, right?" He would stop until the laughter subsided.

"Do you know why?!! Do you know why?!!" he demanded comba-tively. Silence. Once at this point a bum, holding up an empty whiskey bottle, suddenly yelled, "'Cause I ain't got no more booze, that's why, if you wanna know." After an assistant hustled the drunk out, Mighty Adam resumed his routine. "I'll tell you why!! Your bodies are afflicted because they have lost their life fluid. Did you ever see a dog or a cats sit-tin' and squeezin' their guts out like you? No, you didn't, and you won't either, because they still have their life fluid."

Finally, after a few more comments about life fluids, he would weave his hair into a thick braid and, to the music of a Sousa march played on the Victrola, connect it to a rope hooked onto the Chevy. With much huffing and puffing and waving of arms, he would pull it across the stage to a full round of applause. As the crowd was thinning out, a couple of young women would walk around selling the "Life Fluid Tonic." In the many times I stopped by to watch Mighty Adam, I never once saw anyone buy it.

The best relief from the despair bred by futile job hunting was the ten-cent early afternoon double feature. After grabbing a lunch of two nickel hot dogs with mustard and sauerkraut from a pushcart vendor, I would head off to Times Square with all the other discouraged job hunters to get in before the 2:00 P.M. price change. In the thirties there were dozens of double-feature houses around the square filled with the unemployed watching Fredric March in *Dr. Jekyll and Mr. Hyde,* the Marx Brothers in *Duck Soup, The Thin Man* with William Powell and Myrna Loy, or Boris Karloff in *Bride of Frankenstein.* Watching a picture twice could keep you in the theater until four or five o'clock.

Coming home at night was the bad part. It was important to keep up the family's hope that I might actually land a job or I would lose the quarter for car fare and lunch. To do this, I had to invent stories about jobs I almost got. At the dinner table one evening I described seeing a sign "Floor Boys Wanted." (Floor boys were the kids who pushed the hand trucks around the garment district.) "The line was already around the block when I got there at seven, but I got right in it. It took until nine for them to get to me, and they took my name and address and told me to come back next week."

As I told it, it seemed like a pretty good story. Papa, dog-tired from his painting job, paid no attention, but I felt that neither he nor Siegfried believed me. Tanta Bella, though, was her usual lovable self: "You see? He will be working in no time. You'll see."

As usual, my trouble came from Siegfried. He asked casually, "Where was this place?"

"Oh, on 38th Street, just off Seventh Avenue. You know one of those big loft buildings."

"What floor was it on?"

Damn! He was trying to catch me again. Everyone at the dinner table looked up to see if I was trapped.

"Oh, I think it was the twelfth."

"You mean you don't remember the floor?"

"Well, when you spend a whole day lookin' for a job, you can't possibly remember every place you've been."

"But you said they took your name and address and asked you to come back." I knew what was coming. Siegfried put down his fork, wiped his Bismarck mustache, and looked over his bifocals. "Now what was the name of this company?"

God damn him, I thought, he's just getting back at me for all that cellar shit. "I think it was the Botany Robe Company."

Everyone seemed relieved. By God, Bobby had actually talked to a real company. He had an honest-to-goodness job interview. That was a big victory. Tanta Bella bubbled: "See? He got his first interview. Isn't that wonderful? Don't worry, he'll get a job." She turned to Papa, " And how did the painting go today?"

Papa hardly spoke at mealtimes anymore. Either exhaustion or something about the work seemed to silence him. In those days ceilings were painted with a whitewash called calcimine, which was slapped on with a six-inch brush. Before the ceiling could be repainted, the old calcimine had to be washed off with soapy water and a sponge. That was Papa's job. Every day for eight hours a day, six days a week, he washed ceilings. When he first started, it didn't seem so bad; it was a job, and it paid seventy-five cents an hour. Now when Tanta Bella waxed enthusiastic about it, Pop just sat in silence.

One Sunday afternoon at the zoo, as Papa and I were watching the hippos sloshing around in the mud, I asked him why the ceiling-washing job was so bad. He thought for a while. When Papa felt strongly about something he would answer a question as if he were giving a public speech.

"Do you know what it feels like to work for a stupid, ignorant, bigoted fool? That's what I have to do. This man is an animal. He refers to Jews as 'kikes' and says unions are for lazy people who don't want to work. And he thinks Hitler is great! No matter how hard I work, he is never satisfied. He came to the job the other day while I was on the scaffold washing a filthy ceiling. The soapy water was running down my arms, and I was working as fast as possible, soaked with dirty water. 'Otto,' he said, 'what the hell you doing all day? Reading your dumb papers? It's three o'clock an' you're still not done? You shoulda been finished by noon.' I was so mad I had to keep myself from dumping the bucket of water on his head."

"Why didn't you, Pop? He deserved it."

"Well, we need the money to eat. So we have to put up with the fools, ignoramuses, and the bloodsuckers who own the world. It isn't bad enough we're exploited? They need to mistreat us, humiliate us as well? But Bobby, someday—when the workers take power—there will be no unemployment, no exploitation simply for profit. And, most important, no more humiliation."

"Yeah Pop, and no more dirty soapy water runnin' down your arms, right?" I would never, ever forget the indignities that many workers like Papa suffered on their jobs.

On Sundays there was a lot of time to kill. Except for the Zoo—which was free—we couldn't afford many of our old pastimes. People found new games to play to fill up the time. Mah-jongg, a sort of Chinese dominoes, became very popular, because it took forever to play. In between games, attention would shift to the weekend want ads, with my employment, instead of Papa's, as the focus of concern. Everyone would sit around with the classifieds. One of the Tanzer girls might spot something of interest and say, "Hey, Bobby, look at this, 'Wanted: Helper in a Mattress Factory. Learn to Tie Springs.' Why don't you try that?"

"Yeah, sure, I'll go there tomorrow," I'd reply. To myself I thought, "You're going to your nice school on Monday, and all I'm good for is the mattress factory. Well, up yours."

On the Sunday after he cross-examined me about my job "interview," Siegfried revived the subject. "By the way, I happened to be looking in the phone book under *B,* and you know what? I could not find the Botany Robe Company."

"Well, I guess maybe they don't have a phone." With that, I was out the back door.

I could hear Tanta Belle say, "Why do you pick on him that way. You know he's trying."

I stopped outside the door long enough to hear Siegfried say, "Because he is a liar and a thief. He never tells the truth and hangs out with a crowd of bums. You'll see how he ends up."

I went looking for the gang to see if we could figure a way to make some money. Mario, Perry, Al Pupo, and Johnny Buttoli were all sitting on a stoop bullshitting. Except for Al, we were all out of school and out of work. His uncle Louie, the local Mafioso, owned ice wagons, sold wine

grapes in season, and had an olive-oil importing business. Once in a while
Al would get us a couple of days' work unloading grapes from freight cars
at the Bronx Terminal or moving cases from one truck to another. "When
you're handling hot stuff," Al informed us, "you have to move it around a
lot. Mix it up with legit stuff, then nobody can tell the difference. Get it?"

Delivering fresh-killed chickens for Rocco's poultry store was another
way of earning a few dimes. Rocco's was patronized by fierce-looking Italian women who dressed all in black; to me they resembled the penitents in
a medieval painting I saw on one of our regular visits to the Metropolitan
Museum. Roaming purposefully among the cages of live chickens, one of
the women would suddenly point to a chicken as if guided by revelation to
just the right victim. Sensing danger, the chickens would be clucking up a
storm. Rocco would grab the sacrificial bird and, with a resounding
whack, cut off its head. Quicker than the eye could follow, he dumped it
into a garbage can and slammed down the cover. The sound of the head-
less chickens thrashing around inside the can for what seemed like ages
sent shivers down my spine. Finally, Rocco would lift the cover, grab the
chicken as though it still had some potential to resist, and dunk it in a
bucket of boiling water before plucking the feathers. His hands ran over
the chicken like electric shears and in minutes he presented it to the cus-
tomer: "Here you are, lady, clean as your baby's bottom." On a hot day
Rocco's stank of chicken shit, wet feathers, and garbage cans full of blood,
making he whole neighborhood smell like a slaughterhouse.

We would hang around Rocco's until one of the women asked us to
deliver her chickens. A good tip was twenty cents, and fifteen cents was
okay. Mostly we got a dime.

After a pretty good day of delivering chickens, Mario and I sometimes
walked a couple of miles to Morris's candy store in "Jewtown"—as it
was known in Van Nest—for a thick chocolate malted that filled two tall
glasses. On one lovely spring evening, as we meandered up Tremont Avenue feeling pleasantly full of malteds, we came upon a street meeting.
Speaking from the top of a stepladder with an American flag tied to one
side was a nifty-looking young woman. Mario and I stood admiring her
"great pair of boobs," which were nicely outlined by a tight-fitting pink
sweater. On the opposite corner, on a soapbox similarly adorned with
the flag, stood a young man also making a passionate speech.

The sweater girl spoke ardently about what needed to be done to create more jobs, stop evictions, increase unemployment relief, and organize the unorganized. The man on the opposite corner was urging people not to listen to her, because she was "an agent of Stalin interested only in promoting the interests of Russia." He announced that later that evening a major speaker would reveal how Stalin had sold out the Russian Revolution.

Finding the girl a clearly more attractive choice, I suggested to Mario that we listen to her, but he rejected the idea: "Uh-unh! I don't wanna listen to that Red stuff." To me the speeches had the familiar ring of Sunday School, our family dinner table conversations, and the Lincoln Park camp. I tried to explain to him that capitalism was the reason we were out of work and that under socialism everyone would have a job. My interest surprised Mario. We had never talked about socialism before. "Boy, if the priest ever heard you talk this Red stuff you would have to say Hail Marys until your knees was bleedin'. Robishe, I'm tellin' you, don't talk that Red Jew stuff around Van Nest. Anyhow, I'm gettin' the hell outa here. So long."

The crowd on both corners was growing, and people were listening and showing their approval or disapproval by yelling "That's right" or "Go back to Russia" or "You tell 'em." Back and forth I went. The guy from the Socialist Workers' Party was saying that we couldn't trust Roosevelt to stop fascism or the NRA (National Recovery Act) to lift the country out of the depression. Only the power of the working class could prevent fascism and assure jobs and security for all. The young woman communist argued that the people must force the government to do something now about unemployment and hunger.

Like me, some people drifted back and forth across the street listening to both speakers. They started their own little discussions, becoming very animated as they argued about the depression, who was responsible for it, and how to get out of it. I found myself the recipient of an armful of radical literature, including a copy of the newspaper *The Militant* and pamphlets by Trotsky, which mostly insisted on the necessity of a worldwide revolution. The Communist party material was primarily about jobs, unemployment relief, and stopping fascism. I stayed on as speaker after speaker took the platform to talk about women and socialism, youth unemployment, the NRA, and the need for peace. I was amazed at the speakers' skill to field questions from hecklers right in the middle of a speech. The meetings ended late and everyone wandered away, except for a few hard-core believers engaged in violent shouting matches. I thought their arguments sounded like a great game of wits.

Capitalism and class warfare—that was familiar stuff to me. What was new were the ideas for action, the assumption that we could *do* something about our misery. I knew I would be back for more. I was full of questions about myself and the depression, and the tired radicals of my father's generation didn't seem to be offering any solutions. Maybe here were people—young people—with the answers. I wanted desperately to be a part of some activity that would address my predicament of being out of school, out of work, out of money, out of food, out of clothes, out of shoes—and out of hope.

It was a good half hour's walk from the meeting place on Tremont Avenue to our neighborhood, and it was late when I arrived home. Looking up from his book at my armload of papers and pamphlets, Papa wanted to know, "What have you got there?" I showed him the papers. He glanced over them, commenting that they were very interesting but suggesting that I be careful what I get into.

"But Pop, didn't you say it's the system that is rotten and causes all our troubles? So why not overthrow it and put something better in its place? That's what the communists want to do."

"Yes, it's true that the capitalist system is evil. It makes people into exploitative monsters with little or no concern for their fellow humans. But, my dear boy, what you put in its place may turn out to be far more important than the answer to some immediate problem."

A few days later when I met Mario to play stickball, he begged me not to say anything about the meeting on Tremont: "'Cause if my father finds out, I'm gonna get my lumps."

"Don't worry, Mario, I'm not gonna say anything. Christ, you didn't do nothin' but pass a corner where they happened to be meetin'. You didn't sign nothin'. Jesus, Mario, what are you so scared of?"

"Listen Robishe, you don't know my parents. If they ever see me with the Communist Jew *Daily Worker*, they would never let me see you again. That's how they are."

The next day, as always, the clip-clop of the milkman's horses woke me early. I was in the kitchen by 6:00 A.M. Pop had already gone. I had my bread and cocoa, made a leftover-something sandwich, checked my carfare, and picked up the want ad section of the Sunday *Journal American* and made for the subway.

There was an ad in the paper for Western Union delivery boys. I'd often seen these guys running around town in their military-type uniforms. The word was that the pay was lousy but the tips were good. Besides, if I made a lot in tips nobody but me had to know how much I earned. I decided to try Western Union.

I made my way over to Church Street in downtown Manhattan with a new determination. No fooling around—I was really going to get this job. When I came up out of the subway I saw a line that seemed to wind around three city blocks. The men waiting all looked a lot older than me. Learning that the people in the front had been there since yesterday made me feel really stupid. As others joined the line behind me I felt better— at least I was no longer last. The men in line soon became friendly. After all, we were all in the same mess. Everybody was swapping stories about how, "I almost got this job at Macy's," or Bamberger's, or Braunschweiger's, or the Edison Company.

About 9:00 A.M. word came down the line that they were taking applications. People were delighted that something was actually happening. The line moved very slowly. Two or three young men came along handing out leaflets about a demonstration in Union Square. "All out to Union Square for jobs. Make your voice heard. Demand jobs now." Almost everyone took a leaflet, some eagerly, some reluctantly. Most of the people in the line agreed that something had to be done. I put the leaflet in my pocket. If I don't get this lousy job, I thought, I'm going to Union Square to demonstrate. That would be it. I'd show them! Either I got the job or I would demonstrate.

At about noon, Western Union announced that they were closing applications for the day. At first there was disbelief: "How can they keep us standing for hours—days for some people—when they know they're not going to hire this many messengers?"

Then came the anger. "God damn the sons of bitches! They just don't give a damn about us."

"We're just shit. That's it. When you're unemployed, you're just shit. That's all. Just shit."

Frustrated and bitter, the men began drifting away, disappearing into the streets around the skyscrapers in lower Manhattan. I had been standing next to a tired, beaten-looking Jewish man who asked me what I was going to do now. I said I didn't know. He was going to check on some other job possibilities and invited me to come along to keep him company. I agreed.

"Do you expect to land anything?" I asked him as we walked away.

"No, of course not."

"So why do you bother?"

"Because you gotta keep looking. That's the whole thing, looking. Besides, it keeps you busy. Otherwise, you could get in trouble. You know," he said, "President Roosevelt (he said *Roos* like in *rooster*) announced he was starting more public projects for the WPA. Maybe we should apply for that."

I shrugged. "I don't know."

"Listen," he said, "if you keep lookin' for work, even if you don't find it, people will respect you. But, if you don't look, you're a bum and that's the worst. So good-bye and good luck."

At dinner I told about the Western Union line and how I almost made it. Siegfried peered over his glasses with the usual look of disbelief. Papa was worn out and depressed from washing ceilings and said very little. But dear old Tanta Bella was delighted: "See? He will get a job yet. Don't worry. He's a nice boy."

I mentioned the people giving out leaflet s for the jobs demonstration. Right away, Pansy demanded self-importantly who was sponsoring the affair. She read over the leaflet. "Ha! This Workers' Alliance is another Communist front organization. You'd better watch out." Pansy had joined the Lovestone Communist faction, whose major enemy was the Communist party.*

---

*The Lovestoneites were a minor faction led by Jay Lovestone, a Marxist intellectual who was expelled from the Communist party in 1929 for holding that Marxist-Leninist ideas had to be modified to fit the peculiar conditions of America.

I told her defiantly that I would go to the demonstration anyway: "We have to do something about all these people out of work with nothing to eat." That seemed to wake Pop up. He looked at me with a sort of quizzical expression, not quite believing what he heard but seeming to approve of my new interest.

I asked several of my Van Nest buddies to come to the demonstration with me, but the answer was a unanimous "No." In those days, Union Square had the reputation of being a hotbed of radicalism; just going there suggested some kind of left-wing sympathies. My friends gave me the usual excuses: "My father would kill me." "If the St. Domenic's priest found out I'd be doin' Hail Marys for the next year. Robishe, you don't know about this stuff 'cause you ain't Catholic." He was right. The members of our family were hard-nosed atheists. All I knew about Catholicism was the need to go to mass and do Hail Marys—whatever they were. Papa, believing that it would interfere with our freedom to figure things out for ourselves, always insisted that we stay away from religious "hocus-pocus."

When the subway train stopped at 14th Street, a lot of people got out. I could hear the loudspeakers as I ran up the stairs from the station. The street was thronged with what looked like thousands of people. The fellow who distributed the leaflet had said that if there was a big enough turnout the government would have to do something for the unemployed. This was great! The speaker was talking about the capitalists trying to solve their economic problems at the expense of the working class. They had created this army of unemployed, he said, to depress wages even more and to prevent unionization. This was a familiar argument, and I felt right at home.

Still, I wasn't quite sure what you were supposed to do at a demonstration besides just be there. I wondered if there was a special way to cheer or shout. The square was ringed with cops. Some of them were on horses trained to move sideways to push the crowd back. Others were just sitting on their on motorcycles, while the rest were on foot and casually swinging their nightsticks around on the leather laces.

The chairman introduced someone who was the president of the "unemployment councils." Addressing us as "comrades," the speaker said that capitalism was responsible for the high unemployment and that it was the government's responsibility to create jobs for all citizens who wanted to work. Yes, he acknowledged, we want home relief (welfare), but only as a temporary measure. People want jobs. That was exactly what I came to hear, and I was cheering along with everyone else. The crowd had grown and was almost completely filling the square. I wandered around, finally ending up at the outer edges of the square where the various groups were distributing their literature. The wars among the left-wing factions seemed only slightly less bitter than the fight against capitalism.

At the outer fringes of the crowd there were periodic scuffles with the police, who were trying to keep the traffic lanes open. The cops were using their horses or revving up their motorcycle engines to make an opening for the cars to get through. One middle-aged Jewish woman referred to the cops as "dirty Cossacks" The chairman was exhorting the crowd, "Comrades, do not be provoked by the police. They are agents of the bourgeoisie sent here to create a riot and make us look like a mob of undisciplined rowdies. Remember, the revolutionary working class prides itself on its discipline." The crowd, which was mostly made up of middle-aged workers, seemed in complete agreement with whatever the speakers said.

As the demonstration was winding down and people began to drift away, a voice shouted, "Hey, ain't you from Tremont Avenue?" I looked around uncertainly. Yes, someone was talking to me: "Why don't you come with us to the cafeteria." There were six of them, two girls and four boys, singing, laughing, and carrying copies of the *Daily Worker*. They were all excited about the huge demonstration and certain that actions like this would get the working class moving. I was greatly attracted to that kind of talk, but I only had fifteen cents in my pocket and wasn't sure I should go to the cafeteria. One of the girls urged me not to worry about money. "What's your name, comrade? Mine is May."

"Bob."

"None of us have much money, Bob. Whatever we have we share." Laughing, she added, "Besides, there's always catsup and mustard on a slice of rye bread."

The 14th Street cafeteria was half the size of a football field and mobbed with people celebrating the demonstration. May told me to "grab a table over in the corner while the rest of us get what we can." Wow, I thought,

I'm taking orders from a girl I don't even know. They brought coffee, soup, sandwiches, and a Danish. Someone suggested that I buy a nickel order of rye bread as there was enough egg salad in one of their sandwiches to make two. My dime bought the bread and a cup of coffee.

At first the excited conversation was about the demonstration. How many people were there? Was it one hundred thousand, two hundred thousand, or three hundred thousand? All agreed that the police and the bourgeois press would lie and say there were only a few thousand.

My new friends, who willingly shared their cigarettes and food, were all members of the Young Communist League (YCL) branch on Tremont Avenue in the Bronx. I'm not exactly sure when I became a serious smoker. It could well have been at that gathering, where everyone seemed to be in a constant state of lighting up. We were on the coffee and Danish when May asked me to join the YCL and become part of the struggle. I had a strong desire to do something about my own plight as well as that of others. But what? There were so many different radical groups—Communists, Socialists, Lovestoneites, Trotskyites, Socialist Labor Party, the Wobblies, and so forth. I was not an intellectual who could form opinions based on a well-reasoned theory. My primary interest lay in action.

Henry, a tall, skinny, Italian with shifty little eyes, lectured me on the need to study and learn all about Marxism. He kept asking me what I had read? Embarrassed and defensive, I didn't want to appear to be an absolute dumb bell, so I said, I had read the *Communist Manifesto*. In fact I hadn't read much of anything—nor, in truth, paid a lot of attention to the ideas behind the Sunday School discussions. May said not to worry. Once I joined the YCL I could attend a beginners' class and learn all I needed to know about socialism and how to achieve it.

When I asked about the fundamental difference between Stalin and Trotsky, all six of them began talking at once, but May quickly became the dominant voice. She said that after Lenin's death Trotsky had tried to capture the party to use it for his own personal designs and that only Stalin's alertness had kept him from succeeding.* This big talk made me

---

*Leon Trotsky, with Lenin the leader of the Bolshevik Revolution, had numerous ties to the American Left both before and after the revolution. After Lenin's death, Stalin maneuvered him out of power and, in 1929, had him banished from Russia. Trotsky was murdered on orders from Stalin in Mexico in 1940.

feel important, and I promised May I would drop by Tremont and Prospect for the street meeting. So began a lifestyle of going to meetings and sitting afterwards in cafeterias to talk, talk, talk.

I also began to read in earnest some of the pamphlets and newspapers I had collected. Slowly, I learned about the differences among the radical groups. They all agreed, of course, that capitalism was evil. More important, they shared a belief in the basic contradiction within the capitalist system that would ultimately lead to its collapse. That contradiction was between private ownership of the means of production and the essentially social nature of work itself. This would inevitably lead to intensified class warfare and ultimately to the overthrow of capitalism. Under a capitalist system, because workers only received a part of the full value of their labor power, they were deprived of the ability to buy the very things they produced. The "surplus value" they created but did not receive was the profit confiscated by the owners. This contradiction created the cyclical economic depressions that led to unemployment, decreased wages, and war as a way out of the crisis. Meanwhile, under capitalist influence the schools taught children the wonders of the profit system, while cultural institutions like the movies glorified rugged individualism and fostered discrimination, creating convenient sources of cheap labor. Finally, capitalists promoted religion, the "opiate" designed to keep the working class docile.

The middle class was undependable. Because they owed their existence to the profit mode of production, they could not be trusted in the final struggle. Nor could the *lumpenproletariat*—degraded and uprooted individuals such as alcoholics and addicts, who were cut off from their class roots. Artists and intellectuals had a choice; they could be of service to the ruling class or the revolution. Ultimately, however, the revolution could count unreservedly only on the working class because, as the *Manifesto* avowed, "they had nothing to lose but their chains, and a world to gain."

The finer points of difference among the various groups opposing capitalism seemed less important to me than being out of school, out of work, and broke. There was considerable relief in knowing that being unemployed and poor was not my fault. I was a victim of the capitalist system in crisis, which was trying to solve its internal contradictions at my expense. The people on the job lines, the soup lines, those living in shantytowns—all were there through no fault of their own. My realization was a good example of Thomas Carlyle's maxim: "The alpha and omega of wisdom is to know whether to change yourself or the situation." I saw clearly that the problem was the situation. The system was failing. It was a reassuring thought and made me decide to read the basic works of Marx, Engels, Lenin, and the others.

It was inevitable that the dinner table discussion that night would get around to the unemployment demonstration. Pansy wanted to know what had happened there. Describing it as best I could got me into another long argument about the differences among the various radical groups. For me, what was important was the fact that thousands of people had demonstrated for jobs. I found all the discussion about Stalin, Trotsky, and the direction of the Russian Revolution too remote. They were issues in a far-off place called Moscow. At the time I had never been any farther from the Bronx than Lincoln Park, New Jersey. My vision of Russia was of a lot of bent-over men pulling boats along the Volga River.

Not long after this, the miracle happened. After all the desperate hunting, I landed a job as a helper in a furniture factory in Brooklyn. I got the job, which paid twenty-five cents an hour, through a friend of a friend in the Sunday School. The whole family was excited. Bobby was going to work! To be at the plant on Morgan Avenue in Brooklyn by eight I had to leave the house by six-thirty. On my first day everyone in the house got up to see me go off carrying my lunch and overalls.

The company, which made frames for upholstered furniture, was located in a four-story factory building. My first assignment was to move parts from one machine to another for assembly. I was sort of a human conveyor belt. I could have spent a lot of time waiting for a slow-moving freight elevator, but instead I often carried the stuff up and down the stairs. That's when I first caught hell from my fellow workers for working too fast. "Hey, boy! Slow down. Take a smoke break instead of bustin' your ass. You're gonna work yourself right out of a job if you keep that up." The foreman, of course, appreciated my efforts and would periodically reward me by putting me on a machine. The union shop steward objected strenuously as I was not yet a member, not having completed my sixty-day trial period.

In the beginning I was just happy to have a real job. At home even Siegfried was treating me with more respect. Having money to buy a sandwich in a cafeteria or go to a movie or have a double malted on Tremont Avenue was a great feeling. I was very happy to be working and making money. I am not sure how long it took before the work became so monotonous and tedious that I felt as if the clock had stopped; the days never seemed to end. I found talking to my fellow workers at coffee breaks, lunch hour, and in the locker room the most satisfying part of the job.

After work I would rush home on the subway, eat dinner, and be off to Tremont and Prospect for the street meetings.

I now had a new interest. Her name was Barbara.

I first saw her on a June night at a street corner meeting. It was one of those warm spring nights when people are drawn to the streets for the simple pleasure of being outside. I saw a girl who seemed perpetually bubbling with laughter. Though her friends were constantly shushing her, she seemed unable to contain her overflowing joy of life. Her long, wavy brown hair tumbled to her shoulders, and she had an enchanting way of tossing her head back to get the hair out of her face. I will always remember her sparkling green eyes, her well-rounded breasts, and the way her feet turned out like a ballet dancers'.

I had to figure out a way to meet her. Since she was in constant motion, even trying to get close to her was a challenge. I thought about how I could walk home with her or buy her an ice cream cone or coffee. Something. My excitement rose as I tried to keep her in view by wandering casually around the crowd. After a while she became aware of my attention and starting glancing at me quickly with a cute little smile. Soon the glances and little smiles became a game. When the meeting ended, she went off with a group of YCLers, and I saw no way I could possibly join them.

After that—though I didn't yet know her name—Barbara became my chief reason for attending the street meetings. Hauling heavy loads of furniture parts around the plant all day left me exhausted. Even so, I would rush home every day to clean up and change my clothes. As I bolted down my dinner, the family became curious. What's your big hurry? My newly devised excuse was "I have a meeting to go to," and with that I was out the door. It must have been three or four meetings later that I arrived at the corner quite early and found her there alone arranging copies of the *Daily Worker* and some YCL pamphlets on a table

She saw me, smiled, and asked, "Why don't you help me?"

"Of course. What should I do?"

"Just set out the pamphlets and papers in neat little piles." She asked if I was a member of the Young Communist League?

"No."

"Then why do you come to these meetings?"

"Well, I am considering becoming a member."

Handing me a membership card, she suggested that I fill it out. I offered her a cigarette. From the rapid way she puffed it I could tell she wasn't a real smoker. I said I had a lot of questions about the YCL. Would she be willing to answer them? She didn't know if she could tell me everything I needed to know. "Why not join and then attend the new members' class?"

"Could we get together after the meeting and talk about it?" I felt dizzy. My heart was pounding, and I thought my legs would crumble.

"Sure, we can go to the Deli and have a coffee." Wow! She had agreed to have coffee with me.

Hymie's Delicatessen on Tremont Avenue was the place all the YCLers headed for after the meeting. There must have been a half dozen other "comrades" there, and I was outmaneuvered for a seat next to Barbara. Were there other guys interested in her? Was she going out with one of them? Some people bought a Danish pastry and others pastrami sandwiches. It was all cut up and shared around the table as they reviewed the street meeting. The conversation then ranged over FDR's efforts at dealing with unemployment, the rise of fascism in Europe, and the organizing drive of local laundry workers. Barbara told the group that I was not a member of the YCL.

Her announcement focused all eyes on me—a potential recruit. One guy said he had seen me at a number of the meetings. So why didn't I join? I said I wasn't ready to discuss that just yet, wanting to save talk about joining exclusively for Barbara. They continued trying to draw me out, but I was unyielding, and the conversation turned to other subjects—movies, novels, and City College debates. It was after one in the morning by the time we all left the Deli. When I asked Barbara if I could walk her home, she looked around as if checking on whether someone else was available, then said "Sure, why not?"

The walk was shorter than I had hoped. As we walked along, her rapid-fire chatter about the Workers' Laboratory Theater (WLT) was totally lost on me. I was aware only of the thrill of our hands "accidentally" touching. Then she switched to the reasons why I must join the YCL: "This is where the action is. If you really want to do something about unemployment and low wages and that sort of thing you need to join up."

She lived on one of the many streets in the Bronx where the monotonous brick walls of six-story apartment houses were only occasionally broken by a one- or two-family house. The walk-up apartment she lived in was a few blocks from the Bronx River and the entrance to the zoo. As we sat on the stoop she told me that her mother, father, and sister were all party members. Her own all-consuming interest was revolutionary theater, the WLT. "Think of us as the theater of the people, the working class. We go to plant gates and street corners and put on agitprop theater." I looked blank. "Agitation propaganda. We learned it from the Germans. Our skits and plays help workers understand the class struggle." Oh, yes, I knew about that from Sunday School fundraising shows. But this, I sensed, was different.

Right there on the stoop the WLT's latest drama began to unfold. She became excited, explaining the show and acting out bits of it. I was getting worked up too, but not over the theater. I made a lunge to kiss her but missed. My lips landed somewhere between her ear and her chin. It didn't phase her a bit; she just giggled and went right on.

"One of us comes out reading a newspaper. 'President Roosevelt announces that unemployment has dropped to 13 million.' Mrs. Janesi, who lives in a Harlem slum tenement, comes home from standing on a soup line to find her three-month-old daughter dead in her crib from rat bites."

Barbara made believe she was turning the page. "Ah, look at this. 'Mr. and Mrs. Ashley Van Richen announce the engagement of their daughter Pamela to Horace Moneybags at the Rockribbed Country Club. The bride-to-be wore a beautiful silk gown from Bendel's that cost $200. The dinner menu included truffles, pheasant under glass, glazed asparagus, and a seven-foot cake'. The whole thing is done on a dark stage. One lone spot is focused on the action. The spot fades out, another one comes on, and we are in Mrs. Janesi's apartment in Harlem. A few neighbors gather and express their fury over what has happened. Mrs. Janesi is threatening to kill the landlord, whom she holds responsible for the rat infestation."

By now it was around 2:00 A.M. I was sitting on the stoop smoking one cigarette after another as Barbara ran through the show out on the side-walk. A few stragglers came by, stared at us, shrugged, and walked on.

"The spot fades out, then comes on again. We see a meeting where an organizer from the unemployed council is telling the tenants in Mrs. Janesi's building that they should organize a tenants' council to demand their rights. 'You are entitled to decent homes without rats and to jobs at a living wage.'" Barbara was carried away, seemingly able to go on all night. "The organizer passes out cards to the tenants and they sign up."

"The next scene shows a picket in front of the old slum. You see, we use only minimum props, and damn few people; so all we have is a mock-up of a front door. By using the spotlights on a small stage we can sim-ulate a big crowd. Look, this is how we do the pickets. There might only be six of us, but as we walk in a circle in and out of the spotlight it looks like an endless line of people. Oh, it's wonderful! We did this show the other night in Harlem and at the end the whole audience stood up and cheered."

By then, I was clapping noisily. Suddenly an old guy stuck his head out of a window above us and yelled: "If you people are so interested in the working class, why the fuck don't you do your actin' someplace else so this working man can get some sleep?"

I took Barbara's hand and led her into the hall. Standing in silent ten-sion at the foot of the staircase, neither of us able to speak, we leaned to-ward each other and kissed. Slowly, ever so slowly, our arms wrapped around each other and we stood motionless mouth to mouth. My excite-ment was out of control and I was afraid she would feel it and be of-fended. It seemed like forever that we stood clasping each other between the mailboxes and the staircase. Finally we peeled ourselves apart, only to return to kiss goodnight several times.

"Can I see you tomorrow?"

"Oh, no, I have a rehearsal."

"Can I meet you afterwards?"

"It's all the way down on 12th Street."

"Oh, that's nothing. I can meet you there."

"Okay, but you might have to wait around a while. Sometimes we work until after nine."

"I'll be there."

It was early morning. Not a soul was around as I bounded home across the park singing at the top of my lungs:

Ramona, I hear the mission bells above.
Ramona, they're ringing out our song of love.
I press you, caress you, and bless the day you taught me to care,
To always remember the rambling rose you wear in your hair.

Ramona, when day is done you'll hear my call.
Ramona, we'll meet beside the waterfall.
I dread the dawn when I awake to find you gone.
Ramona, I need you, my own.

I passed the old Sheffield Farms stables with its doors wide open and the memory of Miter Howe flashed briefly through my mind. In the still-sleeping dawn, the drivers were getting ready for their morning deliveries, and I could hear the stomping and neighing of their horses.

I managed to tiptoe into the house and up to my bed without kicking over a footstool or slamming a door. I lay in bed, tingling deliciously with my new-found joy and the excitement of Barbara—the kiss, the feeling of her breasts pressing against me. What would happen if I ever got to touch them? It was too much even to think about.

I'm not sure I slept at all that morning. Before long I got up and was off and running even earlier than usual. My euphoria carried me to the factory a half hour early; I could think only of nine o'clock that evening. I was singing at the top of my lungs in the locker room, where other early comers thought I had gone nuts.

That night I was on 12th Street at 8:30. Not right in front of the building where she was rehearsing but a little way down the block, so when she came out I could rush up as though I had just arrived. As I waited, time stood still, stuck. Nine o'clock finally arrived. I expected her to come out on the minute, but nothing stirred. Suddenly I was in a panic. What if I was in the wrong place? Frantically I searched for the slip of paper on which I had carefully printed the time and address. No, it was the right place.

At long last, at about 9:30, the door opened and eight or nine people emerged. They were involved in heated discussion, with Barbara in the thick of it, tossing her hair back as she made a comment. My casual approach, as if I had just come, was completely wasted. Nobody, including Barbara, took the slightest notice. She did say a perfunctory hello and introduce me to a comrade whose name I didn't get before turning back to the conversation. He apologized for her wryly: "Workers' Lab actors are involved in changing the world. You know how that is."

I walked along with them, ignored, to the 14th Street cafeteria. I sat there for the next hour and a half listening to them talk about the best way to portray the benefits of unionism to the city's sailors and longshoremen. Barbara herself said very little, and except for me nobody paid much attention to her.

As the gathering broke up, we said our good-byes to the others and headed for the subway. She was still excited by the rehearsal and talked all the way to the Bronx about the theater and her career as an actress. Looking at me with her shining green cat's eyes, she insisted that "Nothing is going to interfere with my acting career. Understand?" Well, of course, I didn't. I was being put on notice.

It was warm when we got to the Bronx Park station, and I suggested a short walk along the river. She looked at her watch. "Well, it's late. But it's such a beautiful night. It'd be a shame to go inside."

The path along the river was dotted with benches occupied by couples in a variety of mild and passionate embraces, stimulating my own desire to sit down with her. She kept up a stream of stage talk—about Stanislavski and sense memory, the Hedgerow Theater in Philadelphia, Paul Muni, the Jewish Theater—things I knew little or nothing about. I made a mental note to begin learning about the theater or she would lose interest in me. I spotted an empty bench. "Would you like to sit down?"

"Well, just for a little while."

Barbara talked while I fooled with her hair, kissed her ear, her cheek, rubbed her arm. Then, when I was kissing her neck, she turned her head and planted her lips on mine. We stuck that way with our mouths wide open, our bodies exploding. I began to move my hand under her blouse. She remained perfectly still, not helping, not resisting, but letting it happen.

"We had better go now." We got up, straightening ourselves, pulling down the pushed-up clothing. We put our arms around each other and started walking home. I said, "Barbara, I love you very much—I just think about you all the time."

She was quiet for a long while. "My life in the theater comes first. You have to remember that. And my life in the Young Communist League is second. If you joined the YCL, you could spend time at my house, because my parents are active party members."

For many months the walk in the park became a regular routine. We became expert at making love on a park bench, using our coats as covers in the cold weather. We did not get around to the real thing, because, as she explained, she was still a virgin and didn't want to get pregnant. It would ruin her career in the theater. She hastened to add that I shouldn't think she was being petty bourgeois about this. "It's just a matter of being sure that I don't get pregnant, that's all." She didn't trust condoms. "I will go to Dr. Herman on Washington Square and get a diaphragm fitted. He's a communist and understands these things as natural human functions and is not all full of petty bourgeois shit."

"Wonderful! When will you go?"

"Oh, as soon as I get some time from rehearsals and memorizing scripts. By the way, are you ready to join the YCL yet?"

"Well, I . . ."

She broke in, "If you did, you would be as busy with your league activity as I am with the theater and you'd miss me less." Then, in case I was losing interest, she would become kittenish and rub her head on my shoulder.

The more demonstrations, street meetings, and marches I attended the more fun I found them. Singing, "Solidarity Forever," "Hold the Fort," "The International," or "On the Line" was invigorating and raised my hopes for the future. I was seeing Barbara as often as I could—before or after rehearsals, in between performances, on the way home from meetings or work—any chance I could get. Dr. Herman told Barbara that if she was still a virgin he couldn't fit her with a diaphragm, so we were back in negotiation regarding the real thing.

One night she suggested I come by her house after work and have dinner with her parents. "Then we can go over to the Young Communist League headquarters to see if we can get you signed up."

That evening I raced up the five flights to their walk-up two steps at a time. A tall thin woman greeted me at the door. She said, "You must be Bob, I'm Mrs. Jennick, Barbara's mother. And this is her father, Jacob. Come in." She had short brown hair and a long face with eyes set so closely together that she looked perpetually about to cry. Jacob was a stocky, round-faced man They both spoke with heavy Jewish accents.

He gave me a friendly handshake and zipped off his reading glasses. "I hear you maybe join the YCL, that's good." He shoved the book he had been reading at me. "Is a good book. You should read it." I looked at it. It was *What Is to Be Done?* by Vladimir Ilyich Lenin. "You read and understand it you know everything what is to do to make a revolution. What do you do anyway?"

"Well, I work in a furniture factory."

"Good, you're a worker. You're not a student, you're not an intellectual, you're a worker—very good!"

Barbara's mother was staring at me with concern. "Bob, doesn't nobody feed you? You're so skinny! Come in kitchen. Sit down and eat!"

I said that I could wait for everyone else to eat, but she insisted I needed to eat as I had been working. "Barbara? Who knows when she be here. So why not meantime you could eat a little someting?"

I sat down at the enamel-topped kitchen table. She put a glass of milk and a slice of rye bread with American cheese in front of me. "You need eat. You're too skinny, so you're not looking so good. Start eating."

When Barbara came home she was welcomed with questions about the rehearsal and the play. Her parents treated her like a star. Even before she took off her cape she gave us a run-through of the latest WLT production, which seemed very similar to the one she had acted out for me on the front stoop.

During dinner Jacob wanted to know what was going on at the furniture factory. He was not satisfied with my explanation that I was new—

only a helper—and had to be very careful about the union stuff because I got the job through a friend. Most of the workers, I told him, were pretty scared about the whole union business.

The Jennicks had come from Russia and took immense pride in the "great achievements" of the Russian Revolution. Jacob had been driven out of Russia by the pogroms against the Jews led by the Cossacks—Czarist cavalry officers who went on periodic anti-Semitic rampages. They had beat him and tortured his mother, father, and other relatives. Now, he assured me, it was all different. Workers were in control of everything and were showing the world the way to socialism.

He could not say enough in praise of the industrialization that was going on in Russia. He went on and on about the new factories, steel mills, and mines, and the great shipyards that were being built. Backward Russia was being industrialized—all in the name of socialism. Soon the Russians would outstrip not only the Americans but the world!

I tried to stay interested, but what I really wanted to do was get Barbara on the bed in her room. No, no, that wasn't any good, she told me; her mother would come in periodically to check on us.

After a bit, her father commented that tomorrow was a work day, and I figured that was my cue to go home. He would let me know when the next new members' class was starting. Primarily because I was a worker, he was convinced I had a big revolutionary career ahead of me. The Party, he said, was looking forward to getting more workers into this working-class organization. As I left, I realized I didn't understand what he was talking about.

In the communist world, being a worker was a badge of honor. After all, the future society was to be run by workers. It didn't occur to me at the time, but the funny part was that—with few exceptions—the leaders of the Party were all intellectuals, most of whom had never been inside a factory.

6

Portrait of a Young Communist

The ideal potential convert (recruit) is the individual who stands alone, who has no collective body he can blend with and lose himself in and so mask the pettiness, meaninglessness and shabbiness of his individual existence.
Eric Hoffer

The Party's determination to recruit more workers won me a warm welcome at the Young Communist League (YCL). May, whom I had first met at the Times Square demonstration, introduced me to the section organizer, Comrade Seymour. A small man who seemed too old to be a leader of young communists, he looked something like Charlie Chaplin. He smiled as we shook hands and called me by my first name. May told him that I was as an honest-to-goodness worker who was not Jewish, and that seemed to please him. May explained that most YCL members were Jewish students, intellectuals, or white-collar workers.*

In 1934 the YCL's headquarters at Tremont and Prospect was a dingy apartment over a dry goods store. The old living room had been converted into a meeting room and was full of folding chairs. Its peeling, cream-colored walls were covered with banners and portraits of communist heroes. A mimeograph machine sat on top of the enamel sink in the kitchen, and the two bedrooms had been turned into offices.

About twenty of us squeezed into the living room for the new members' class. Up front, Comrade Seymour sat behind a rickety old table

*The YCL, along with its campus counterpart, the National Student League, was the most important radical youth organization during the 1930s. In 1934 it staged a massive national antiwar strike that caused 15,000 to 25,000 students in New York City alone to boycott their classes.

and welcomed us to "the movement." He explained that that we would refer to each other as *comrade,* because titles like *Mr., Miss,* and *Mrs.* were decadent, bourgeois expressions. Familiar talk to me. When describing any party organizational structure Seymour had a strange way of pronouncing *the* as *dee.* Some years later when I heard high-class midwesterners talking about "dee Parrrty" with the accent on the *r* so that it came out like a growl, I realized they had picked this up from European Marxist theoreticians like Seymour.

Seymour proceeded to explain "dee party structure" and how it worked. The primary unit was the membership group; immediately above it was a section, which covered a specific area. We were in the northwest Bronx section, which had about twenty-five hundred members. Above us were the county, city, and state committees, and—most important of all—the American Central Committee, which laid down the party line for the whole organization. He was very emphatic about its preeminence: "The Central Committee is the highest authority of the Party in the United States. It is superseded only by the Comintern, that is, the Communist International in Moscow, which spells out policy for all the world's Communist parties."

Comrade Seymour was very serious. He spoke in a confidential manner, as if he were sharing precious information. The Party's system of establishing a policy, he explained, was *democratic centralism.* After a period of free and open discussion of an issue, the Central Committee set a policy to which all members were expected to adhere unconditionally. Communist discipline was a fundamental requirement for membership. "You all need to learn it. Any questions?"

Someone asked what happened if you disagreed with the party line. Seymour laughed: "Why would you? After we all engage in a thorough discussion I'm sure you'll find youself in agreement."

The major themes of our classes were very similar to the Marxist ideas I had heard so many times before. Because the profit motive was clearly the source of all evil in society, once it was eradicated everything would change. "In a socialist society," Seymour declared, "we will work for the good of all instead of the profit of the few. Exploitation will cease when workers receive full value for their labor."

Marxism-Leninism was presented to us as the "science" of socialist theory. This was an idea I had never heard from Papa or the Wobblies. Seymour used the example of water being heated and changing from a liquid to a gas as a metaphor for revolutionary change. "Just as science can measure the rising temperature of water until, at a critical point, it changes into the gaseous state of steam, so we as Marxists can scientifically predict when social unrest becomes intense enough to change so that a revolution occurs and creates a new state." Believing that we were part of a foolproof scientific historical process, he emphasized, separated us from utopian socialist dreamers and reinforced our fundamental Marxist beliefs.

Although I had heard many denunciations of the "dictatorship of the proletariat," I had never understood why communists saw it as so essential. Seymour described Lenin's revision of this concept of Marxism as his greatest theoretical contribution. Lenin realized from his study of earlier revolutionary movements that the ruling class would not give up its power through the ballot box or any other peaceful means; the working class had to be ready to seize power by military means and hold it through "iron discipline." The intervention of world capitalists against the Bolsheviks in the civil war that followed the revolution further convinced Lenin, as well as Trotsky, that the evolution toward the classless society Marx had envisaged could only proceed under the protection of a large military force, the Red Army. In the meantime, under the dictatorship of one class, the proletariat, socialism in Russia would operate under a system of democratic centralism similar to that used in the Party in the United States. I was certainly no intellectual and could not argue the theoretical issues involved; as a practical matter, it sounded pretty reasonable to me at the time.

In addition to reading some of the basic writings of Marx, Engels, Lenin, Stalin, and Earl Browder (the head of the American Communist party), we had to learn how to carry on the day-to-day functions of the YCL under all kinds of conditions. Although I expected to acquire the ability to make speeches and write leaflets, I didn't realize that I would also learn how to build a homemade mimeograph machine out of household objects, make ink, and use a window screen and a wooden frame to "publish the voice of the revolution no matter how serious the repression." To do this, we needed to be independent of capitalist suppliers of printing equipment.

In times of real crisis, the teacher explained, getting our message to workers would be the key to our success. We heard many stories of how courageous revolutionaries in Italy, working under fascist oppression, managed to publish some kind of underground paper to keep the struggle alive. A common theme was how these heroes risked their lives for the cause by printing a leaflet or a newspaper. The eighteenth-century radical writer and pamphleteer Thomas Paine was held up as an example of someone whose ability to get the message to the masses had a decisive effect on a war of liberation—our own American Revolution.

After a while I found attendance at the new members' classes a real drag. My problem wasn't learning the material, it was staying awake. Working in the furniture factory, plus the hour-long subway ride to Brooklyn and back, left me worn out at the end of the day. Usually I managed to find a seat in the back of the room, preferably against the wall, where I could tilt the chair back, lower my head, and doze off. This seating arrangement became my pattern for most future meetings. Endless hours of droning talk became an agreeable opportunity to catch a little nap.

Toward the end of one of the last classes, I drowsily heard a call for volunteers for a waterfront flying squad to help organize sailors and dockworkers. I perked up and raised my hand, "Yeah, I'll volunteer for that." I wasn't sure what a flying squad was, but it sounded exciting. I soon learned that—in this case—a flying squad was a group of people who went from pier to pier holding impromptu meetings and explaining the need for unions to longshoremen and the sailors coming off ships. Since ships docked and were unloaded every day of the week, the flying squads could work on weekends.

I asked Seymour why the Party was interested in unions; "What do they have to do with socialism?" He approved of my question and used it to explain the Party's current policy on organizing the unorganized. Because unions empower workers and sharpen the class struggle, they create the necessary context for workers to learn the fundamental truth of the *Communist Manifesto*: "They have nothing to lose but their chains, and a world to gain." He went on to criticize the American Federation of Labor (AFL) unions. They sold out the workers' interests by seeking only minor reforms and higher wages and not recognizing the class struggle. He said there was a major debate going on in the Party over the issue of whether it is better to work inside the existing reformist unions (boring from within) or to create new, more militant unions. At any rate, a flying squad sounded like fun.

I had been eager to tell Barbara about the new members' class, but most of the time she claimed to be too busy with her theatrical work to see me. We did have a date for that Saturday night, though. I was feeling self-important about my first revolutionary mission when I called to tell her casually that I might be late for our date because I was going to be on a waterfront flying squad that day. "We have a lot of ships to meet," I said. "The action might even go on all night." For the first time in many days, I heard real enthusiasm in her voice. She thought it was "just wonderful!" No matter what time I finished, I should call her at home if she wasn't at Hymie's. I felt our relationship now had a purpose.

The flying squad was to meet at noon at the United Fruit piers on West Street—the same United Fruit that Papa had denounced in Sunday School as the worst kind of imperialist exploiter. But that was just talk; our action was the real thing! One of the ships, the *Santa Rosa*, had docked with its cargo of bananas from Central America but had not yet been unloaded. When I got to the pier I looked around for the others on the flying squad but didn't see them.

Forty or fifty husky, mean-looking longshoremen were standing around with their big hooks, hoping to get work. The boss man walked along tagging certain individuals; he knew exactly which men he wanted to work the ship. I had heard that to get picked for a job the longshoremen had to kick back part of their pay to the bosses. It was simple as that—no kickback, no work. The sight of those big tough men groveling before the dock boss was beyond belief.

While the gang was being picked, the other members of our six-man flying squad showed up. The squad leader, who looked like a sailor himself, told us that step one was to board the ship and step two was to distribute our literature to the sailors. A couple of the guys on the squad were ex-sailors and knew the insides of ships. I told one of them, Arthur, that I knew nothing about ships. He said, "Okay, kid, you stick with me. I'll show you how we do this." As the longshoremen walked up the gangplank we followed along behind them. Before anyone noticed we were on the ship.

Arthur said, "Follow me, we'll go to the fo'c'sle. That's the crews' quarters in the bow of the ship." Although most of the sailors seemed to have left, there were still a few on board. We handed out our literature, gave them cards to sign for the Maritime Union, and explained that we were organizing all the ships out of the Port of New York. In rapid fire, Arthur told them that this was their chance at "higher wages, better working conditions, shorter hours, and job security." He had an endless repertoire of slogans. After listening to him for a while I decided to try it on my own.

Up on deck I found a couple of men—longshoremen not sailors—working the winches used to unload the cargo. They were mildly interested in what I had to say about unions and about "finally getting those stealing dock bosses off your backs." I handed them cards and told them about all the things needed to improve waterfront working conditions.

We were moving around the deck in a pretty relaxed manner, nodding to each other as we passed. Suddenly the sound of whistles blowing seemed to come from everywhere, and I caught sight of nightstick-wielding security guards. One of them yelled something about looking for "those fuckin' union agitators." They were stopping longshoremen to check their identification. Trying to remember the way out, I started to run up the catwalk stairs. With security men waiting at the bottom, I thought the gangplank would be a trap. Luckily, Arthur came by and yelled, "Follow me!" Half way down the gangplank he ducked under the rail and jumped onto the dock below. It looked a hundred feet down, but there was nothing to do but follow. We ran down the pier and onto West Street with the security police close behind. Arthur hollered, "Grab a truck and get out of here." As a big flatbed came by, I ran alongside, leapt up, and was gone.

I was scared as hell, and my heart was beating like a tom-tom. A dozen blocks from the dock I climbed down off the truck and sat down on the curb to recover. We had agreed to meet at the 14th Street cafeteria after the action. I waited there a long time. Finally a couple of guys from the flying squad showed up to report that Comrade Sam had been badly beaten by the security guards and was in Beekman Hospital. "Running away without paying attention to what was happening to the other comrades was a serious mistake," they said. I realized for the first time that this class struggle stuff could get you killed. Arthur and I protested. We had been told to get out of there as fast as we could; nobody said anything about watching out for the others.

We agreed to pay Sam a visit, but by the time we got to the hospital visiting hours were over. We found out that he was okay. There were no fractures, only some light internal injuries; he could go home in a day or so. We sent him a note saying that the operation was a great success as we had signed up some sailors and a few longshoremen.

The next day the six of us on the flying squad had to meet with the Party's trade union director, Comrade Jack, to review the operation. I found him very intimidating. He never smiled and was constantly blinking his eyes as he regarded us severely through the smoke of his cigarette. He was harshly critical of the action. We had failed to plan it like a military action. First, we lacked a clear objective. Second, we hadn't figured out the geography—the ways of getting in and out. Third, most important, we hadn't made a contingency plan of what to do if things went wrong and we had to get everyone out. He was angry that we had left our comrade behind.

The more annoyed Jack became over our lack of revolutionary knowhow the faster he blinked. He chewed us out good for giving our real names at the hospital and told us to choose new names. We became Brahms, Plaza, Bookworm, and so on. "Okay, now empty out your pockets." He pointed to all the things we carried that would have given away our true identities. He clearly thought we were a bunch of amatuer revolutionaries who simply had no idea what they were up against.

This cloak-and-dagger, class warfare stuff was exciting. I could take on a new identity and engage in a grim game of cat and mouse with the ruling class. They were the capitalist bad guys; we were the working-class good guys. Anything went. As fighters for social and economic justice, we would win the working class to our cause by supporting their struggle for higher wages and better working conditions. It was the greedy bosses who hired thugs and made this a life-and-death struggle. We were only responding in kind.

After a couple of weeks my excitement over the waterfront caper receded, and I was again longing for Barbara. One night at Hymie's Deli she breezed in with her cape flying. My joy at seeing her instantly erased any anger I had felt over her neglect. After a peck on the cheek she sat down and in her usual breathless manner started talking about the Stanislavsky method of acting. All I wanted to do was kiss her.

"No, not yet," she insisted, "I have to tell you about the Moscow Art Theater director who is coming to visit the Lab Theater. This could be my big chance! I have to work on some monologues. By the way," she threw in enthusiastically, "Burt drove me here in his car. It was great!"

As she continued babbling on about the theater, I had a revelation: A car, by God! That's it, that'll get her. At that moment, I moved up by a year my childhood resolve to have my own car as soon as I reached eighteen.

I looked up Vinnie, one of the Van Nest Steamrollers. I was sure he would give me good advice about getting a car. He took me to a junkyard and introduced me to Mario, the owner, a short, heavy-set Sicilian. He was clad in a pair of shiny overalls that were caked solid with years of accumulated grease. I told him I was looking for a roadster, in good shape of course.

As we walked around his acres of wrecked cars, he listened carefully to my requirements, nodding in agreement. Then he stopped, pointing toward the fence. "See the green one in the back? It's a '26 Chrysler roadster, needs some work. You know about cars?"

Remembering a few things I had learned from Mr. Ruh and from helping a couple of the guys around Van Nest, I said, "Sure I do."

At this point Vinnie stepped in. "No bullshit now, Mario. Does that fuckin' heap run or is the block cracked and is the rear end gonna fall out? Now Robishe here, he's no *paesano*, but he's one of us. *Capisch?*"

"If he canna drive it outta here, would I sell it him? Never I do that." The junkyard man wanted to know how much money I had. I told him ten dollars. He shook his head. "You come tomorrow with twelve dollar and you drive her out, okay?"

I had driven Papa's car in and out of a garage a few times, but I was still too young to drive legally. As we left the junkyard I started to get nervous. "Vinnie, how do I get license plates? Suppose I can't drive it? What do I do?"

"Don't worry," he said, "we're gonna get you license plates from a car dumped in a lot, and tonight we teach you how to drive." That night in Al Pupa's 1925 Essex, Vinnie and Al taught me to drive and presented me with the license plates for my dark green Chrysler roadster with the rumble seat.

The next day I went to pick up the car. The junkyard owner threw a missing left front fender into the rumble seat said, "Here, getta couple screws an' you got perfect. I even give you a fifty cents a gas." I stood on the running board looking down at the crumpled black leather seats and the shiny dashboard instruments. It was hard to believe this grand old automobile was really mine.

I was so excited I damn near hit a peddler's horse as I was backing out of the junkyard. "Hey, whatsa matter, you crazy? You wanna kill my horse?" I stopped long enough to push down the folding roof and drove off. I was hoping to pass someone I knew so I could blow the horn and wave like a king from my new-old green roadster. Everything was great until I stepped on the brake pedal and it went straight to the floor. Only the emergency brake prevented me from meeting a trolley head on.

The 1926 Chrysler was one of the first cars equipped with hydraulic brakes. I had to learn quickly about master cylinders and wheel cylinders, brake fluid, plungers, and seals. During the depression, taking a car to a repair shop was out of the question. You either fixed it up yourself—taking trips to the junkyard for the parts—or gave it up. Gas being a nickel a gallon, for a buck you could say, "Fill 'er up."

I had to keep the car a secret at home. I was certain they wouldn't approve, especially as I wasn't old enough to get a license.

My affair with the Chrysler roadster even caused me to neglect Barbara for a time. Buying my first automobile was a rite of passage and the beginning of my lifelong passionate identification with the automobile. For decades I had recurring dreams about cars. In one of them I have parked the car on a New York street while visiting a friend. When I want to go home, I can't for the life of me remember where I parked it. My anxiety building to nightmare proportions, I desperately search the streets, calling for the police and ending up on a curb crying like a baby. Years later, in therapy, I would discover that I myself was the lost car of my dreams.

The roadster was polished up and running pretty good, but I was feeling uncertain about showing up with it at the YCL office. My comrades might see car ownership as petit bourgeois. Instead, I called Barbara and picked her up at her place for a ride around Bronx Park. Her reaction was disappointing. Sure, she thought the Chrysler was okay, but it couldn't compete with the impending visit of someone called Jasper Dieter from the Hedgerow Theater in Philadelphia. This could be another big opportunity for her acting career. Although the roadster did a hell of a lot for my state of mind, it did nothing to improve our romance.

In spite of her deadly serious theatrical whirl, I did manage to take Barbara to an occasional free Saturday night symphony concert in the front hall of the Metropolitan Museum of Art. During the depression years these concerts, along with the twenty-five-cent New York Philharmonic summer concerts in Lewisohn Stadium, were the best entertainment deal in town. There were only a few chairs in the museum's entrance hall, and we left them for the "old fogies." Most of the YCLers attending the concerts found cozy corners to spread out a blanket or a coat to listen to Brahms, Mozart, or Rossini. Barbara and I usually took advantage of a semi-private spot behind a large Egyptian statue of Tutankhamen's wife to create some crescendos of our own.

After the concert the YCLers gathered at yet-another cafeteria—this one on 86th Street—for a earnest review of the concert. Everybody had an opinion. David Mannes (the conductor) lacked emotional rapport with Wagner, or with Brahms. The tempo was bad. One night there was general agreement—after prolonged discussion—that the horn section was suffering from arteriosclerosis. Periodically, someone would ask me what I thought and I would repeat what someone else had already said: the tempo was too fast, or too slow, the strings section lacked luster, and so on. Often I just shrugged and said "I guess it was all right."

A good part of the time, I had no idea what these City College students were talking about. I was sure they had read everything from ancient Babylonian tablets to the *Encyclopædia Britannica* and all the great literature in between. It seemed essential for them to have an opinion about everything—philosophy, economics, art, history, drama—and, even more important, to analyze everything from a Marxist point of view. There might be an interminable discussion of whether the 1812 Overture was simply Russian "nationalistic jingoism" or a "great celebration of the people's liberation." Was Freud an apologist for the bourgeoisie? Was Wagner a true revolutionary or the anti-Semitic glorifier of Germany's barbarous past? In their presence I felt very dumb. Outside of a few Marxist tracts, I still hadn't read a book. How I wished they knew something about cars so I could get into a conversation about carburetors or clutches. I kept resolving that I would start reading.

While I was preoccupied with Barbara, my Chrysler roadster, and the Young Communist League, the sounds of fascism were getting louder— and closer to home. In the summer of 1935, glad to leave the furniture factory, I worked as a counselor at the Sunday School camp where I had spent so many childhood summers. As a budding young Marxist, I was eager to promote the ideology of the class struggle among the children and grandchildren of my father's friends. On the first or second Sunday that summer, the camp was crowded with Sunday School families. The pastoral calm of our little utopia was completely shattered when one member, Hans Ritzen, showed up wearing a swastika armband.

Bruno, the camp director, was furious. He hollered at him in German, "Take off that Goddamned swastika or get off this campground!" Ritzen, a very tall, gaunt-looking man with deep-set eyes, remained calm. "Before you condemn me," he said, "let people hear what I have to say." It was close to dinner time, and most of the campers and visitors were gathered in front of the dining hall. There were shouts of "Let him speak," "Let's hear what he has to say." Bruno seemed stunned. The unexpected support for Ritzen left him unable to respond.

Ritzen, feeling more confident, strode forward to address the group. "All of us here are for socialism, *ja?* Well, so is Hitler. Why do you think his party is called National Socialist? He is against the rich and the bankers, and so are we." His voice rose as he hit his stride. "He's putting Germany back to work. People are not starving anymore. You people here in America, you don't understand what it means to be hungry and to watch your children starve. Hitler is ending all that." He was very convincing.

First there was a long silence, then applause—scattered for sure, but there it was. The Nazi issue was out in the open. Some of the old German radical socialists had become supporters of National Socialism and its leader. It was the start of a debate that would tear this once-harmonious utopian community apart and come close to breaking my Papa's heart.

Bruno and others took turns answering Ritzen. Hitler and the Nazis, they declared, were tools of the capitalists; they were exploiting the grievances of the German workers to realize their own dreams of world power. The applause for this position was now greater than it was for Ritzen's, and the argument continued, even though most of the onlookers went into the dining room to eat. The confrontation ended when Ritzen took off the swastika armband, announcing that he had no intention of leaving but would stay to continue the fight for National Socialism.

Papa, who hadn't been there to argue the antifascist position with Ritzen, arrived the following weekend in time for an enlarged meeting of the Camp Committee. After a stormy debate on the right of free speech and a very close vote, the committee asked Ritzen to leave the organization. Papa looked very sad. In response to my queries, he reiterated what was becoming his constant theme: "We are in for terrible times. People do not want to understand what Hitler and his gang of evil Nazi thugs are up to. There are very dark days ahead." I hadn't seen Papa this depressed since after Mutter died.

All German immigrant organizations in the United States suffered the same process of disintegration over the pros and cons of Hitler and Nazism. Along with the various radical political organizations, sports and hiking clubs and singing societies were caught up in the argument. Once German tanks started to roll into Czechoslovakia, and then into Poland, I believe many Germans felt a welcome relief from the depression and humiliation of World War I and its aftermath of unemployment, hunger, and disease. Their desire to see Germany as a proud nation, at least initially, gave even some of the Sunday School radicals an almost-subconscious wish to see Hitler victorious. You could sense the terrible conflict between their feelings for the Fatherland and their socialist ideology.

In spite of the war, the decisive defeat of a postwar attempt at a socialist revolution in 1919, and the social and economic degradation of the

Weimar period, the Germans I grew up with—including Papa—were extremely proud of Germany and its culture. Papa's deep dejection after 1933 stemmed from his belief that the Nazi movement reflected "the dark side of the German character, a love affair with death through heroism." He thought that many Germans were bitterly resentful that the world did not recognize their superiority. "That's why they are always so eager to march off to war under some Prussian general." Again and again, Papa and Bruno explained that fascism was simply capitalism taken over by the state in order to deprive the working class of its power. It might have been a more effective argument if it had not had to compete with the newsreels of the Nazis' beautifully orchestrated mass rallies. For some of our Sunday School people, the exhilaration of a reawakened Fatherland was intoxicating enough to justify their support of Hitler. For Papa, who prided himself on following the humanist tradition of Goethe, Schiller, and Mann, the Nazi phenomenon was so painful that he began a slow withdrawal from his involvement in politics.

While the political storm over the swastika incident was boiling, I was busy teaching the kids under my supervision all about the evils of Nazism. A big antifascist demonstration was being held in New York City on a Wednesday that happened to be my day off, and I told Bruno I wanted to go. He refused to give me permission; even though it was my day off, I was supposed to stay around in case of some kind of emergency. I protested at his unfairness. If it was my day off I should be allowed to do whatever I wanted. We left it at that. Unsure of whether I would be fired if I went, I met with the kids and, after telling them what Bruno had said, asked for their support in "our fight against fascism." The eight- to twelve-year-olds urged me to go.

I caught the train into the city, attended the rally, and was back in camp by nightfall, only to be told that I was fired for disobeying an order. Feeling victimized, I marched into the dormitory, announced to the kids that I had been fired for attending an antifascist meeting, and challenged them: "So what are you going to do about it?"

They were great. They immediately elected a committee to go see Bruno and demand my reinstatement. I sat and waited while they went off to negotiate. When they returned I knew from their hangdog looks they had not succeeded. Bruno had told them that I had not been fired for attending an antifascist meeting but for disobeying an order. He had concluded by stressing the absolute need for discipline to prevent chaos.

Throughout my childhood I had been brought up to defy authority when it was unjust. Though I was sorry to lose my job, I was proud of my defiance. I had run up against this German authoritarianism before. Behind the commitment to equality of even true socialists like Papa and Bruno lay an authoritarian personality that surfaced when their power was challenged. Fortunately, though I was now out of work, I had been promised a job as a plumber' s helper that would start in a few weeks.

By the time I arrived back home Papa had learned about my political activities at the camp from Bruno. He was furious. I wasn't sure if it was the Nazi problem or me being fired that bothered him so much. I tried in vain to explain to him why it was important for me to participate in the demonstration. "For Christ sake, Pop, I was trying to add my voice to the antifascists. What the hell is wrong with that?" He didn't care about the demonstration. It was my lack of respect for Bruno that really angered him. It was as if I had defied him.

His voice full of anger and contempt, he erupted: "So now you're a big shot Stalinist organizer! Well, let me tell you a few things. Stalin is as power-crazed as Ivan the Terrible was. He has murdered more great Bolsheviks than all the world capitalists combined. The dictatorship of the proletariat is completely contrary to the tenets of socialism. It has reduced a noble idea to nothing more than a system of power over the masses. In the United States the IWW is the only true adherent to the socialist ideal, and that is why they have been the most persecuted of all the left-wing organizations. While the Russian Revolution is being betrayed, Hitler and the fascists will march across Europe." I couldn't remember ever seeing him quite so angry.

When he paused, I said, "Yes, that's the reason we need a united front against the fascists." He looked over his glasses and lit his hand-rolled cigarette. "Well look who's making speeches! When did you become an authority on how to beat fascism? You listen to some idiot on the street corner and, whataya know, you're ready to march. Well, you know what? I think you better go make your own way. No Stalinist lives here."

I couldn't believe what I heard. It didn't make sense. "I got fired from a job and now you're telling me to get out of the house?" I was confused and scared, but I had to defend myself. "I went to an antifascist demonstration and you accuse me of being a Stalinist. I don't get it? All my life you preached that a person should be willing to stand up for his beliefs, alone if necessary. I can't understand why I'm being punished for doing what you taught me."

For Papa it wasn't the demonstration; it was my membership in the Young Communist League and my lack of loyalty to a very old and dear friend. We argued long into the night, but it didn't matter. His mind was made up, and I was not going to beg him to let me stay. I thought about saying I would quit the YCL, but I couldn't bring myself to do it. The next morning as I was putting my few belongings into a couple of cardboard cartons, I still hoped he would change his mind. He didn't.

I didn't know where to go. I loaded my stuff into the roadster and drove over to YCL headquarters. Harry, one of the Bronx YCL leaders, invited me to sleep on his family's living room couch until I could find a place to live. Luckily, my new job as a plumber's helper would enable me to pay room rent in a couple of weeks.

One evening shortly after I left home I ran into Barbara at YCL headquarters. It was an all-too-familiar scene. She was excitedly enacting a new street theater piece on unemployment for the comrades gathered around her. "It' s so great. You see, we are in these rich folks' mansion," and so on, and so on. When she finished, her little audience clapped. Pleased, she smiled gaily and said she really had to dash. In her usual breathless rush out the door she threw me a little wave and promised to meet me at the Browder meeting the next night.

Living with Harry made me part of a little group of young Communists—his friends Henry, George, Joe (the one Italian in the Bronx YCL), Leo, and myself. After most meetings we would end up at Hymie's Deli. They were all City College students and referred to me as "the worker." Their conversation was the traditional YCL intellectual ping pong game of references to everything from the works of Plato, Hegel, and Dostoyevski, to the speeches of William Z. Foster, Browder, and FDR. Whatever the subject, from free love to the meaning of existence, they could quote something a great mind had to say about it.

One night, we got into a big debate over the Party's new policy—the Popular Front to stop fascism. Henry thought it was justified by the immediate need to stop fascism, simply to preserve an opportunity for socialism to develop. But in the process, Leo argued, we were giving up the class struggle to make common cause with some very dubious partners. I said I thought that because of the worldwide economic depression the capitalists saw fascism as a way of dealing with working-class discontent. With the Russian revolution staring them in the face, the capitalist countries had a terrible fear that any organized protest could lead to revolution. Wow, I thought, where did that come from? For a moment, the guys stopped eating their pastrami sandwiches. "Hey, Schrank, you're really ready for the soapbox."

The group was split about Roosevelt. Was the NIRA (National Industrial Recovery Act)—which had just been struck down by the Supreme Court—a move toward fascism or a sop thrown to the masses to keep them quiet? Or both? Leo and Henry saw FDR as a capitalist reformer, while Joe was sure he was "embarking on a program of state capitalism, which is what fascism is all about." And so began a debate that would go on within the Party for years, even while the official policy was cooperation with the FDR administration.

The Browder rally took place at the Saint Nicholas Arena, a large hall used mainly for boxing and wrestling matches. By the time I got there with Harry and his friends it was packed with thousands of people. A huge banner over the stage read "Build the Popular Front To Defeat Fascism." A band was playing some marches and the atmosphere was more like a political convention than a Communist meeting. In those days, citywide party meetings were huge; the Party was one of the few organizations that could regularly fill Madison Square Garden.*

The meeting got underway with speakers proposing an intensified effort to organize the unemployed and a campaign for Home Relief. Each time someone called for an action—a march on Washington, a petition campaign for unemployment benefits, organization of unorganized workers, or a new subscription drive for the *Daily Worker*—the place broke

---

*According to one historian (John Patrick Diggins, *The Rise and Fall of the American Left*), membership in the Communist party increased from 7,500 to 55,000 between 1930 and 1938; another perhaps 30,000 unregistered members were affiliated through various youth groups and trade unions.

into enthusiastic applause. The more militant and strident the speaker, the better the audience liked it.

Michael Gold, a columnist for the *Daily Worker* and editor of the *New Masses,* dramatically described the humiliation of workers who all their lives had been able to support themselves and their families but were now desperately picking through garbage dumps looking for food for their hungry children. Looking up at the audience, he asked whether it was fair for U.S. Steel to make a net profit of $220 million while honest working people had to pick garbage for their children to eat. The audience rose to its feet yelling "No, No, No!" as Gold concluded with a call to organize workers for a new and better socialist world.

During a pause in the speeches I noticed that Barbara was no longer in her seat but was on the stage talking excitedly to some man. I became anxious about whether we would get together after the meeting. For the first time, it dawned on me that she really didn't care for me.

Just then Earl Browder, the general secretary and party leader, was introduced to the usual wild standing ovation. Browder, a midwesterner from Kansas, was the new face of communism in the United States. This soft-spoken man looked more like an English schoolmaster than a dangerous revolutionary. In a speech that lasted for more than an hour, he laid out the Party's new line on the Popular Front strategy for "defeating fascism at all costs." After listening to Browder, I believed we would unite with the devil himself if he was against fascism. The crowd was on its feet cheering and whistling as the band struck up the "International," the song I had first learned at the Modern Sunday School not so many years before.

Arise ye prisoners of starvation,
Arise ye wretched of the earth
For justice thunders condemnation
A better world's in birth.
No more tradition's chains shall bind us
Arise ye slaves no more in thrall.
The earth shall rise on new foundations
We have been naught, we shall be all.
Refrain
'Tis the final in conflict.
Let each stand in his place
The International UNION shall be the human race.

The Party, however, sang that last line as

The International SOVIETS shall be the human race.

As I was leaving the meeting, Seymour, our section organizer, stopped me to say that there would be a section meeting to plan our Popular Front work in a few days and he wanted me to be there.

I left the meeting all fired up about the new strategy, my suspicions about Barbara forgotten for the moment. I was sure this was the way to stop fascism. All the next day, while working on a plumbing job in a West Side Manhattan apartment, I tried to figure out how we could apply the Popular Front strategy to our North Bronx community. In the following weeks and months the comrades in our YCL section held regular planning meetings in the cramped headquarters living room. We decided to focus our efforts on the unemployment councils, neighborhood youth clubs, and the local National Guard Armory.

The first step in intensifying our organizing of unemployment councils was an extensive campaign of leaflet and membership-card distributions at soup kitchens and unemployment relief stations. To do this we put into operation the careful methods of planning an action we had learned from Seymour. We also organized the many youth social clubs of the Bronx into a federation. In the past a number of them had been harassed by the police for not having liquor or club licenses. We believed that a federation would help them deal more effectively with the police provocation and heighten their consciousness of the threat of fascism in all its forms.

In 1933, the Party created a new national organization called the American League Against War and Fascism. The hope was to get local organizations representing all shades of political opinion, including the neighborhood churches, to join together in the antifascist struggle.

At one of our planning meetings Seymour, speaking in a hushed conspiratorial manner, asked whether there were any nonmembers present. "No? Then please shut the door." He explained that there was a National Guard Armory on Kingsbridge Road. Most of the guardsmen were working-class kids who joined, primarily, for the few bucks a month they got for it. We could make them our allies in the fight against fascism. He went on to define our mission as "making sure that these sons of the working class never became our very own fascist stormtroopers." We would try to unite them with us by organizing a new Popular Front group. Of all the ideas for uniting various groups against fascism we devised, cracking the National Guard was the weirdest and the most secretive.

The plan called for sending our prettiest YCL girls to distribute literature outside the armory. The hope was that over time we could form a highly secret party unit inside the guard. The YCLers doing this work would only be known to and would report to the section organizer. Although there was something very exciting about this clandestine business, I also found it very troubling.

The questions and discussions regarding the Popular Front strategy went on for many weeks and months. The major problem was how we could unite with people—including other socialists—who a short time earlier we had characterized as "social fascists" and enemies of the working class. Nonetheless, the Party had decided that we should set aside our traditional hostilities in support of the primary goal: halting what we perceived as the ever-rising tide of fascism. Once that was accomplished, we could reevaluate our friends and enemies. For the time being, we would join forces with anyone: Socialists, Trotskyists, Republicans, reformist trade union leaders, and churches—as long as they were against fascism. As a practical matter, of course, uniting with many of these organizations was highly unlikely. The Trots, for example, were not at all interested in reuniting with the Party, so there was really no issue, although the guys at Hymie's Deli concluded that it was now okay to screw Trotskyite girls.

As part of the new antifascist drive, we launched a massive effort to increase the number of street corner meetings. It was spring in the Bronx and that meant we were out on the street corners as often as possible. I was especially useful because I could use the car to cart around the ladder, platform, literature, and, if we were very lucky, an amplifier. The amplifier was particularly useful when there were simultaneous competing meetings on the same corner. The corner of Tremont and Prospect avenues was one of these multi-meeting places.

On a night I will never forget, Norman Tallentier, president of the newly formed American League Against War and Fascism, was scheduled to speak. He was a immensely popular speaker, and we had put up signs and distributed leaflets about his appearance. There was a good turnout for the meeting, which started around seven. May, who was a regular YCL speaker, held forth first on women's role in the fight for jobs and equal pay. Then Leo spoke about disarmament and stopping the arms race. By then, it was getting late, and Tallentier still hadn't shown. Esther was desperately telephoning all over town trying to locate him. Because he was in such great demand as a speaker, he often spoke to several different groups over the course of an evening.

Returning from her last call, Esther looked me straight in the eye, gave me a big smile, and said, "Schrank, there is no one left here who can speak. It's your turn."

Flabbergasted, I quickly lit up a Camel. "You gotta be crazy. I never made a speech in my life. What the hell will I say? The idea is absolutely nuts!" I could hear my voice rising in pitch as I protested.

She didn't reply but just climbed onto the platform. I heard her announcing that "the next speaker is a real son of the working class, a worker himself, a plumber's helper, who will pinch-hit for Norman Tallentier, who is tied up in Brooklyn. Comrade Bob Schrank."

I could either run away, faint, have a heart attack, or get up on the platform and start talking. That's what I did. I have no idea how it happened. I just began to talk about the dangers of fascism and what we needed to do about it. I kept smoking, and that seemed to give me some measure of composure. The crowd was growing; it now spilled out into the cross street. I experienced for the first time the adrenaline of audience approval. With growing confidence, I hammered away at the dangers of complacency and doing nothing in the face of the threat of fascism. Finally—was it a half hour later?—I stepped down, dazed and unsure, to a round of grand applause. Esther and May were ecstatic about their new working-class hero. They kept saying to people around the platform, "He's a worker and has never spoken publicly before. Isn't that remarkable?"

While I was still recovering, an elderly woman worked her way through the crowd toward me, pointing to the air above my head and holding out a little Virgin Mary medal. "Your life is watched over by the Virgin. I saw her just behind you as you were speaking. I want you to have this medal so you will always remember to trust her." The YCLers around the platform were somewhat embarrassed as I thanked the old lady and assured her I would take good care of the medal.

Walking home that night, I wondered where the speech had come from and how I had known what to say. It was as if some part of me had made contact with what the audience was thinking and put their thoughts into words. That part of myself always remained something of a mystery, but I experienced it on many occasions. At the time I wasn't sure why, but I did save the old lady's medal.

All the next day at work I was preoccupied with that speech. Was it a fluke? Could I do it again? For that matter, what did I say? I really didn't remember. That night at YCL headquarters I was welcomed as a hero. Suddenly I was a different person. Leo, the first to greet me, said, "I hear you knocked 'em dead on that street corner. God, that's great! We need soapboxers who can talk to the workers."

In the thirties the "movement" had an extended social life of parties, dances, lectures, concerts, picnics, outings, theater parties, and so on. The major source of information about these activities was the "What's On" column of the *Daily Worker*. That next weekend, with my new status as street speaker, I was looking forward to a Saturday night party being given by Audrey, a member who lived in the fancy or "bourgeois" part of the Bronx called the Grand Concourse. I had tried reaching Barbara to tell her of my street corner success, but she was becoming increasingly elusive. I hoped she would be at the party.

As I got off the elevator I could hear the strains of Benny Goodman's swing band and see through the open door a room packed with young people. Outside the door a couple of YCL members were collecting for the section fund drive. One of them, a pretty girl with black hair pulled back in a braid, gave me a big smile. "Hi! Aren't you our new street corner speaker? And you really work in a factory? That's just great."

In the smoke-filled living room the music was blaring, and a few couples were trying to get the dancing going. The couches and chairs were crammed with people. I spotted Leo and Henry in a corner having a heavy discussion on the real meaning of the Popular Front tactics. I asked Leo how all these people knew each other? Most, he said, were students at City or Hunter College. The crowd kept changing as YCLers and friends dropped in, looked to see what was happening, and decided to stay or to move on to another party.

Not wanting to spend the evening in talk, I tried looking for Barbara, but no one had seen her.

Most YCL parties split into three distinct groupings—the dancers, the singers, and the talkers. I tended to end up with the singers. Enthusiastically, if not harmoniously, we would belt out "Peat Bog Soldiers," "Kevin Barry," "I've Been Working on the Railroad," "Solidarity Forever," and "Long-Haired Preachers." When it was late and people were leaving, I got up to go too, but Audrey suggested that I stick around and help her move the furniture and the rug back. "And anyhow, you can stay over. Of course, that's if you want to." I think her boldness surprised her as much as it did me, for she turned away quickly and hurried to the door to say goodnight to her guests. As they left, Henry and Leo asked me if I had any rubbers and slipped a couple into my pocket.

With everyone gone, we put the furniture back, unrolled the rug, and, before long, ended up on the bed. We covered our uncertainty with violent kissing and touching, trying to undress in the midst of our headlong passion. We rolled around half undressed, and she kept moaning "have you got the rubber on?" As the night faded into dawn and we lay there exhausted, she leaned over me and said, "You'd better leave now. My parents are coming home early. Incidentally, your girlfriend Barbara never showed up tonight because she's having a hot affair with some actor."

My heart sank and a terrible dread began to engulf me. I said a quick good-bye and took off. In the beautiful early morning light, I walked along the concourse trying not to believe Audrey's report. Yet it explained all too well my inability to make contact with Barbara. The words "How could she? How could she?" were echoing inside my head, and tears were streaming down my cheeks. I walked faster and faster until I was running. When I stopped to look around I saw that I was in front of her apartment building. Oblivious to the hour, I bounded up the five flights and rang the bell. A voice called "Who is it?" It was Barbara's mother. She opened the door, looked at me in alarm, and said, "What's the matter, you poor boy, what happened to you?"

"Is Barbara at home?"

She paused, glanced apologetically at her old checked housedress, and said, "Come in, I make you some hot cocoa. Come, come."

Her failure to answer my question added to my panic. I sat at the table and she fussed around the tiny kitchen. Slowly she began to talk. Her voice came from some far-off part of her and was full of pain. "Barbara is no good. You should forget her. She is not here. She has gone to live with some actor. She doesn't tell you because when he throws her out, which he will, she wants to have you. She is a very selfish. Forget her." I barely managed to say thanks, get to the door, and make it to the street before I threw up.

For a long time I stood on the Bronx River bridge staring down at the swirling water. It was the second time I had felt the pain of a broken heart. The loss of Barbara's love caused a replay of all the fearful emotions I had experienced when Mutter disappeared. For the rest of my life, it was always the same: the loss of love reactivated that childhood nightmare in full bloom. This time, slowly, the pain of loss retreated, and I again became interested in girls. Still, many years passed before I ventured again into that state of ecstasy called "being in love."

When I met up with Leo and the gang at Hymie's a few days after Audrey's party, their welcome was different—not because of my speaking ability, but because I had made it with Audrey. "So give us all the details." I described a delicious night of indulgence in an unusual sexual smorgasbord. Not a word of it was true. Young communists were like most other young men; any opportunity to strut our sexual stuff was not to be missed. It was just another form of boyhood pissing contests. My new status as a lover at least allowed me to forget my pain over Barbara, if only for a few hours.

According to my FBI file, I was appointed youth secretary of the American League Against War and Fascism primarily because I was a successful street speaker. The job gave me an opportunity to plan meetings and work with Norman Tallentier, who was head of the league. He was a powerful speaker, but after hearing him many times I realized that he had only one script, which he repeated over and over. His jokes told the story: they were delivered with the impeccable timing of a practiced vaudevillian. When I began listening to myself critically, I recognized the same pattern. I was getting bored with myself. After that I decided to introduce one new idea in every talk—not necessarily new to the world but new to me.

Speaking against fascism was exhilarating. We were waging a clear, uncomplicated fight against pure evil. The theme I liked the best was the connection between fascism and capitalism—the twin devils. I maintained that the crisis of world capitalism—with its rising unemployment and homeless, starving people—offered fertile ground for extreme social unrest. The situation was laden with revolutionary potential. The capitalist solution to the risk of insurrection was establishment of a state of terror. That, I argued, is what we have in Nazi Germany and Italy, fascist states terrorizing the population into submission and using the Jews as convenient scapegoats.

Building to my dramatic end, I would bellow "What is our solution? What is our solution?" Like any good evangelist, I had one ready: "Only a Popular Front of all antifascists can guarantee that it will never happen here." Only by securing the peace could we deny the fascists the opportunity to destroy the Soviet Union. For Party and YCL members, the U.S.S.R. was our New Jerusalem, the hope for the future.

7

Organizing Against Fascism

What I think held young people to the Movement was the sense that they had gained, not merely a "purpose" in life but, far more important, a coherent perspective upon everything that was happening to us.
Irving Howe

In Europe, fascism was on the march in 1936. Mussolini, the Italian Il Duce, had invaded Ethiopia in 1935 and was consolidating his control over one of the few independent nations in Africa. The shaky republican government of Spain was under attack from the Army of General Francisco Franco, who was aided by tanks and troops from Italy and Nazi Germany. On the other side, international brigades of leftist intellectuals and idealists from Britain, France, and the United States were beginning to pour into Spain, along with Soviet money and supplies.

In the United States, the Communist party's fear of fascism was being fueled by homegrown rabble-rousers and protofascists peddling instant economic cures. Louisiana Senator Huey Long's Share Our Wealth program gained support from the poor by proposing to expropriate the property of the very rich and distribute it equally. Only his assassination in 1935 removed what FDR considered a serious threat to democracy. Father Charles Coughlin, the Detroit radio priest—egged on by automotive magnate Henry Ford—was blaming Jewish bankers for the depression. The American Liberty League was attacking FDR and the New Deal as a threat to states' rights, among other things. Painting Russian communism as the real threat to America, the Hearst newspaper chain defended the fascists in Spain and elsewhere.

Every day the radio and newspapers carried stories the Party's leaders interpreted as signs of growing right-wing strength. Because leftists in

Europe were always the first victims of fascism, American Communist officials' paranoid response to the rise of local fascist movements seemed justified. In Europe, after all, the Party had been all but wiped out.

None of this dampened the spirits of the Bronx YCL members as we prepared for the annual May Day parade. Although the parade served a serious purpose, for Young Communists it was always the equivalent of a Mardi Gras celebration. The night before the 1936 parade I was working with Leo, Henry, and a dozen other members at YCL headquarters, painting banners and placards and choosing the central themes for our Bronx contingent. I was still singing "Smoke Gets in Your Eyes" and secretly pining for Barbara, but I had a renewed interest in female companionship. My hopeful anticipation that evening centered around a tall young woman named Miriam blessed with a luscious mouth and an enticing figure. Although we had met only once before, we both felt the immediate intimacy of being members of the same crusading army. The excitement of a cause can be quite an aphrodisiac.

It must have been 2:00 A.M. by the time we had all eaten our sandwiches and painted what felt like hundreds of placards and banners with such slogans as

Workers! Unite and Fight For a Living Wage
Build the Popular Front to defeat Fascism
Down with Hitler and Mussolini's Fascist State!
Free all political prisoners. Free the Scottsboro Boys!
Pass the Social Security Bill—Extend Unemployment Insurance
Defend the U.S.S.R.
Black and White, Unite and Fight

Exhausted, but stimulated by the thought of the next day's festivities, we washed the paint from our hands and promised to meet in the morning. "Don't forget," someone yelled, "we gather at 38th Street west of Eighth Avenue." As I headed toward my car, Miriam snuggled into my arm, whispering, "If you think you're going home alone, you're nuts."

The next day was a beautiful, sunny first of May. Our Bronx contingent waited on West 38th Street while the parade proceeded down Fifth Avenue. We couldn't see much of it, but periodically we got reports of a "massive turnout." The public relations campaign of the previous weeks seemed to be paying off.

Finally the Fur and Leather Workers union, the contingent ahead of us, moved into the procession and we followed right behind. The furriers had a couple of bands, which made marching very exhilarating. As we came around the corner onto Fifth Avenue singing "Hold the Fort For We Are Coming," we saw the sidewalks packed with animated onlookers cheering us on.

As we paraded ten or twelve abreast down Fifth Avenue, stopping periodically for crosstown traffic, we chanted: "Black and white, unite and fight." "What do we want? Jobs at decent pay! When do we want them? Now!" "Fight fascism, don't read the Hearst papers" With our YCL banners held high, our flags snapping in the breeze, and thousands of people applauding us, we marched past the reviewing stand at the north end of Union Square singing the "International." "'Tis the final conflict, let each stand in his place." God, how we believed those words! Urged on from the reviewing stand by the party leaders, with an quarter of a million people cheering as if we *were* all one, we felt no doubt. The future was ours.

Our contingent now merged into the Union Square crowd where the speakers were describing capitalism as the cause of the present unemployment crisis and socialism as the way to guarantee a job for everyone. Huge public gatherings of this kind always made us feel that victory for our cause could not be far off. We came away convinced that the lives of working people were being vastly improved by our actions.

And in fact they were—often at the office of the Home Relief Bureau in the old Bronx Borough Hall. A couple of times a week YCL or other party members working with the unemployment councils went there with people who had been denied benefits. I occasionally served as a family's spokesman in meetings with the local bureau chief. Aided by comrades who worked at the bureau, we had mastered the rules and regulations in detail and often ended up educating the bureau staff about the rights of their clients. In most instances we succeeded in winning benefits for the families and gained strong community support for our work.

Oddly enough, we were helping weave the safety net that ultimately rescued the very capitalism we were pledged to overthrow—as the Trotskyites and the most radical members of the Party charged. At street corner meetings, I was often heckled by leftists accusing me of "saving the capitalist system with your reforms."

"No," I would reply coolly, "we are helping workers become class-conscious through their everyday struggles, which will make them more aware of their strength. When they finally realize how totally dependent the system is on their labor, they will be ready for socialism."

"Baloney," came the heckler's reply, "You're patching up the system by squeezing out some crumbs from the tables of the rich—just enough to quiet any social unrest."

And so the argument raged. I believed in our everyday efforts to make people's lives better. I found solving immediate problems much more appealing than dreaming of the wonderful world to be, "come the revolution." I still think there was a lot to the reformist argument. Our organizing efforts in support of social programs made a major contribution to humanizing the system. We had followed the old Wobbly slogan of "Fan the flames of discontent," and our actions resulted in strong support for the New Deal's social agenda—if not for revolution.

In the 1936 elections, though, the Party leadership had a tough time making up its mind about FDR and the New Deal. Some saw the programs Roosevelt had introduced during his first term as a means of halting the spread of the Right. Others believed that the New Deal was itself a potentially fascist movement and saw in the Civilian Conservation Corps (CCC) a strong resemblance to the Hitler youth camps. Depending on the perspective, the New Deal was either a humane rescue of capitalism's victims or the seedbed of American fascism.

Fearful of undermining Roosevelt's chances for a second term but not willing to endorse him publicly, Party Secretary Browder ran for president himself on the odd slogan "Defeat Alf Landon at all costs; vote for Earl Browder." Translated it meant: "If you can't vote for Browder, for God's sake don't vote for Landon." Browder was nominated at a huge rally in Madison Square Garden. The bands and combined choruses of scores of party-organized workers' clubs, ethnic associations, and Friends of the Soviet Union thundered out songs of protest. Left-wing theater groups presented a pageant dramatizing the need for people of all political persuasions to unite against war and fascism. For fifteen or twenty minutes, the garden exploded in a rapturous demonstration as the YCL chapters marched around the floor vigorously waving banners and proclaiming "Browder for President." Then someone introduced Browder as "the new John Brown from Kansas." (The real John Brown, ironically enough, was hung in Virginia for leading a failed slave insurrection!)

Sounding more like a professor than a revolutionary, Browder explained the Party's complex policy of working for the defeat of the Republicans while avoiding outright endorsement of FDR. That position sat well with many at the rally who were working as a result of Roosevelt's Works Progress Administration (WPA). For those on the far left, however, there was general discomfort with the implied notion that FDR was our bulwark against fascism. Browder himself believed that a Roosevelt defeat would spell disaster for the Left.

For once, the Party was somewhere close to the mainstream of American politics, and I was surprised to learn how good that felt. For eighteen years I had been an outsider—not standing or the saluting the flag, not singing "The Star Spangled Banner," not attending church or synagogue or celebrating Christmas, and expressing only scorn for patriotic Fourth of July hoopla. Feeling a little closer to the majority turned out to be a tension-relieving experience. Not having to stand alone, I could let my guard down, be part of the everyday scene, just swim merrily along with the crowd. Of course, this comfortable situation didn't last long.

Roosevelt won the election by a landslide. Plenty of people on the Left continued to enjoy the benefits of the New Deal. The WPA and Public Works Administration (PWA) programs employed people on an extraordinary variety of projects. In an average month more than two million people were working to produce plays, offer adult education courses, perform with symphony orchestras, and build parks, post offices, bridges, and highways. My sister Alice and her boyfriend Will were in the Federal Writers' Project, and many actors from the Workers' Laboratory Theater ended up in the Federal Theatre Project.

In spite of FDR's success at the ballot box, Congress was constantly nibbling away at the appropriations for New Deal social programs. It fell primarily to the Left to organize public support for federal relief programs. Our constant agitation for unemployment insurance and expanded funds kept the pressure on Congress. Nobody understood this situation better than FDR; he knew that the backbone of his support were the militant, newly organized blue-collar workers in the auto, steel, rubber, and electrical industries who were benefiting from the provisions of the Wagner Act to build their unions.*

As youth secretary for the American League Against War and Fascism, one of the new Popular Front organizations, my major responsibility was to run all over the city making speeches about how crucial it was to hold back the rising tide of fascism. Starting in 1936, members of fascist organizations like the German American Bund were strutting around in Nazi uniforms, displaying the swastika and boldly claiming whole streets and neighborhoods as their turf. The league decided that it had to challenge these guys in their own territory.

By then the Bund had branches in Manhattan, Yorkville, Ridgewood, Brooklyn, and the West Bronx—wherever there was a large German immigrant population. In 1937 they also opened a full-scale youth training camp, Camp Nordland, in Lake Hopatcong, New Jersey.**

We decided to hold a street corner meeting in one of the strongholds of the Bund, the St. Nicholas Avenue neighborhood in the Bronx. That's how I met George Lohr, a tall, skinny, chain-smoking German who was also working for the league. Some years later he became editor of the western edition of the *Daily Worker*.

George had a crippled left arm as a result of his escape from Nazi Germany. He spoke with a slight accent and had a humorous but confident manner that made me happy to be with him when we held meetings in fascist-controlled areas. He was determined "to make it clear to these bastards that we will concede nothing to them without one hell of a fight."

*The National Labor Relations Act (Wagner Act) was passed in July of 1935. It established the right of workers to a union of their own choosing, and created the National Labor Relations Board (NLRB) to administer labor law, conduct union elections, and compel employers to bargain in good faith. After numerous challenges, the Supreme Court upheld the constitutionality of the act in 1937.

**Information on membership of the German American Bund is unreliable. In April of 1939 the U.S. Justice Department estimated that there were 4,529 members in the metropolitan New York area. That same year Bundesfuehrer Fritz Kuhn claimed that there were 20,000 members nationally, plus three to five times as many sympathizers.

We met before the meeting in a coffee shop on St. Nicholas Avenue. The local comrades reported a rumor that the Bund was planning to show up in strength—uniforms, jackboots, swastika banners, and all. George insisted that we make detailed plans for defending the speakers from "the scum," who would probably try to break up the meeting. He knew from his experience in Germany how these guys operated. He reminded us that Bund members were fed a rich diet of propaganda films about Hitler and his stormtroopers and had come to believe they were just like them. "We need to teach them that this is not Munich or Berlin."

The local league committee had turned out about a dozen people to help with the meeting. George, looking around the coffee shop at our companions, whispered to me, "This is a nice bunch of kaffeeklatschers. I'm not sure they're gonna be much help against the Bund gang. But we go on, yes." He gathered the group together and instructed them to form a circle around the speakers' platform and under no circumstances to allow the Nazis to break into the ring. He would speak first to build up a crowd, and then "Robot"—that's how he pronounced my name— "then you give 'em hell. Okay, we go."

The platform, American flag, and amplifier had all been up set up beforehand. A few people began to gather in response to our leaflets inviting them to an antifascist rally. The local chairman of the American League introduced George as someone who had seen Hitlerism at firsthand and was there to tell us about it. George spoke slowly but precisely of how Hitler had come to power; how he had skillfully manipulated the politicians and used the economic crisis to convince people that he alone could end the misery of the German workers. From the beginning, he had blamed the Jews for the workers' terrible suffering.

The crowd had grown quite large when the Bund began to show up in uniform, swastikas on their arms. As George continued, they began to heckle him, yelling, "Are you getting Moscow gold?" "Go back to Germany, Jew lover." "The Jewish bankers are paying you."

George didn't flinch, or respond to them. He simply went on with his talk. He knew that hecklers, among other things, attract the curious to a meeting. (Once when we were unable to draw a crowd any other way, we resorted to lighting a fire in a large garbage can.) On St. Nicholas Avenue, though, the crowd was already large enough to overflow onto the street, and the cops asked us to move our platform back. When George stepped down I was introduced as a young American worker. I was well into my description of how capitalism caused the depression and might now try to get out of it by creating a fascist dictatorship when an egg burst on the side of my head. I was furious. As the heckling turned to catcalls, I felt a tug on my jacket. It was George, saying in a reassuring voice, "Keep cool. Don't respond to them. Keep going. I'm in back of you, don't worry." Was I ever worried! My speech kept coming out of somewhere. I don't know where. The crowd now seemed to be mostly composed of men in Bund uniforms. George kept encouraging me, and I kept going until suddenly someone blew a whistle and I was pelted with a shower of eggs, rotten fruit, and other garbage. My only injury came from a hard apple that hit me square in the face and made my nose bleed.

The Bund members loved it. They cheered and yelled, "This is only the beginning for you commie Jew lovers." We had no choice but to conclude the meeting before they caused a riot. As I came off the platform with a bloody handkerchief over my nose, George dismissed the incident with a little laugh. "It is nothing. Our problem is to get out of here without getting our heads cracked." George was sure the "little fascists would love to beat us up, so they can win high praise at the next Bund meeting." One of the local comrades went for a car and got us away without injury. I was discouraged, but not George. He insisted that once we got better organized we would hold a successful meeting.

Though I was scared, it was exciting to venture into the enemy's camp with George. He seemed to relish challenging Nazis on their own turf, as if he were getting even for what the Nazis were doing in Germany. His organizational planning improved after the egg-and-fruit shower on St. Nicholas. Now he showed up with old coats or smocks and safety glasses. "It's okay if the little Nazis want to throw stuff at us," he would tell the crowd derisively. "As long as the rest of you will listen to what we have to say, we will never give up the streets to the fascist bums." And so, night after night, we organized and spoke at antifascist street meetings. Most of the time, the league, the Party, or the YCL could muster enough local support to prevent the bastards from doing what they always managed to do on St. Nicholas Avenue.

As a worker and natural soapbox orator—and probably because I was non-Jewish ("composition" in party parlance)—I was tapped for the YCL Bronx section committee. Long before affirmative action policies or talk about diversity, Communist organizations were practicing them by trying to be representative of the communities they worked in. The Bronx section was concentrating on recruiting Irish, Italian, and black members. Once recruited, they, like me, rapidly moved up in the party hierarchy.

Our section covered most of the North Bronx. At the time we had over three thousand members, and the Party had over twice that number in the same area. It was considered a real honor to be on the section committee; Seymour advised me to consider my section work as the most important thing in my life. The committee met monthly to review and plan the work of the section and to divide up responsibility for the various actions. A typical meeting agenda might cover topics as various as changes in the party line, boosting *Daily Worker* sales, improving the organization of the unemployed, increasing Home Relief benefits, organizing tenants' councils to stop evictions, and planning one of the never-ending fund drives.

Not long after I joined the committee, we decided to try reducing the growing numbers of evictions for nonpayment of rent by staging a demonstration in support of the local tenants' council. The idea was to mobilize tenants to defend themselves against their greedy landlords. After a lengthy discussion of how to organize an antieviction action, we agreed to issue three leaflets, bring in a sound truck, and use enough YCL members to keep the police from attacking our furniture movers.

The team chosen to "return the furniture" were my buddies from Hymie's Deli. At the appointed hour we gathered on Southern Boulevard. To our surprise, the family had already been evicted. The mother, father, and two kids were sitting forlornly on the sidewalk with their furniture and belongings piled around them. We assured them that we would either get them back into their apartment or take them to the Home Relief Bureau to get emergency shelter.

A pretty good crowd gathered as our speakers condemned the landlords for their inhumane act of putting these poor, hardworking people out on the street as though they were dogs "No, not dogs. We treat dogs better than that!" the speaker contended. We started the action by carrying the furniture back into the apartment. The marshals then carried it back out. For most of the day, it was like a scene from a Mack Sennett comedy: we carried the furniture in, the government marshals carried it out again. In, out. In, out. With the loudspeakers blaring denunciations of "the greedy landlords and their lackeys, the police," things were heating up.

Finally a large police reinforcement created a line in front of the building and denied us entrance. By the end of the day, the furniture was on the street. We had lost. The best we could do was take the family to the emergency shelter for the night and to the Home Relief Bureau in the morning. All through the depression years, the Party initiated actions like the one on Southern Boulevard. The results were nearly always the same.

At the next section committee meeting, of course, there was a detailed analysis of our eviction demonstration. There was considerable criticism of us for taking over the action instead of involving local tenants. This was the first time I was asked to engage in what the YCL and the Party called "self-criticism." Unsure what that meant, I merely reported, "We were given an assignment, and we did it. So what's wrong with that?" In response I got a lengthy explanation of the need for individual members to constantly examine their individual behavior to make absolutely certain it was consistent with the Party's larger purposes. I expressed the view that, as we had not reinstated the family in their apartment, we had lost. "Not at all." countered Seymour. "Our real objective is helping people understand the class struggle. Now they know who the government really represents. And it isn't them."

Another form of self-criticism, replying to charges of sexual misconduct, was originated by the Party long before present-day antidiscrimination laws. Not too long after the eviction action, I found myself in the dock at the section committee, accused of "male chauvinism."

Some of the female friends I had made in the YCL subscribed to the notion that being straitlaced was nothing more than petty bourgeois nonsense, and they often enjoyed a little sexual dalliance. Other women, however, were as prudish as their Victorian predecessors. I was too young to know the difference. On a warm summer evening I met Rebecca at the mimeograph machine. She was wearing a loose-fitting blouse, and as she bent over, there they were—those exquisite mounds. I stared at them appreciatively, then looked up at her big brown eyes, not noticing their outraged expression, and said, "Jeez, you got a beautiful pair there." She pulled her blouse shut and spat angrily, "you are a rotten male chauvinist" and stormed out of the room.

A few weeks later I was asked to do some self-criticism for demeaning Comrade Rebecca. To me, it felt like my Catholic friends having to say Hail Marys to atone for their sins. I apologized and tried to explain that I really thought women's breasts were beautiful. "Of course, I shouldn't have said what I did, but . . ."

At this point Rebecca took off at me: "You're a classic example of a bourgeoisified worker! I think you should be suspended and given some strict control tasks to demonstrate that you have learned your lesson before you can be reinstated."

This really set me off. I was steaming and completely lost my temper: "Why don't you give yourself a control task—like a good fuck! Then maybe you wouldn't be such a bitch." I was out of my chair and out the door when I heard Seymour say, "Bob, take it easy. Come back."

Afterward I was sitting in Hymie's with Leo and Henry explaining what had happened. They were sympathetic: "It's too bad you didn't know that Comrade Rebecca is the embodiment of the party prude. You're in deep trouble, Schrank."

The case went all the way to the state committee. The state secretary suggested that I apologize to Rebecca and accept some control tasks—such as helping organize women laundry workers. The secretary, a tall, soft-spoken man, explained to the committee that "we are dealing here with a son of the working class who brings all the sins of the bourgeoisie with him. We need to be tolerant and help educate him, not chase people like him away."

But Rebecca was not satisfied. "This is just another male whitewash," she fumed. "I'm going to the National Office to settle this." After she stalked out, the meeting was adjourned and I was told not to worry. I was assigned to help organize the women's Laundry Workers Union, and eventually the charges disappeared. Rebecca never forgave me. Whenever we encountered each other, she would turn beet red, spin around quickly, and walk away.

At West Farms and 180th Street, not far from YCL headquarters, there was a big amusement park and swimming pool called Starlight Park. It was a small version of Coney Island and a popular blue-collar hangout. One day a group of YCL members, two of them black, were denied admission. When pressed, the person in the ticket office said, "We don't want no niggers in this pool."

The issue of what to do about Starlight Park was discussed at the next section committee. Should we picket the park and force the owners to admit blacks, or carry on an education campaign to convince the blue-collar guys that it was in their best interests to unite with their black brothers? We were divided. Many of the guys I grew up with in the Van Nest Steamrollers frequented the park. I was certain that picketing would simply inflame them and end up in a brawl. I favored the educational effort.

Many meetings later, the Red Starlight Campaign began. The name came from a poem Leo was inspired to write over a pastrami sandwich at Hymie's. It described a future world in which all working people were brothers and Starlight Park was called Red Starlight. The deli gang was delighted. In his usual earnest way, Harry turned to me: "You see? The revolutionary struggle produces art!"

We started leafleting the Park and asking people to sign a petition demanding the admission of blacks in the name of fairness and constitutional rights. To say that we got an icy reception would be a gross understatement. At times we had to run for our lives as young toughs threatened to "hang you fucking commies with the niggers. This place will never let 'em in. If it does, we burn it down." We didn't win that campaign, although some years later blacks were admitted.

About the same time, the Party was making an major effort to recruit black members. It had also developed the idea of a separate "Negro republic" in an area of the South identified as the "Black Belt," where blacks were in a clear majority. If there was ever a far-out intellectual exercise that had nothing to do with reality this was it. The Party assumed that because black Americans were the most oppressed people they would, with a little encouragement, flock to the cause. They never did, although a few black intellectuals—for example, W. E. B. DuBois—were sympathetic to Marxism. I believe that black workers, like a majority of white workers, simply wanted to be equal partners in the existing order of things. Nonetheless, the Left's recognition of the need for unity regardless of race, creed, or ethnicity was an important factor in the successful organizing drives the Congress of Industrial Organizations (CIO) carried out in the thirties.

Toward the end of 1936, the plumbing business, like everything else, was bad, and I was laid off. By then I was living with my sisters Hattie and Alice, Alice's boyfriend Wilfred, and an assortment of others in a YCL "commune" on Daly Avenue. Our six-room apartment was a hangout for left-wing activists, especially those working on WPA projects. On any given evening you could find a dozen or more people there in a heated argument over a Federal Theatre production of "Turpentine" or "Julius Caesar." What was the premise? What did the author say? How did the director and actors interpret it? Was it overacted or emotionally convincing? Was the staging right? And on and on into the night.

I hadn't been out of work too long when Alice's boyfriend made a lucky contact that got me a job as a "grease monkey" at Packard Motor Car. The plant on Fordham Road installed accessories in new cars—radios, heaters, extra lights—and was also a general service garage.

Employment at Packard had the immediate effect of ratcheting up my YCL status. I was now a worker in a "basic industry," one of the primary producers of wealth that was absolutely critical in the struggle for a socialist society. Without the support of workers in mining, steel, rubber, railroads, utilities, and automobiles, there could be no social revolution. For this reason, the Party was establishing an elaborate system of "concentration units" aimed at organizing them. It was not a markedly successful policy. The Party wielded some limited influence in a few basic industries through its access to the leadership of some unions, and communists were known as indefatigable workers in the CIO's organizing drives. Yet the Party could claim substantial memberships in very few unions—principally the maritime, municipal, and transport locals.

I was directed to join Local 259 of the United Auto Workers (UAW) and work with the comrades already there. My work at Packard was pretty boring, changing oil and shooting grease into dozens of little fittings under the car. I was never much good at repetitive tasks that presented no challenge, and I soon became bored. But because I was compulsive about arriving on time and was a dependable worker, my responsibilities at Packard were gradually increased. I was allowed to install optional equipment on new cars, and I learned to do simple repairs. As the job became more interesting, I actually began to like it.

The Packard was a prestige automobile owned by rich people. When Lou Gehrig was playing first base for the Yankees, he had a twelve-cylinder Packard roadster that I loved to service. Gehrig would hang around the garage talking with the mechanics and generally making all the guys feel good. Everyone who worked on his car was sure to get a dollar tip— a lot of money in those days.

A Local 259 organizer began to pressure me about getting my coworkers to sign union authorization cards. My interest in cars was strong enough to cause me some conflict between jeopardizing my job and doing my duty as a disciplined union supporter. The conflict was intensified by a beautiful 1932 Packard touring car with double windshield, leather interior, two spare tires on each side of the running boards, and a powerful straight-eight engine. When it was traded by the Tommy Manville estate, my boss, the service manager, called its low mileage to my attention. The used-car price to me was $125, but I didn't have it. My boss, seeing my fierce desire to own it, made an informal arrangement for me to pay it off in installments. And I was trying to organize a union right under his nose! I felt like a heel.

When I told the gang at Hymie's about my dilemma, they warned me against letting sentiment get in the way of understanding the true nature of the class struggle. No matter how nice he was, the manager was a tool of the Packard Motor Car Company and therefore—by definition —an enemy. My comrades were often critical of me for being overly sentimental, especially about my Packard touring car with the double windshield.

My new car could easily carry six of us, and we took to driving up to Provincetown on Cape Cod for summer weekends. On one of those trips, the Packard almost got me shot, and I learned a painful truth that cleared up a long-standing family mystery. While six of us, including Alice and Will, were returning from Provincetown we made a coffee and bathroom stop at a diner in Willimantic, Connecticut. As I returned to the car, two guys with guns appeared suddenly out of nowhere, saying "We finally caught up with you. We'd know this fuckin' car anywhere." Feeling the barrel of the gun stuck in my ribs, I was scared shitless. I tried not to move, or even breathe. "We've seen this getaway car in a dozen robberies around here, and this time we got ya."

Just then Alice arrived from the diner and, with the full force of outraged indignation, snapped, "What the hell is going on here? Put that gun down. That's my brother. Who do you think you are?" Slowly, as the rest of the group showed up, the two plainclothes police realized that this was a case of mistaken identity between a gang of bank robbers and a grown-up "Our Gang Comedy." From then on, the Packard was known as the "getaway car" and Alice, who was so fearless in the face of police terror, was our very own heroine.

As I drove away from the diner, I could still feel the barrel of that gun sticking in my side. Alice was sitting next to me. Tired from a couple of days in the sun and surf, the others in the car gradually fell silent and dozed off. The two of us talked about the precariousness of life. "Just one little squeeze of that guy's index finger and I would be laid out on a marble slab right now," I said.

"No," Alice said, "It wasn't meant to be, that's all."

For some reason it popped into my head to ask, "What about Mutter? Why did she die? Was that meant to be?"

"You mean you don't know?"

"Was it cancer?"

"What? Where did you get that idea?"

I tried to think. "I don't know. I thought Papa said so."

For some time we rode silently through the approaching dark with only the sound of the wind and the engine. Slowly, Alice began. "Mother was pregnant. Papa didn't know it, and I think she didn't want him to. You may not remember, but we were pretty poor then. Papa was blacklisted, and there was very little money coming into the house. I believe Mother thought we didn't need another mouth to feed. Without telling Papa, she and a woman friend went to some back-alley abortionist. She hemorrhaged and died that evening in French Hospital."

I was completely dumbfounded. Alice couldn't believe I hadn't known. She said, "Why do you think Papa was on the verge of suicide?" Not waiting for a reply, she continued, "He blamed himself for what happened—and probably still does."

This new-found source of grief shed a glimmer of light on what had happened that terrifying night thirteen years ago. I had a terrible urge to stop the car and run screaming into the woods. That would have to wait. I had to continue the long drive home so that we could all be at work Monday morning. Finally I knew what had happened and could begin the long, confused journey of trying to understand its impact on me.

It was taking a long time, but we were gradually getting the Packard workers to sign union authorization cards. The local union officers reminded me that until we had enough members to petition the National Labor Relations Board (NLRB) for an election my job was in jeopardy. I needed to be extremely careful not to screw up and give management an excuse for firing me. I heeded their advice, but not long after I sensed a chill between me and the boss.

We never did get enough signed cards, and I was fired for supposedly leaving a crankcase oil-plug loose, causing the car to leak oil and burn out the engine. Some of my fellow workers whispered that I had been set up, and they claimed to be with me; "but I got a family and I need this job. You're just a kid. You can afford to get bounced. I can't."

The case of Packard *vs.* Schrank was one of the first cases to go before a recently established state labor board. As it was only my word against the evidence of a burned-out engine, the union lost. It was great to be hailed as a hero and a victim of class warfare, but after a few days the reality of being out of a job began to sink in.

While hanging out at the UAW local 259 office, I volunteered to help the union's organizing efforts at the Ford Plant in Weehawken and a Chevrolet dealership in Westchester County. Periodically I would distribute leaflets or lend support to a picket line. The work contributed to my education as a union organizer. I learned how to size up a plant for an organizing drive and devise a plan to move it toward unionization. One of the most important efforts was devoted to understanding the workers' situation by developing a relationship with them so they would feel comfortable feeding us information about their major gripes. This helps organizers gain a familiarity with the plant and lets them mention workers' real problems in the leaflets, so that workers don't view the union as a bunch of outsiders. In years to come, the lessons I learned in this introductory course in union organizing came in very handy.

At other times, having nothing much to do, I killed time at the union hall, just schmoozing and nursing the illusion that a job might miraculously emerge from somewhere. Especially during a strike, the union hall was in a perpetual smoky haze from the cardplayers who hung out there. It was during the strike of the Chevrolet dealer that I learned to eat raw oysters and clams.

The local union was running out of money, food, and morale for supporting the strike at the dealership. Remembering what Papa had said about strikes running "on the bellies of the strikers and their families," I had volunteered to help a group of local members solicit food donations. We were getting a good supply of rice and potatoes, but after many weeks of picketing, the strikers were showing signs of boredom. A brother suggested that they needed a change of diet, and someone suggested going clamming. In no time, two groups were formed—the clammers and the oyster diggers.

That afternoon they returned to the picket line with baskets full of oysters and clams. Someone came up with a bottle of Tabasco sauce, and someone else got horseradish and lemons. The picket line took on a celebratory mood as the fresh clams and oysters were shucked and strikers lined up enthusiastically slurping them out of the half-shells. One of the brothers noticed that I wasn't eating: "Hey kid, whatsa matter? Come on, have some. They're good for your thing, make it stand up good."

Suddenly I was the center of attention. "Hey, I betcha this kid never ate one of these. Right kid?" I nodded yes. He called to the crowd to gather round to "see this boy eat his first raw clam and oyster." Leading me over to the shucking table, he asked, "You want Tabasco, horseradish?" What did I know? I nodded. He handed me an oyster on the half shell. Looking at this slimy thing, I was sure I would throw up if I ate it. I hesitated.

The strikers were yelling, "slurp it, slurp it in" and laughing. Somebody next to me said, "Just hold your nose, shut your eyes, and slurp." I did, and a broad cheer went up. Next the clam. It went down a little easier, and before the afternoon was over I had made it through a half dozen clams and oysters. Thank you UAW. Every time I eat a clam or an oyster I remember that Chevrolet strike with fondness.

Occasionally our Daly Avenue commune was used as a hideout for political refugees. One day a party functionary brought over a long, thin man who chain-smoked and spoke no English. He was José Amaro, a Cuban communist who had escaped from jail and, with the help of sailors, stowed away in the icebox of a freighter. He was a very handsome man, and once he thawed out and had a few good dinners he enjoyed teaching YCL girls Latin American dances.

He was also very superstitious. One hot, humid summer night I was sleeping up on the roof when José awakened me yelling something in Spanish—"No sleep in full moon, you get loony." He insisted that I get out of the moonlight, which he believed was far more dangerous than the heat. All our attempts to explain that as scientific Marxists we didn't believe in "peasant superstitions" of that kind didn't convince him. He didn't think Mr. Marx knew anything about such things. He was probably right.

We arranged for José to speak to a YCL section membership meeting through a translator. He described to the packed meeting hall the horrors and tortures suffered by political prisoners in Cuba and Central America. In great detail he told us how they insured their mental and physical survival in the overcrowded jail cells by organizing their daily lives. They held regular exercise sessions, classes in astronomy, cooking, geography, languages—whatever subject someone knew something about.

José Amaro was an inspiration to us; he embodied the ideal of a revolutionary hero, a saint in our socialist crusade. One day he left us, just as suddenly and mysteriously as he had arrived. A party leader told us that we must never, ever speak of his presence among us. Doing so could endanger his life. José's brief presence and the need for silence made us feel part of the worldwide struggle against the evil imperialists.

There were all kinds of other folks coming to and going from Daly Avenue. One of them was Eddy, who was working as a stagehand, designer, and general factotum on a Federal Theatre Project. He didn't pass muster in our socialist commune, because he marked his name on food that he left in the refrigerator. We launched a surreptitious game of trying to steal a little from Eddy's stash; when we began watering his milk, he finally caught on and became angry. We tried to laugh it off, but Eddy wouldn't. After a lengthy discussion, we agreed that there was no way to survive in a commune without a good sense of humor. Eddy was invited to leave.

A more amiable housemate, Robin Winthrop, showed up at a YCL meeting one night looking for a place to flop for a few days. We had trouble figuring him out at first. He was a guy of average height with an upturned nose and a long tuft of hair that was forever falling over his eyes. He looked like the epitome of the all-American high school class president, and he came from a well-to-do WASP family. If there was ever an unlikely communist, it was Robin. Ethnic intellectuals and working-class revolutionaries made sense to us. We were the exploited and, as the *Manifesto* said, had nothing to lose but our chains.* Robin insisted, though, that his father was such a rotten bastard only a radical change in the system could do anything about people like him. The commune residents remained suspicious. Could Robin be an FBI plant? The YCL leaders decided to test his loyalty by giving him some tough assignments.

At the time we were conducting a mass campaign against the Hearst press for its support of fascist movements and its anticommunist propaganda. As Robin was a talented graphic artist, we assigned him the job of painting "Down With Fascism! Don't Read Hearst" in three-foot-high red letters on the Hearst building. I was assigned to go with him to help out and observe his performance. Robin was great with the paint brush. When he was finished, the slogan—printed in big, bold letters—was very impressive. The problem was that working at such high speed had left him splattered with paint. When the sirens and whistles blew, we had to make a run for it. If the police caught up with us, he would be caught literally red-handed.

We ran along the East River, where, to our great good luck, the Fulton Fish market was just opening for the day. We ducked in behind one of the fish stalls to hide until things calmed down. Crouched behind barrels of

---

*Most of us didn't realize then that a number of American radicals of the preceding generation—for example, John Reed and Jessie Ashley—had come from prosperous backgrounds.

pickled fish, we looked up to see a big guy in hip boots standing over us, hands on his hips. "Hey, what the fuck you guys doin' there? Stealin' fish, uh?"

"No," I said, "we're on the lam for painting the Hearst building."

He looked at us quizzically: "Oh, stealin' paint. Okay, stay there. I'll tell you when you can get the fuck outa here before the cocksuckers try to shake you down."

"You see, Winthrop," I said, "this is working-class solidarity."

When we got out of the fish market, Robin was still smeared with paint, and we both stank of fish. We got lots of space on the subway ride home. The next day's newspapers carried a front-page picture of "the defacement of the Hearst building, probably carried out by Russian Communist agents."

Robin's decoration of the fascist press building and his defiance of the capitalist police made him the YCL star of Tremont Avenue for a while. He had passed the test. His citation might have read: "For demonstrating courage as a Young Communist by going into the enemy camp to broadcast an antifascist message."

Living in a commune, you get used to strange people coming and going. I seldom arrived home before midnight or so and didn't know who might be there when I crept quietly into bed. One memorable night my homecoming was like the beginning of a fairy tale. Fast asleep in my bed was a very beautiful young woman. For some time I sat and stared at her. Her delicate, perfectly proportioned features seemed carved out of Carrara marble. Who was she? I vaguely remembered Robin saying something about a sister who was getting as fed up with life at home as he had been; he'd mentioned that she might join us one of these days. Could this be her? Not wanting to wake her in case she decided to leave, I crawled carefully into bed and, in spite of superhuman efforts to stay awake, fell asleep. In the morning she was gone. Dressing quickly and heading for the kitchen, I found her sitting at the table, coffee cup in hand, staring out the window.

"Hi, so who are you?" Her beauty was simply overwhelming. For a time I just sat studying her perfectly chiseled features and haunting blue-gray eyes.

"I'm Robin's sister, Abigail. I hope you didn't mind me being in your bed. Your sister thought you wouldn't."

"Mind? How could I? Please feel welcome anytime."

Abigail and I spent that day visiting the zoo and talking. As we ate dinner at a cafeteria, she told me about her mother's death and her father's remarriage to a woman with children of her own. The new wife resented Robin and Abigail, and their father had become increasingly distant. "That's why Robin left. Without him, I couldn't stay. They can't force me to come home," she declared defiantly. "I'll be eighteen in a few months. And anyway, I won't go back."

"Suppose your father decides to come after you?" I asked. I was concerned about the effect of her presence on the commune.

"Oh, he's glad to be rid of us. His new wife has her own kids, and she hates us."

Her matter-of-fact tone, her coolness, and her seeming maturity fascinated me. I had never met anyone like her. Her whole five-foot-six figure was as perfect as her face. Wherever we went in public—on a trolley, in a cafeteria, just walking in the street—I was aware of people staring at her. Unlike her brother—who saw himself as an earnest revolutionary eager to right the wrongs of the world—Abigail was not interested in the Party. She was sympathetic, but "all that meeting stuff is so boring. You people seem to be saying the same things over and over all the time. Don't you ever get tired of it?"

"No, not if you really believe it."

After the first night, to my regret, she insisted on sleeping on a couch in the living room.

In spite of her lack of interest in politics, we spent a lot of time together. She often met me after a street corner meeting to walk home with me. One night I told her I loved her. We stopped and kissed. She remained distant; nothing seemed to happen. After many weeks of trying, and with a little help from some cheap Chilean wine, I coaxed her into bed. We hugged, kissed and touched. I was all worked up and ardent, but she just lay there as if nothing was happening. I thought of all the advice I had read about being a good lover and the importance of foreplay. I tried everything, but she remained indifferent, motionless.

"Don't you feel anything?" I asked.

"No, nothing," she answered, then added, "but you're okay?" I assured her I was.

Like so many men before me, I was sure that with the proper technique I could somehow free Abigail from the icebox she was locked in. I continued to try for many months, but it was always the same—she just lay there staring up at the ceiling. After a time, she got a job modeling in the garment district and moved out. She showed up periodically on the cover of *McCall's, Vogue,* and other prestigious fashion magazines. The bunch at Hymie's Deli had great fun ribbing me about the "pretty, frigid WASP lady even our working-class hero couldn't defrost."

8

Evolution of a Political Activist

After being fired from Packard, I didn't have much to do but speak at street corner meetings of the American League Against War and Fascism. In the winter of 1938 the YCL leadership decided it was a good time to make me a paid "functionary." Going on the payroll was a badge of honor, though my job as Bronx YCL educational director was only half-time.

I still don't know how I came to be appointed to the position. No one could have confused me with a Marxist scholar or an intellectual; it must have been my speaking ability and my status as an authentic member of the working class. I was sure most of the college kids in the leadership training classes I taught knew a hell of a lot more about the subject than I did. I had to scramble to stay at least one session ahead of the students.

Someone—I don't know who—also arranged for me to get a second half-time job with the National Youth Administration (NYA), a New Deal work program. Some years ago, when I requested and received a copy of my FBI file—750 pages with about a quarter of it blacked out—I learned that the bureau began recording my activities regularly the day I joined the NYA. For the next twenty-five years, sometimes under the direct supervision of J. Edgar Hoover, it kept close tabs on me.*

The NYA assigned me to work for a Jewish Federation organization called the National Desertion Bureau. Its mission was to locate husbands who had run out on their wives and arrange, at best, reconciliations or, at least, financial support of the mother and children.

---

*I now consider this file a sort of very expensive personal diary kept at considerable cost to taxpayers. I will occasionally share some of its contents with the reader.

I met the director, Mr. Mandelbaum, in his tiny office cluttered with piles of brown legal-sized folders. He was a short, stocky man with jet black hair, a hearty handshake, and a handlebar mustache. He greeted me in a friendly manner while clearing a stack of folders off a chair for me. "It's our job to get these deserters to accept their family responsibilities," he explained earnestly. "But first we have to find them, and then we turn them over to the authorities." He hastened to add, "Not to lock them up, of course—what good would that do?—but to put them on probation to us so we can counsel them. Get it?" Mandelbaum leaned back in his chair, looked me in the eye, and said, "Robert, for two weeks a month we're going to make a detective out of you. So what do you think of that?"

What did I think of that? "It sounds great," I replied. I was mentally conjuring up my new image. I already smoked Camels. I just needed to add the trench coat and fedora hat and cultivate some gumshoe talk.

Mandelbaum reached into a huge pile of file folders and pulled one out. "Now this is a wrestler named Sam the Butcher. He had an affair with Sadie, an immigrant woman who was working in a Philadelphia restaurant. Like most immigrant girls, Sadie was desperately looking for a husband. After a series of dates, he proposed to her. Poor woman! Little did she know he was a *ganef*; he just wanted to get her in bed. In his selfish little mind he figures she'd just forget him afterwards." He paused, looking at me quizzically: "You know what is a *ganef*?" I shook my head. He leaned back on his chair and looked up at the ceiling. "A *ganef* is a combination of a con man and a bum. Trouble is, poor Sadie can't forget him, because he left her with a son. Periodically we catch up with him, he gives her some child support, and then he drifts off again. Well, he's in one of his drifts, and we want you to find him. Then we'll try to make him responsible for what he did to Sadie."

I must have appeared as dumb as I felt. Mandelbaum hastened to assure me, "Oh, it's not so hard. First you interview Sadie. She keeps track of where he is wrestling from the newspapers, and we can always get his license number and address from the motor vehicle bureau. Then we get a subpoena, and you serve him. That's all there is to it." I didn't say anything, but I guess he read my doubts about serving subpoenas. "Look, he'll make some payments, and that will help Sadie. That's what we're after—making people be responsible. It's not revolutionary or world-shaking. It's just making things a little better."

I wanted the job. "Of course," I said. "I'm sure we can help Sadie."

I arrived at the woman's apartment early the next morning. She came to the door in an old padded housecoat, with a sad-faced little boy pressing himself against her side. Their dark, groundfloor rear apartment looked onto an air shaft. I introduced myself and told her why I was there. She gave me a cup of coffee and insisted on making herself "presentable." While she was in the other room, the child stood leaning against the doorjamb and stared at me.

When Sadie returned she was wearing a low-cut blouse, dangling earrings, lipstick, and all varieties of bangles and beads. She had pulled her glossy black hair back with a comb. She reminded me of the gypsy fortune-tellers I had seen on the Coney Island boardwalk.

In answer to my questions, Sadie told me she had last heard from Sam about six months earlier and that he had given her no child support since then. Yes, she had a part-time job, in a "nice kosher restaurant in the neighborhood. You should stop by for a sandwich." She showed me a box of news clippings about wrestling matches and explained that she watched the match schedules carefully. It was important to look for pictures, in case Sam was wrestling under a different name. "But you can always tell Sam. He's got a funny tattoo on his left arm. Like a hook or somethin'."

She thought he might be wrestling in an upcoming series at the Ridgewood Grove in Brooklyn. "Please tell him I don't like chasing him. I would like we should live together like a real family. Look at this nice boy. Wouldn't you be proud to be his father?" The child still stood leaning his head against the door frame, staring and silent.

As I got up to leave, Sadie wanted to know "What's your hurry?" She was lonely, she said, and liked company. If this had been the movies she would have looked like Lauren Bacall or some other gorgeous femme fatale. She didn't. I left.

Some time later, after visiting the motor vehicle bureau and various wrestling arenas and gyms, I caught up with Sam the Butcher at the Bronx Coliseum at West Farms. Mandelbaum's detailed instructions were to go to the arena, wait until after his match, then, when he was on his way to the locker room, hand him the summons. "Damn," I muttered to myself. "Now I'm a process server. This is a shit job. What kind of detective work is this?"

I had never seen anything like this funny show called a wrestling match. It consisted of muscle-bound men tossing each other around like beach balls while groaning and moaning loudly. In the end, miraculously, nobody was hurt, but the spectators screamed and yelled as though they were witnessing a fight to the death.

I caught up with Sam as he walked to the locker room. I felt sorry for him. He was older than the other wrestlers, and he looked very tired. As we reached the dressing room he stopped, looking at me with his sad eyes. "All right," he said, "so give it to me, I'm not stupid, I know what you come for. Tell her I give her some money come next week." He gestured wearily toward the arena. "You know, with all the yellin' and screamin' out there, we don't make nothin'. It's all for the promoters. Us, we get peanuts. So what does she want from me already, my blood? You know what? She could have it."

He was probably lying. It didn't matter. I was instantly on his side against the promoters. "Why don't you guys organize a union," I suggested.

Fearful, he looked around to make sure no one was in earshot. "Listen kid, you wanna ruin me? Anyone hears that kind of talk around here, Sam is a dead duck. Not just a little dead, all dead. They wouldn't even let me be a sweeper in here if they hear that word. So I like girls, and I got in trouble with Sadie. You make a mistake once and you pay, pay, and pay. Good-bye and good luck, kid. Don't make my mistakes."

I decided the detective job was not for me. As I explained to Mandelbaum, it seemed ridiculous to chase down one "poor exploited soul to try and get him to help another exploited person, when the real problem is the system."

Mandelbaum smiled. "Of course, you want a revolution to change the world into some kind of paradise here on earth. And me, I'm just a guy who wants to fix things up, make them a little better. It's okay. At your age, you *should* have higher goals. So what will you do now?"

"I have some friends"—actually they were comrades—"who are on the WPA. They think they can get me a job as a first-aid man at the Orchard Beach project. And they're gonna tutor me so I can pass the test."

"Well, good luck, kid. God knows the world needs idealistic young people like you."

The Orchard Beach job was also part-time, but it paid a little better. The project employed thousands of men building bathhouses, walkways, a pavilion for food stands, and a immense parking lot. The first-aid shack was a great vantage point for watching a strange assortment of men—tailors, accountants, bakers, factory hands, carpenters, plumbers, bankers, mechanics, bookkeepers, and cooks—doing plain old manual work. They were digging up the ground with pickaxes and shovels, raking, and pushing loaded wheelbarrows. The skilled workmen needed on the project were still the elite; they got the highest pay and worked fewer days than the unskilled laborers.

On cold, nasty days it was a crummy job, but when the weather was good the place took on the cheerful air of a summer camp. At lunch break there were ball games, chess and checker tournaments, and card-playing. I and my comrades kept busy organizing, giving out leaflets about the need for higher pay and more jobs, and touting socialism as the solution to all our ills. Their own circumstances made many of the WPA workers receptive to what we had to say.

In the late 1930s, the Wagner Act and the CIO were transforming the union movement. The legislation had created an entirely new playing field for labor by guaranteeing workers the right to join a union of their own choosing and requiring employers to negotiate with the unions' elected representatives. To gain recognition, however, a union had to collect a certain number of signed authorization cards and petition the NLRB for an election. At Packard we had failed to gather enough signatures and, without the union, it was still easy to get rid of employees who, like me, were organizers.

In 1935, the same year the Wagner Act became law, eight AFL unions under the leadership of United Mine Workers President John L. Lewis formed the Committee for Industrial Organization, the CIO. After years of imploring the AFL leadership to get off their collective fat asses and organize all the workers in the mass-production industries—instead of forming craft unions of skilled workers only—Lewis decided to act. The

AFL expelled the unions that had formed the committee, and the CIO was born.

The Wagner Act made it respectable to be a union member, and soon there was a tidal wave of workers wanting to join. "Hell, the government, the Congress, and the president say it's okay" was the way one worker put it. The CIO was primarily interested in organizing the mass-production industries. In any given industry, such as automotive manufacturing, all the workers in the plant became members of the same CIO-affiliated local—the United Auto Workers (UAW) in this case.

The AFL remained a federation of craft unions that organized only skilled workers. Moreover, when the AFL organized an industry, like the building trades, the workers ended up in a dozen different craft unions, weakening their bargaining power and causing jurisdictional conflicts. The AFL unions used as much of their energy fighting each other as they did fighting the employers. Talk about the Hatfields and the McCoys!

During 1937, using a new strike tactic, the "sit-down strike," CIO unions had made organizing gains in the steel, automotive, and rubber industries. By 1938, three years after passage of the Wagner Act, the CIO was in desperate need of trained organizers. The left-wing political organizations, fiercely committed to the cause of the working class and skilled at organizing, were exactly what the new labor movement needed. That's why the CIO unions had such a disproportionate number of leftists and Communist party members in leadership positions in the late 1930s and early 1940s. The Transport Workers' Union was organized by comrades Mike Quill, Doug McMahon, and a lot of other party people. The Socialist Workers' party organized the Teamsters in Minneapolis, and the Socialists worked among government employees throughout the country. The leftists not only became leaders of their respective unions—way out of proportion to their representation in the rank and file—they also supplied the ideological base for these unions. Their departure in the post–World War II era was a major factor in the decline of the labor movement. Soon after losing its ideologues, the movement ran out of ideas.

All this union activity meant that a major part of my job as Bronx YCL education director was putting together courses on how to organize workers. One evening while I was teaching a session on the need to understand the culture of a community or workplace before attempting to organize it, the county YCL organizer showed up. After a lengthy pre-liminary speech on the wonderful opportunities for getting our message to workers in basic industries, his round, cherubic face broke into a grin as he told me I was to leave for Georgia the next day. I would work with the CIO's Textile Workers' Organizing Committee in checking out the potential to organize a cotton mill down there.

He also suggested that I use an alias for this trip; we chose the name Bob Hayes. The Party had the conspiratorial notion that by changing our names we could avoid identification. The FBI file, though, reveals that the government knew exactly when and where every name change occurred. Whom were we hiding from anyway?

This new assignment caught me by surprise, and the idea of venturing into the South scared me. I protested to Comrade County Organizer that my car, a 1934 Ford roadster, wasn't in shape for a long trip. It would take time to get it ready. He replied that I was supposed to be a grown-up revolutionist and should be ready to move at a moment's notice. "Sure, I'm ready," I said defensively, "but my car is not a revolutionist, and I got to . . ."

He interrupted me: "Just do whatever you have to." After a quick cal-culation, I figured I needed tires, new plugs, points, and a couple of other things, and he impatiently handed over two ten-dollar bills.

"Once you're on the road," he explained, "Harold will take care of everything."

"Who the hell is Harold? And when will I be back?"

Frustrated, he snapped, "Harold is the education director of the Party. He's from Texas. And if you're successful down there, you may never be back. You could even be the new leader of the Southern Textile Work-ers' Union."

A few days later, the work on the Ford complete, Harold and I were off to Georgia. Harold was a pleasant surprise. Unlike the southern red-neck I had expected, he was a short, congenial man who wore horn-rimmed glasses and looked like a schoolteacher. What distinguished him from most party leaders was his sense of humor. He was an amateur his-torian too, and as we drove south he gave me a running commentary on the landscape and the people. He was intensely interested in the every-day lives of the farmers and workers.

In Baltimore, he wanted to find the house at Fells Point where Frederick Douglass had lived as a slave. We did not find the house, but listening to Harold talk gave me a glimpse of Douglass's heroic fight against slavery. With the help of his master's wife, he had learned to read, Harold said, and that had changed his life. His contacts with freed slaves in the Baltimore shipyards helped him resolve to gain his own freedom. The twentieth-century workers and sharecroppers of the South, Harold believed, could only be converted to socialism the same way, through learning. Like Douglass, they first had to learn to read.

Harold's talk about Douglass gave me an interest in the great abolitionist that is still active. In his autobiography, Douglass has a passage about the antislavery struggle in which he distinguishes among "the ideal, the real, and the actual." In my years of learning about work groups, I found Douglass's distinction very useful. First, I would ask, What is the *ideal*, as set forth by the company; for example, "We are one big happy family." The *real* is best exemplified by accounts of a work situation in employee surveys; that is, what workers say about it. The *actual* is how the people in the workplace experience their jobs. I found Douglass's conception a valuable tool for learning what is really going on in a work environment

Around noon one day we were driving through the Virginia countryside when Harold suddenly yelled "Stop the car." Whatever was the matter, I asked. He smiled. He wanted to show me what had made the Confederacy rich, what had built its great mansions, and what had caused its downfall. He walked over to a fence and, leaning into a field of bushes with little white flowers, he picked one and held it out to me. Did I know what it was? I did not. "This is King Cotton, which kept these folks stuck in their feudal plantation world long after the industrial revolution was closing that chapter of history."

The South was the world Harold loved and understood. When we reached the Carolinas, he explained, we would start meeting with members of the Sharecroppers' Union. Then I would get a real earful of the unbridled greed and exploitation that was the legacy of King Cotton. In the soft spring air, his words didn't make a lot of sense to me. I just wanted to sit under a tree and doze off while smelling the flowers and watching puffs of cotton clouds drift by.

From North Carolina we drove west through the mountains to Tennessee. Harold was from Texas, but he knew the Tennessee hills as though he had lived in them. Near Chattanooga we drove up and around the twisting country roads until he motioned me to pull into a church parking lot. The building's sides were adorned with signs advertising Moxie and Bull Durham chewing tobacco. Only a rickety wooden cross on its roof peak identified the poor little structure as a church.

As we were early, Harold suggested that we take a walk. Along the narrow dirt road we came upon shacks that looked like chicken coops, surrounded by cotton plants. I refused to believe that the sharecroppers lived in such hovels, but Harold assured me that they did. When we came upon a little shanty with a porch covered with signs for Coca Cola, Durham Snuff, and Burma Shave, he suggested that we get some "real southern eats." When we came through the broken screen door the Negro woman behind the counter looked alarmed. With his broad Texas drawl and a big smile Harold said, "Good day Ma'am. Can we get a little grits and chitlins or what you got that's real down home good?"

It was beginning to dawn on me that I was in that terrible part of the country I had only heard or read about, the home of lynch mobs, cross-burnings, greedy exploitation of sharecroppers, and vicious hatred of "come-unists." When we left the store Harold said he was sure this Negro woman had never, ever had a white person in her place before. Going there was Harold's way, as he told me many times, "of breaking down barriers put there by the ruling class to keep us divided." He never tired of explaining how sharecroppers, the "agrarian working class," needed to be united with their white wage-slave brothers so that the bourgeoisie could not pit them against each other.

We sat on wooden crates eating our grits and chitlins off a wobbly table. I was doing my disciplined best to eat this stuff, but my first encounter with southern cooking was a failure. The grits tasted like uncooked Farina covered with bacon grease, and the chitlins were some kind of rank-smelling fried guts. I simply couldn't swallow them. A mangy dog that loved chitlins came to my rescue. Harold asked the woman how much we owed her. Without looking at us, she replied in a whisper, "Ten cents." He gave her fifteen cents, she thanked him, and we left.

When we got to the meeting at the church, we found six or eight black sharecroppers. Harold explained that we had come to listen and to help, but the men seemed extremely reluctant to speak in our presence. Later Harold told me that, with the exception of the leader, none of these men had ever been in the same room with a white person before. Harold was at home with them, but I felt like a stranger in a foreign land.

Reluctantly one or two of the men explained their problem: "We're not gettin' enough for the cotton to pay the boss man and eat and pay the rent. So what is we gonna do?" From the way they spoke, I had the impression they thought Harold could actually do something about their immediate situation. In Alabama, Harold told them, the Sharecroppers' Union had managed to raise the price of raw cotton. Later Harold told me privately that the Party had organized the Alabama Sharecroppers' Union, but he didn't mention it to these men. To them, he stressed repeatedly the importance of signing up all the sharecroppers on their plantation. "Otherwise the boss man's just gonna fence you off." Looking at these powerfully built black farmers, I wondered about their paralyzing fear of the white boss man. I had a lot to learn about the South.

In the next few days we met with a number of similar groups of sharecroppers in the area. Harold was always cheerful and optimistic as he explained the potential of the Sharecroppers' Union. Although the men seemed glad to see Harold, I could feel their fear like a dense fog hanging in the air. I breathed a great sigh of relief when we finished the last sharecroppers' meeting.

In Chattanooga, Harold said, he knew a great rooming house where for twenty-five cents a day we could get a good, clean room and breakfast. He looked at me and laughed, "Where you gonna beat that? The South ain't all bad, eh?"

That night after dinner on the rooming house's round oak table, Harold introduced me to the regional director of the Textile Workers' Organizing Committee, who explained my assignment. They had a few contacts in the Clarks ONT mill, a cotton-thread mill in Trion, Georgia, about fifty miles south of Chattanooga. They would give me the workers' names, some leaflets, and a stack of authorization cards. I was to give them out, and then "we'll see if we can get something going." I asked a lot of nervous questions about the workers' sex, race, age, and so on, which really annoyed the regional director. "This guy worries me," he said to Harold as if I wasn't there. "Why didn't they send someone from the South?" The more Harold reassured him of my organizing skills, the more frightened I got. I thought this was a ridiculous assignment and began asking myself "What the hell am I doing here anyway?" I can't count the number of times in my life this phrase has circled around in my head in similar circumstances.

The next morning, Harold said good-bye in his most cheerful voice. "It's been great working with you. Be careful now. This is not the Bronx." That was reassuring! He was taking off for his home in Texas, but I felt like I was being sent to the end of the world.

It was a beautiful spring morning as I drove south past the Civil War battlefield at Chickamauga. The road to Trion runs alongside the Chattahoochee River with its portal of old willows draped along the banks. The tranquil scene made it easy to forget why I was there. Around noon I spotted the sign for "Trion, Home of Clark's Cotton." The town was on the far side of the river. Blocking the approach to the bridge was a big, fat white man with a red flag in one hand and a long-barreled shotgun in the other. An honest-to-goodness chain gang, dressed in horizontally striped suits exactly like those I had seen in pictures, was laying new planks on the bridge. Holy Christ! I was in panic. What the hell do I do now? Slowly I drove up to him.

As the shotgun man approached, he looked at my license plate and then at me. I was sure I was face to face with a Ku Klux Klan lyncher. I was strangely relieved to realize that there were no whites in the chain gang. The fat man said something that sounded at first like a foreign language: ". . . bawds in l'il bit, for was y'all doin in thees heer parts?" I figured he'd said, "We'll have the boards down soon. What are you doing here?"

"Visiting a friend," I replied. Oh, oh, I thought, what a mistake! Suppose he asks who? Fortunately, he didn't. A few minutes later, as he waved me across the bridge, I wondered whether I would get back across the river alive.

The town square lay just beyond the bridge. I drove around it, hoping to find another twenty-five-cent rooming house. I rang the bell on the front porch of a house with the sign "Clean Rooms, Running Water." A friendly old lady showed me a room and had me sign a little school notebook. "Oh, y'all from Chattanooga? Well, you sure coulda fooled me. Are y'all with the mill?" Trying to speak southern, I said, "No, just visitin' a bit." I spent the rest of the day walking around town, checking out the plant location, the main gate, the coffee shops, and the streets with their row on row of little A-frame company houses.

After a few days getting to know the town, I decided it was time to visit one of my contacts. As I opened the garden gate, a sweet evening smell of flowers filled the air. Just for a moment, I was moved by the peaceful tranquillity of this southern mill town. I knocked on the door. It seemed forever before a tall, gaunt-looking man came to the screen door.

He looked at me quizzically. "What can I do for you?"

I told him I had been sent by the Textile Workers' Organizing Committee.

He was immediately alarmed. "Come in quickly! Shut the door," he exclaimed. "My God, mister, you shouldn't come here. If they found out you was visitin' me I'd lose my job." He went to the window and looked out. "Is that your car out there?" Before I could answer, he asked, "What kinda plates you got on her?"

"New York."

"Damn!" he exploded. "Don't you have no sense parkin' front of the house? Where'd you get your organizing learnin' from? Not down here, that's for sure." He kept shaking his head. Finally he asked, "What do you wanna do now?" I told him about the leaflets and cards and how I planned to distribute them in the morning. "And then what?" he wanted to know. I said if we didn't get a response I would keep going back every day until we got enough cards to petition the NLRB for an election.

He was incredulous. "Just like that? Y'all think the company is gonna just sit there like a bump on a log while you're signin' 'em up. Mister, you don't know what you are doing, and whoever sent you must be stupider than you are. Go ahead and do what you wanna do, but don't come near this house ever again." He walked to the window, looked out, and said, "There's no one around. I guess you can go now."

Back at the rooming house, I called my Chattanooga contact and told him what had happened. I was hoping he'd say forget it and go home, but he didn't. He had thought the union development was further along than it now appeared to be, but he saw no harm in giving out the flyers and the cards that people could mail in if they cared to.

The next morning I was at the plant gate early, giving out the flyer that said "Join the Textile Workers' Union for Higher Wages and Better Working Conditions. Stop the Stretch Out That's Killing Us," and so on. I figured that nothing happened because nobody in the company expected to see a young man alone distributing union literature. I tried to detect some reaction as the workers took the leaflets, but they accepted them with absolutely no comment or expression. It was a strange experience. I hadn't the slightest idea how they felt about the union. By the time the shift was in, I had distributed most of the material and felt pretty good.

I stopped at the local coffee shop, ordering bacon and eggs and eating my second helping of grits. The South didn't seem so bad after all. I could even get to like grits. On my return to the rooming house, I was welcomed by a committee of three men who all resembled the fat flagman with the shotgun.

"What are you doin' here, boy?" they wanted to know.

"Nothin'."

"Nothin'? That why you're givin' out this here communist union stuff? Did you think you was just gonna come down here and stir up folks with your Yankee propaganda?"

The three of them were standing real close to me, and I was using all my resources not to piss in my pants. I was thinking, 'So this is a lynch mob.'

"How much money you got, boy?" I asked why he wanted to know. He said if I didn't have twelve dollars I could be locked up for vagrancy and they could take my car. It turned out I had a little less than ten.

"All right, boy, here's what we're gonna let you do. We're gonna let y'all get your New York Yankee ass out of here right now. And if you don't like that, we're gonna let your ass set in the county jail for a while." Remembering my legal rights, I asked if I could make a telephone call. Sure I could, but from right here. The other two guys kept muttering something about "runnin' his ass out of here." I called my New York contact and told him of my predicament. He advised me to do whatever they wanted and come on home. The time was probably not right for this particular organizing effort. Did I ever agree!

As soon as I packed my bag, the three men pushed me out the door and down the stairs. By now I was both furious and frightened, a bad combination. I knew if I gave them any excuse at all they would kick the shit out of me. They shoved me into the Ford and told me to follow them. "If you make a bad move, we'll show you some real southern hospitality." As they led me out of Trion by a back road I was still worried that I was headed for a hanging tree. After what felt like fifty miles, they stopped in the middle of nowhere. One of them ambled back to my car with a gun in one hand. "Okay, boy, just you remember. Next time we ain't gonna be so nice. And tell that to the rest of those New York communists."

With a huge sigh of relief I pressed down on the gas pedal and was off to New York City. Driving straight through the night and stopping only for coffee to keep me awake, I had lots of time to think about the outburst of union activity resulting from the Wagner Act. It was causing organizers to make some pretty poor judgment calls. My experiences in the South should teach us that some places were not going to be organized just yet, in spite of the Wagner Act. What a relief it was to read the sign "to the Holland Tunnel."

Some time later I ran into Comrade Harold at a meeting and told him what had happened. He smiled and in his most cheerful drawl he said, "Well, y'all got a darn good lesson in how the southern bourgeois functions. Now you understand the problems of building a mass movement down there."

I wanted to tell him how stupid I thought my assignment was and point out that I could have been killed, but I didn't. I figured it was probably a symptom of lack of commitment when your ideological zeal doesn't cancel out your concern for personal safety. Harold reminded me that Comrade Marx had told us we had nothing to lose but our chains. He laughed as he said, "but remember, soldiers in a cause must always expect casualties."

I still believed we were primarily propagandists selling a cure for society's ills. I had not yet grasped that we were in a life-and-death struggle. In the Bronx, what we were doing felt a lot more like a game of wits than a war. You might get hit with a rotten egg, punched, shoved, or whacked by a police club, but you didn't get killed. That's not the way it was in Georgia—or in Europe.

9

War and Betrayal

What makes people raise their fists in the air, puts rifles in their hands, drives them to join struggles for just and unjust causes, is not reason but a hypertrophied soul. It is the fuel without which the motor of history would stop turning.

Milan Kundera

My understanding of what was at stake in the antifascist struggle, as well as my personal political philosophy, were both confused and clarified by momentous events taking place in Europe in the late 1930s. The fascist military attacks on the republican government of Spain were a central concern for everyone on the Left. After the conflict in Spain became a full fledged civil war in July of 1936 and the western democracies—Britain, France, and the United States—refused to intervene, the Party decided to take action. It called a closed leadership meeting for a Saturday afternoon at the Manhattan Center.

The hall was packed. The presence of all the party top brass on the stage made it clear that this was an important session. A banner reading "Stop the March of Fascism in Spain" stretched across the stage. As usual, party leaders made long speeches explaining the desperate need to unite the antifascist groups of Spain and Europe into a united front. To me, the descriptions of Spanish antifascist factions—anarchists, communists, socialists, and liberals—made it sound as if they hated each other more than they did the enemy. I couldn't understand all the ideological differences among them and was fearful that Spain would turn out to be like pre–Hitler Germany, where the Left, including the communists, spent more time bickering among themselves then they did resisting the Nazis. Perhaps for the first time, I wondered whether the factional disputes over power might be at least as important to the participants as the cause of freedom itself.

At the end of the meeting a party official proposed that we organize a battalion of Americans to join the Spanish government in its fight against fascism. What became known as the Abraham Lincoln Brigade was born to thunderous applause and a standing ovation.

One Saturday afternoon a week or so after the rally, I and my YCL friends—Leo, George, Henry, and Robin—were sitting around at Hymie's debating whether to volunteer for the Lincoln Brigade and looking for some weekend entertainment. On the spur of the moment we decided to drive up to Camp Unity at Sylvan Lake, New York, one of the Party's camp resorts. We didn't have reservations, but if the camp was full we figured we could find a cabin or tent to share, preferably with some nice girl comrade. If worse came to worse, we could always sleep in the car.

For a while during the drive to Camp Unity, we avoided the question of "Who's going to Spain?" Instead we sang "Die Heimat ist weit," the song of the Ernst Thälman Brigade of antifascist Germans fighting in Spain.

Die Heimat ist weit. Doch wir sind bereits
Wir kämpfen und siegen für dich, Freiheit!
Spanish heavens spread their brilliant starlight
High above our trenches in the plain.
From the distance morning comes to greet us.
Calling us to battle once again,
We'll not yield a foot to Franco's fascists.
Even tho' the bullets fall like sleet,
With us stand those peerless men, our comrades,
And for us there can be no defeat!

After a thoughtful silence, George said he would go, because sooner or later we would all have to fight Hitler and we might as well stop him now. Harry, though, was convinced that with Hitler and Mussolini enthusiastically supporting the fascists, the republic couldn't hold out unless the democratic countries came to its aid.

The whole subject was giving me a tough time. When asked what I would do, I explained that in our family all militarism was considered evil. My Papa said he would not be found dead in a military uniform, which he believed was a mental straitjacket. Anyone who puts on a uniform stops thinking, he said, which is exactly what the militarists want.

One of Papa's favorite pacifist quotes was from Clausewitz: "When my army begins to think, the war is over." For Papa, that meant that no thinking person would ever go into the military. To make certain we got the message, Papa took all the kids to see the film of *All Quiet on the Western Front* often enough to be sure that the message "War is hell" was deeply imbedded in our psyches. I simply couldn't see myself, I exclaimed, wearing a uniform and obeying orders. Embarrassed by my pacifist outburst, I added hastily that in class warfare, of course, violence could not always be avoided. I further hid my reluctance to join the Lincoln Brigade behind the argument that factional fighting among the republic's supporters made it difficult to see how they could defeat the united might of Hitler and Mussolini.

When George asked me how I thought there could be a revolution without a military strategy, I replied that gaining power through the general strike made far more sense than getting a lot of innocent people killed. Shut down the whole system and make workers' control a condition for returning to work. A military strategy held no allure for me. In spite of our disagreements about the Party, Papa's influence was strong.

Part of me felt very much like a coward, yet I heard an inner voice— what the old lady at the street corner meeting called my guardian angel— saying it was okay. I could be an antifascist and not go to Spain. I'd never make much of a soldier anyway; marching and drilling were so unnatural to me I was sure I couldn't be one even if I wanted to.

For a communist, this was another paradox. Every November we saw pictures of the huge military spectacle in Red Square celebrating the anniversary of the revolution. The whole military business, including the songs we sang in praise of the Red Army, always made me uncomfortable. How could a true socialist society celebrate military might? Whenever I raised this point, comrades were eager to explain that the Soviet Union was surrounded by hostile capitalist forces and that the military was its only hope of survival. But then, I always retorted, doesn't maintaining its military might rather than building a socialist society become the country's raison d'être? The question was never answered.

Leo, who had grown up in the Hebrew Orphan Asylum where he had organized a YCL unit, was going to enlist, because he thought as revolutionists we needed to understand military action. He was convinced that in the end we would have to fight. Moreover, if the fascists weren't stopped, he, as a Jew, would be one of their early victims. All this made sense, but didn't help me resolve my dilemma.

When we got to the camp gate, Leo told the guard we were part of the evening's entertainment, and he waved us in. It was dinner time, and the cavernous dining hall was packed with weekend vacationers. We agreed to separate to search out people we knew who might let us bunk with them or sleep on the floor.

As twilight began to fall I met up with May, my first YCL contact, on the lakefront. As we talked of politics and the events in Spain, the soft summer evening turned my thoughts to one thing. She must have guessed what I was thinking about, for before I had made a move she started to lecture me about the clean-glass theory of sex dreamed up by Lenin's wife, Krupskaya. Comrades like me, May chided, were responsible for the public's impression that the YCL was full of people who believed in free love. I asked defensively if she was subscribing to all the bourgeois nonsense about the evils of sex that was based on a lot of religious humbug. That's when she explained Krupskaya's parable of the dirty glass. When questioned about sexual freedom, she had responded, "If I am given a glass of water to drink, I want it to be out of a clean glass, not one that anyone might have drunk out of."

It was tough to argue with Lenin's wife, but I gave it a try: "May, I don't know what sex has to do with a water glass." I'd heard the clean-glass theory before, from a number of YCL prudes. Henry, who knew some Greek mythology, said it was like the oracle at Delphi, which answered questions from underneath a waterfall. Listeners could interpret the answer any way they wanted to. I told May I thought Lenin's wife meant you should take a bath before having sex. She didn't think that was funny and told me to forget any ideas I might have about fooling around with her. I did.

As we approached the great lawn in front of the dining hall, we could hear the strains of music. What looked like thousands of people were spread out on the lawn under a starry sky. The entertainment started, as almost all party occasions did, with a folk singer leading the crowd in song. On the lawn that night we sang "The Peat Bog Soldiers," the old union tune "Hold the Fort," a depression ditty "Zoup" ("Soup, they gave us a lousy bowl of soup"), and lots more. Like evangelists before us, we sang our message at any and every opportunity. Only the black churches sing as much as we did in the heyday of the Party. You can always tell when a movement is losing its steam. It's when the singing stops.

Next came the Group Theater actors led by Will Geer performing a hilarious living-newspaper script called "Don't Shoot Your Mother on Mother's Day, It's Not a Propitious Time." These skits poking fun at the day's news were regular events at mass meetings, rallies, parties, and cultural affairs. Then the Ukrainian Workers Chorus, decked out in native costume, sang and danced, followed by thirty or forty members of the Russian Workers Mandolin Club, who plucked their strings in perfect synchrony. Finally, dancers from the Anna Sokolow Troop presented a modern dance with political significance. In the 1930s artists and entertainers directed enormous creative energies toward making the world a better place.

As people walked toward their cabins and tents singing, the haunting lines of the Irish Easter rebellion song, "Kevin Barry," floated through the woods: "Shoot me like an Irish soldier; do not hang me like a dog." Suddenly in the dark a familiar voice called out, "Hi, Bob." I knew who it was. I wanted to run away but forced myself to exchange greetings with her. It was Barbara.

"Gee, I'm glad to see you. How did you like the show? Conway and I worked on the production."

All the old emotions came rushing back. What could I say? I told her I was in a hurry to meet some friends and hurried to the car. No one else was there. Huddled up in the back seat, I covered myself with a blanket and cried myself to sleep over this damn woman I could not stop loving.

On the drive home the next day, we continued our discussion of the Civil War in Spain. Aside from my unhappy encounter with Barbara, it had been a wonderful weekend of swimming in the crystal-clear lake, playing volleyball, and arguing about politics, art, and literature. In that setting, it seemed ludicrous to talk about going to war. Leo, our poet, raised the same point. "Why, with all the potential for joy we glimpsed this weekend, would we want to go fight in Spain?" He answered his own question: "If we don't, a darkness will descend on us, and we will never laugh again." I knew he was saying that "it could happen here." But, like so many things we said in our propaganda efforts, I don't think I ever really believed it.

Still, after 1936 the Civil War in Spain focused our energies on developing a broad popular front to stop fascism there before it engulfed all of Europe. The Party undertook a major relief effort, holding fundraising affairs throughout the city. Broadway and Hollywood celebrities gave generously of their time. The results were huge shipments of medical supplies, ambulances, and the organization of an American medical corps.

Send-off parties for comrades leaving for Spain became the model for later similar "celebrations"—if you could call them that—after December 1941. I was on the way out the door after one of these parties, feeling the cheering effects of cheap wine, when comrade Dave stopped me. He absolutely had to talk with me. I tried brushing him off with a joke, but he was very serious. "It's not funny, Schrank. We have to talk."

Dave was a devoted, very earnest comrade of remarkable innocence. He seemed to see most issues in terms of life or death. That wasn't my outlook. A good fight was one thing; putting your life on the line and getting killed was something else again.

Standing there in the street, he told me he had decided to join the Lincoln Brigade and go to Spain. The problem was his mother, who was grief-stricken and threatening to kill herself if he went through with it. He was asking me what he should do. I couldn't think of anything to say. For a long moment nothing but the incessant clang of the trolley bells broke the silence. Finally, embarrassed, I told him, "Look, Dave, how can I tell you what to do when I don't know what the hell to do myself?"

He was puzzled. "But you make all those great speeches about the threat of fascism and how we've got to defeat it now or it will get us later for sure. I believe that too. Shouldn't I?"

"Well, yes, of course. I believe it too," I said. "But making speeches is one thing. Going off to war is something very different. It's a very personal decision. I sure haven't made that decision for myself. How could I possibly make it for you?"

For weeks Dave continued to press me for an answer, and I kept waffling. Ultimately he decided to go. He told me he'd finally realized that nobody was going to tell him what to do. In his gut he knew he had to go, even though he was scared to death. He paused, looking at me and sensing my ambivalence and—yes—my guilt. He reassured me that it was important for me to "stay right here and keep rallying the people against fascism while I do my part fighting in Spain."

We held the usual going-away party for Dave and sent him off with presents and a hearty rendition of "Die Heimat ist weit." A few weeks later I got a letter from Dave. He wanted me to show his letter to all the comrades who were his friends and asked us to send him cigarettes and chocolate to share with other soldiers. Here is the enclosed letter.

Early in June

SPAIN

Rumbling trucks speeding through the night; starry skies and parching suns; women garbed in black; clenched fists and moist eyes; majestic mountains and snow white caps; dusty roads and marching feet; laughing boys and snatches of fleeting songs; the stamping of feet and the clatter of mess kits; tired bodies and willing minds; cocky hats and deep-tanned faces; beans and beans and chunks of bread; wine; hidden spots of cultivated lands and half dried up little streams; the "campesinos," those heroic Catalonian peasant soldiers speeding through the night in huge trucks—gaily singing their songs of attack and victory; little bare-foot children in old torn clothes; *Salud, salud*, and !*Viva la España democrática*!; flashing white teeth and upraised fists; cherry trees filled with ripe cherries and sticky fingers; lines for rations and a mouths full of bread; search for a cigarette and washing of clothes; rickety villages and hard parched soil; stone houses and tiny, unpaved, mysterious streets; holes in sides of rocky mountains and small burros pulling large-wheeled carts; broken bridges and shell-torn streets; tears and laughter; song and mourning; bugles and more duty; camouflaged trucks; broken wheels and bandaged legs; limping boys and eager hands; beautiful vistas and smoking ruins; beans and bread and wine; dusty guns and determined hearts; shaved heads and bearded boys; fiery spirits and more clenched fists; solidarity—anti-fascists—peasants—workers—communists—popular front——SPAIN—WAR-TORN SPAIN.

Yes Comrades—I have been in Spain now for the past ten days, ten days of rapid motion [amidst] slow moving surroundings. I am now a soldier in the 15th Brigade of the 35th division of the United Spanish Peoples Army. I and hundreds of other foreign comrades are part of the International Brigade and now are learning the rudiments of war in a section of the country that looks as restful as the Bronx Park. We have a wonderful collection of German, Austrian, English, Scandinavian, Polish, Latvian, Argentinean, Mexican, French, Italian, and one

Negro—all gathered here from every section of the world to wipe fascism off the Spanish soil. There is so much to say of the life of a Spanish soldier. It is a hard and callous life but at the same time a pleasant and desirous life. Here I have learned the true meaning of INTERNATIONAL SOLIDARITY, of *Red Front*, of comradeship, of hardships easily and willingly accepted, of the clenched fist, a salute here loved by all from cradle to grave. Of course we have little variety in foods, mostly beans and bread, occasional meats and salted fish, but we have sufficient and it is wholesome. Of course we don't have feather beds or bacon and eggs—yet the comrades take it wonderfully and in good spirit. We have some really true and good comrades, comrades to the nth degree. Even Schrank would think me justified in saying so. Outstanding indeed are the German and Polish comrades, those who went through the most horrible and toughest experiences life can possibly offer. How useful they could be in the States so as to familiarize our comrades as to how difficult Communist work really can be. How generous and willing they are. How frightful the scars upon their backs look. We have some comrades who were soldiers in the American army and you ought to hear them rave about our new army. How great and powerful proletarian discipline can be you cannot imagine unless you experience it. Our lives are well regulated according to a spirit of freedom and initiative. We have a daily political hour, practice in the field, practice on the blackboard. All unnecessary discipline and compulsory hardships are gone. You walk, talk, and live as a human being and that makes you a damn good soldier. I cannot say too much about our lives and army for these letters do pass through fascist hands and might contain some valuable information. Also, I have only a pencil to write with and little time—so wait until we meet, and I will be willing to tell you tales right through the night.

What you are mostly interested in is the political angle and Spain in general. Well! Political training is very important here. We have political commissars, cultural leaders, bulletins (voluntary), we are encouraged to read and study and live as comrades should. We are trained to live not as individuals but [as] part of a movement. We are here not only as soldiers of war but soldiers of explanation, sacrifice, understanding, proletarian discipline, unselfishness, pep, and comradeship.

Of course we have a few rotten apples, but they are few and lost. Most of us are tried communists and trade unionists—from New York, Tennessee, San Francisco, and Chicago—and we live up to the revolutionary traditions we represent.

Spain is united, determined, strong, and unbeatable. (Right now the comrades rest and are singing that famous Irish Revolutionary song—an Englishman leading.) Spaniards are great people. Hard working and kind. Their land is dry, and parched, and stony. Not one inch of fertile land is wasted and you see Spaniards working away into twilight wrestling out of stony nature—green bliss! It is indeed wonderful to see the little plots of land found in between rocks, amongst the hills, far apart but sparingly cared for. Water is scarce and irrigation waters the land. Just like their fight against Fascism, their struggle with nature is hard and determined. The peasant bends all day over his land, works diligently, and is never defeated. His determination is carried into the battles of war and there he is never defeated. Here I fully understand what unity means for Spain. The fascists have, because of their large number of trained men and war materials, made advances. Yet they were costly and small by comparison. Then the nation was still divided. Now with fascist superior aeroplanes and guns . . . practically at a standstill— held back by poorly armed and little trained Spaniards—Spaniards who are united. Training is becoming more complete. Things are fairly well centralized, traitors are weeded out and people want to fight to a finish.

(I am writing this letter at intervals, thus it might lack cohesion and clarity and maturity. We have little time to spare.)

As for myself—I am doing well. I rapidly adapted myself to conditions. I am the interpreter here when German is spoken. German and Spanish is mostly spoken here, and my knowledge of both comes in handy and [is] useful to the Brigade. (Some teachers are German.) I also was made a temporary corporal—thus am I representing the Bronx YCL in Spain!!!!

There is *great shortage* of cigarettes here and lack of smokes causes many trying moments. Comrades, I would like to see this letter be a stimulus for a bigger drive to aid Spain materially—in our country anyway.

. . .

Just returned from the political period, where André's speech to foreign Communists in Spain was discussed. Sacrifice and comradeship were stressed. The need for hard training and study also was pointed out.

Just came back from a three-hour climb. Boy—you can get a swell tan here!!!

Well! I feel that I have written enough. Thus I'll say so long comrades back in New York and carry on your work so that the American people will not have to go through the hardships that the Spanish people are.

Salud Comrades. Dave Lipton

As the war intensified, young men continued to leave for Spain, and we began to receive regular reports on the fighting. At YCL headquarters I heard that Dave was killed after a few weeks in action. According to the report, they sent these kids into battle with so little or no training. Among party members, crying was considered a sign of revolutionary weakness, sentimentality, and lack of communist discipline. I have no idea how long I sat in the toilet and cried for Dave—at least long enough for people to start banging on the door.

Some time later at a street corner meeting at Tremont and Prospect I was giving my call for continued support for the fight against fascism. I pointed out that our own government, by failing to help a democratic government defend itself, was aiding the fascists. I was interrupted by a woman making her way through the crowd, waving her arms in the air and screaming, "He killed my son, he killed my son, murderer, murderer, he killed him." She repeated the accusation, over and over. Stunned, I just kept talking. Several YCL members were trying, with little success, to move her out of the crowd. I was thrown into confusion, and when someone finally told me to finish up I was glad to climb down from the platform.

The comrades had managed to form a circle around the woman and move her to the outer edge of the crowd, which had grown considerably as a result of her screaming. The police arrived, and we assured them we could handle the situation. The last thing we needed was for the police to arrest some grief-stricken Jewish mama. Esther told me quietly that the woman was Dave's mother. "She's been grief stricken since she heard about his death. She yells at all the comrades, accusing them of killing her son. It isn't just you." She was trying to be reassuring, but I wasn't at all sure I believed her.

For a long time after that I avoided speaking in the Tremont area for fear of hearing Dave's mother screaming her accusations. Though my friends in the Deli were saying I shouldn't feel responsible for Dave's death, in some strange way I did. Her face screaming "You killed my son" became another nightmare image of death that showed up periodically in my dreams of the darkest night of my childhood. In the dream I go down the cellar steps and see an arm sticking out of the basement floor. Frightened, I grab a shovel and desperately try to dig a hole to bury it, but it's hopeless. The arm keeps coming back.

George and Leo, like Dave, were among the earliest volunteers from our crowd to cross the Pyrenees to become part of the Lincoln Brigade. Leo was killed not long after. Each death of a dear friend made me feel cowardly and ashamed As the months went by and the fascists gained more ground, I couldn't help wondering whether my friends' deaths were in vain. I never found a satisfactory answer.

When the republic's situation grew more desperate, so did our relief efforts, meetings, and demonstrations. Then came those fateful days of 1938 as the fascist victory unfolded. In all the antifascist meeting places in New York, we kept a silent vigil, hoping—some even praying—for a way out for "our boys," for France had closed its border with Spain. In one of the final battles fought by the international volunteers, remnants of the Lincoln Brigade were forced to retreat to the Ebro River, the only escape route. Good swimmers like George Watt made it across, but others did not.* When it was all over, 1,600 members of the Lincoln Brigade were dead and virtually all those who had survived had been wounded at least once.

We now, sadly, had our own honest-to-goodness war heroes. In every May Day parade and left-sponsored demonstration or meetings, veterans from the Lincoln Brigade stepped out in their uniforms with their flags and banners flying. Cheering our veterans, we too could express patriotic pride in our cause.

Now, inevitably, there ensued a long debate about Spain. Whenever the Party suffered a defeat, in endless discussions, arguments, position papers, and meetings, members would attempt to dissect what had gone wrong. Because we operated on the assumption that Marxism was a science, we thought that a proper scientific analysis would always uncover the mistakes. Mostly we ended up blaming others for not doing what we thought they should have done.

Long before the final defeat of Spain's republican forces, it was evident that Europe was disintegrating. The Nazis reoccupied the Rhineland, annexed Austria, and, with the concurrence of the appeasing democracies, rolled into Czechoslovakia in 1938. A shaky United Front government in France was struggling to hold itself together and maintain democracy against its own right wing. There was a growing realization that the fascists were poised to take over all of Europe, while in the United States isolationists were determined to keep us out of the world war that was now certain to come.

Adding to our fears and our growing sense of doom came shocking news from Moscow. As I passed Hymie's one day on my way to YCL headquarters, I heard someone yelling, "If you want to believe that Bukharin was a traitor to socialism, you can. But I never will. You hear me? Never." There were Henry, May, Harry, Esther, and Joey sitting around a table looking as though they had lost a beloved friend.

"What happened?" I asked.

---

*George Watt became a captain and a commissar—a sort of combined information and morale officer—in Spain. In World War II, as a bombardier, he was shot down over Belgium and rescued by the underground to fight again.

"Haven't you heard of the arrest of the old Bolshevik, Bukharin?"

Nikolai Bukharin was not, of course, the first. Since 1936, Stalin had systematically purged thousands of old Bolsheviks. The Moscow trials of increasingly important Bolshevik leaders of the November Revolution had presented the ludicrous spectacle of many of Lenin's closest cohorts confessing to treason. Now Bukharin, the editor of *Izvestia,* whose *ABCs of Communism* was considered a classic of Marxist literature, stood accused of being a traitor and an agent of imperialism. His trial was certainly one of the strangest in history. The same man who had withstood all kinds of persecution and threats as a revolutionist stood in a Moscow courtroom mumbling the words of his forced confession.

As I read the reports of the trials I could hear Papa's agonized voice whispering in my ear, "What did you expect? Are you satisfied now?" This news was hard to swallow. I was sure it couldn't be true. Like many others on the Left, I had a real fear that darkness was closing in and the world we knew was coming to an end.

I remember John Little, the quiet and gentle New York State YCL chairman, trying to convince a group of YCL leaders that their serious misgivings about the Moscow trials were unfounded. Very patiently he explained that we needed to understand that capitalism would never rest until socialism in the Soviet Union was destroyed. Its very existence was a threat to the capitalist world; every industrial step forward in Russia meant that socialism was growing more secure. He quoted statistics on the achievements of the latest Five Year Plan and—as party officials always did—pointed to the success of industrialization as evidence of socialism's strength. These successes, John argued, were responsible for the increase in imperialistic plotting against the Soviet Union. That, he claimed, was the great revelation of the Moscow trials.

Many of us still had reservations as we left the meeting. Henry said that although he wasn't sure about what was going on in Moscow, it shouldn't keep us from carrying on the struggle to create a better world here in the United States. His declaration expressed the feelings of many of us who were deeply involved in building unions and neighhborhood organizations, marching for the unemployed, and being part of a close-knit community of like-minded people.

One night I came home late from a street corner meeting where I had tried to talk about the dangers of fascism while being heckled about the

Moscow trials. There was a letter waiting for me. It was from Papa. It had been years since we had spoken. Though I was happy to hear from him at last, I was very troubled by what he had to say.

Dear Son,

Bruno heard you speaking at a street meeting in Brooklyn. He said I would be proud of your speaking skills but not happy about what you had to say. He said you made eloquent pleas to stop the march of fascism across Europe. You were not put off course by a Nazi heckler. Then Bruno says someone hollered, "What about the Moscow trials?" Bruno says you then went into a long explanation of why these old Bolsheviks must have been guilty. Bruno said he was really sorry that you had swallowed that Moscow baloney. He wanted to know how you could be so willing to accept the Moscow party line with an independent thinking father like me. In trying to find an answer for Bruno I have thought the following.

Most of your life has been lived in one of the worst economic crises in the history of capitalism. The worldwide nature of this economic crisis has made it unique. In the past, capitalist crises as described by Marx usually occurred in one country. That meant that other countries might help stimulate the economy through trade or colonial expansion. Colonial expansion was the easiest way to get new sources of cheap new raw materials. After World War I the colonial world was pretty well divided up so there was no longer any cheap sources of raw materials. American capitalism used to feel immune from all these troubles because it had its own frontier. It could carry on an expansion within its own borders. Since the '29 crash that doesn't seem to work anymore. The depression here has just become endemic. It does not want to go away. You're wondering what's this got to do with you?

Throughout your entire childhood you were taught the evils of the capitalist system. How it exploits workers and deprives them of life's elementary essentials. How it legitimizes greed by extolling the virtues of the rich and their worship of money. This was the message of your childhood. Whatever was wrong in society, we were able to show how capitalism was responsible for all its evils. I believe you learned these lessons well and for that I am proud of you.

Do you remember how proud we were of our Wobbly comrades? The Wobbly model of the new world of the brotherhood of man was to never have a government bureaucracy. In the IWW you could only serve one term as a full time official and then it was back to the shop or mine. Why did they insist on that rule? Because of what has happened in Russia and every bureaucracy since the beginning of recorded history. People get into positions of power and they never, yes I said never, want to give it up. That's what Karl Marx did not understand. Only the anarcho-syndicalists knew that unless you find a way to keep power from accumulating it will eventually corrupt. That's what has happened in Russia, and that society has absolutely nothing to do with the noble ideal of a socialism.

Now I come to the continuation of the Moscow trials of old Bolsheviks. In 1936 it was Zinoviev and Kamenev, in '37 Radek and Pyatakov, and the latest, the most bizarre of them all, Bukharin and Rykos. Let me say that my concern is not so much for these men, who supported that atrocious idea of the Dictatorship of the

Proletariat that has turned out to be simply the terror of Joseph Stalin—Ivan The Terrible. What I cannot understand is how you can stand up on a soap box in Brooklyn and say that Bukharin was guilty of plotting against socialism. How dare you little snot-nosed kid dirty the name of that old Bolshevik? Whatever he did wrong he does not deserve to be shot. Each bullet that killed one of those old revolutionaries put another nail in the coffin of socialism.

When you were a child growing up, do you remember how we sang the praises of freedom? That's what our socialism was about—freedom. We read Goethe, Schiller, Heine, and Walt Whitman as part of our love of freedom. We detested capitalist curbs on freedom to speak, think and act on what we believed. Do you remember these things? If you do, how can you stand up on a street corner and try to justify that evil terror being perpetrated in Russia called the Dictatorship of the Proletariat? When the history of this century is written, the evil of Stalin and Hitler will stand together as equally guilty.

I write this in the fervent hope you will see that what has emerged in Russia is simply a new ruling class in place of the old. Our greatest tragedy is that it grew out of a revolutionary effort of the people for socialism. The revolution has been betrayed by Stalin and his henchmen in the communist party. Why can't you see that? Or are you too caught up in what you are doing to understand where you are going? It does hurt me to see you using your talents for an evil cause. I know you may never forgive me for what happened to your mother, but please try to at least hear what I am trying to say to you.

Father

I read Papa's letter many times. I did not want to believe that what he was saying might be even partly true. My hatred of the capitalist system of exploitation and love of the ideal of socialism made me unable to see that the terror of Stalinism had destroyed the ideal. Besides, the YCL and the Party were my extended family, my support system. Having read so little myself, I was humbled by the Marxist intellectuals and party officials. It was very flattering that these same intellectuals had recognized my leadership qualities. Somehow my whole life, everything I believed, had become intertwined with the huge web of the movement. The thought of leaving the YCL or the Party felt like contemplating suicide. I couldn't do it.

My inability to desert the Party was reinforced by something else. Something that Papa himself had taught me: the conviction that deserters are by definition stool pigeons, informers. When I was a child, Papa had defined absolute evil, not as Satan or the devil, but as the informer. Why was Papa so preoccupied with the informer as the devil? I do not know. I do know that the only time I saw the nasty side of his character was when he spoke of stool pigeons. Once, in referring to an informer in the Mooney and Billings case, he claimed, "I could shoot him in the face, sit on his stomach, and eat my liverwurst sandwich and feel absolutely no remorse." After *All Quiet on the Western Front,* Papa's favorite movie—which he took me to see many times—was *The Informer.* Papa wanted to make sure I understood how to avoid the temptations that led to the quicksands of informing. As a result, any situation—real or imagined—that even hinted at informing scared the shit out of me. Besides, I felt certain that what we were doing here in the Bronx was the right thing, so why should I be concerned about Moscow?

I would not hear from Papa again for a long time.

As the world outside our movement grew increasingly hostile, we huddled more closely together. Crowds at street corner meetings were becoming less friendly. In some places our supporters were so few we had to give up holding meetings altogether.

Then, in August of 1939, came a political thunderclap—the Nazi-Soviet Nonaggression Pact. It felt like the end of our cause. Maybe it was. How could we explain this treaty between a socialist country and the most hated fascist regime?

As the headlines were screaming out the news of the pact to divide up Europe, I made my way in a state of total confusion to YCL headquarters. Everyone was there, looking for explanations. Seymour told us that the Politburo of the Central Committee was in session at that very moment to consider the Party's position. He was sure they would come up with a clear explanation of why the Soviets had signed the pact.*

On our way to a meeting at Webster Hall that evening we were besieged by a group of Trotskyites waving copies of their paper, *The Militant.* Its headline read "Socialism Betrayed—Stalin Signs Pact with Hitler." An argument with the Trotskyites invariably ended in a screaming match. Even to me, my arguments sounded limp, and I was glad when someone pulled me away: "C'mon Schrank. It's a waste of time. Nobody is going to convince anyone else of anything."

---

*The Politburo was another party organization on the Russian model. In American parlance, it would be the executive committee of a board of directors. The insistence of officials of the Communist party of the United States on copying Russian party structures might have pleased the Soviets but it did nothing to integrate the CP into the American cultural scene.

In the packed, hushed hall, hundreds of party members leaned forward in their seats as Earl Browder, the general secretary of the party and our very own midwestern college professor, quietly began to explain. Ever since the rise of Hitler in Germany, he said, the central objective of the imperialist powers had been, directly and indirectly, to support and build German fascism in order to prepare for an assault on the Soviet Union. It was no accident that the West had stood back as Hitler marched across Europe. The Munich agreement, Hitler's invasion of Czechoslovakia, the failure of the West to act—all convinced Stalin that Russia should not, as he put it, "pull their [the capitalists'] chestnuts out of the fire." Browder explained that at times socialism had to take many steps backwards in order to move forward. This was such a time. Stalin's agreement with Germany would defeat the capitalists' scheme of letting these two powers destroy each other while Britain, France, and the United States looked on, licking their chops in anticipation of the spoils.

The hall broke out in wild applause. Of course! That was it! It was a brilliant maneuver!

But did we believe it? At the cafeteria after the meeting, we were not so sure. Henry pointed out that intellectuals like Browder could explain anything. It was a Faustian gamble. Could we sign a pact with the devil and not be destroyed by him? Hitler was now ready to move east against Poland, and Churchill was saying that World War II was about to begin.

To those of us in the American Communist party, Moscow was something like the Vatican to Catholics. It was a far-off place that periodically issued directives—papal bulls or the party line—about subjects followers in distant lands may have known or cared little about. With the exception of high party officials, most of us in the movement had never been outside the United States. To me, Europe was a place Papa had characterized as cursed by an incurable and deadly nationalism. Looking back, I think the outlook I learned from him didn't give me much hope for Europe, and even less for Russia. I suppose I was a provincial American. I was humbled by the intellectuals in the party leadership. I simply assumed that they knew things I couldn't possibly understand and continued to think of myself as dumb worker. Whatever doubts I had about the wisdom of the Nazi-Soviet Pact, I continued to believe in what we were doing in the United States.

10

Apprenticeship

Late in 1938 a new person moved into our YCL commune on Daly Avenue. Edith was a model as well as a dancer in a WPA theater project. She became the next and, in some ways, the most important, woman in my life. Our relationship, though, did not begin with a glance across a crowded room that strikes lightning to the heart. I remember us as more like two troubled and lonely children huddling together for comfort. At the time I was exclusively preoccupied with my own importance in the revolutionary vanguard. Edith was a person to share a bed with and not a hell of a lot more.

Even after we got our own apartment together in 1939, I periodically found it necessary to explain to her that the revolution was my first love and to reaffirm the Marxist notion that marriage was an invention of capitalism to provide a steady supply of workers for the factories. Capitalism, we believed with Friedrich Engels, denied women their freedom by making them the property of men. Whenever either of us felt unhappy in the relationship, I reminded Edith, we were free to leave.

Politics aside, neither of us had much of an idea of what marriage was about. For me, being in love was full of dangers. What with Mutter dying and Barbara running off, love felt like a treacherous minefield. Any notion of permanence put me in a state of high anxiety; intimacy and commitment were all too clearly related to the handmaiden of death and abandonment. Edith was equally disinclined to expect happiness in a relationship. Deserted by her father as a young child and raised in a tiny one-bedroom apartment by her Russian immigrant mother and grandmother, she had grown up poor and terribly insecure. As a result, there was very little in life she trusted—including me.

I don't ever remember either of us using the word *love* in those years. In my childhood, I had heard the word exclusively in the context of poetry, drama, myth, literature, or opera. It was a mystical word; at the very least, it was dangerous. I am sure my own inability to express love contributed to our marital difficulties. Yet Edith was a very beautiful young woman, and in those early years, while we may not have succeeded in creating a secure little family, we did have a lot of fun in bed.

In the fall of 1939 I met a man who worked in a powerhouse substation, and he managed to get me a job. I started as an oiler, but before long I was promoted to the machine shop. I was apprenticed to "Minnesota," a kindly old Finnish machinist from Duluth who was an alcoholic. He taught me an awful lot, and in return I covered for him when he was soused.

About thirty or forty men from a wide variety of crafts worked at the powerhouse, which primarily generated electricity for Montefiore Hospital. They were a mix of Germans, Italians, Poles, Jews, and nonimmigrant Americans. Because it was good steady work, most of the men had been employed there for quite a while and seemed to get along pretty well. With the war in Europe heating up, however, that was about to change.

While the German Panzers rolled across the Low Countries, events in the powerhouse reminded me of what had happened at the Sunday School camp. After news of the Blitzkrieg came over the shop radio, a couple of our local Germans, Becker and Weber, began to strut around, crowing like roosters over the victories of the Fatherland, puffing themselves up—particularly to a couple of Jews who worked there.

It happened again at lunch time one day, while fifteen or twenty men were sitting around the workbenches in the machine shop. A quiet, six-foot Polish watch engineer named Joe Mikoski usually suffered the Germans in silence. On this occasion, though, he told Becker firmly, "I'm tired of your pickin' on the little Jew electrician and braggin' about what the Führer is gonna do to them. So cut it out." Card games stopped. Radios were snapped off. All attention was on Mikoski. Someone had finally challenged the loud-mouthed Nazis, but we all knew there were quiet ones in the shop too.

Becker made the mistake of losing his cool. "We wipe out all the ver-
min scum like you. If you Polacks are so great, where were you when the
Germans went through your country like shit through a pipe? Answer
that, big shot."

Everyone now took sides, and to my surprise most seemed to side with
Becker. The two Jews were looking scared. Harry, the electrician, spoke
directly to Mikoski: "Look, I don't care what he says. He's not very
smart anyhow. He's a boiler cleaner. What kind of brains does that take?
Why not leave him alone?"

Becker went into a towering rage. "You see? The little Jew bastard
thinks he smarter than everyone. Well, we see what Hitler do to them."
Then, looking at Mikoski, he spat, "What he do to the Polacks" and
turned to leave. He had not taken two steps when Mikoski was on top
of him.

Men gathered quickly to where the big Pole had Becker pressed up
against the wall. With his hands around the German's neck, he was
slowly lifting him off the floor. There was an uneasy silence broken only
by the sound of Becker's foot hitting the wall and the hum of the gener-
ator. Becker tried to yell, but Mikoski's grip got tighter and Becker
couldn't make a sound. He seemed to hang there forever. He was no
longer kicking. His face was turning blue, and his eyes looked ready to
pop out of his head. Finally, Mikoski dropped him to the floor, looked
down, and said, "If you ever talk your Nazi shit around here again, I feed
you like a piece of wood into the steam boiler and nobody, even your
wife, ever know what happen to you." He then turned to the group of
startled men as if addressing them: "Let this be a lesson to anyone who
wants to practice Nazi shit here. Now we go back to work."

As we drifted off back to our machines, it became clear that the men
were somewhat evenly split between the Pole and the Nazi. I think some
of them sided with Becker for the same scary reasons I had heard at the
Sunday School camp years earlier. Hitler had become a hero to many because he had put people to work and ended the terrible misery of the depression years. An impression was growing that the Germans were
superior at solving economic problems. It was not that unusual to hear
workers say things like, "Maybe that's what we need in this country to
get us out of the depression."

I became politically interested in Mikoski. Who was he? Was he a potential recruit? Because he was on rotating shifts, I only met up with him once every few weeks. One lunch hour he told me he had been a sailor on several Polish and Greek ships, which he described as "tramp rust buckets not fit even for cattle, with slops that pigs wouldn't eat." One day, he said, "I get so fed up with this whole shit, I jump ship in South Seas."

Wow! Big, quiet Joe Mikoski was hiding a great story! I was hungry for details, and in between tasks I pumped him for more. "What island? How did you live there? How long did you stay?"

He seemed surprised that I wanted to know all this. Out of the blue, he said, "You a Red, and you want I should join."

I acted surprised, "I don't know what do you mean?"

"Oh, yes you do. On ships I meet many you kind. Don't worry. I think that okay. I know all about Lenin, I read him on ship. He good man, but it never happen. In Bora Bora, I live in socialist paradise right on beach. Go sleep in hammock under tree. No need for blanket, never. In morning wake up, take swim in nice ocean, make little fire on beach, cook oatmeal, have coffee. Later go with men to fish. We come back, clean, cook fish, find beautiful girl she eat with us. Then go walk up beach. Under nice tree, we fuck maybe all afternoon. Those people all happy in socialism. Everybody own everything, nothing is private property. Then we come and ruin it all with religious shit. Those people so beautiful, with no shame, till we come. You see, the world already have socialism long time ago. We never go back there."

I tried to explain that what he had experienced was called primitive socialism, but he didn't care about that. He was certain that it would never work in our civilization.

"Why did you leave?" I asked.

He rubbed his chin and looked at me: "You know, is very hard to give up life you used to. Now I think many times how I lie naked in hammock on beach. Sun shine down and you get good sunburn. At night have fish dinner, find a plenty pretty girl, we have wonderful time, maybe love. She and me never forget that, but still you gotta go home."

Now, he told me, he was living with a nice "dumb woman" in Connecticut who "has good pussy like nutcracker." Would he like to read the *Daily Worker,* I asked. No, he says, he knows all the arguments, and "they don't mean nothin'," because people are no good for socialism, and that's why it never works.

Still, I had made a friend of Mikoski, and we would periodically talk—not about politics, but about women. Mikoski's favorite saying was, "Politics, it's nothin', same shit. When you make love with woman, this make you happy, you born again. That's why we here. Never forget this."

Nothing—not politics nor the tides of war—interfered with the powerhouse gang's parties. Any excuse would do: anniversaries, retirements, Thanksgiving, Christmas, whatever. Drinking in the shop was supposedly forbidden, but Peter the Irishman and Frank the Dutchman had rigged up a unique bar system under one of the workbenches. At party time the barrel would arrive in a wooden box marked "American Standard Toilet Bowl." Peter would be in his glory as he maneuvered the box under the bench, flipped up its hinged top, poured in the ice, pulled the plug out of the bench top, and slid the tap through the hole into the barrel. Unable to resist, he would draw off a glass as Carl scolded, "It's only ten o'clock, for Christ sake. Don't start now. We all get fired. Use your head, stupid."

"Oh," he said. "I just want to make sure it's not flat."

Of course we all knew about Peter. His preferred beverage at coffee break was a can of beer. With a whole barrel camouflaged under a workbench, Frank said, "Peter is happy as a pig in shit just thinking about all that beer right there under the bench. It's his heaven on earth."

The parties usually started around three. The bologna, franks, chips, bread, potato salad, and pickles arrived in the afternoon, and by three o'clock we were all washed up and ready to celebrate. Peter uncovered the tap and kept the barrel pumped up to make sure that "we return this mother empty. And I mean *empty,* so let's get drinkin' here."

As quitting time was 4:30 P.M., we had an hour and a half for eating, drinking, and bullshitting. After the Mikoski–Becker fracas, we carefully avoided discussions of politics and war. That left baseball and sex. The former was easily dispensed with, as the fans of the Yankees, Dodgers, and Giants (then all New York teams) loudly expressed confidence in their favorite teams.

Sooner or later when the beer was flowing and the bologna and franks were being devoured, the talk of these blue-collar guys would drift to women.

Sharing the same shower and locker room, there was very little we did not know about each other's anatomy. I have to admit that the first time I saw Carl's I gasped. It was a good foot long and provoked no end of admiration. Carl delighted in our wonder: "You guys with those little pinkie dicks are jealous, that's all there is to it."

At one of the powerhouse parties, Little Tony had a bright idea: "After the party we should all go down to 116th Street and get laid. Whatta ya say fellers?"

There was some division of opinion among guys who were single, married, or didn't much care one way or the other. In the meantime, the beer kept flowing. By quitting time, two cars had been recruited for the 116th Street caper. One of them was mine. Trying to be one of the boys—after all, I was in the "working class," wasn't I?—I agreed: "O.K., I'll drive you, but no thanks to the whores. I don't wanna get the clap an' go blind and crazy."

"Hey, kid," taunted Carl, "if you never had the clap, you're no man." Laughter. I was embarrassed, and I had a real yen to do it in a whorehouse. But Papa's warnings of the terrible consequences of gonorrhea and of Beethoven going deaf from syphilis were enough to scare me away from brothels for life.

By quitting time, the barrel was empty, but Peter had found a couple of bottles of beer and was feeling no pain. We helped him into the Chrysler, and four others climbed in. At 116th Street I parked the car across the street from a certain brownstone and the whole gang—except Peter—went off to have what Tony called "a fuckin' good time, Schrank, while you pull your meat and he sleeps." Next to me on the front seat, Peter contentedly slept, snored, and stank, for he had pissed in his pants.

As I sat in my car across from the whorehouse, half asleep, I wondered how in hell we could ever think these working-class guys would be the saviors of the world. It was probably around this time that I began my quest for the working class Karl Marx wrote about and my intellectual friends talked of but didn't know a damn thing about. Fat chance these guys could create, or even participate in, a socialist society.

Dozing with my hat half pulled down over my face, I could vaguely see something that looked like flashing lights across the street. I woke up to see four police cruisers parked in front of my shopmates' favorite whorehouse. I couldn't believe it. While I was sitting there they were raiding the joint! Carl and two of the other guys came out of a house the police hadn't yet entered, motioning for me to drive down the block to pick them up. But where was little Tony? As I was starting the car I saw a fantastic figure on a fire escape across the street. Was it a mirage? No, it was someone waving frantically. Could it be? Sure as hell, it was Tony, all dressed in his hat, coat, and tie—with no pants! I was laughing like hell and trying to figure out what he wanted me to do. He kept pointing first to his lower body and then back to the whorehouse. Obviously that's where his pants were.

By that time the cops were swarming all over the street, and I could already see the headline, "Man arrested for aiding and abetting a whorehouse escape." Shit! What kind of a heroic end is that? Papa would be mortified. And what would the comrades say? Hell, I thought, I'll tell them I was cavorting with the working class. Finally Tony came streaking down the fire escape with his coat wrapped around his waist and leaped into the car. Pete was still fast asleep, and I couldn't stop laughing.

Deadly serious, Tony urged me to go to "Yvonne the nigger's room" and get his pants. His wallet and his license and everything were in it. He was afraid the cops would find it and come to his house and his mother would find out. "She's a good Catholic, Bob. She'll kill me. Please, Bob! Please!"

"Tony, no way in hell I'm goin' into that whorehouse to recover your pants. The guys are waitin' on the corner an' the cops are lookin' over here."

I drove down the block, picked up Carl and the others, and got out of there. They asked Tony what happened to him. Their laughter was uncontrollable when he replied, "Oh, you know, I always jerk off first, otherwise I come too fast and I don't get my money's worth."

They were laughing so hard I had to ask them about finding pants for Tony several times before they could answer me. Somebody suggested we could buy him a new pair, or find some bum about the same size and buy his pants. In the meantime, Tony was talking about "jumping off a bridge before I'll go home. My old lady will kill me. You guys don't know what a tough guinea mother can do. Holy Christ! If she tells my old man, forget it, I'm dead."

We finally decided to drop Tony at the shop and let him put on his work pants. The bigger problem was Peter. I wanted to fill him up with coffee and send him home on the subway, but Frank said he'd never make it: "He'll end up sleeping in the subway yard, and his poor Irish wife will go crazy wondering what happened to her darling Peter. You gotta take him home, Bob. It's just over the Brooklyn Bridge."

It was already after seven, and I had a meeting to go to. "C'mon, fellas, how about a couple of you guys taking him home?"

Carl said, "Bobby boy, you got the gift of gab. You can give his wife some bullshit. You're a nice kid. She'll believe you."

"Yeah Bob," they all chimed in. Flattered, Bobby boy said, "Okay. Who's got the address?"

An hour later I found the house in the middle of Brooklyn and pulled Peter out of the car. He was wobbly, and I had to use my shoulder to hold up all six feet of him while shakily negotiating the steps. Finally, relieved and feeling noble, I pressed the doorbell. When the door opened, a very large woman with a square face glanced at Peter slumped over my shoulder and then glared at me in anger. "So you're the drinkin' buddy he's always tellin' about," she burst out in a powerful Killarney accent. "Shame on you for what you've done to this good man." I could not believe my ears. Slowly it sank in. My whorehouse buddies had set me up. That's why they were giggling like a bunch of schoolgirls and yelling "and give our very best to the missus" as I drove off.

"All you bar bums with your boozin' is destroyin' this nice man." My good Samaritan spirit draining away, I withdrew my shoulder. Peter, still mumbling something about "anotha drink," sank to the floor. As I turned and bounded down the stairs, I shouted "He's all yours, mamma. Next time put a diaper on him so he don't piss up the next poor sucker's car seat."

Later that evening I entertained the Deli comrades with my latest working-class adventure. These City College YCL members loved to hear about the sex-craved working class. They responded to my doubts about such workers' ability to run a socialist society by lecturing me in a well-read tone of voice: what I was experiencing was the impact of bourgeois culture on the working class. But what, I wanted to know, would make them change come the revolution?

On Monday morning, I was the locker-room joke. Frank asked with a big grin, "So did you get 'im home okay?"

I was pissed. "To hell with you and the rest of you shitheads for getting me crapped all over for being a nice guy—besides ruinin' my evening." They couldn't stop laughing. "Okay, you guys, have your laugh. But the next time you want to get laid on 116th Street, you can walk or crawl there." Peter came in all happy and zippy, as though nothing had happened. Somebody whispered, "Watch out for alcoholics. They'll do it every time."

As the Nazis marched across Europe, many Jewish doctors were catching the last escape routes out. They were forced to leave behind every piece of medical equipment—from the tiniest scalpel to the most complex exercise machines for treating polio sufferers. The hospital we supplied power for had set up a special unit to help the doctors recreate equipment they had left behind. Our skills would have to meet some new challenges, and for me working with the doctors was a new opportunity.

I was still serving my machinist apprenticeship under Minnesota, the soft-spoken Finn from Duluth, and I was feeling terribly conflicted. I was hungry to learn as much as possible from this kind old man. Machinist craftsmen were a dying breed, and Minnesota was one of the last. He was often very sad, watching his craft degenerate into what he called "replacing parts that any monkey could do. What you need machinist for? I make the part fit; it make machine work like new. That is craftsman, not monkey. I drink to forget."

Explaining the problems of the doctors to Minnesota, I asked him if it would be okay if I went to work in the special unit. My apprenticeship with Minnesota had evolved into a partnership: I was learning from a master, and whenever he was too drunk to run a machine I would cover for him. "I'll only be a few blocks away" I assured him. "If you need me when you don't feel so good, I can be back in a few minutes."

He looked at me, touched by my concern. As he put his arm on my shoulder, he turned his face away so I wouldn't see his tears. "Bobby," he said. "You mean when I drink bottle whiskey, can't stand no more, you come do the work. Thanks, that's good. But you go do what you gotta. Old pal here be okay, and I help you with the doctor stuff."

The technical support unit, as it was called, consisted of a medical technician, an electrician, and me. There must have been over a dozen refugee doctors. After many failed efforts to get them to produce simple drawings of what they wanted us to make, John, the chief engineer, made a suggestion. We could ask the doctors to just make a rough sketch on the blackboard or show us what they wanted on their own bodies. Then we would see if we could make a drawing or a mock-up of the equipment.

We made surgical instruments, respirators, pneumothorax machines for collapsing tubercular lungs, and a variety of external metal frames for people with bone diseases. Since most of my work was in the machine shop, I felt good that I was able to maintain contact with Minnesota by asking advice, even when I didn't need it. I am not certain how I came to hold craftsmen like Minnesota in such high regard. I suspect it was the influence of the Wobbly tradition that only people who produced something really matter.

One day I was busy cutting a gear in the machine shop when someone said one of the doctors was there to see me. Doctor Harpuda, an orthopedist with a hunchback condition he'd had since birth, was no taller than a ten-year-old child. As I shut off the machine, he smiled at me over his granny glasses and asked, "Where is your bench?" At the bench, he dumped out the contents of a brown paper bag while others in the shop gathered around to see. "Do you know what this is?"

Sifting through the broken pieces, I was able to identify a couple of microscope lenses. "It's an old microscope."

"Yes," Harpuda nodded, "It was my father's. At the airport in Vienna an SS officer, looking at the wooden box, asked me, '*Was hast du da?*' I told him it was just an old microscope. He grabbed it from me, opened the lid, and took it out. Then, looking at his compatriots, he held it up in the air, and as they applauded and laughed in delight, he smashed it to the ground. I was numb with rage. I got down on my knees, picked up the pieces, and put them in my pocket while my fellow passengers were yelling, 'Harpuda, *macht schnell* or they leave you here.'"

Those who had gathered round to listen to this little man were stunned into a reflective silence. None of the Nazi supporters were there. Looking at the heap of broken parts, I wondered what he could possibly want us to do with them.

"Is it at all possible to fix it?" he asked. "You see, it was my father's. He gave it to me when I graduated medical school. As a modern microscope it is nothing," he went on. "I know it is silly, but I have this strong sentimental attachment to it."

While I was apologizing, doubtful that we could do anything with this pile of broken pieces, John had been sorting through them. "It's a Zeiss," he announced. He suggested that Dr. Harpuda leave the parts with us and we would see what could be done. John was a bright young Cooper Union graduate who enjoyed a challenge. A six-footer with pale blond hair, he was very self-conscious about his lack of facial hair—as though it somehow signaled a lack of virility. He would regularly comment on how lucky I was to be so hairy.

After some careful inspection of the pieces, we concluded that the lenses were okay and that the parts that had been broken might be available from Zeiss. We even recovered a number stamped in the base, which we hoped might identify the model. Rebuilding the smashed microscope became a group anti-Nazi effort. I was sent down to Zeiss's New York office with the broken pieces. The instrument was too old for existing parts, but they thought they might find some old blueprints we could use to make new parts. Some weeks later, Zeiss called to say they had found the prints. Working at the lathe under a large magnifying glass, I learned to cut very fine instrument threads.

Months later we presented Doctor Harpuda with his father's fully restored microscope in a carefully varnished mahogany case. With many of the refugee doctors in attendance, John spoke of "our pride in what we were able to do for the dear friend to all our sore backs." Others praised his great contributions to humanizing medicine. The little man, in his blue suit and his perennial bow tie, had tears streaming down his cheeks as he thanked us, "for your kindness in restoring my sentimental nonsense. I will never forget this moment as your spirit redeems me. Thank you, I will never forget." He never did. For many years thereafter, whenever Edith or

I sent someone with a bad back to see Dr. Harpuda he would accept no payment, saying he had already been paid.

In spite of his terrible experience with the Nazi terror, Doctor Harpuda seemed to have not a trace of anger or bitterness. When I asked him about that, he said hatred was a waste of time and good energy. He believed that the best we could do as humans was to try to treat each other with respect and kindness. Then, as if he knew about my political ideas, he said he did not believe that class warfare would bring any real solutions; it would just replace one set of bureaucrats with others. At the time I hoped fervently that he was wrong.

Politics was still the most important part of my life, but I began to develop a new interest in becoming a machinist. I believed I would win more respect as a member of the working class if I had a genuine skill. In spite of Minnesota's opinion that "book learning don't teach you nothin'," I purchased a machinist's handbook. One day he looked around to be sure no one heard him, then asked me to look up air compressor ring clearance in my book.

The work I was doing in the shop was based on very basic scientific principles—coefficients of expansion, heat loss, and so on. Comparing that science to what Marxists called *scientific socialism* left me with serious doubts about the latter. In my work with steam and diesel engines, there were predictors based on data that could be calculated and depended upon. I could never find such predictors in Marxist analysis. Could the whole idea that there was a scientific solution to the social and economic problems we were dealing with possibly be wrong? At the time I had read only a few of the basic works of Marxism; I knew more about the coefficients of expansion than I did about Marxist theory. Until then I had just assumed that party intellectuals knew what they were talking about.

By the summer of 1940 we had completed many of the tools, appliances, and mechanical units the refugee doctors wanted, and I was only working part-time in the medical engineering unit. One day John called me to his office overlooking the floor of the power station to give me an assignment that changed my life.

France had fallen to the Nazis. Every day we listened to Ed Murrow on the radio describing the bombing of London and saw pictures of the devastation in the morning papers. John told me that when one of the London hospitals was hit, radium needles—then used to treat cancer—were spread around, exposing people to dangerous levels of radiation. An unsuspecting person could sit on some radium and be exposed to a lethal dose without ever knowing it. Because our hospital had a major radiation department as well as a medical engineering group, the government had asked us to build a bombproof radium container.

John was a soft-spoken man, but now he spoke very emphatically: "I want you to take on this project." I was flattered, but I also realized that I knew nothing about radium or bombproofing. "That's all right," John assured me, "neither does anyone else. The military wanted no part of the job and decided it should be done as close to a radium supply as possible." He became conciliatory: "Don't worry, you'll be working closely with an experienced radiologist, Dr. Sandra Shuman. She'll teach you what you need to know." And, with a silly little grin on his hairless blonde face, he added, "Besides, she's real cute. So be careful."

She was standing in front of a wall lightbox looking at an X-ray plate when I introduced myself as the machinist who was supposed to build a bombproof radium container. She continued looking at the X-ray, periodically running her hand through her short curly black hair. She was about five foot seven and was wearing a long white coat. When she turned around and introduced herself I was sure I was dreaming. Her brown eyes danced with delight as she smiled, and she laughed a little nervously, as if embarrassed by what was going on between us. Then, as if to shake off our mutual chemistry, she asked, "So, what do you know about radium?"

"Nothing," I said.

"Okay, then, let me show you what it looks like, how it is stored, and what a bombproof container will have to do."

She hung a lead apron and a name tag with a radiation exposure indicator on me. By now, I was reeling from our physical closeness and wasn't listening very well. I think she said, "If the indicator starts to turn red, you're being overexposed," or something like that. The only exposure I was feeling was to her, and it was overwhelming.

Opening a huge lead box, she used a three-foot-long forklike pincer contraption to remove a small tray containing what looked like a few nails. She placed it behind another lead shield.

"Doctor," I asked, "what do you do with those rods?"

"First of all," she said, "let's stop this doctor stuff. Let's just call each other Sandra and Robert, okay?"

It was not just okay, it was wonderful. "So what do you want me to do?"

"Because this war can spread anywhere, we need to build an external steel container that can withstand a direct hit. Obviously this lead box can't do that."

Before I went back to the shop, we had coffee together. We were in that animated state that comes when two people discover common interests and become certain they are made for each other. We liked the same romantic music, both thought capitalism was rotten, enjoyed the outdoors, and appreciated good food. I had lost my heart.

Returning to the shop, I ran into John, who took one look at me. "Boy, I told you to be careful, but I can see you weren't. Better go take a cold shower." I laughed and kept walking toward the drawing board to make a first rough sketch of the radium container.

The design we came up with was a round steel cylinder with a very heavy threaded cap that was screwed in and out. After several consultations, Sandra thought it took far too long to open and close it. Besides, neither of us was sure it was bombproof. It was then that John endeared himself to me by casually suggesting that we go down to the Army Proving Ground in Aberdeen, Maryland, for a day to see what they could suggest. Smiling with delight, we blushed simultaneously. "What a great idea," I said, a little embarrassed, and we all laughed.

That night—to avoid Edith—I hurriedly ran off to a meeting, establishing a pattern that came to pervade our relationship.

We had agreed to catch the 7:30 A.M. train to Aberdeen and to meet at 7:15 under the big clock in the main waiting room of Penn Station. When I arrived it was only 6:30. I had another cup of coffee and tried to read the *Times* but kept looking up to see if she was coming. As the clock crept toward 7:15 she still had not showed. "Suppose she forgot? Maybe I have the wrong day or I should be in Grand Central not Penn Station. No, the ticket says Penn Station." Finally, at 7:25, there she was—her curly hair shining, her body bouncing along in a completely uninhibited manner. This was the first time I had seen her without her white lab coat, and I realized she was a large woman—not fat but big-boned, with full breasts and wide hips. Her smile exuded the joy of her whole being, and the simple blue-and-white skirt and blouse emphasized her tremendous energy. Over time I learned that the source of her enormous life force was a complete acceptance of herself as a person, body and mind. She delighted in who she was, and it made everyone feel good just to be around her.

On the train, trying to avoid the fierce attraction we had for each other, we spent all our energy in intense conversation. First, we made a list of questions to ask the "munitions makers," as we called our Army consultants. Then we reviewed the war in Europe and the mess the world was in as a result of fascism. Finally, we moved on to movies, plays, books, music, and art. By about 10:00 A.M. we were in Aberdeen.

We were greeted at the station by a couple of Army majors, who outlined the day's program: information on what the British had learned in the Blitz, what was known about storage of critical materials, like gold at Fort Knox. "Finally," the major said, "we'll give you a tour of the facility, so you folks"—he quickly corrected himself—"that is, you doctors—can familiarize yourselves with our operation." I started to correct my status but got a poke from Sandra. We were now "doctors." It was fun.

During the tour we passed a group of field artillery pieces. I asked if I could look at how they worked. "Why certainly," came the reply, "but they're old stuff. Would you like to see the new ones?" Sandra was looking very curious. I whispered to her, "I think I got it, we can go home." She smiled, gave me another poke, and shook her head. As we walked along I whispered, "The breech block on the cannon is our radium container solution. The block has split threads that open and close with half a turn. If it can take the shock of an exploding shell, it could certainly withstand a bomb hit." Sandra suggested I say nothing until the end of our visit as she was very interested in the other things they did there.

During lunch at the officers' club we were briefed on the force of various sizes of bomb hits and the kind of damage they caused. We were both surprised by how casually the Army engineers described the amount of bodily damage inflicted by different size "projectiles" at varying distances. Toward the end of our visit, I described the radium container we proposed to build, and they made a few suggestions. They were confident it would survive even a direct hit.

When we were alone on the train, we decried the waste of money and energy that went into producing the tools of destruction we had seen at Aberdeen. In our vision of the new world, all such military bases would be converted to serving mankind instead of destroying it.

Still, we were feeling good about our mission. As we settled into our seats, our hands met and stayed together. We looked at each other, we kissed, and that went until Philadelphia, where I suggested we get off and spend the night.

Sandra thought for a long time, then said, "No, we will always be dear friends, but there are too many other people in our lives who would be terribly hurt. We can't create a little paradise of our own on the wreckage of others' lives. The guilt would be too destructive."

I suggested that I was not thinking of forever, just tonight.

"Well, of course, we could jump into bed, have a good time, and then what? If I didn't feel as deeply as I do about us, I would sure think that was a great idea. But for now anyhow, it would create too many conflicts for me." God, I thought, she does love me. This great woman loves me! I could hardly believe it.

She went on, "I love you, but I respect you too, so we will always be dear friends. Someday, when we won't have to disappear for a night or a weekend and make up endless lies about it afterward, we will have our time."

The flattery was overwhelming when this doctor, this woman who was considerably older than I, said, "I love you." After all, I told her, I was "just a dumb high school dropout. What could you possibly want from me?"

"I don't want anything," she said, "I just want to love you—and your closeness to the earth." She was laughing: "That's what really excites me. Your being a plumber and a machinist! What can beat that?"

We built the radium container, though I'm not certain it was ever used.

11

Allies at Last

In June of 1941 the Nazis invaded Russia. The Nazi-Soviet pact was forgotten, and the Russians became good guys on the side of the Allies. At least for the duration, all the old anti-Soviet hostilities were put on the back burner. When, only a few months later, the Japanese bombed Pearl Harbor and the United States entered the war, defeat of all the Axis powers became the single worldwide objective of capitalists and imperialists, socialists and communists. In the Party, we redirected our energies from the class struggle to all-out support of the war. Although I was happy with our new alliance, I did not for a minute think I could publicly declare my politics. Still, it felt good, for a change, not to be an outsider.

As the war effort went into high gear, my decision to become a machinist turned out to be well-timed. There was a growing demand for machinists and lots of opportunities to contribute to the war effort. At the powerhouse, Minnesota's drinking had became so bad he had to be let go. John, the chief engineer, had taken the risk of allowing me to replace him in the machinist job. I hadn't been in it long when I decided I could make a lot more money at a war plant. When I told John, he was furious: "So that's how you repay all we did for you? We'll have a tough time trying to find a machinist, even a half-assed one. You know that. You're a user, that's all."

I felt terrible. John was right. I *had* used the situation. But, feeling defensive, I shot back, "What about the war effort?"

He looked at me incredulously and—in his quiet Swedish way—got mad. "A short time ago you were head of a peace organization." I must have looked surprised. "Oh yes, the FBI told us all about you and asked us to keep an eye you. We told them we didn't give a damn about your politics as long as you did your job. Now that the Russians are attacked, whata ya know, you're for war the same way you were for peace. You're for whatever the Party is for, so go make some real money in the booming war industries. And good luck, 'cause you're gonna need it."

Shocked by the FBI stuff, I sort of stammered "I'm, I'm really sorry." I wanted to ask why he hadn't said something about the FBI before but was too scared. John turned his back on me and walked off, saying, "Just give us your leaving date."

Without difficulty I got a job at the Voss Ice Machine Company, a nineteenth-century factory that looked like something out of Dickens's *Hard Times*. It was cavernous and poorly lit by single lightbulbs hanging over huge old machines driven by a crisscross system of overhead belts. Before the war, the company had manufactured commercial ice-making machines. Because of its giant-sized machine tools, this antiquated old factory was suddenly transformed into an around-the-clock, seven-day-a-week operation turning out propeller shafts, couplings, gear boxes, and all kinds of power units for the U.S. Navy.

At the time, Voss was recruiting new machinists almost daily. I made friends with a couple of the young guys in the plant, and before long we were circulating authorization cards for Local 402 of the International Association of Machinists (IAM). Because of the war effort, it was relatively easy to organize plants like Voss. The employer just passed the costs on to the government. I had started at a higher hourly rate than I'd received at the power plant. As a result of the unionization, we got generous overtime pay: time-and-a-half after eight hours, double time for Saturday afternoons and Sunday, 10 to 20 percent extra for the night shift, and so forth.

The men who worked in what we called the dungeon were a mix of Young Turks—Teddy, Paul, and myself—and some real old-timers who chewed tobacco, smoked corncob pipes, and called the new guys "bottle babies," "pip-squeaks" or "bookies." The latter label referred to our penchant to use the Machinist Handbook when dealing with shop problems. Because the IAM, an AFL affiliate, was almost exclusively an organization of journeymen, new members had to pass a craft test administered by a local lodge committee.

Lodge 402 was a small local made up primarily of German-speaking craftsmen at factories scattered around the city. Besides passing the machinist's test, all of us Young Turks had to learn the lodge secrets—for example, how to enter a lodge meeting by standing at the door with your right hand held over your heart until the local president gave a similar salute—and swear a secret oath never to propose any but white men for union membership. All this mumbo-jumbo was leftover from times when unions had to be secret societies to protect their members. Under the protection of the Wagner Act, unions had become organizations recognized by law; that didn't matter much in the IAM, where tradition did not die easily.

The Voss plant was a great place to learn what it meant to schmooze. There were forty-foot lathes for turning propeller shafts; a cut on these antique monsters could take days. That left lots of time to walk around, think up things to pass the hours, play tricks, and figure out gadgets to decrease the need for our presence at the machine. The Marxist argument that "de-skilling" the workforce was a capitalist plot against craftsmen sure didn't hold in my factory experience. We were automating machines to make the job easier. I believe that since the invention of the plough there has been a fundamental human drive to find ways to get the work done with the least amount of human effort.

Teddy, Paul, and I also began using our schmooze time to develop schemes for waking up this sleepy little Local 402. Within a year we had decided that I should go to work at a nonunion plant and try to organize it for the IAM. The Nathan Manufacturing Company on 106th Street employed about fifteen hundred workers. We succeeded in unionizing that plant without too much trouble; then, as shop chairman, I led negotiations that resulted in a pretty good agreement.

It was a wonderful time for unions. With defense industries expanding like crazy and the government footing the bill, we were able to win quickly real concessions for the newly organized workers. The following year I ran for lodge president, Paul ran for business agent, and Teddy ran for secretary. We were all elected. Becoming president of a local wasn't all that difficult. It was an unpaid position, and most guys wouldn't take it if it was offered. Besides I was quite verbal and even knew how to run a meeting. Union elections were hotly contested only after offices became full-time paid positions. Then the competition could be fierce.

With Russia and the United States allied in the war against Hitler, being a party member seemed to become acceptable almost overnight.

Stalin's picture was on the cover of *Life* magazine, the Benny Goodman and Count Basie bands were playing at YCL dances, and Hollywood stars were doing benefits for Russian war relief.

Paul, Teddy, and I became close friends and spent many evenings after work thinking up ways to build the local and, at the same time, shake the IAM out of its traditional lethargy. Paul, a tall, skinny, blue-eyed westerner, had survived the depression by knowing how to work the Skid Row missions; by saying a few prayers he could get a hot meal and a clean bed. Unlike me, he was married and had a couple of kids. Like so many people who experienced the miseries of poverty during the thirties, Paul was haunted all his life by fear of losing his job. He thought that having good steady employment with lots of overtime was a good deal.

One night over bratwurst and sauerkraut at the Ideal Restaurant on 86th Street, Paul wanted to know how I had learned so much about running a meeting. I looked, he said, as if I had been born with a gavel in my hand. I told him of my membership in the Party. He didn't say anything. Looking back, I realize that Paul found this news very troubling. I was his friend. I had helped him learn everything he knew about organizing, and he was enjoying his new status as business agent of the lodge. My party membership would always bother him. He would one day be caught between loyalty to a friend and his own survival as a union business agent.

As a result of my election as president of an IAM local, the party leadership took a renewed interest in me. All the major union positions being won by comrades were in the new CIO unions. In the AFL, well-entrenched old leaders left no room for new men, least of all communists. In many of the old craft unions, like the Carpenters or Teamsters, running for office was laying your life on the line. Not so in the Machinists. It was, and probably still is, one of the more democratic of the old-line AFL unions.

One night, because of my union status, I unexpectedly found myself at a meeting with the Party's top trade union leaders.* They criticized me for being too open about my politics with coworkers. Many people in

---

*My FBI file indicates that the Party then considered me one of their most important people inside the AFL.

the Party were sure the honeymoon with the Soviet Union would not last forever and that once the war was over we would once again be confronted with a hostile government. There was a split in the leadership over whether the U.S.–Soviet friendship would last and whether the American Communist party under Browder should pursue a course independent of Moscow. I was instructed to go further underground and to avoid open connections with the Party. I could no longer speak from party or YCL platforms.

From then on, I lived two separate lives: one in the labor movement, as president of a rapidly growing local union, and another in the private world of communists and fellow travelers. In the years ahead, the need for secrecy would haunt me with the nightmare of being exposed as a perjurer. In a recurring dream, I found myself naked on a crowded street trying desperately to cover my genitals. People were pointing at me and laughing hysterically. A crusader in the cause of socialism, I feared being revealed as a perjurer, liar, agent, or spy. Above all, the dream told me that if I wanted to keep my job I needed to be extremely careful to conceal my politics.

With the demands of wartime production on the metal trades, the local union was now growing by leaps and bounds. In the few years I was president, the membership doubled and then tripled. We were very successful in organizing the many small machine shops that dotted the city. At the time, I attributed part of our success to advice I was getting from Bill (William Z.) Foster, the Party's top trade union leader. He had led the 1919 steel strike and was considered by trade unionists one of the best labor strategists in the country. Because IAM had been involved in the steel strike, Foster had a good working knowledge of the union. He considered the IAM leadership a nice bunch of namby-pamby guys. They were not as corrupt as the men in the building trades unions, but they had no guts for the class struggle. Throughout the years of class collaboration to win the war, Foster never lost his enthusiasm for the class struggle. He believed workers would only respond to militant trade unionism and taught me that to win the workers' support a union had to fight every single grievance as though it were a life-or-death issue. I followed his advice and, by pursuing a very militant policy emphasizing the class struggle, built a very broad base of member support.

In that period of dramatic union expansion, belief in the class nature of society and the resultant conflict was the major reason so many lefties like myself rose to positions of leadership. For us, class conflict was the equivalent of the Apostles' Creed for Christians. Being militant, tough on employers, and incorruptible put us in sharp contrast to the old-line conservative, do-nothing AFL leaders who sometimes had their hands in the till.

Two other factors contributed to making party people and Marxists extremely effective as union leaders. First was our intensive study of how the capitalist system worked. Second was our deep ideological commitment to correcting what we saw as the terrible economic injustices of capitalism by increasing the power of the working masses through their trade unions. In the long run, we hoped, workers' experience of the class struggle in the unions would make them realize that the only real solution to the unfair distribution of wealth was establishment of a socialist society.

While I was organizing machinists, Edith was dancing and modeling. One evening early in 1941, as we sat around the kitchen table, she said, "I think I'm pregnant." My reaction to this news was nothing like the joyful response of fathers in the movies. I didn't feel anything at all. I thought, "So what does that have to do with me?" I didn't want to talk about it, but Edith insisted that we needed to make a decision, as time for an abortion was running out. I got up abruptly: "I'm going to walk the dog."

At the time we had a German shepherd puppy. As we walked along, he was, as always, eager to play. This made me so furious that I began hitting him hard with his leash. "Say," a stranger asked, "Aren't you being a bit rough on that little feller?" Embarrassed and overcome with shame, I rushed away and began to cry. The incident reminded me of my fierce anger at the pigs on the camp farm. I wanted to give the dog to anyone who would take him, and I did.

The next morning, Edith and I resumed our discussion. We agreed that I probably would be drafted soon and might never return. She wanted to have the child. Okay, I thought, with a war going full blast, it's her gamble. I couldn't guarantee her anything beyond today. Should I be killed, though, we needed to assure her of veterans' benefits. That's how we decided to get married. After completing the necessary blood tests, we picked up a couple of YCL friends for witnesses and took the subway to City Hall. We gave the clerk two bucks, he mumbled something, we said "Yes," and he pronounced us man and wife. As he handed me the license, I felt the need to reiterate my contempt for this, "whole idiotic bourgeois ritual." I wasn't at all happy to assume responsibility for a child, but what could I do? For me, the alternative, an abortion, was impossible even to suggest.

Edith's pregnancy only began to show in the seventh and eighth months, and she continued dancing until then. The pregnancy didn't interfere with our sex life until her ninth month. A few months before Elizabeth was born, overwhelmed with the impending responsibility of a child, I went canoeing in the Adirondacks with some YCL friends. Edith, obviously hurt, said nothing. This became the pattern of our relationship: I did whatever I needed or wanted to do and she, feeling insecure, said nothing.

As a result of our successful organizing efforts, we in the local leadership were feeling very cocky. In the months between organizing factories, Paul, Teddy, and I began thinking of ways to shake up the whole IAM. We learned that local Machinists' lodges in many states had formed state councils but that there was currently none in New York. The functions of the councils were primarily legislative and political. After extensive consultation with locals around the state, we concluded that the council idea had enthusiastic support. The Party too welcomed the idea, immediately interpreting it as an opportunity to expand its influence within the international union and throughout the rest of the state's AFL locals.

In the spring of 1944, my local, Lodge 402, called a meeting of state lodges to discuss forming a council. Because our lodge was one of the fastest growing in the state, it had won lots of respect from other locals, and the meeting, held in New York City, was well attended. Representatives of a couple of dozen locals came from Buffalo, Jamestown, Rochester, Elmira, Oneonta, and numerous other towns.

Local 402 delegates presented the reasons for reestablishing the council: the needs to make our voice heard in state politics, to influence legislation in both Albany and Washington, and to provide an apparatus for local union cooperation on issues like strike support. The New York State Council of Machinists was accordingly reborn, and an executive board was elected. I served as the first president. The new officers of the council were sworn in by Harvey Brown, the president of the international. The act was widely interpreted as his blessing.

The major actions taken at that first meeting were preparation of a lengthy statement on the need to plan for conversion from wartime to peacetime production and, most important, a resolution strongly endorsing Roosevelt for a fourth term. The newly elected officers were instructed to launch a statewide campaign to reelect FDR.

Sometime early that summer the council's conversion resolution led to a meeting with Vice President Henry Wallace and to a very strange, wholly unintended consequence of it. Because FDR had not yet announced for a fourth term, there was a lot of speculation over whether he would—or should—run and whether Wallace would again be his running mate. Wallace was a committed New Dealer, and I believed we needed to fight to keep him on the ticket, especially as there were grave doubts that FDR would live out the term. For the same reasons, a well-organized conservative effort inside the Democratic party wanted to dump Wallace in favor of a more acceptable traditional machine politician like Harry Truman. On one of the council executive's many trips to Washington, we had a meeting with Wallace to talk about converting war industries to peacetime production.

Some time later I got a letter from an old YCL friend thanking me for getting him out of a Navy brig. It seems he had slugged a junior officer for calling him a "Jew boy" and was serving time. From time to time I wrote to comrades in the service; in a letter to this friend I had mentioned the meeting with Wallace. When the Navy censors saw the reference to "meeting with the vice president," my friend was instantly released.

The traditional AFL union leaders were very hesitant to declare their support for FDR. The New York State Council of Machinists was the first AFL affiliate to support him in 1944. After several lengthy discussions of what we could do to actually advance his reelection, the council executive board decided to distribute a pamphlet setting forth the reasons "why labor needs FDR now more than ever for the rough times ahead."

The council also decided that we needed a voice both in the Machinists and in the labor movement generally. We planned to support our monthly newspaper, the *IAM Beacon*, through bundle sales to locals throughout the state. As state president, I was assigned the editorship, a task I knew absolutely nothing about. Since none of the rest of us knew beans about putting together a newspaper, we clearly needed some professional help.

Through the Party, I had recently met Howard Friedman, a journalist working for the Federated Press, a left-wing front organization devoted to reporting "labor news ignored by the capitalist press." Howard was a big, cheerful, soft-spoken man with a pockmarked face. He seemed to me to have read every book ever written and to have total recall of their contents. He was a sort of walking encyclopedia.* Howard urged me to contact a left-wing publisher, the Trade Union Press, which published papers for the United Electrical Workers, the Building Trades Press, and others

At the time I was working in a machine shop that made parts for locomotives and did development work on jet engines for General Electric (GE). The plant had recently received an Army-Navy "E" award for its contributions to war production. I was putting in, at a minimum, a forty-four-hour week. The council wanted me to take some time away from the plant to carry out my new duties as state president. Not wanting to be accused of neglecting the war effort, I resisted the idea as long as possible. Yet when Howard called and asked me to meet him at the Trade Union Press on Saturday morning, I was more than willing to forgo Saturday work. He told me to bring some cheap wine, and we would all have lunch. In a few hours, he said, I would be a full-fledged editor. I was nervous about this new assignment and hit a local bar for a quick one to settle my nerves. Somewhat fortified, I made it to the Federated Press building at Fifth Avenue and 25th Street.

The press's office was in a second-floor loft. It was crowded with a dozen well-worn desks, piles of tabloid-size newspapers, and shelves sagging with papers. There was also a water fountain and a table holding a battered coffee pot, a box of sugar, and some heavily stained coffee cups.

*The FBI file says that Friedman was then my main contact with the party leadership. I knew he was in the Party but not that he was my "contact person." That's how secret my political life was becoming.

Howard greeted me with, "Here's our new editor, the emerging Thomas Paine of the IAM."

Holding a pencil between his teeth like a pirate knife, he introduced me to the gang. Betty Goldstein, feet up on the desk and her pink panties unashamedly visible, nodded and went back to reading. Howard said she was a Smith College graduate but that shouldn't scare me. "And this is Beecher, a descendant of Harriet Beecher Stowe, still trying to free the slaves—wage slaves that is." In contrast to Betty, who was plump, Beecher was a skinny string bean with a New England accent. She too was deeply involved in what she was reading. Last was Mike, whose only comment was "Watch out for these girls. They're really hot to trot," to which Beecher retorted, "Don't you wish!"

All five of us gathered round a table to talk about the first issue of the *IAM Beacon*. We ate sandwiches, drank the cheap wine, smoked a lot of cigarettes, and talked union. Those three recent college graduates were very impressive. From their reading, they knew as much as or more about the labor movement than I did. Betty knew the details of GE's antiunion efforts, and Howard had intricate knowledge of the jurisdictional fights in building trades unions as well as of the feud between Harvey Brown of IAM and William Hutchinson, the dictatorial president of the Carpenters. I was in awe of their knowledge. "How the hell do you guys know so much about unions?"

"Shit, Schrank," said Beecher, "we're reporters. That's our job, keeping up with what the sellouts are up to. Otherwise we're useless to people like you."

Even as they heaped praise on me as an "honest-to-goodness worker," they scared the hell out of me. Beecher said admiringly, "Hey, this guy actually makes something." Howard added, "Makes something? He worked as a plumber on some of those tall West Side apartment buildings. He can make a toilet work! Imagine that!" They had finally met someone who fit their intellectual myth of the working class. I told them that being in the working class wasn't as great as they made it sound, and they laughed when I pointed out that "working in a factory can be pretty fuckin' dull and boring."

Betty, who spoke in a rapid staccato voice and was the most serious of the group, wanted to know "What are the major things bothering the members?" Beecher asked, "What's the union leadership up to?" While I tried to answer their rapid-fire questions, one of them was always busy writing down what I said. Betty, who came across a bit like a tough but friendly Jewish mother, handed me a bunch of clippings from the wire services and other newspapers and magazines: "I thought we might use some of these stories. Read them over and put a check on any you think we should use." Howard handed me the proposed masthead for the *Beacon*.

Working at a table off in a corner, I began to enjoy being an editor. The air was filled with our cigarette smoke and the rat-a-tat-tat of the typewriters. Periodically someone would hand me a piece of paper with, "see what you think of this." Marking up articles with a red pencil, I added, subtracted, changed, rephrased, rejected, and approved. Between the wine, Betty's panties, Beecher's sweet smile, the smoke, and the clack of the typewriters, this was for sure a Hollywood movie. Late in the afternoon I was learning how to paste up the pages when someone exclaimed, "Christ! We forgot all about the editorial." All eyes turned to me.

"Hey, it's one thing to read and suggest, it's another to write," I said. "Shit, I'm not a writer. I'm a machinist."

"Listen to me," Betty instructed. "If you can speak and express yourself the way you do, then writing is simply a mechanical problem." She told me to just close my eyes and imagine that I was in a bar, at a union meeting, or talking to some guys in a plant. If someone asked me a question like "What's the union need a newspaper for anyway?" what would I say?

I closed my eyes and the words came pouring out of that same strange place that they did when I was on a platform. I began by explaining why we needed an educational organ to keep members informed about what is going on in the union, the economy, and government. I went on:

No doubt, all of us will not agree all the time. We want every member to feel that this is his BEACON and that he is free to state his opinions and pleas. The columns of the BEACON will always be open for this purpose. Naturally, the Editorial Board feels the great responsibility of presenting the views of our organization and always serving the best interests of our members.

While I was speaking, Betty was typing. As I finished, she pulled the sheet out of the typewriter with a grand flourish and handed it to me. "What do you think?" I read it. It sounded good. I read it again and suggested a few changes. The others read it and nodded their approval.

Betty assured me that I was a writer. I just had to remember to always write as if I were speaking on a street corner, explaining a contract or grievance, or telling a joke after dinner. I should imagine my audience, listen to my inner voice, and write down what it said. "Believe me, it will work. Maybe not for everyone, but for you." It was my first and most important writing lesson from Betty. Some years later she got married and, in 1963, became well known as Betty Friedan, author of *The Feminine Mystique*. I wonder if I ever thanked her for that lesson.

By the end of the afternoon, the *IAM Beacon* was laid out, pasted up, and ready for the press. I was thanking everyone on my way out when Howard, ensconced in his corner at a desk piled high with papers, articles, magazines, and photographs, yelled out, "Schrank, come here." I saw that he actually chewed up pencils and then sort of spat the pieces of wood into the wastebasket. Grinning broadly, he congratulated me: "I want to say you carried this off beautifully. Now bring me an outline for the pamphlet on FDR you mentioned, and we'll give you whatever help you need."

That night there was yet another ritual party for Arnold, a YCL friend going off to war. We were peace-lovers celebrating a good war. Our lives seemed extremely vulnerable. Who would live? Who would die? We were living in "a big crap shoot."

That's what Dolores said to Arnold as they sat together on the couch drinking cheap Chilean wine. Her husband, like so many other comrades, was somewhere in Europe. He was working for the Office of Strategic Services (OSS), the forerunner of the CIA.* As the party grew merrier and the singing and dancing more boisterous, Dolores and Arnold became more and more tipsy. She kept mumbling, "What difference does it all make now? Christ, let's have some fun." I saw them get up and make their way through the crowded room into the bathroom. A minute later I heard the shower running and knew exactly what was happening. After a while they emerged, laughing at how they had put it over on the rest of us. Between the cheap wine, the songs, the talk, and the dancing, no one but me

---

*William "Wild Bill" Donovan, who headed the OSS, considered the Spanish Civil War veterans particularly useful for planning insurgent actions and assisting partisans behind the lines in fascist-controlled countries.

had missed them, though Esther asked Dolores why her hair was all wet. "Dunked my head to sober up a little," she replied with a giggle.

In wartime, with so much death staring us in the face, our usual anxieties about life and death were lifted to a level of intensity that made many of us do things we would never have done in peacetime. War is a hell of a reminder of our mortality. Living for the moment, we were glad to be alive and were making the most of it. We said good-bye to Arnold, who became a B-17 tailgunner. Like many other Young Communists, he returned a hero and took advantage of the GI bill—to become a doctor.

The wartime honeymoon on the homefront was proceeding just fine. The Party, with its firm commitment to the all-out effort to help the Soviet Union, was satisfied with the way we were influencing the AFL. And the CIO was growing by leaps and bounds. The unions in the newly organized mass-production industries were exhibiting a new militancy, a natural result of the promises made during the agitation and propaganda phase of the organizing. Such promises, not unlike those made during political campaigns, could not always be kept, and we had to contend with lots of wildcat strikes. For the most part, we were able to control them, and war production was not affected.

A major issue for the Left was the delay in opening a second front in Europe to relieve the Russians. A lot of leftists believed that the allies were intentionally letting the Russians bleed so that when the war was over they would be too weak to be a major factor in postwar alignments. When, on June 6, 1944, a vast sea and airborne force of American, Canadian, British, and French troops began landing on the beaches of Normandy, we breathed a sigh of relief.

The FDR pamphlet was driving me nuts. For one thing, I did not know how to deal with the Truman problem. What could I do? He was hated by the Left. We thought of him as a Democratic party hack with a lot of ties to big oil people. I decided to ignore him.

Though by then I had written leaflets and editorials, the idea of writing the pamphlet loomed over me as if I had been ordered to write a novel. I kept reminding myself of Betty's advice to write as if I were talking to some machinists. In fact I wrote much of the pamphlet talking to the lions in the Bronx Zoo. Sometimes on cool Sunday mornings I would take Elizabeth, then about two years old, to the Lion House. As I sat thinking on the comfortable benches across from the tigers, leopards, lions, and jaguars, Lizzie would run around and talk to the keepers. One Sunday I addressed the assembled big cats on the subject "Why members of the AFL are supporting FDR again." I had to overcome the reluctance of, especially, the leaders of the New York AFL, to support FDR. "This great surge of support." I began, "is for Roosevelt and not necessarily for the Democratic party. We back FDR because he is our friend."

With some good suggestions and editing from Howard, Betty, and Beecher, I managed to finish the FDR pamphlet, and on July 16, 1944, the state council enthusiastically supported my draft. We advertised the pamphlet in union papers and journals and were overwhelmed with orders. The first printing of twenty-five thousand and then a second printing went quickly; we could not keep up with the demand. At five cents a copy, our first pamphlet-publishing endeavor was a huge success. Harvey Brown and Sam Newman, respectively president and vice-president of the IAM—both quoted on the opening page—were happy with the results.

In the meantime, as we began to gear up for the election, we encountered an unexpected problem at our own local union. Members were beginning to worry about what would happen to their jobs when the war was over. As our local's organizing drive kept rolling along through 1944, we held mass initiations of hundreds of new members, often including Asians, Hispanics, and Negroes. We had simply dropped all the old tests for entry into the union, including the pledge to propose only members of the "white race" for membership. The dues kept rolling in and nobody at IAM's Washington headquarters paid any attention; after all, for them it meant increased income from the per capita tax.

The problem started when Joe, a tall, handsome young light-skinned Negro, came into the union at one of the newly organized plants. Sometime later he applied for a machinist's job at the Schlitz brewery in Brooklyn. At the time there were over a dozen major breweries in New York, and their maintenance machinists were all in our local. One day I received a message at the union office saying, "if the nigger starts to work at the Schlitz brewery, the shop committee cannot guarantee his safety." The old-timers hanging around the union hall said there was a lot of tradition about who comes to work in the breweries. They thought it was the old German brewmasters who objected to letting in anyone who wasn't a relative, let alone a black man.

That night we held a meeting in the brewery locker room. The old-timers were very emphatic: "You guys (referring to the new leadership) were wrong to send him here." I responded that he was a brother, a member in good standing, and a full-fledged machinist. The response was emphatic: "Fuck you and his good standing. He's a nigger, no matter. So find him a job somewhere else."

"You poor fuckin' assholes don't understand this ain't some dumb stamping plant," fumed another man. "This is a brewery. We're a family here, not a bunch of fuckin' Spicks and niggers."

The deep hatred of these workers toward a fellow worker solely because of his skin color troubled me. All the benefits of this brewery job had come as a result of unionization. Why didn't the lesson of brotherhood carry beyond their narrow definition of who was worthy to be a member? Maybe workers were different when the visionaries I had grown up with dreamt of a socialist future. Each time I confronted a situation like the Schlitz brewery brouhaha, my faith in a socialist future eroded a little more.

Joe did go to work at Schlitz, but only after we brought in the union lawyer to tell our brothers that it was probably against the law to keep him out and that they just might be legally liable if they did. It was mostly the latter that scared the shit out of them. It didn't keep the "brothers" from making his life miserable though. We had to meet him regularly for a drink to plead with him to "hang in there, they'll come around." Eventually they did accept him as "our nigger" but warned, "Don't send us no more."

At the next convention of the International, it was the few Communist party delegates who led the fight to take the word *white* out of the initiation pledge. As at Schlitz, it wasn't the moral argument that won the debate; it was the opinion of a liberal Jewish lawyer that it was probably illegal to discriminate on the basis of race.

12

FDR's Last Campaign

In spite of a cool, even hostile reception by the leaders of many AFL unions, orders for the state council's Roosevelt pamphlet kept the presses running overtime. Harvey Brown, president of the IAM International, told me he thought AFL leaders were unwilling to support FDR because they blamed him for the rise of the CIO. Brown himself saw the CIO's growth as a direct result of the AFL's own failure to take advantage of the Wagner Act to organize the mass-production industries. The IAM, an exceptional AFL union in this respect, *was* beginning to organize workers along industrial lines. This effort brought in thousands of new workers but also created numerous jurisdictional disputes inside the AFL. At the time, Brown and Bill Hutchinson, president of the Carpenters, were quarreling bitterly over which union controlled various jobs in the nation's shipyards.

After publishing the pamphlet, I took a leave of absence from my job to stump the state for FDR full-time, assisting local unions to set up organizations for registering voters in every town and hamlet of New York. To the train crews of New York Central's Empire State Express, I became the "president's friend, Brother Bob." Many nights, as the train rattled its way north along the Hudson, they helped us win the election by finding me an empty sleeping compartment to grab a good night's sleep.

During that summer and early fall, the state council of Machinists became a major political force in the state. As a result, Brown asked me to serve on the staff of the Democratic National Labor Committee for the last weeks of the presidential campaign. The chairman of the committee was Dan Tobin, president of the Teamsters and an ardent Roosevelt supporter. I was delighted to accept.

Bright and early the next Monday morning, I reported to the Hotel Biltmore headquarters of the Democratic National Committee (DNC). Tobin occupied a large corner office with half a dozen adjoining rooms. He had a hoarse bass voice, and when his secretary told him of my arrival, he boomed out "Bob, come in here." Before amplifiers, the voices of public speakers had to reach the people in the top balcony. Probably out of habit, Tobin's everyday conversation sounded as if he were addressing the assembled multitudes.

Tobin, a short, heavyset man with a head of gray hair and thick eyeglasses, had worked as a coal wagon driver behind a team of horses. In his gravelly voice he told me how much he liked the council's pamphlet. "When I saw that FDR pamphlet I couldn't for the life of me figure out who on God's earth woke up those old fuddy-duddy Machinists. Now I see. Shit, they just slept while you guys were busy. Well, damn good for us!"

Tobin had a way of taking you into his confidence by moving in real close. His face in mine, he said emphatically, "We have to go into every mine and factory. I want you to go to Pennsylvania and carry it for Roosevelt. Lewis thinks he can carry the state for the Republicans. Well, we're gonna teach him a lesson or two about loyalty. Win it and you can name your prize."

John L. Lewis, the tough, highly respected president of the CIO's United Mine Workers, had broken with FDR after his second term. Pennsylvania being a major coal-producing state, Lewis had a strong political base there. This talk of beating the pugnacious labor leader was heady stuff, and I ate it up, every minute of it.

I was assigned an office, a secretary, and charging privileges at the Biltmore. On many mornings I would have half a dozen union guys in for breakfast to talk strategy.

Some time later, a few staff people were gathered around a table looking at a map of Pennsylvania, trying to figure out the details of the campaign. Tobin turned to me: "Bob, come on. I want you to go to Washington for the Teamsters' dinner with the president." I was thrilled. I had heard about the upcoming dinner, but it was billed as a strictly Teamsters' affair, and I never imagined I would be invited.

On the evening of September 23, 1944, I was seated at a table in the main ballroom of the New Statler Hotel with some of the people from the union's research department. Discussion at the table centered around the internal politics of choosing a successor to Tobin. Dave Beck was the candidate most often mentioned, but there seemed to be a desire for someone "cleaner, less connected." I certainly knew about the mob presence in the Teamsters, but their tough, antibusiness attitude put them on our side in the class struggle. It was expedient to maintain a good relationship with them.

The main ballroom, as well as every meeting room and lobby of the New Statler, was packed with Teamsters. They had come from every corner of the United States to hear FDR's first major speech of the campaign, which was also being broadcast nationwide. When Tobin introduced him, I was sure the discharge of human energy in whistles, clapping, foot-stomping, table-slapping, and cheering would cause the building to collapse. I marveled at what an unusual leader this president was. He was as relaxed with this bunch of truck drivers as he was at a lunch with cronies at the exclusive Metropolitan Union Club or having cocktails with landowner friends at Hyde Park. The dinner was a huge fund-raising success for the Labor Committee.

The best story of his masterful speech that evening came at the end of a long litany of ridicule of Republican propaganda and misrepresentations. It was about a rumor that somehow his Scottie dog, Fala, had been left behind in Alaska on a recent military inspection trip. The Republicans and the press were accusing the president of sending a Navy destroyer up there for the sole purpose of bringing the dog home.

He paused as his warm smile had the desired effect on the audience, then said: "These Republican leaders have not been content with attacks on me, or on my wife, or on my sons. No, not content with that, they now include my little dog Fala." As the audience roared, he went on. "Well, of course, I don't resent attacks, and my family doesn't resent attacks, but Fala does resent them. . . . He has not been the same dog since." The place was wild with laughter. It became the joke of the campaign: You can attack me, but leave my dog out of it. FDR's skill at getting the audience laughing at the opposition was an early lesson for me in the uses of humor.

The dinner was a wonderful celebration of a great president, and I consider myself very lucky to have been part of it. Watching him that night, I realized why some of the politicians that hung out at the Biltmore, as well as large conservative business organizations like the National Association of Manufacturers and the U.S. Chamber of Commerce, no longer trusted him. He had probably become a bit too liberal, too comfortable with these blue-collar union brothers. The Teamsters' dinner was a sure sign that labor was a vital part of his coalition.

Word came to me at the Biltmore that the party leaders were delighted with my appointment, though they emphasized strongly the importance of keeping my affiliation strictly secret. During the campaign, the FBI file shows, the bureau received a number of queries about me from someone (whose name was blacked out) wanting to know who I was and how I came to be working at the Biltmore. I had heard that Jay Lovestone, a former Communist party leader, was working as the principal red hunter for the AFL, and I assumed the inquiries came from him. Unlike later queries about me, they do not seem to have received an FBI response.

At the Labor Committee, we were making the IAM railway locals our bases of operation throughout the state, giving us excellent access to all the railroad unions. In going over our Pennsylvania strategy with Howard one day, I asked if he had any additional suggestions. He promised to think about it and get back to me as soon as he could. A few days later he brought me an invaluable list of Pennsylvania labor leaders that indicated where each one stood on the political spectrum. The list specified who could be contacted directly and who needed a go-between. There were also lists of potential financial contributors and of union officials who could deliver manpower for door-to-door electioneering—not to mention names of people who would say good things and do nothing.

The Party took pride in their analysis of what it called "the relationship of forces," a way of differentiating between people according to their political positions, from the far Left through the middle to the far Right. The schema is based on a Marxist class-analysis paradigm—where do various groups and individuals stand in terms of their social and economic interests?—and is a fairly reliable method of forecasting a voting outcome. In addition, by separating people into groups and interests, it can tell campaign workers where to focus their efforts in order to *change* the relationship of forces and so produce a shift in voting.

By applying this schema to the 1944 election campaign, the Party was able to come up with a winning combination of forces that supported FDR in the Pennsylvania campaign. In many electoral campaigns, unknown to the public, the Party's behind-the-scenes network and expertise made a real difference.

We also found the relationship-of-forces schema a very useful tool in union organizing drives, because it allowed us to concentrate our efforts on the uncommitted. Early on, I observed that it was a lot more fun to campaign among supporters than to face the cooler audiences of the undecided. I learned to forget those who can never be converted and devote the union's resources to persuading the fence sitters.

A month before election day, I was in Philadelphia for a meeting of our newly established Pennsylvania Labor Committee. With the help of the Party, we had brought together over two hundred union officials from all over the state to plan our strategy for the final weeks of the campaign. As the author of the pamphlet *This Is F.D.R.*, I was introduced to a standing ovation. After my short talk about what we needed to do to win Pennsylvania for the president, the meeting broke into geographic working groups. We decided to concentrate all our efforts on the mining districts where Lewis had a strong union following.

What emerged was a detailed plan to cover every minehead and every factory and mill with literature, buttons, posters, and get-out-the-vote committees. The Railway Brotherhood unions, who fully supported the president, acted as our delivery system. A huge map of Pennsylvania on one wall of my office had hundreds of red pins indicating key railroad distribution points. As each area was covered with election materials and meetings, the pins were changed from red to orange. When the local election team pronounced its area safe for the Democrats, a green victory pin—accompanied by an enthusiastic cheer of "We won another one!"—was substituted.

The Pennsylvania campaign was expensive. At one point, Tobin told us we were doing a great job but that we might have to cut back because we were running out of funds. Besides, he said, the "goddamn leadership of the party don't give a damn about the Great White Father." It was depressing news. A few days later, Eleanor Roosevelt came to the Biltmore to rally the supporters. She walked around headquarters pleasantly inquiring, "How are things going?" When she asked me, I told her we could lose Pennsylvania because the Democratic party's national treasurer was not releasing funds to the Labor Committee. She looked a little surprised, thanked us for our support, and said she would see what could be done.

The next morning while we were planning a rally with some union people from Buffalo, Tobin came in and started yelling at me: "What the hell were you doing talking to Eleanor about our troubles with this gang?" I was mortified in front of the union people and began to apologize, though I wasn't sure for what. Tobin, dropping his voice a few decibels, got more conciliatory. He explained that he had enough trouble with Robert Hannegan (chairman of the DNC) and the "rest of these wardheelers" without Eleanor, whom they hate anyhow, riling things up. Then he laughed, winked at me, and said, "But we got what we need for Pennsylvania—and some to spare for other hot spots."

The Buffalo meeting—I think it was for Truman—turned out to be every rally organizer's nightmare. When the train pulled into the station with Tobin, the two New York senators, and Truman, a band was there to meet them. The problem was that the band was on the wrong side of the station; as the politicians were walking toward the south passageway, the band and welcoming committee were moving to the north passageway. When someone realized what had happened, both groups were turned around and simultaneously marched to the opposite passageway. (Remember we had no walkie-talkies in those days.) Each group was turned around often enough to have us falling all over ourselves laughing at the Mack Sennett comedy routine. Tobin commented that "If we never meet the mayor, the band, and the welcoming committee it won't matter, because if they can't figure out which track we're arriving on, how the hell they gonna know how to mark the ballot?"

Whenever something like this occurred, Tobin would turn to the nearest staff person—in this case it was me—and say, "Bob, get up here and straighten things out." All the staffers had learned to say "Yes, sir" and pay no attention.

On October 21, FDR made his only New York appearance of the campaign. As his motorcade slowly made its way through a drenching cold rain in the Seventh Avenue garment district, I caught a glimpse of the president looking pale and sickly. Instead of the ebullient, smiling hero that was etched in my memory from the Teamsters' dinner, I saw a tired old man who seemed to fade into the leather seat of the open touring car. I was sure he did not have long to live.* Tobin agreed and said we needed to think of Harry Truman as president.

"But why," I asked, "Why did he run?"

He put his arm around my shoulder. "Bob, when you get the kind of power a president enjoys, you begin to think that if you can only hang onto it you'll live forever. Kings and dictators, and even some union leaders, think that all the time."

Two weeks later, on election night, I was at the Biltmore with Tobin and the dozen or so people who made up the Labor Committee staff. We had a great dinner of shrimp cocktail, huge steaks, and Cuban cigars to reinforce our feelings of success and power. After dinner we went up to the chairman's suite to wait for the returns. The party chairman and several New York politicos, including Jim Farley, the Bronx party chief, were getting numbers over the phone and beginning to predict the state outcomes. Through the dense cigar smoke I had a tough time making out the numbers as they were posted on a blackboard. The research director of the Teamsters explained to me how they could call the election once returns came in from key counties in each state: "That's all they're waiting for. Once they are in, they will call the election." Who were these men in this smoke-filled room? I wondered. I had never seen them in the day-to-day campaigning and now they seemed to be taking over.

Tobin shrugged: "Well, we did our job, now the politicians are back." As he left, he promised to see me in Washington at the inauguration. Then,

---

*By the time he reached Manhattan that Saturday, FDR hand endured a four-hour drive through the relentless downpour, refusing to speed up or close the car because people had lined the streets in the expectation of seeing him. That evening, he gave a foreign policy address that contained a ringing endorsement of a United Nations powerful enough to carry on the difficult "enterprise of waging peace."

almost as a parting shot, he warned me to watch out for Lovestone, the red hunter.

On January 20 I attended the inaugural ceremony on the south lawn of the White House, later receiving a handshake from a very tired-looking president. The day ended with an inaugural party thrown by the Teamsters. Everyone seemed aware of how poor the president's health really was, and that put a damper on our celebration. Still, attending the inauguration of the "capitalist president" turned out to be a rewarding experience for me. FDR was an unusual leader and, as other campaign workers will attest, being involved in an election campaign arouses feelings of friendship for the candidate. It felt surprisingly good to be part of the establishment, although I thought my presence on the Democratic Labor Committee was a sort of freaky mistake. Sooner or later, I was sure, my true identity would be revealed and I would be booted out on my ass.

It was obvious from his comment about Lovestone that Tobin knew about my party connection, and it hadn't seemed to matter. When we met at the Mayflower for a good-bye drink, Tobin first talked about how tired and worn FDR looked and predicted that the country was headed for tough times. As a result of his campaign efforts, Tobin had control of a number of patronage appointments, including some judgeships in Minnesota. He apologized for not offering me anything like that but said I should seriously consider an opportunity to be the administrator of Yellowstone National Park. "Out there," he thought, "they" would probably forget about me. "Besides they won't figure on you making much trouble looking after grizzly bears and big trees. Think about it, boy. Once this war is over, it's going to be rough." He was certain that once FDR was gone, the antilabor Wall Street crowd would launch an all-out offensive on New Deal legislation, particularly the Wagner Act.

Yellowstone Park? At the time I hadn't the slightest idea were it was, but it had the ring of a place called Siberia. I told him I would think it over and call him in a few days. Some years later I would have fallen all over myself getting out there.

When I told the party leaders of Tobin's offer they laughed. "Well, of course. That's an easy way to get you out of their hair." But I was sure Tobin was thinking of my best interests. I felt he genuinely cared about me and was expressing real concern for my future. The party leaders thought I was still suffering from bourgeois sentimentality.

Riding high on the tide of our success in the FDR campaign, the Machinists' council hosted a fortieth-anniversary memorial dinner for Harvey Brown, our International president, on March 23. In the spring of 1945 it was clear that the war in Europe would soon be over. If victory over Japan soon followed, there would be serious cutbacks in production and the loss of millions of jobs. Coupled with employers'antilabor sentiments, the effects of the impending victories confronted the labor movement with a serious choice—to accommodate or fight. Our agenda for the Brown dinner was to bring together the progressive forces of the IAM to talk about these issues.

The Hotel New Yorker ballroom was jam-packed with IAM leaders from all over the United States. As the toastmaster, I looked down from the dais at the hundreds of people and wondered what the hell I was doing there. On my left were Senator Claude Pepper of Florida, labor arbitrator Ted Kheel, and William Green, president of the AFL; on the right sat U.S. Army Major General Ulio Harvey Brown and the entire national leadership of the IAM. We received long telegrams of greetings from FDR as well as from Senator Bob Wagner, who was prevented from attending by poor health. With the help of the Federated Press, the council had put together a very slick journal as a tribute to Brown. Of course, it had a message—the need to fight for jobs as part of the peacetime conversion and to maintain friendly relations with the Soviet Union.

Spread out above the podium was a huge banner honoring Brown and the IAM. As we came to the coffee and dessert, I rapped on my coffee cup a couple of times, told a joke, and introduced AFL President Green. The audience was generous with its applause. Senator Pepper, with his impassioned plea for support of the new world peace organization, made the most effective speech of the evening. When he warned the employer organizations not to try to undermine labor's hard-won gains, the crowd was on its feet. Between speakers, folksingers led the audience in a lot of union songs, including the anthem of the labor movement, "Solidarity Forever."

The dinner was a huge success. As this remarkable evening came to an end, people stood around talking about maintaining high employment

during the transition to peacetime production and about the growing antilabor sentiment of a Congress now dominated by conservatives in both
parties. One of the state council officers approached and told me to look
over at table 54 for a surprise. At first I was unable to believe it. But, yes,
there was Papa! Except for his letter after the Moscow trials and a few
brief telephone conversations, we had not seen or talked to each other
since the fracas at the Sunday School camp.

Slowly, I made my way through the crowded ballroom. Papa stood,
his hand-rolled cigarette dangling from his lips, his eyes shining from
welling tears. "Hi, Papa," I said.

He took both my hands and, regarding me with proud approval, said,
"If only your mother could be here to see her little curly-haired Bobby
sitting up there with generals and senators." Embarrassed by his tears,
he was nervously searching his pockets for a handkerchief.

I was glad when someone tapped my arm to remind me of a meeting
of state council presidents. Papa's tears brought back the memory of that
terrible day so many years before. I thanked him for coming and said I
hoped we could see each other again soon. Overcome with emotion, he
nodded his good-bye.

After the election, as Machinists' state council president, I remained deeply
involved in New York State politics. As a result, I was wined, dined, flattered, gifted, and cajoled. I spent very little time as a working machinist. It
was intoxicating, and I hoped it would never end.

The council was focusing all its efforts on the problems of the transition to peacetime production. We made regular trips to Washington with
delegations to present petitions supporting legislation to provide severance pay to laid-off workers. Most of our friends on the Hill considered
the outlook for labor gloomy. Several of them—including senators Pepper, Wagner, and James Mead and congressmen Emanuel Celler, Vito
Marcantonio, and Hugh Delacey—permitted us to use their offices as our
lobbying headquarters.

It was around this time that I got several odd inquiries about the Manhattan Project, ostensibly from party officials. Several machine shops in
the city were involved in what one union business agent told me was a top
secret endeavor to build a "super bomb" as destructive as all the bombs

dropped on Germany since the war began. I said it sounded like "a lot of machine-shop bullshit." In that case, he wanted to know, why was it being kept so secret? He was probably right. The machine shops that built brewing equipment were doing subcontracting work—probably on the uranium-purification process. I had seen big red-lettered signs in those plants: "Restricted Area—Only-Security Approved Personnel Permitted Beyond This Point. Show Your Security Badge At All Times." I took the signs very seriously. I kept out.

The casual questions about the Manhattan Project troubled me. I didn't like to think that the Party was trying to collect information on a top secret weapons project. That would be very different from representing the best interests of the working class. Yet I had met party officials who put the interests of the Soviet Union before anything else. I became so paranoid about the Manhattan Project that I mentally blocked out the names of plants that were probably doing no more than making special piping for uranium purification. Being a communist and fighting for the working class was one thing; "innocently" supplying information to the Russians was something else again.*

On the afternoon of April 12, 1945, Roosevelt died in Warm Springs, Georgia. Just weeks before, he had apologized to a joint session of Congress for sitting down to report on his Yalta meeting with Stalin and Churchill: "It makes it a lot easier for me not having to carry about ten pounds of steel," he said, referring to the iron braces he had worn on his legs for most of his adult life. Until then, the general public was unaware of how difficult it was for the president to walk. Now he no longer seemed to care about concealing his real condition from the citizens.

In his report on the agreements reached in the Crimea, he expressed profound sympathy for the sacrifices of the Russian nation. Forty to fifty million people were dead and two-thirds of their country's industrial base was in ruins. He was emphatic in his desire to see a postwar continuation of our collaboration with the Russians.

---

*My FBI file indicates that the bureau alerted the local field office to the fact that many machine shops I had access to were involved in "highly classified work."

The day after FDR died, I awoke with a feeling of great uncertainty. In my overwhelming grief, I realized how much I had come to care about this man. Our great leader was dead. Would things just go on as though nothing had happened? As my daughter Lizzie and I had our very same, everyday breakfast, the radio played dirge music, reported worldwide reactions to the president's death, and assessed his contributions.

Historians may consider his leadership of the war against fascism his major achievement. The FDR legacy I remember is his empowerment of working people: through public works programs that gave the millions of unemployed a new hope; through the Wagner Act, which resulted in a growth in union membership from 1.5 to 14 million workers and incomes that rose from an average of $18 to $43 weekly; through the Social Security Act, which gave many working people economic security in their old age; and through rural electrification, which forever changed life in rural America. In my editorial for the *IAM Beacon* I wrote, in part,

We have lost our *best* friend. Workingmen and women everywhere regarded Franklin D. Roosevelt as their champion. . . . To him we owe most of the social and labor legislation on the statute books: the Wagner Act, unemployment insurance, social security, public works, minimum wage legislation. . . .

He died with his work unfinished. But he left us a program. The Economic Bill of Rights . . . 60 million new jobs at decent wages. . . . Every local should immediately contact all Congressmen and state legislators and let them know that we stand solidly behind FDR's program.

That morning as I walked to the union office on 84th Street still in tears, I was startled to find that life seemed to be going on the same as always. The subways, buses, cars, and traffic lights all worked as if nothing was changed. Damn it, I thought, don't they know that our leader, our hope, has died? Why haven't things come to a crashing halt? On the subways, in the street, people were troubled. Some cried openly, others just looked at each other and shook their heads in disbelief. Yet everything seemed to move normally, as if, yes, it was a sad day, but we have to go on with our various routines—check the mail, have coffee, answer the phones, go to another meeting. Watching people's reactions to this important death was a terribly important learning experience for me. Individual leaders may be important to causes and countries, but in our everyday lives no one person seems to be of much consequence.

For a time after FDR's death, politics as usual seemed to be on hold. It was if we all paused to see what would happen next. Or was it just a period of national grieving?

That April, two weeks after the president's death, I was asked to speak at a Carnegie Hall rally in support of the United Nations. I have never forgotten the miracle of the acoustics that sent my unamplified voice into every corner of that great hall. Thanks to the FBI, I have a full copy of my speech. In the final summary, I said that the best assurance of world peace was a continuation of the wartime collaboration between the United States and the USSR. To this end, I argued that we should heartily support President Truman and the new United Nations.

The report on my Carnegie Hall speech was the first of many similar accounts of "subversive" actions in my FBI file. From then on I was under strict surveillance. It looks as if J. Edgar Hoover knew, long before anyone else, where we were heading. Or was he helping shape the future? I wasn't saying or doing anything subversive or in any way inflammatory, but it didn't matter. The mere fact that I was under surveillance suggested that anything I said or did could be viewed as suspicious.

A few weeks after Truman became president we heard the wonderful news of the allied victory in the war against German fascism. The Left clung to a slim hope that he would carry on in the FDR tradition of friendly relations with the Soviet Union. Truman was a product of the Missouri Democratic Pendergast machine, which was considered as corrupt as any big city political machine. I associated him with the Hannegan crowd that had occupied so much space at the Biltmore during the campaign but had done so little to reelect Roosevelt.

We were treated to pictures of joyous American and Russian soldiers meeting on the banks of the Elbe River, the ruins of the Berlin bunker where Hitler and Eva Braun had destroyed themselves, and the final Nazi surrender on May 8.

There was a spontaneous outpouring of joy in the land. The scenes in Times Square, where strangers sang, danced, and hugged each other, were a reflection of what was happening everywhere across the country. The war in Europe was over. Good had triumphed over the evil plague of fascism. The Allies—that strange alliance of capitalists and socialists—had rid the world of a terrible nightmare.

When the newsreels and pictures of the Nazi atrocities began to arrive, I reacted, like everyone else, with shock and disbelief. We simply were not prepared for the visual evidence of those inhuman acts. There had been other holocausts in history—though not on this scale—but people had never before had to look at anything like those scenes of horror at the extermination camps. The evidence of the movies and still photographs went far beyond anything we could have conceived in our worst nightmares.

Papa was devastated. From Nazism's inception, he had never wavered in his firm conviction of its evil character. Yet even he had not foreseen the barbarism the Allies' cameras exposed to the world. Whatever pride or faith he had left in the Germany of Goethe, Schiller, Heine, Beethoven, Marx, and Liebknecht died in those grisly revelations. From then on, Papa retreated into his own private world. He began to paint pictures of bucolic nature, spending most of the rest of his life in the scenes he created with canvas and oils.

As I looked into the face of the Holocaust, I experienced a profound sense of shame—shame that our world had not known or, knowing, had done so little to help the victims. Early in the war I had not believed all our own war propaganda. The radical Germans I grew up with recalled clearly the well-oiled propaganda machines of World War I. Papa told us how the press in Britain had concocted stories of German soldiers eating Belgian babies, and how the Hearst press and other American newspapers passed on the stories.

Radicals like Papa saw the propaganda as designed solely to recruit young men to be slaughtered in the name of one or another greedy imperialist nation, and, as a result, he embraced pacifism. That was why the novel and film *All Quiet on the Western Front* became our Bible. Having grown up in this fiercely antiwar atmosphere, I had suspected that some of the horror stories about the Nazis were nothing but good-old wartime propaganda. This may partly explain the shock many of us experienced when we saw pictures of the real thing. But suppose there had been no pictorial records from Auschwitz and the other camps? Would we have believed that so many people had perished there? Might we have thought the accounts were nothing but wartime propaganda?

Three months after the end of the war in Europe, Truman decided to drop the atomic bomb on Hiroshima and Nagasaki, ending the war in the Pacific in a few days in August. The bomb had a chilling effect on those of us still dreaming of a postwar brotherhood of wartime allies. On the Left, the dream dissipated rapidly in face of our belief that the United States had dropped the bomb as much to impress the Russians as to defeat the Japanese. Truman, it turned out, was not just another nice clubhouse politician.

On the evening of my 28th birthday in October I was told to attend an important meeting at the Manhattan Center. When I arrived I was pleasantly surprised to be welcomed by hundreds of our local union members singing, "Happy birthday to you." It was a happy occasion. We were celebrating our victory over fascism, and the depression was behind us. In the months ahead, many of the veterans at the party would return to school under the GI Bill—the Readjustment Act of 1944—to become doctors, lawyers, engineers, accountants, psychologists, and so on.

The biggest surprise at the party was the presence of Marcel Camus, president of the Machinists' Union for metropolitan Paris. We had corresponded but had never met before. He was a handsome young man with a winning little smile and very gentle eyes. Even though he spoke in French and we heard his words through a translator, he radiated a kind of warmth that easily won over the meeting.

Camus described the many problems they were having rebuilding the union, but he was most concerned over the plight of the Maquis. These independent fighters, who had led the Resistance against the fascists, were in desperate need of our help. He told me privately that many of the Maquis were communists and that the French government was pursuing an intentional policy of starving them out of existence. I assured him of my commitment to the international solidarity of metal workers and asked him to send me a letter on union stationery requesting our help. The letter, which arrived a short time later, ended with the words "We are desperate. Please send help."

I called on many union officials for help, including a well-known mobster who was head of the New York Longshoremen. "See Schrank," he said to me, "sooner or later everyone needs a favor. You get one 'cause we owe you one." I was puzzled. He went on, "When the DA's office was asking questions about us you refused to get cozy with them. That gets you points."

"How the hell do you know that?"

"Listen boy, we know everything."

He gave me a thousand bucks. In a short time, I collected five thousand dollars to send to Camus. For months afterwards, we received letters from ordinary French machinists expressing their heartfelt thanks for "saving our lives." Some years later when I went to Paris I was wined and dined by the Metal Workers Union in appreciation of our help to the Maquis.

In November of 1945 the 21st International Convention of the Machinists Union brought about eight hundred delegates from every state to New York City. After the Brown dinner in the spring, the state council presidents from Ohio, Illinois, and Missouri, Joe Cronin of the New England council, a number local presidents, and I, as New York council president, had met to plan strategy for the convention. We considered ourselves the true representatives of the Machinist rank and file and saw the national leaders as nice, tired old men who lacked the will to put up a real fight. It was us against the bureaucrats. As we talked, we became excited by the possibility that we had enough votes to win on some of the important issues. Someone said, "Hell, we might control the whole damn convention!"

The night before the convention, I also had to meet with the half dozen party members in the IAM to discuss our strategy. Jack, the same chain-smoking and constantly blinking comrade I had met after the flying-squad fiasco, was the Party's official trade union representative. He would hole up at a hotel for the duration to be available for day-to-day discussions of the proceedings and to advise comrades on which resolutions to support, oppose, or ignore. This was standard party practice at union conventions and meetings of any importance.

At this convention, the little party caucus concentrated on a couple of resolutions on international affairs. One, which was severely critical of the lack of democracy in the new Romanian communist government, was obviously a set-up. I and the other union comrades thought we should just ignore it.

It was not at all unusual for bitter arguments to erupt between the comrade participants and the party reps. In this case, Jack lectured us on the importance of defending the new socialist countries, especially during this period of transition. We Machinists argued as vigorously as we could for ignoring the resolution because "it's obviously a fucking set-up and we shouldn't take the bait." It was of no avail. Finally, in exasperation, a comrade from Ohio said, "You want us to behave like lemmings? Okay we will." It was a prophetic statement.

For the next few days things went smoothly as the convention carried out its routine union business. The success of our emerging state council alliance was beginning to show up in winning votes. We were able to deliver block votes to defeat the International's effort to increase the per capita tax—the portion of the membership dues that goes to the International Union—and had prepared several resolutions dealing with severance pay for workers in the war industries. These resolutions spelled out a series of steps the leadership would be required to take in support of members subject to layoffs.

Nobody in the council group wanted to get tangled up in this Romania business. There had been a quick shift in the political winds. A few months back we were all celebrating the Allies' victory, but now the Russians and East Europeans were emerging as the new enemy. Just before the resolution calling for free elections in Romania was scheduled to come up on the convention floor, I tried to convince other state council presidents that "this resolution is a slap at the whole idea of the new United Nations, and we should oppose it."

Joe Cronin, president of the New England council, looked at me with his quizzical smile and wanted to know if I was kidding. "Why not just forget it?" he said. "If their life depended on it, most guys in this union couldn't locate Romania on a map." He paused, laughing. "Come to think of it, I don't know if I could myself. Where is it Schrank?"

IAM vice president Roy Brown had bragged that he was going, "to smoke out the commie rats." Now, "the commie rat catcher" was strutting back and forth across the stage looking out over the convention floor to see who would bite the bait. There was a lot of parliamentary maneuvering on the Romania issue: motions to table it, lay it over, refer it back, and so on. The delegates were restless and couldn't figure out what

was going on. One delegate at the mike asked, "With all the layoff problems we got, who gives a fuck about Romania?" He brought down the
house.

It's hard to explain why I went along with the Party on this issue, other
than to say that I simply didn't trust my own judgment. In spite of the
severe doubts that were sticking in my guts and giving me a headache, I
asked for the floor. Assuming I would speak against the resolution,
Brown was very solicitous in yielding it to me. He was mistaken. I introduced an amendment calling for democratic elections in all countries.
It was seconded, but Brown ruled it out of order on the grounds that it
was contrary to the resolution. I appealed the ruling of the chair.

While the appeal was being voted, Howard, who was at the press table
representing Federated Press, handed me a note. It read: "There are two
FBI agents in the balcony on your right." He had heard some of the reporters at the press table talking about them and wondering why they
were there.

I shouted, "Brother Chairman, point of order! Would you please direct
those two men up in the balcony to identify themselves as members of this
union as required by the constitution." The two guys I pointed to immediately got up and started running, and Brown instructed the sergeant at
arms to determine whether they were entitled to be in the hall. In the
meantime, I was telling the delegates that the men were FBI agents invited
here by the leaders of this union to spy on the activities of its own members. Delegates were yelling, "Throw the bums out."

The sergeant at arms reported that he was unable to identify them before they fled the hall. Nonetheless, the uninvited presence of the FBI
agents was clearly resented by the delegates and worked to our benefit.
My appeal of Brown's decision on my amendment carried, and it was put
before the delegates. To the deep chagrin of the leadership, we won.

The FBI incident was reported in the press and had J. Edgar Hoover
ripping mad. Many pages in my FBI file are devoted to trying to find out
who had assigned the agents to the convention and why they weren't
given proper identification. More important, I think he was pissed because the press reported the Keystone Cops scene at the convention—the
agents sprinting out of the hall with the sergeant at arms in hot pursuit.
Some time later we learned their identity.

We won the amendment, but I still I felt as if we were lemmings going over the cliff. Joe Cronin said, "Okay, are you happy now? Can we get on with the serious convention business?" I suspected we had won some kind of an absurd victory that would come back to haunt us. The party rep was happy, because he could announce to party leaders that another anti-Soviet attack had been turned back.

A major part of these union conventions were the long nights of drinking, eating, telling dirty jokes, cigar smoking, and—for—some brothers, whoring. Most of the convention delegates worked in factories and had few opportunities to be away from home on their own. The sudden freedom of being out of town had some brothers behaving as if they were Hollywood playboys out for a night of fun.

Late one night near the end of the convention I was getting ready to call it quits when there was a knock at the door of my hotel room. It was an obviously very troubled comrade who looked as though he had lost his best friend. At first he was silent. Then, slowly, he said he couldn't belong to the Party any longer. His first loyalty was to the union. After watching the fiasco over the Romania resolution, he had decided he couldn't accept any more directives from the Party. I asked him, "What about socialism?" He said he couldn't think in terms of a great ideal that was so far off in the future; he believed that the most we could do was to improve things in the present, as we were doing in the union.

A part of me wanted to do the same thing, but, I told him, another part of me refused to give up on the dream of socialism. We shook hands and agreed to remain friends, which we did. It was hard for me to believe that he did not have to pay the price of some informing as a mea culpa for his past sins. But as the FBI file showed, it didn't matter. With the help of Jay Lovestone, I was sure Hoover knew the identity of all party members. Years later Lovestone became head of the AFL's international department. The idea of leaving the Party always scared me, because I knew that "getting clean" meant informing. For me, that was beyond the realm of possibility.

13

Strange Union Business

It was during this time at the end of the war that I remember receiving a strange telephone call. In those days, union officials were often called upon to do things that would now be considered far outside their normal responsibilities. It was a warm, sleepy afternoon in that lull between lunch-hour plant visits and after-work meetings. I was at my desk in the 84th Street office of our local when the secretary announced that someone from the Queens district attorney's office wanted to speak with the local president. My paranoid response was, "Christ, what the hell did we do now?"

"No" she said, "It's not another investigation of union crooks. The DA says it has to do with one of our members and a statutory rape charge."

"So what does he expect us to do? Reverse the action?"

She laughed, "I bet you know how to do that."

An assistant DA informed me that one Victor Rosario, a member of our local, was under arrest. At two o'clock in the morning a police officer had caught him screwing a girl in the back seat of a parked car. What, I asked him, does this have to do with the union?

"The girl, Magda, is sixteen." He paused. "With a pair of tits that would make your twenty-five-year-old cousin jealous." Rosario, he explained, was a seventeen-year-old Puerto Rican kid "who doesn't know a soul in this country who gives a shit about him. Under state law he's gonna do time. Don't matter if she begged him to fuck her. The law has no forgiveness. She's under age. You fuck her, you go to jail."

"So, why are you telling me all this?"

When Rosario and his girlfriend were at the station house being booked, the poor kid had kept flashing his union membership card. "He really thinks it's gonna get him off. Can you believe this? I was trying to explain the statutory rape law to this poor illiterate Puerto Rican, but he just but kept saying, 'It is not rape because she liked it very much.' Magda just stood there nodding her head in agreement."

"Look," he went on, "he's a nice kid without a record. We don't really want to send him up. It'll just make another nice dumb kid into a hardened criminal. He has no one but his union, and he trusts you guys. How about coming down here, and we'll see if we can figure out something to keep him out of the can?"

I found Rosario awaiting arraignment in a holding pen at the Queens County courthouse. He greeted me with a big hug like a long-lost brother. He was a handsome young man of medium height whose brown eyes and big smile reflected a perpetual sense of delight in the world around him. He was a lovable innocent. It was easy to see how even a hardened DA might be taken with him.

I didn't recognize him, but he said he got his job through the union local and reminded me that he had been in a tough strike at the Benson Machine Company in Maspeth, Queens. The owner's grand scheme for keeping out the union was to buy plane tickets for Puerto Ricans to come and work in his factory; he then put them up in his own boarding house conveniently close to the plant and proceeded to deduct the cost of both the plane fare and room rent from their paychecks.

The payroll deductions were illegal, and the boarding house proved to be his undoing. We turned it into our union organizing headquarters. It was Rosario who had convinced his countrymen that Benson was, "Out to screw us good. So now we fuck him with this union." I remembered him as a impatient kid who every day of the strike wanted to "burn up some trucks, is easy, then we win strike."

When the newly organized union threatened a strike, Benson had tried to evict the worker-tenants, but we stopped him in the housing court and used his boarding house as strike headquarters. With a place to live and all the ingredients for *arroz con pollo* (chicken, rice, and beans), the strikers figured they could stay out forever. We won the strike, and the plant was unionized—though we didn't burn any trucks.

Now here he was, a union brother in trouble. Regardless of the right or wrong of it, we had to help out any way we could. The assistant DA urged me to come up with some kind of workable scheme that would convince the judge to go along with it. "That won't be easy, because the stupid statute has a mandatory sentence." The DA said he would talk with his boss and the judge to see if they could come up with something.

As we were leaving, Rosario laughed and said to the DA, nodding toward me, "My presidente, he's gonna fix. You see, he is mucho big man."

A few days later, the DA telephoned to say that he could keep Rosario out of jail if he and Magda were married "retroactively." He paused, "Hell, there's nothing illegal about a married couple humpin' in the back seat of their car."

My job, he said, was "to convince big titties Magda. There's no way we can do that out of this office without getting into trouble. Christ, we're already far out on a limb as it is. So what do you say?"

"But suppose she doesn't want to. She's only sixteen. Is this a good idea?" There was a long moment of silence.

"Well, I don't know if it's a good idea or not, but it's either that or your Puerto Rican brother is lookin at doin' time. So you decide."

At Magda's address in Queens, Magda's mother, a plumpish, round-faced woman, answered the door. They lived in a small one-bedroom walk-up. When I told her who I was and that her daughter's friend Rosario was a member of our union local, she didn't seem upset by the mention of his name. She politely got me a cup of coffee and went to fetch Magda from the bedroom.

Meeting Magda confirmed the assistant DA's observations. She was about five feet five and round all over. She was wearing a tight blouse that left at least half of her breasts out for show and tell. She was certainly proud of them, and I thought, Well, why not? It's better for Rosario that way. Just looking at her, who wouldn't want to fuck her? That, of course, was not the issue. So where to begin?

When I questioned her about Rosario, the girl told me she had met him the previous summer at a picnic at Reiss Park. Lots of Puerto Ricans were there singing and dancing. She threw back her shoulder-length hair, and a smile lit up her face as she remembered. "There was this boy, playing the guitar and singing. He was having such a good time that I just fell in love with him, right then and there."

Her mother interrupted, "You see how it is with her? She sees some good lookin' guy and, bingo, she's in love. She's been like that since she was twelve. Can you believe it?"

She went on without waiting for an answer. "We've been lucky that with all her bouncing in the back seats of cars—that's her favorite place—she didn't get knocked up." She stopped quickly. "Excuse me," she says, "I mean get pregnant." I assured her I knew what she meant.

Everything seemed to be going just fine, so I made my pitch: "Since the two of you are a couple of love birds, why not be married and live happily ever after?"

Magda seemed to like the way "being married" sounded. Not realizing that they had met, I was relieved when the mother too said she liked Victor but was concerned about how he was going to support Magda.

I had become so obsessed with keeping Rosario out of jail that I lied a bit about his good job at the Benson Machine Company and his good union wages. That was at least partly true, if you considered a buck over the minimum a good wage.

To my delight, Magda had already moved on to wondering about a wedding dress. "I ain't gonna get married in my regular street clothes. For marryin', you gotta have a gown." Her mother chimed in with "and we ain't got the kind of money for stuff like that." I hadn't the slightest idea how, but I assured them that somehow she would have her wedding dress.

Lying a bit more, I told them it would be a great honor to be married by a judge in his courtroom. Her mother, though, said she would have preferred a church and added as a sudden afterthought, "By the way, is he Catholic?"

"Of course," I said, "aren't all Puerto Ricans?"

Feeling jubilant that my mission was accomplished, I headed for the nearest telephone to tell the assistant DA of our success. He agreed to speak with the judge and, if he consented, to fix a date for the ceremony as soon as possible, before anyone in the legal system found out what we were up to.

The wedding gown problem he left to me, but it was soon solved. Some of our union sisters, intrigued with the romantic challenge of a young girl in love with a brother but too poor to buy a wedding gown, were almost

Bobby with Papa in Bronx Park, 1923. Our family was part of New York's large radical community of socialists, anarchists, and freethinkers. Not long before this photo was taken, Papa, an immigrant from Mannheim, Germany, was blacklisted for his work in helping found the Amalgamated Clothing Workers' Union.

With Edith and Nine-month-old Elizabeth, 1942. Edith, a model and dancer in a WPA theater, later became an accomplished musician and teacher. In the 1930s when our relationship began, the revolution was my first love and I held to the Marxist notion that marriage was a "bourgeois ritual" invented by capitalists to provide workers for the factories.

New York State Council (IAM) Officers Review Tribute to Retiring International President Harvey Brown, March 1945. We put together a very slick journal for the dinner in Brown's honor. It emphasized the need to fight for jobs during peacetime conversion while maintaining friendly postwar relations with the Soviet Union. (Front row, l. to r.: Council Vice President Paul Kessler, Rochester; Secretary-Treasurer Harold Fitzgibbons, Buffalo; President Robert Schrank; and Vice President Reginald Newell, Buffalo. Second row, l. to r.: Vice Presidents Robert Hanson, Jamestown; Joseph Bernard, Plattsburgh; and William O'Brien, Elmira; Legislative Director Erick Witzke, New York City; and Educational Director Fred Swick, New York City.)

Conducting Union Leadership Training, April 1945. During the war, heavy demands for production in the metal trades provided rich opportunities for unionization. As president of local 402 of the International Association of Machinists (IAM), I and other lefties in the unions pursued a very militant policy emphasizing the class struggle. Membership grew by leaps and bounds. *(Photograph by Joseph Strul)*

The Stamford, Conn., General Strike, 1945. An opening shot in the postwar anti-union war was fired by the Yale & Towne Manufacturing Company, which simply refused to bargain, even though the IAM local had been certified as the workers' bargaining agent by the National Labor Relations Board. After a long strike, the local aroused support for Yale & Towne workers by successfully organizing a general strike that shut down the city for an entire day. *(Seaf Photo Service, Stamford, Conn.)*

Remington Rand Strike Meeting, Elmira, N.Y., May 1947. Lack of access to a local meeting hall lent a holiday atmosphere to early strike meetings at Dunn Field, home of the local bush-league ball club. But as payless paydays accumulated, the strike slipped into the doldrums and the company started sneaking women strike-breakers into the plant—until local members devised a unique way to discourage the "scabs."

Back Cover of Pamplet "This Is Aimed at You!: An Exposé of the Taft-Harley Plot to Bust the Unions and Hijack the American People," by Robert Schrank. (*New York State Council of the International Association of Machinists, Robert Schrank, president, 1948.*)

Speaking in the Miners Hall, Butte, 1954. In the longest, coldest winter of my life I worked to reorganize and restore the Montana local of the Mine Mill and Smelter Workers' Union, which had been taken over by the Steelworkers' Union. What did I know about Rocky Mountain hard-rock miners? Nothing! *(Photograph by C. Owen Smithers, Butte)*

March to Take Back the Union Hall, Butte, 1954. The peaceful restoration of the hall, which had been taken over by the Steelworkers, symbolized Mine Mill's renewed strength and unity. It was a turning point in our efforts to win back the copper miners. *(Photograph by C. Owen Smithers, Butte; reprinted from* Life *magazine)*

Celebrating the Victory: Mine Mill Convention, Denver, 1954. Although Mine Mill had won the Montana election, there was a general acknowledgment that Mine Mill's militant tradition was past. A short time later, the union ceased to exist as an independent organization and was absorbed into the Steelworkers.

in tears over her plight. If I produced Magda, they promised, they would make the gown. Happy with all the attention, Magda showed up with bells on. By piecing together parts of several old dresses, the women created a lovely white wedding gown and showed it off proudly. A few even attended the wedding in the judge's chambers, where he solemnly declared Victor and Magda man and wife and so made the illegitimate copulation legal. Rosario gave me a big hug and said something in Spanish that I think meant, "You will be my best friend forever."

A few years later I encountered Rosario at a Benson Machine Company union picnic. There he was, smiling, laughing, and playing his guitar left handed while he sang songs of lust, love, and beauty. Since I played guitar I could not believe what he was doing; he had not even reversed the strings as left-handed players usually do. Being completely self-taught, he didn't know there was any other way to do it.

In a break from his entertaining, we walked away from the crowd. He confided that his life was "just wonderful. Look, I live in their house with both of them." He winked at me happily, laughing. "The mother is much better than the wife, so, me, I am very much tired. But is wonderful. You are great man. Some day, you see, I do something for you. *Muchas gracias, amigo.*"

War production was grinding down and, as Dan Tobin had predicted, the unions were confronted with an all-out effort by a conservative Congress to undermine the gains labor had made in the last decade. The National Association of Manufacturers (NAM) and the U.S. Chamber of Commerce were loudly proclaiming that the Wagner Act and the war emergency wage and price controls had tipped the labor-management scale heavily in labor's favor. The time had come, they said, to "even the playing field." A wave of strikes in late 1945 in the steel and automotive industries was followed in early 1946 by deadlocks in negotiations in the coal and railway industries resolved only by threat of federal intervention. Newspaper headlines fueled the belief of a war-weary public that the widespread labor strife was the result of the unions' excessive power.

The result was the introduction of a slew of antilabor bills in Congress. The Machinists' union, facing the layoff of thousands of members, was a major supporter of severance-pay legislation to ease the burden of transition on laid-off workers. It all added up to a big fight ahead in Congress and kept the state council busy holding rallies all over the state, getting people on record in opposition to the antilabor legislation, and sending lobbying delegations to Washington.

Just as serious was the antilabor crusade employers were launching at the individual plant level. Without the War Labor Board to serve as the final arbiter of disputes, and with the premature end of effective wage and price controls, employers figured it was a good time to take on the unions. In the Northeast, the opening shot in the antiunion war was fired by the Yale & Towne Manufacturing Company of Stamford, Connecticut, in the late fall of 1945. They simply refused to bargain or to even continue to recognize the IAM or any other union. Years earlier, the IAM had won an election and had been certified by the NLRB as the workers' bargaining agent. The local at Yale & Towne, faced with the company's refusal to negotiate, had no alternative but to strike to defend the workers' right to be represented by a union of their choice.

Week after week, around the clock, picketing kept the old classic red brick factory in Stamford shut tight. Joe Cronin, president of the New England Council of Machinists, Joe Ficaro, president of the Yale & Towne local, and I spent many hours figuring out ways to build support for the strikers. We picketed the company's New York offices, started a boycott of Yale locks, and tried desperately to get the building-trades unions to refuse to install Yale products. The latter effort failed completely, for the Machinists and the building-trades unions, particularly the Carpenters, had a long history of jurisdictional disputes. There was no such thing as solidarity when it came to the old craft unions defending what they believed was their turf. Sadly, the craftsmen were being wiped out by technology but did not want to believe it.

The strike had been on for six weeks and it was nearly Christmas when Joe called to say the strikers' morale was slipping. "We gotta do something. Some people are beginning to talk about returning to work."

That night I drove up to Stamford and walked around the plant with the two Joes. In the cold, dark night, with the strikers huddled around oil-drum fires, it was like a scene from a medieval crusade. The strikers spoke of their fears of a giftless, hungry Christmas for their families: "The kids would never understand, and the wives are beginning to get discouraged. We gotta do something. We can't just stay out here forever," they pleaded with us.

The two Joes and I sat in a bar for what seemed like hours, going over every possible option. We agreed to do two things. First, with Christmas close at hand, our priority was to get enough food to strike headquarters so that not one family missed a single meal. We decided to rent a couple of trucks and ask union locals in New York and New England to start collecting food for what we now called the union's life-and-death struggle. Union members across the region were totally committed to winning this strike, for they recognized its importance for the labor movement as a whole. Second, we agreed on the need to create a crisis big enough to force Connecticut's governor to act. That would mean sending in the National Guard and would, I hoped, lead to an arbitrated settlement.

In addition to the food drive, we launched a major effort to collect toys for the kids. We were very successful in both endeavors. The Christmas party in Stamford was a great morale booster, and every child received at least one nice gift. The gifts from union locals all over the New England and New York areas demonstrated union solidarity at its best. Edith, after giving up the theater for motherhood, had transferred her talents into organizing children's parties. She arrived with her guitar and a sack full of instruments for the children to play and for a whole afternoon led the strikers and their families in an enthusiastic singalong. By the end of the afternoon we all felt good enough to cope with anything Yale & Towne might throw at us.

Driving back to New York on U.S. 1, I kept wondering how we could shake up the situation. Picket lines that go on with no end in sight tend to become routine and often end up in back-to-work talk. The Stamford Machinists were basically nice peace-loving folk. When company trucks began to slip in and out of the plant, I suggested that we might have to get a little rough with the scabs. This surprised some of the strike committeemen, who sternly reminded me that they were law-abiding citizens. After the meeting, though, a couple of brothers took me aside and said they understood what I was talking about; all they needed was some guys to get the rough stuff started and they would sure as hell join in.

Thinking over this comment, I asked myself who knew about rough stuff? Of course, I remembered, Marc would know exactly what to do.

Marc was Vito Marcantonio, our liberal congressman from East Harlem and Fiorello La Guardia's old law partner. I used to think of him as the Italian prince of 116th Street or the don of East Harlem. For most of my years as local president, the plant I worked in was at 106th Street and First Avenue, in Marc's district. Periodically he would call to ask a favor, usually for some guy who needed a job. Marcantonio had a great way of speaking that made you feel he was just another old friend, and we had occasionally run into each other at meetings protesting or demanding one thing or another. After getting a few of his needy friends jobs, I learned that they were in jail upstate awaiting probation, for which they needed a promise of employment. Of the many companies we had under contract, there were one or two I could touch for such a letter of promised employment.

One of these was a machine company located in what is now called SoHo. The owner, a little wiry German who had invented some bombsight instruments before the war, hated unions. He thought they made people lazy and believed that anyone who was willing to work could be as successful as he was. After we organized his company, I had become friendly with his son, who made sure to let me know that he too was a Marxist and was sympathetic to everything I stood for. He was extremely helpful in supplying employment references as well as promises of a job for those in need—especially for some of Marc's friends.

When these men got out of jail, their first stop was the union office to pick up the card for the promised job. What were they doing time for? I wondered. I knew it wasn't for union organizing. After many beers and a lot of bullshit, they admitted to being collectors, soldiers, or "wheelmen" for one or another of the crime families. How did they know Marc? They didn't, but "the boss" did. I realized then that Marcantonio had many different kinds of connections and that one of them might help me with the Yale & Towne problem.

So I called him and said I needed a favor but would rather not talk on the telephone. When we met in his headquarters, I explained about the picket line. Would it be possible to get a few guys up to Stamford to push some scabs around? Maybe send a few to the hospital. "But for Christ sake, don't let them kill anybody or we'll all be in deep, deep shit."

His coolness was scary. "Just give me the details, exactly where and at what time. The rest will be taken care of."

A few days later the newspapers reported a small riot at the strike-bound Yale & Towne plant in Stamford, Connecticut. Seven local union members and one international union representative were arrested for disturbing the peace. During the "disturbance" at the plant loading dock, none of the "New York toughs"—as the locals called them—were caught, but their mission was accomplished. The strike was back on the front pages, and Governor Baldwin, acting to curb the threat of continuing disorder, dispatched a company of state troopers to Stamford to keep the peace.

Over the years, I continued to provide employment for Marcantonio's friends.

A visit to the picket line a few days later brought many laughs and a lot of "thanks for the help of our New York brothers." Support for the strike was at its peak, but it didn't matter to Yale & Towne. The company remained adamant, refusing even to meet with the union. I agreed with the two Joes that we were at a turning point, but I wasn't sure what we should do. They were both convinced that the strikers could not hold out much longer.

A few days later we were sitting in a bar. Our talk was taking on an increasing air of desperation—reflected in assorted fantasies of blowing up City Hall, kidnapping the chairman of the board, or torching the plant. Sometime late in our reveries, someone said, "Why don't we call a general strike in support of the Yale & Towne strikers?" What a great idea! But how would we pull it off?

Stamford had two citywide labor councils—the AFL, representing the traditional conservative, craft unions, and the new, more militant unions in the CIO council. The Machinists' local was affiliated with the AFL council. Cronin believed that the CIO could be fairly easily convinced to support a one- or two-day general strike, but that our problem would come in convincing the "old farts" in the AFL. Ficaro, thinking out loud, mentioned that both councils met on the same night, the first Wednesday of the month. With this coincidence in mind, we cooked up the following scheme.

Cronin would go to the AFL council meeting and tell them that the CIO council had voted to support a one- or two-day general strike in support of the Yale & Towne strikers if the AFL council agreed to join it.

Simultaneously, Ficaro and I would be at the CIO council telling them the same story. It was a simple matter of daring one group to be tougher than the other. Admittedly, it was a long shot, but it just might work.

When we met at the bar after the Wednesday meetings, we were delighted. My God, it had worked! Each of the labor councils had appointed five members to a general strike committee, which would meet the following day to lay the plans for a one-day work stoppage.

In 1946 Stamford was an industrial factory town, and its unionized workers were eager to show off their strength and demonstrate to the public the importance of their work. The utility workers were even itching to shut down the generators just so that people would recognize what they did, but the strike committee hung tough: there would be no power stoppage. The general strike, they insisted, must be handled responsibly. The committee also had to spend a lot of time convincing hospital employees, milkmen who delivered to hospitals, food suppliers for the sick and elderly, and others eager to join the strike to stay on the job.

Mayor Moore, who was anxious to cooperate with his blue-collar constituents, gave over the City Hall as headquarters for the general strike committee and agreed to let the committee maintain law and order during the strike. As a consequence, World War II union veterans in their uniforms were set up as a policing committee to take charge of all patrol functions.

The strike was set for the start of the workday on January 3, 1946. The night before the strike found all of us peering over maps and making final preparations. The veterans' patrols were deciding which roads would stay open and which ones would be closed, giving the strike the appearance of a military operation. Great care was taken to ensure that emergency vehicles would receive right of way. Here was a real payoff for the veterans' military experience. For the first time, I was able to see the relevance of military training to a workers' revolution.

The City Hall strike headquarters was crowded with people from all the different unions making signs and preparing packets of materials for the press. The strike committee was going over the last-minute details of who would work and who would not. With adrenaline flooding our bodies, sleep was out of the question, and while we worked the night faded into morning. The dawn of the worker's revolution, I thought, would feel like this. For me, the general strike felt like a rehearsal on the road to social-ism. Here was the working class, the producers of all wealth, in charge of their own existence. The scene at strike headquarters reminded me of a song we used to sing at Sunday School, the "Commonwealth of Toil."

When our cause is all triumphant
And we claim our Mother Earth,
And the nightmare of the present fades away,
We shall live with Love and Laughter,
We, who now are little worth,
And we'll not regret the price we have to pay.

But we have a glowing dream
Of how fair the world will seem
When each man can live his life secure and free;
When the earth is owned by Labor
And there's joy and peace for all
In the Commonwealth of Toil that is to be.

As the day of the strike dawned, nothing moved. No clocks were punched, and there was an eerie feeling in the air. As the city came to life, people began to gather in small groups along Main Street. Friends and strangers were shaking hands, congratulating each other on their great vic-tory. I kept hearing comments like "We showed 'em, didn't we though?" "They never believed we could do it." The day turned into a joyous cele-bration of working-class strength and dignity.

By afternoon the square in front of City Hall was packed for the meet-ing. Speaker after speaker denounced Yale & Towne for its union-bust-ing. I spoke about how we had won the war against fascism in Europe and were now faced with an employers' war against the unions here at home. "Today is just the beginning of our response," I promised. In my best street corner style, I paused, looked out at the crowd, and said, "If the employers and the manufacturers' association don't believe we will defend our hard-won rights, what is happening here today is just a little dress rehearsal. For if they keep up their antilabor drive, the next step will be a general strike across the state of Connecticut and, with Joe Cronin's help, right up into the rest of New England." The crowd went wild, yelling "Strike, strike, shut 'em down."

The meeting over, people returned home jubilant, uplifted and proud of what they had accomplished. Workers on the night shift went back to

work. The general strike was over. I was criticized by the IAM representative for being too provocative. "This is not a class war," he said. "We
believe in living together, not killing each other."

"Yes," I said, "and that's why the leadership of the AFL has always
opposed the use of the general strike. It is far too empowering for the
workers." My God, I thought, how right the IWW was when it argued
against military revolution à la 1917 Russia. It believed workers' control
could be achieved by workers simply "downing their tools" and letting
the system grind to a halt. What happened in Stamford that one day
made me think that maybe the IWW had something.

Hearst's *New York Journal-American* called the Stamford general
strike a revolution and was particularly distressed that it had occurred
right in the backyard of the rich and powerful. It quoted me as threatening a statewide general strike. One reporter called the union office asking who was this rabble-rouser Schrank to threaten a Connecticut-wide
general strike. The governor appointed an arbitration board headed by
Mr. Fuller of Brush Company fame—no friend of labor—and the Yale
& Towne strike was finally settled through arbitration, though not without serious concessions by the union.

As a result of the Stamford general strike, the Party's trade union leadership took a renewed interest in me. The FBI file reports that early in 1946
I attended a Central Committee meeting held at a "secure place" in
Brooklyn to discuss the Party's strategies in the AFL.* The primary subject of the meeting was foreign policy and how the AFL leadership was
responding to the new eastern European socialist governments. Party
officials saw the union comrades' resistance to fighting the Romanian resolution at the IAM convention as evidence that they did not understand
the Party's primary responsibility to defend the Soviet Union and the new
socialist countries of eastern Europe.

The meeting was just another occasion when I felt inadequate to argue
with all the very smart people on the Central Committee. I wasn't at all
knowledgeable about the foreign policy issues inside the AFL and could

---

*The FBI file contains a transcript of my remarks at that meeting; so much for
"security"!

contribute little to the discussion. However, the file does quote me as saying that American workers didn't give a damn about the Soviet Union or eastern Europe or anything but their own bread-and-butter issues—certainly not a class struggle of the European variety. The file says I was also critical of the Party for its lack of influence in the AFL, which left people like me extremely vulnerable. There was general agreement that the Party needed to do more work inside the AFL unions.

I thought a lot about that Central Committee meeting afterwards. Why did I feel so intimidated by the intellectual capacity of the committee members? My fierce hatred of the capitalist system was part of the culture I had grown up in, and just as important was the personal experience that had led me to embrace Marxism. Unlike the Party's leaders, I did not have a love affair with intellectual concepts learned primarily in the library. Still, I believed I would understand better and have fewer doubts if I had read more books.

My everyday experience was teaching me that the American worker could be as militant, tough, and mean as any movie cowboy, but only when it came to the economics of wages, hours, and working conditions. I was beginning to seriously doubt that this defined them as class-conscious or that they would ever make the leap to the barricades of a socialist revolution. Of course, whenever I expressed such doubts I was criticized for "reformist thinking" or a failure to grasp Marxist-Leninist theory fully.

All during the war, wage and price controls had, in effect, outlawed strikes. In the face of record-breaking corporate profits, workers considered the wage and salary increases they were granted puny. In the early months of 1946, their pent-up resentment and frustration created a wave of strikes that rolled across the country like spring thunderstorms.

For three months General Motors remained on strike. The company claimed that it simply could not afford the union's wage demands. When Walter Reuther, president of the United Automobile Workers, suggested that the company open its books to prove its contention, GM characterized the idea as absurd and absolutely refused. Even so, it was the first sign of a very new idea in labor relations: that the union, as a vested interest group, had a right to know how the company is run.

We had slowed the antiunion attack at Yale & Towne, but the effort to gut the labor movement was continuing in Congress. Over fifty antilabor bills were introduced during the Eightieth Congress. If anyone still had any doubts that the wartime honeymoon was over, they were soon dispelled. Unable or unwilling to meet the onslaught, Truman tried to slow things down. He submitted his own proposal for a cooling-off period before a strike could be called and vetoed several of the most flagrantly antiunion bills.

In May of 1947 another showdown similar to the Yale & Towne strike was about unfold in Elmira, New York. The Remington Rand Machinists' local was an active, militant supporter of the state council and myself as president. With well over a thousand members, it was one of the largest single-plant locals in the state. The plant's primary product was typewriters, though during the war they made gunnery instruments.

The company was seeking the same union-busting concessions as Yale & Towne had achieved. After lengthy negotiations with no progress in view, the local voted to strike. The strike started out in the usual picnic-like atmosphere. In plants where workers have put up with years of abuse, the strike offers an opportunity to finally, "get even with the bastards." The abuse could be real or imagined; it didn't matter. It was the workers' turn to take charge. There is always a great rush of energy when workers—with a shout of "Hurray, we shut her down"—experience their power over the company, even if only for a short interval.

It was late springtime in Elmira, and there were lots more enjoyable things to do than walk back and forth on a picket line in the noonday sun. To begin with, though, lack of access to a local meeting hall helped create a holiday atmosphere. The union held its meetings in Dunn Field, home of the local bush-league ball club. At a noisy and enthusiastic strike meeting at the ballpark I pledged the full support of the state council and went home.

A few weeks later I received a call from the president of the local union asking me to come back to Elmira. As he put it, "too many members have gone fishing or are out playing golf. In the meantime, the god-damned company is making moves to bring in scabs." By midnight I was ensconced at the Mark Twain Hotel in Elmira, my home for the duration of the strike.

The local union leadership was an odd mixture of ex-coal miners from Pennsylvania, a number of southern women—over half the work force were women—and a lot of church-going Catholics. The local president, a charismatic leader when sober, was an alcoholic. Members of the local's executive board told me that when he drank they had to "find him quick before he fucks things up but good." Once after he hadn't shown up for a week, a rumor spread that he was involved in some shenanigans with the company. It was time to get him out of the way before it became public knowledge that the local president was a souse. Fortunately, he was a member of Alcoholics Anonymous, and they assured us that they would handle the whole matter. Sure enough, they found him and took him away somewhere for the duration. It was my first encounter with AA members, and watching them handle the tricky situation gave me a life-long respect for the organization.

Although it was now summertime and local farmers were contributing more fresh corn and vegetables than we were able to give away, the pic-niclike atmosphere was dissipating as payless paydays accumulated. The strike was slipping into the doldrums as boredom and indifference set in. Wives were beginning to gripe, and every day fewer people showed up for picket duty. We had a serious morale problem in the making.

I also began to get urgent telephone calls from Jim Matles, an organizational director for the United Electrical Workers (UE) I had met at various left-sponsored gatherings. He was regularly charged with being a communist and, like me, he ducked the question or denied it outright. I figured he probably was a communist, but I didn't want to know for sure. The UE, a CIO affiliate, also had a Rand plant under contract, and he was concerned that IAM might get a better settlement than the UE had. I told him we were going for the best contract we could get and refused to consider taking less just to make the UE look good. Some time later, the UE was expelled from the CIO for being communist-dominated.

My room at the Mark Twain became a regular hangout for some of the local's officers when they weren't at the plant. One sleepy July afternoon one of the officers, Paul, burst in and announced, "We gotta have an executive board meeting fuckin' quick." He said he had just gotten the word that the company was getting ready to bring in a busload or two of scabs the next morning.

The executive board decided to meet without me, so I wouldn't be involved in whatever they planned to do. They did tell me that the company had in fact been quietly sneaking busloads of women scabs into the plant for the past few days. Paul said, "They figured we wouldn't do nothin' about girl scabs. Well, you're gonna see they're outa their fuckin' minds."

The next day at breakfast he told me that he and some of his buddies from Pennsylvania had cooked up a plan to "stop the bitches from scabbin' our jobs." I would see what would happen the next morning at the main gate. On the way out, he said, "See you in the morning, but after it's over we're goin' south."

"Hey," I yelled after him, "What are you guys gonna do?"

"I'd rather not say." He was laughing uproariously. Whatever escapade he was up to, he was sure having a lot of fun thinking about it.

At six the next morning I stood watching the main gate with nothing but sweet summer-morning thoughts and birdsongs in my ears. What could possibly happen on such a lovely morning? I was quickly jolted out of my dream by the approach of two yellow schoolbuses. I couldn't tell how many people were inside them. Just then a whistle blew and the pickets flew into action to block the buses from entering the plant. A few of the pickets were waving good-sized bricks, and the drivers got the message and stopped; they opened the bus doors. Looking embarrassed and frightened, women began to get off the bus.

The air was tense as the pickets waited silently for a line to be crossed. Then, at a signal from Paul, a small group of women strikers descended upon the would-be scabs with military precision. In the broad daylight of that lovely summer morning, they proceeded to tear the clothes off the strikebreakers. For a few moments, shock and surprise over this bizarre scene left those of us who were watching absolutely dumbfounded. No one—least of all the police—had a clue about what to do. The scabs were running around trying to cover their variously exposed parts. The police, totally embarrassed and confused, were trying to give some of the bare-breasted women their shirts and push them into the police cars.

It was another great scene from a Mack Sennett comedy. Once we got over the shock of what had happened, we were unable to stop laughing. I wanted to congratulate Paul for a beautifully executed—and highly original—scab-busting tactic, but when I looked around for him and his associates, they were nowhere to be seen. They seemed to just disappear. Gone south I presumed. The scabs were shamed, but they were not hurt; they just wanted to get back on the buses and go back where they came from.

The newspapers reported that company President Jimmy Rand was furious. He demanded that the culprits who had perpetrated "this heinous act" be brought to justice. The local cops, many of whom had strong union sympathies, were politely interrogating folks about the whereabouts of the "perpetrators." Of course no one knew. I had a vague idea that Paul and his cohorts were holed up in a mining town somewhere in Pennsylvania, which was, Paul liked to say, "real union country." The plan had worked, and the company gave up the idea of hiring scabs to break the strike. Rand himself kept fuming about the "thugs and hoodlums" and swore he'd never negotiate a contract with any of those implicated in the great undressing. That was not a problem, as Paul and his group stayed out of Elmira until the strike was settled.

The victory on the picket line resulted in a jubilant atmosphere around the Mark Twain Hotel, and soon a federal mediator arrived from Washington. A couple of weeks later he helped negotiate a settlement that established the union's right to negotiate for the plant's workers.

Not long before the end of the strike I was sitting in my hotel room reading at around eleven o'clock when there was a knock on my door. I had been waiting for it for some time. I had met Margaret, the daughter of one of the board members, when I rode to a meeting of the local strike committee in a members' car. In the crowded front seat, with our legs pressed against each other, there had been no mistaking our intense attraction to each other. When I flung open the door to the hotel room she just stood there, all five feet four of her, with a little knowing smile.

Afterward, looking at her lying naked next to me, I admired her beautifully formed breasts and realized that she was far too experienced to be a virgin. But, I suddenly wondered, how old is she? Was this a set up? Had loneliness and pent-up sexual desire gotten the best of me? It was obviously too late to worry about it; I would just have to savor the delights of that night and take whatever consequences came with them.

In the morning I watched her dress with a very satisfied smile on her face. "Why are you smiling like a cat that swallowed the canary?" I asked.

She laughed: "I was thinking my mother would kill us both if she knew where I had spent the night." But I didn't need to worry, she assured me; her mother had gone south until the strike was over.

A city slicker union organizer out on the road and away from home for weeks or months gets lonely. To local women, he may come off as a hero defying the big, bad company. In small towns where nothing much happens anyway, many frustrated women dream of great romance, creating opportunities for a little seduction. It might be just a little dalliance, or it could be a set-up for a quick ride out of town. It never again happened quite as spontaneously as it did on that lovely summer night in Elmira.

It felt strange to go from the harsh reality of the Remington Rand strike in Elmira to the rarefied atmosphere of the first Aspen (Colorado) music festival. Edith and our daughter Elizabeth had gone there earlier in the summer to study music and dance. Edith was taking master classes with Richard Dyer Bennett, the well-known countertenor. She was as steeped in the culture of music and dance as I was in the union movement.

We were a folk-singing, guitar-playing family. Edith studied with a variety of teachers, and Elizabeth played the piano as well as the guitar. I loved to sing too and had learned to play the guitar well enough to play simple folk tunes and cowboy songs and to accompany the singing of "Hold the Fort," and "Solidarity Forever" at union organizing meetings. Wherever we went as a family we sang, especially during long car rides. Our repertoire ranged from "Clementine" to classic Elizabethan love songs. Edith and Elizabeth harmonized while I carried the melody. Those were the happiest times in our family.

These were the days of the folk song revival and Burl Ives' "Erie Canal" and "Go Tell Aunt Rhodie the Old Gray Goose Is Dead." In difficult times, singing was always a balm that soothed me and reaffirmed my faith. In the Sunday Schools, the Young Communist League and the Party, and in the labor movement, we sang. A movement needs the inspiration of full-throated singing, whether it's the "International" of the socialists, "We Shall Overcome" in the civil rights movement, or "Ain't

Gonna Study War No More" of the anti–Vietnam War movement. You can tell when a movement has run out of steam. The singing stops.

In the Party, there were regular singing parties at the home of a rich comrade who lived in Nyack. A bunch of guitar players and singers would sit in a big circle, each one of us singing a new song as the music went around and around the circle. I remember one night when we started with champagne, had a sumptuous dinner, and sang through the whole night until morning, when a great pancake breakfast was served. Our hostess had inherited a couple of oil wells and was married to a leading member of the Party.

That first evening in Aspen I walked around town looking for my family. Aspen, an old silver-mining town, was then still very much a ranching community. At the bar of the Hotel Jerome I came upon a bunch of cowboys drinking it up after a hard day in the saddle. Embarrassed as hell, I asked, "Where can I find the music festival people?" I could see they were kind of puzzled about what someone in old workboots and dungarees would want with that crowd. I wondered about it myself.

One of the cowboys asked, "Do you hear that pig whistle? Just follow it and you'll find them." Sure enough, I could hear the sound of a flute coming from a room off the bar. Inside, a small group of people were listening to the music with such rapt attention that my entrance wasn't noticed. Standing next to the cowboy bar was Dyer Bennett singing an intense Elizabethan love song in his high alto voice, accompanied by a flute. It was so incongruous that I had to leave for fear of bursting out laughing.

I was a million miles from my world of blue-collar machinists, but Edith was very much at home in that world. That would always remain a major difference between us. Coming from a labor strike in Elmira to a music festival in Aspen was for me a living demonstration of the huge differences between the cultured intellectual and the average blue-collar union member. Commuting across these cultures, I realized then they knew absolutely nothing about each other. I believe that it is even more true as I write this. If anything that gap continues to grow. The artistic and intellectual communities have lost completely any connections they ever had to the world of industrial workers.

14

Antilabor Crusade

During my presidency, the state council had grown from a few locals to over thirty affiliated locals. It had also become an important political influence. All through 1946 and 1947—when not on strike duty at Yale & Towne and Remington—I pounded my beat in the halls of Congress in my role as a trade union lobbyist, trying to win votes to hold back the antilabor tide. Congressman Marcantonio was one of the most active members on behalf of labor. During the fight over the Taft-Hartley Act in the spring of 1947 we met often. He explained the intricate ebb and flow of how a bill makes its way through the legislative process. At one of the most frustrating of those times he laughed and said he wished we could use "some of the guys we sent to Stamford on the southern Neanderthals on this hill."

Another of labor's staunchest supporters, Senator Bob Wagner, ran for reelection for the last time in 1946. AFL officials, however, withdrew their support of him in favor of a conservative Democrat, Joseph Curran. When Wagner's campaign manager asked if I would head a reelection labor committee, I accepted immediately. Speaking at the state AFL convention, I pointed out that Wagner had been FDR's most trusted ally in the Senate and was the best friend labor ever had. Betrayal by the state AFL leadership, I said, would make every political friend think twice about going out on a limb for labor. I was proud to chair the labor committee to help him win reelection.

As I had several times before, I was finding my new-found public reputation troubling, as well as flattering. I was certain that being in the spotlight would make me more vulnerable to being found out. My growing political influence also meant that I was getting an increasing number of telephone calls and visits from politicians, union leaders, and rank-and-file workers—all looking for some kind of favor. During this period, I also received invitations to meet several "famous men."

Though I never knew for sure, it may have been the Party that arranged for me to become acquainted with important labor leaders I would not have met in the normal course of events. Could it be that the arrangers thought these meetings would help me to better navigate the waters of my dual existence? If so, the encounters should have strengthened my position in the labor movement. They turned out to do just the opposite.

The first such meeting resulted from a telephone call asking me to meet Arthur Horner, president of the British Miners' Union, for a drink in the bar of the Hotel Plymouth. Horner, a short, muscular coal miner with a round cheerful face, a hearty handshake, and a great smile, had grown up in Wales. He was a member of the British Communist party. In the best tradition of British pub life, Arthur and I met several times and spent many hours drinking and talking. He could drink old fashioneds until closing time. Then we would have a sausage-and-egg breakfast and call it a night.

These meetings were very flattering. I greatly admired Horner's militant leadership of the Miners' Union, and we soon became fast friends. Whenever he came to the United States, we would spend an evening talking endlessly about the differences between the British and American labor movements. One night after a lengthy discussion of the east-west division of postwar Europe, we got down to what I considered a nitty-gritty issue. How did the miners respond to his party membership?

"Oh, they don't give a hoot. What they care about is how well I fight for them."

"Are they really as class-conscious as we are led to believe?"

He threw back his head and laughed heartily. "Britain is a class society. Hell, so is Europe. You're born into a class, you stay there. Of course, you're class-conscious—unless you're daffy. If you're a young man born in the Welsh coal country, you're going to grow up and be a miner. You don't think about it. It's just accepted as a fact of life. That's your class, and that's where your loyalty lies."

"How about your being a communist?"

"For the average miner, that puts me squarely on the right side of the class struggle. They're sure of where I stand. Even if they don't always like my support of socialist causes, it's more important to them that I will fight for their interests down to the very marrow in my bones. That's what they care about."

Horner, on his side, wanted to know why I couldn't operate openly as a communist. "I don't see why, with your record of achievement, you couldn't just say 'Yes. I'm a communist and damn proud of it.'"

I explained to him that American workers are militant when it comes to their wages and working conditions but do not think in terms of overthrowing the existing system and replacing it with socialism. "They're not class-conscious. What they want above all," I said, "is to be part of the existing order of things. There's a myth in America that if you work hard enough you can make it. And, you know, there is some truth to it. The unions have been very successful in getting the workers a larger slice of the American pie. If tomorrow I acknowledged my party membership I would be out on my ass as fast as they could get the ballots printed and counted. So I spend my life ducking and weaving. I hate it. It's a dreadful existence."

Arthur laughed, "You might be surprised how many workers already assume that you're a communist."

I agreed. "It makes no difference as long as it stays our dirty little secret. It's like a respectable member of a family who was a whore before she got married. The family members know it, and as long as nobody mentions it and it is never acknowledged it doesn't exist. It's the same story for a lot of communists in leadership positions in the American labor movement. Our excuse for secrecy is that our political beliefs are nobody's business but our own. Unfortunately that's not quite true, is it Arthur?"

"Of course not, every leader is guided by some underlying belief or value system that is reflected in his leadership."

Horner was a firm believer in the orthodox Marxist notion that capitalism could not continue to make the concessions necessary to avoid social unrest by satisfying workers' demands. Like the party people I had met during the depression, he was sure that sooner or later capitalism would fail when it became unable to solve its inherent economic contradictions. "The new socialist countries," he assured me, "are going to show us a new way. That's what will change the world." He really believed that, and I sure wanted to, but my doubts kept growing.

Not long after meeting Horner, I received a call suggesting I meet the president of the West Coast Longshoremen's Union, Harry Bridges, at the Prince George Hotel bar. Bridges was a tall, skinny Australian that the federal government was endlessly trying to deport as a communist, a subversive, or both. He was accused of being a communist or a fellow traveler. I think that this meeting, too, was arranged to teach me more about surviving as a lefty in a basically conservative union.

Bridges, though, was more interested in what I could tell him about the in-fighting in the AFL than in how I might best survive the red-baiting. "After all," he said, "they only just started red-baiting you. I've been living with that forever." I wondered if he was a party member, but I didn't dare ask.

Bridges was most concerned about getting people like me in the AFL to lead the fight against the innumerable antilabor bills showing up in Congress. He referred to the AFL leaders as "a bunch of sell-outs" who couldn't be counted on. He was sure they just wanted to show employers what nice guys they were. The AFL leadership—he said the word *leadership* with so much contempt that it dripped from his mouth— would "shit in their pants" before they took any effective action against the bills. As a result, union members didn't realize what a threat these proposals were to their hard-won gains. "What do you think we can do to wake them up?" he asked me.

The mere fact that Harry Bridges was asking for my opinion was very flattering. But, though I talked as if I had some real power in the Machinists, the truth was that as a local president and state council president I had damn little. Because there were so few lefties in the leadership of AFL unions, I think the Party saw me as a desperate hope, a left-wing beachhead to be nourished and supported in any way possible. I figured that maybe these meetings with important labor leaders were the Party's way of advancing my standing within the AFL.

The last eminent leftist I met with, again at the Plymouth Hotel bar, was William Z. Foster. In the years when he was on the outs with the party leadership I used to schmooze with him in his Bronx apartment. He and Earl Browder, the former party secretary, agreed about nothing. By the end of the war Browder, an intellectual theoretician, came to believe that the Communist party of the United States had to develop its own path to socialism; it could only become a real influence if it adjusted to American conditions by becoming a reformist-oriented political association. Foster, by contrast, was a inflexible Stalinist and Sovietophile and remained fervently convinced of the need for revolutionary tactics.

I liked Foster for his trade union background and his classic book on strike strategy, *The Great Little Steel Strike and Its Lessons*. Having lived all his union life in the AFL, he had a detailed knowledge of and interest in all the affiliated unions. We had a number of fascinating conversations about the 1919 strike and the role the Machinists played in it. In our Plymouth Bar talks, Foster wanted to explore the possibility of remaking the IAM into a militant industrial union on the CIO model. I told him that that was already happening because of the need to compete with the CIO.

He found the Machinists an interesting union because of its old liberal tradition. In the days of Debs's American Railway Union, he said, the Machinists had a strongly militant membership but "a bunch of fuddy-duddy, pansy, gutless leaders. They weren't corrupt, just gutless."

"How do you explain that gutlessness?" I asked.

In Foster's opinion, the Machinists liked to think of themselves as highly skilled craftsmen and didn't want to be identified with the great mass of industrial workers. For a Machinist to be called a "production worker" was an insult, an attitude Foster thought was a millstone around labor's neck. "The damned craft union philosophy just divides workers instead of uniting them against their common enemy."

Having become a skilled worker myself, I was inclined to defend the craftsmen and think they deserved respect for the sacrifice and discipline they demonstrated in achieving journeymen status. "It's not that different from the sacrifices doctors or engineers have to make to get their certification. I see nothing wrong with that." Although I firmly supported the industrial-union model, I also believed that skilled work deserved the same high regard given any profession requiring an extended learning period. In the mass industrial unions, the craftsmen have not fared so well, primarily because they are overwhelmingly outnumbered by unskilled assembly line workers.

Foster thought I was incredibly naive. "Thinking like that won't help you build support in the union." As far as the Machinists were concerned, we didn't agree about much of anything. I thought Foster was stuck in the "one big union" philosophy of the IWW, which was based on a definition of the working class as one homogenous mass from floor sweeper to instrument maker. In the real world, workers accepted the fact that there was a distinct hierarchy. He was reliving 1919, and this was 1946—a very different time for unions. Just how different it was, I was soon to learn.

In early 1946 Winston Churchill had made his famous, "Iron Curtain" speech in Fulton, Missouri, warning the world about the growing threat of communism. The establishment of socialism in eastern Europe under the protection of the Red Army was a big problem for the American Left, as the Romanian issue had so clearly indicated. Socialism was supposed to be won by the oppressed masses within their own country, not by an invading army. The party line was that the takeovers were essential to Russian security and would in turn help these countries find the road to socialism more quickly.

The Roman Catholic Church was mortified by its suppression in these predominantly Catholic countries, and a majority of blue-color workers in the United States were Catholics. Spurred on by the clergy, they became increasingly leery of anything labeled, "red," "pinko," or "fellow traveler." Many of my former supporters began saying they could no longer go along with me. Across the country, a wave of anticommunism that went hand in glove with antilabor efforts was picking up supporters both in the mainline political parties and in society as a whole.

When IAM president Harvey Brown called me prior to the state council meeting in early 1947 to suggest meeting for a drink, I was suspicious. Harvey didn't drink, so what was this meeting about? We met in his room at the Hotel Pennsylvania. He had coffee; I had a Manhattan. Harvey was very much one of the "fuddy-duddies" referred to by Foster and

Tobin. But he was also a decent sort of fellow and was clearly uncomfortable with what he was about to say.

"Bob, we have a problem. We've received some serious allegations about your communist connections. Rather than making an issue of it . . ." he paused. Then, looking me in the eye, he said, "we would win in the end. We have the evidence. But rather than a bruising fight—after all you have to think of your family. By the way, how is your daughter?"

He doesn't give a damn about my daughter, I thought. This is just the old soften-'em-up shit before the heave-ho.

"What I'd like to do is offer us all a nice way out of this mess."

Embarrassed, but also pissed, I asked him if he had gotten this shit from the FBI, Lovestone, or both. He insisted that it didn't matter and refused to get into the source of his information.

He went on, talking about the period of extreme conservatism the country was entering. The reactionary wave could decimate all the labor gains of the past decade.

I agreed. "So what we need to do is stand together and fight the bastards."

No, that was not what he had in mind. In spite of my acknowledged talent, he said, the IAM could not afford to be publicly associated with me. My politics now made me a terrible liability to the union.

I thanked him for the flattery and asked what he suggested we do, emphasizing the *we* as he had indicated that this was *our* problem.

"Before you say no, think over very carefully what I am about to propose. Talk it over with your wife. It will be a great opportunity for all of you." In a few weeks, he said, I would receive an offer from the Schlitz Brewing Company to become their vice president for maintenance at a salary three times what I was then making, plus lots of benefits. "Think about it. It's a great opportunity and will avoid a terrible knock-down, drag-out fight from which nobody will gain anything." He paused, looking at me with sincere sympathy. "You're a young man. You have the most to lose."

For some time we sat in silence. I was in shock. I thought about Schlitz. I liked their beer. Hell, it *would* be an interesting job. But after that, how long would it take them to blackmail me again?

"Harvey, this is just a form of blackmail, so forget it."

"Well, no one has ever accused me of that." He stood up, shaking his head in disbelief. "They told me I was wasting my time."

I interrupted, "Harvey, who the fuck are 'they' anyhow?"

Mostly, I think, it was the "fuck" that bothered him. "That makes no difference. You will find out in time," he said brusquely. He got up and opened the door for me to leave.

He was obviously sorry that his efforts had come to naught. I left scared, and confused about what would happen next. The gauntlet had been dropped, and the fight was on.

A short time later, in February, the New York State Council of Machinists' held its annual meeting in Albany. Brown notified the secretary of the council that he would be in attendance. Prior to the Albany meeting I met with the Party's trade union leadership to devise a strategy. As the country moved rapidly to the Right, the Party was increasingly concerned about its own survival. For people like me, the anticommunist attacks meant going deeper underground and being more careful about the people I met with. In my gut, the whole thing made me very uncomfortable. I had not as yet made any connection between my recent meetings with Horner, Bridges, and Foster and Brown's Schlitz proposal.

About a hundred delegates from locals representing approximately seventy-five thousand members attended the Albany meeting. It was highly unusual for the International's president to show up at state council meetings, especially accompanied by a dozen or more representatives of the International from all around the country. Their presence, it turned out, was strongly resented.

Brown requested the privilege of being the first speaker, and it was granted. Traditionally the state president opened the meeting with a talk on the state of the union in New York. Brown began his speech by describing the role of the state councils. They were formed, he said, primarily to deal with legislative matters and were never intended to be involved in day-to-day collective bargaining or the internal policy of the union. Under Robert Schrank's leadership, the New York council was moving into areas, including international politics, where it simply had no business.

Having no idea what was coming, I was intently watching the audience reaction. So far Brown was going nowhere. Then came the first bombshell. He held up a booklet published by the Chicago Chamber of Commerce entitled *Radicals and Communists in the Unions.* Reading from it, he described what it called the "communist takeover" of various CIO unions. Then he paused and looked over the audience before reading: "In recent years the most dangerous radical communist to emerge inside the AFL is the president of the New York State Machinists' Union, one Robert Schrank."

There was now a hushed silence in the room. The end had finally come. I was overcome with fear; my body seemed to freeze to the chair. As Brown paused to let his message sink in, Dan, an old pipe-smoking Erie Railroad machinist from Oneonta, not bothering to ask for recognition from the chair, stood up. "Excuse me, Brother Brown, but since when do we give a hoot what a Chamber of Commerce says about one of our brothers? Hell, if that notorious antilabor outfit don't like him, maybe he ought to be struck in bronze." While Brown was protesting that he had not finished, the hall broke into applause. I relaxed a little. Maybe we hadn't lost yet.

As the hall settled down, Brown continued. "It isn't just these reports or his support of communist causes in the debates at our recent International convention. There is hard evidence of his communist connections." He held up an eight-by-ten glossy photograph: "Here is Schrank having a drink at the Plymouth Hotel bar with Arthur Horner, president of the Welsh Miners' Union, an admitted and proud member of the British Communist party." Someone yelled, "So what?"

"Let me continue." He pulled out another eight by ten and held it up, seeming certain that it would clinch the argument. "Guess who he's having lunch with here? None other than William Z. Foster, head of the American Communist party. Now this has got to mean something, and it is embarrassing this union." He sat down.

There was a tense atmosphere in the hall. One delegate stood up and complained that we had a lot of business to transact. "Then there will be an election. If the members don't like their president, they can vote him out. Period."

Then Dan was back on his feet asking "Brother Brown" whether "it's any of this union's damn business who a member has lunch with. Christ, I had lunch with Bill Foster and Eugene Debs in the days of the American

Railway Union. Am I now suspected of being a subversive? Why don't we just judge the man on what he does as a leader of this organization and not who he's having lunch with?"

Yells of "that's right," applause, whistles, and calls of "let's get on with it" rolled through the hall. As I had earlier relinquished the chair at Brown's request, I now asked for the privilege to reply.

Using all of my rabble-rousing street corner skills I went after Brown like a Southern Baptist minister chasing the devil. "Brother Brown," I shouted, "Who is supplying you with this information? Who took those pictures? Did you take them? Do you sneak around in bars with a spy camera to catch members at lunch with someone you identify as a devil? I challenge you, Brother Brown, to tell these Machinists where you got these pictures."

I paused. He sat there in silence. "Was it J. Edgar Hoover? If so, you tell him to keep his FBI pig snout out of this union's business. Or was it Jay Lovestone who took 'em, who gave them to you?" After each name he shook his head. "Brother Brown," I said, "We ought to just sit here and wait until you tell these members who took those pictures and how they got to you." I paused again, waiting to see what he would do, but he just sat there. I lowered my decibels. "It's a sad day for the union when our leaders become concerned over what the Chamber of Commerce thinks about a state council president when we should be fighting for severance pay for our laid-off members." I sat down to a standing ovation. Brown, clearly unhappy, walked out of the hall, leaving his representatives behind. By the end of the council meeting I had been overwhelmingly reelected state president. Round one had been fought, and we had won it.

I was now sure that my unexpected meetings with famous men had been set up to entrap me. How else could I explain the photographs? As I sat alone in my hotel room after the meeting, I felt very strange. Who was setting me up? All of this couldn't be a coincidence, as Howard Friedman suggested when I bitterly asked him "what the fuck is going on?" Of course, I reminded myself, I shouldn't assume he would know if it was a setup.

We had won, yet I felt increasingly vulnerable. I had been exposed but had admitted nothing. In the days to come, I was overcome with shame for being dishonest with the people who trusted me so completely.

The toughest part of dealing with the constant political attacks was the need to simultaneously fend them off and continue doing my job as president of the council and the local. My only hope, I realized, was to continue to act in ways that would assure me the support of the members.

With the political winds shifting far to the right, there was plenty to do. Truman had become uncertain about holding together the old New Deal coalition. Harold Ickes, a Roosevelt stalwart and fighter against the utilities trust, quit the cabinet over Truman's appointment of some big oil men from his old Missouri political machine. Truman's man Hannegan was attacking the president of the Brotherhood of Railway Trainmen. The president himself—trying to forestall even stricter antilabor legislation—was now proposing a bill requiring a "cooling-off period" before a union could call a strike. The slew of antilabor bills in the Eightieth Congress culminated in a bill that became the Labor-Management Relations Act (Taft-Hartley). One day New York Senator Jim Mead, a good friend of the Machinists' State Council, called to invite us to an emergency meeting in Washington to organize a campaign against the proposed antilabor law.

Besides Mead, the meeting was attended by a number of New York congressmen, their staffs, and representatives of major unions. There was a detailed review of the provisions of the proposed statute and a lengthy discussion of their implications for the labor movement. I was very troubled by the tenor of the discussion, sensing a growing acceptance—like a debilitating fever or sickness—of the "new facts of life," a resigned questioning of how we could live with the bill. I argued determinedly that we couldn't live with it, that it would slowly but surely undermine the labor movement as we knew it. It would set up a whole series of obstacles to prevent unions from representing their members. If, for example, employers were given the right to replace strikers, the strike weapon would become meaningless. If the union could be made liable for an illegal strike, it would bankrupt us. Moreover, I pointed out, the law unfairly picked on the unions for government regulation, while employers and such organizations as the National Association of Manufacturers (NAM) and the Chambers of Commerce were not subject to regulation. Why not? And why should union leaders be singled out to sign affidavits to prove their political loyalties? Why does being union officials make us second-class citizens? When I had finished my denunciation of the bill, most of those present seemed to think I was terribly naive to believe the antilabor crusade could be stopped.

Underneath my protestations against the bill was a real fear of one particular provision: the requirement that any elected union officer swear an affidavit that he was not a member of the Communist party or any organization on the attorney general's subversive list. I saw in the directive the end of my career in the labor movement.

Someone suggested that we consider supporting the stand of John L. Lewis, president of the United Mine Workers (UMW). He had said he was not going to dignify the idiotic law by signing an affidavit to prove his loyalty to the country. His solution seemed an easy way out. If nobody signs the affidavit, there's no law. The room was silent. I remembered what Brown and Tobin had said about dark days ahead. It looked like the labor movement was about to convince the employers of its unflinching loyalty by denying much of its militant heritage.

The legislation passed in the spring of 1947. When Truman vetoed it, Congress overrode the veto and it became law. There was then a lot of legal talk in the unions about the effects of Taft-Hartley, and lawyers had a field day giving lengthy technical explanations of what the law could and could not do. They had suddenly became an important part of the labor bureaucracy as the emphasis changed from economic to legal means for unions to win their demands.

The law virtually outlawed sympathy strikes and boycotts and permitted state legislatures to ban the union shop and pass what are now known as right-to-work laws. Most of the right-to-work laws of twenty-one states in the South, Plains, and West were passed in the months after Taft-Hartley became law. The law also gave the president the right to declare an eighty-day cooling-off period if he deemed a strike a national emergency.

On the shop floor, workers were saying that they "didn't give a shit about all this legal crap." Someone suggested that I write an explanation of what the law meant to the average guy in the shop. I wrote a draft and sent it for comment to my friends at the Trades Union Press. They made their usual valuable suggestions and arranged for an illustrator. The revised draft then made the rounds of lawyers, union members, sympathetic public officials, and, finally, the executive committee of the state council, which enthusiastically endorsed it.

When I saw the final proof of *This Is Aimed at You* I could not believe the startling effect of Jules Brazelton's dynamic illustrations, particularly the cover art, which looked like something from a pulp western. Printed in bright orange and black on white paper, it shows the barrel of a gun aimed at a worker's head and carries the sensational subtitle, *An Expose of the Taft-Hartley Plot to Bust Unions and Hijack the American People.* Inside, the text begins with a description of plotters from the NAM and Congress planning to destroy the Wagner Act. Profusely illustrated in the best traditions of protest art, the thirty-five-page pamphlet was a great success. It sold for fifteen cents, and the first printing of 25,000 was gone in a couple of weeks.

The essence of the story is summed up on the back cover. The illustration pictures a classroom of the "NAM School." The instructor is pointing to a blackboard and saying, "It's really quite simple gentlemen!" The blackboard reads:

One Example of
HOW IT WORKS
(one of the many ways)

1. TAFT-HARTLEY LAW HOLDS COMPANY **NOT** RESPONSIBLE FOR ACTS OF ITS SUPERVISORY HELP
2. SUPERVISOR PROVOKES UNION MEMBERS . . . WHO . . .
3. WALK OFF THE JOB
4. THE UNION IS HELD LIABLE
5. THE WORKERS ARE <u>FIRED</u>
6. SCABS ARE HIRED
7. SCABS HOLD AN "ELECTION"
8. "<u>GOODBYE UNION!</u>"
9. EMPLOYER CAN SUE UNION FOR DAMAGES
10. THE LAW PROTECTS THE EMPLOYER <u>ALL THE WAY</u>!!

Anxious to demonstrate their patriotic ardor and disassociate themselves from *This is Aimed at You*, IAM leaders in Washington wasted no time in signing the noncommunist affidavits. They hoped their haste to sign would be taken as ample evidence that there were no left or subversive influences in the Machinists' union.

This is Aimed at You was the only thing like it, and we could hardly keep up with the demand. The Teamsters alone ordered five thousand copies. As a result of its popularity, I received requests to speak on Taft-Hartley from all over the country.

Besides speaking and sending delegations to the White House and Congress, the state council was conducting extensive petition campaigns against the new law. In the middle of all this feverish campaigning against Taft-Hartley, I arrived back at the office one day and was told I had had a call from Senator Robert Taft's office. Sure that this was some sort of joke, I replied, "Yeah, and the Pope called too, right?" It turned out, however, that the call was genuine and that Taft wanted to meet with me to correct some of the "errors" in *This Is Aimed at You.* The senator's secretary suggested that we get together the next time I was in Washington.

Against the advice of my friends I agreed, and we met for breakfast in the Senate Dining Room, where on previous occasions I had met with anti–Taft-Hartley senators. The very distinguished-looking man—he looked something like the kindly grandfather in Norman Rockwell's Thanksgiving painting—inquired politely about my family and complimented me on the booklet. He then went into great detail about the errors, distortions, and exaggerations he thought it contained. I talked with him about the law's philosophical implications and tried to show him that the law would destroy the unions' ability to represent their members. He was more concerned about the underworld elements the saw infiltrating the unions, and I found myself agreeing with him about the need to control corruption, though we strongly disagreed about the method for doing so. It was a surprisingly civil discussion, and I left actually liking this man for his integrity. We didn't agree about much of anything, but he listened to what I had to say and seemed to respect my opinions. More surprisingly, I respected his.

I had come face to face with my arch enemy, and he did not seem nearly as bad as I had portrayed him. Several times in the course of union organizing I had met employers who did not fit Papa's favorite characterization of bosses as "bloodsuckers." My doubts were growing that it wasn't all black-white, good guy–bad guy. When union colleagues asked about my meeting with Taft, I pooh-poohed it as just his effort to straighten me out. But I was being dishonest. He had made me think about the failure of unions to deal with corruption, as well as about how we could resist Taft-Hartley by simply refusing to sign those dreadful affidavits.

At Washington headquarters, IAM leaders became increasingly angry over my criticism of their rush to sign the affidavits and my praise of John L. Lewis's declaration that he didn't need the approval of the government to be president of the UMW. In April of 1948, Brown decided to act. Without a hearing, a trial, or anything resembling due process, he suspended me from all my union offices. He did so, he said, for numerous reasons: my apparent support of communist causes; my criticisms of the International's leaders for signing the noncommunist affidavits; my self-aggrandizement; and my opposition to the deportation of John Santo, a known communist. Although the local union and the state council organizations voted their full support of my leadership, the suspension stood.

According to my FBI file, I was a consistent supporter of Santo. He was an officer of the Transport Workers' Union who was among a number of people accused of being communists and therefore subject to deportation. Although I barely remember the case, the file reveals that the FBI used it in their effort to establish a clear connection between me and known party members. About this time, the Party, concerned about my survival as the state president of the Machinists' State Council, cut all open contact with me.

By 1948 the country was in the full grip of a red scare, a political sport justified in the name of "internal security." As the 1948 presidential election drew near, Truman sought to convince right-wing conservatives that he wasn't soft on communism. Early in the campaign, any New York taxi driver could have told you that Truman was in deep trouble. The Republican candidate, former "crime-buster" Governor Tom Dewey of New York, was going to "whip his ass." New Deal days were over, and Truman was badly in need of new allies. With the antilabor crowd firmly in the saddle and riding herd in Congress, the president embraced the red scare. He instituted a loyalty oath for all federal employees, directed the attorney general to draw up a list of subversive organizations as a way of exposing communist front organizations, and frightened the country by suggesting that at any moment the Russian reds might be on their way over the North Pole. It was his use of the rising tide of fear that the "Reds are coming," I believe, that won Truman his legendary victory that fall.

Former New Deal vice president Henry Wallace ran on the Progressive party ticket and was supported by the Party and the liberal Left. The fact that both the AFL and the CIO strongly opposed Wallace's candidacy further isolated leftists inside the unions. The Party itself, preoccupied with survival, began planning a completely underground organization. Events were increasingly forcing it to become more of what it had always vigorously denied being: a secret conspiratorial organization and an agent of a foreign government.

In this atmosphere, my suspension from union office was front-page news. I soon received a telephone call from Boudin, Cohen, and Glickstein, a law firm that had successfully represented local unions resisting efforts by their internationals to take them over and put them in trusteeship. The senior partner, Louis Boudin, was a professor of constitutional law at Yale. He was a very old blind man. When we were introduced, he asked me to come close so he could feel my face. Ever so gently, he ran his fingers across my face, then turned toward the other lawyers to assure them that I was a nice young man with a kind face.

Boudin explained that he was eager to represent the local because he wanted to teach union bureaucrats that they did not operate outside the bounds of the Constitution. He thought I and the local were being punished for criticizing our leaders' decision to sign the Taft-Hartley affidavit. But the freedoms of speech and publication, he asserted, were protected by the Bill of Rights. No union bylaws, rules, silent rituals, or anything else could deny a citizen those rights.

The law firm was clearly of a left liberal persuasion. One of their lawyers, Hyman Glickstein, had run for office on the American Labor party ticket. I did not know whether any of the lawyers were party members and did not ask. Glickstein, a short, restless man who looked and moved like James Cagney, would be in charge of our case, assisted by Lurie and Myer.

Hy was soft-spoken but firm. We had a lot of work to do, he said, and it needed to be done very quickly. First of all, I had to get immediate approval for the firm to represent the local, and the costs could be high. Then, he said, looking stern, we had to execute an end run to prevent the International from taking over the local and putting in a trustee. The first step was to gain immediate possession of the local's assets and put them in a secure place. If the International got control of the money, I, and the local, were out of business. There would be no money for payrolls, bills, stamps, telephones, and—he laughed—lawyers. We were to get whatever authority we needed from the executive board to pull all the local's cash, bonds, and investments out of the bank and hide them somewhere the International's officials couldn't get at legally. Safe-deposit boxes in banks were no good, as they could get a court order to seal them. He paused. "That's how the International unions win these fights. They get control of the locals' finances and paralyze their officers."

Rushing back to the union office, I wondered if we could pull this off. I called a special meeting of the executive board for six o'clock that evening, and all fifteen members showed up. After telling them what the lawyers had recommended, I asked for authority to withdraw the $240,000 dollars in our various accounts and hide it from the International. The local secretary-treasurer, Pete Lynn, a forty-five-year union member, was a nervous, wiry little man who wore frameless glasses. He was strictly apolitical, extremely loyal, and completely trustworthy. Someone suggested that he and I alone be responsible for hiding the local's treasury, and with remarkably little discussion the board voted unanimously "yes."

Pete and I spent that evening trying to figure out where to hide the money. Bank accounts, which could be traced, were ruled out, as were bank safe-deposit boxes. We began to think about wild schemes, like placing the money inside the walls of Pete's house or in his backyard. No, that was too precarious. Neither of us wanted to be accused of misusing a single cent. The money had to be kept somewhere absolutely safe. Then one of us thought of a moving company, Cuneo Storage & Warehouse Company on Third Avenue, which advertised safe-deposit boxes.

Bright and early the next morning we were at the bank. Although the bank's officers were obviously surprised by what they considered a most unusual action, after lengthy questioning they let us withdraw all the funds. We used most of the money to purchase U.S. Treasury bearer bonds—which Pete stuffed into his briefcase—then took a cab to Third

Avenue. It was noon by the time we were finished, so I offered to buy Pete a well-deserved bratwurst lunch at the Ideal Restaurant on 86th Street.

He grinned at me, his eyes twinkling, "Christ," he said, "never in my more than forty years in this union did I ever think I'd do anything like this. Are you sure we won't go to jail?"

"No, Pete, I don't think we will. And, hell, if we do, we'll go together. Then we can play two-handed pinochle." He laughed, and we ate our bratwurst and went back to the office.

Glickstein said that our next step was to get the court to issue an injunction to stop the International union from interfering with the local. I was very ambivalent about going this route. Unions looked upon injunctions as employers' weapons against strikes, picketing, and boycotts. "Isn't there another way?" I pleaded. "What will the members say? If we lose their support, the fight's over."

Glickstein replied that it was our job to explain to the members that the local and state council will be out of business if we don't stop the International. "They're not going to play according to the Marquis of Queensberry rules. And as you know, they're getting all the help they want from the FBI." He paused and looked at me with exasperation. "Why did you have to refer to J. Edgar's pig snout? He'll never forgive you for that. It got you on the front page of the *Times*, but sure as I am standing here it may also get you on his most-wanted list of subversives." I had to promise Hy that, at least for the duration of our court fights, I would refrain from any comments about Hoover's nose.

Within the week we were petitioning the state court to issue a temporary restraining order against the International to keep them from putting the local into trusteeship. A couple of representatives were sent by the International to take over the local, but by the time they arrived the office had been emptied of all files, financial records, and membership lists. We had moved them out the night before.

The guys from the International were livid. "Where's the money? Where's the files? How dare you? You'll all be expelled for this! It's illegal."

We felt very smug about the whole affair. By God, we had licked the Washington bureaucrats, at least for the moment.

Justice Ferdinand Pecora issued the restraining order declaring that "Fair criticism is the right of members of a union, as it is the right of every citizen. A provision of a union constitution which would suppress protests of members against actions by their officers which some members regarded as improper or opposed to their best interests, would be illegal and unenforceable." The court's action was precisely what Louis Boudin had in mind when he said he wanted to teach union leaders about the Constitution. The International was enjoined from interfering with local union or state council functions.

At IAM's Washington headquarters, Brown and the other officers became increasingly furious. They were doing their best to eliminate me, but, as one of them put it, "those damn liberal New York courts keep defeating our efforts to clean up the union."

According to my FBI file, there was also a lot of pressure from the White House to do something about the band of union troublemakers in New York. John Steelmen, Truman's economic adviser—who had dealt with the rash of strikes that hit the country in 1946–47—wrote to Hoover on White House letterhead asking what he knew about Robert Schrank. Hoover told Steelmen that he should know better than to request that kind of information directly and instructed him to make his request formally through the attorney general. (Hoover did upon occasion insist that things be done through proper channels.) Why was all this fuss coming from the White House? I can only guess that it was the "Repeal the Taft-Hartley Law" campaign I was spearheading.

The International now proceeded again to bring charges against the local for going to the courts before exhausting their rights in the union, as well as for "issuing circular letters to other locals maliciously representing the International president of the union." The International executive council appointed a committee to bring charges against three of the local leaders, including me, for supporting communist causes and impugning the motives of the International president of the union. The three of us they chose were in fact party members. I can only assume they got this information through the AFL's chief red hunter, Jay Lovestone, or from the FBI.

Hy Glickstein couldn't believe they were doing this. "Are these people really so stupid as to think they have the power to do whatever they want?" he wanted to know. Back we went to court, and once again we won. The judge ruled that the International was violating the procedures of the union's constitution and that the plaintiffs were within their rights in coming to the court for relief. The International was enjoined once again from interfering with the local. For a couple of months things remained pretty quiet—until the union's 1948 convention in Grand Rapids, Michigan.

In the meantime I was confronted with the most difficult decision of my life. The local union election was coming up. If reelected, I would have to sign the noncommunist affidavit as a condition of holding office. My choices were limited: either sign or give up office and return to the rank and file. My inclination was to avoid signing the affidavit and to refuse to run for office.

At the top levels of the Party's trade union leadership an intense debate on the issue of the affidavits ensued. The Party's lawyers advised union officers to take the legislation seriously. If we signed the affidavit and continued as party members, they said, our chances of going to jail were very good. But to the Party's leaders, leaving the Party and giving up union office were equally unacceptable. Both would mean surrendering what little influence the Party had inside the labor movement.

I tried to convince party leaders that returning to the rank and file was the best course for me to follow. In *This is Aimed at You* I had argued with all the conviction I could muster that no one in the labor movement should even think of selling his soul by signing this affidavit. In the face of all I had written and said, how could I turn around and sign my soul away? The Party's position was that since the leaders of the AFL and the CIO were falling all over themselves to sign we were left with no choice. The only holdout was still John L. Lewis. They argued that if people like me did not sign the affidavits it would mean a full-scale exodus of left-wing leaders from the labor movement, which, of course, was precisely what the law was designed to do. In the long run that's what happened, and loss of the labor zealots who had driven the movement had a chilling effect on the unions.

Party leaders believed that even if we publicly denied membership, our election to union office would somehow indicate that the working class supported the Party. I thought that a strange rationalization. One party trade union specialist told me that "the working class understands that we cannot come out and declare our belief in socialism without suffering capitalist vengeance." That was their rationale for signing the affidavits. I knew they were deluding themselves if they believed for a minute that the workers in the Machinists'union would vote for me knowing I was a party member. I kept repeating the same old argument: that the support I enjoyed from the Machinists came solely from my ability to organize and represent workers at the bargaining table and that, if anything, my politics were seen as a terrible burden to my union friends.

It was this deeply imbedded illusion of a "revolutionary working class" that had for years stoked the fantasies of many party leaders. I remember reading a speech delivered in Moscow by the "beloved" woman party leader, Mother Bloor. She said some very silly things; for example, that American workers were ready to man the barricades in defense of socialism. Some time later at a World Peace Conference, Paul Robeson reportedly said that American Negroes would not fight against the Soviets in a war with the United States, an absurd statement that would isolate him from the black community for years. I think he got that idea from hanging around with a lot of party leaders and intellectual followers, neither of whom had the slightest understanding of the average worker. I believe that kind of talk caused the Soviets to make some bad estimates of what was going on in the United States. The Russians wanted to believe that American workers were getting ready to mount the barricades, and American Communist party leaders anxious to win praise from Moscow told them fairy tales about the revolutionary potential of the American working class.

Glickstein had warned that if I decided to sign the affidavits, I had better make sure I was out of the Party and any of the organizations on the attorney general's subversive list. He looked me in the eye and speaking slowly for emphasis said, "If you sign that affidavit, get it on the record that you have resigned from any and all organizations designated subversive by the attorney general. I will prepare the registered return-receipt letters for you."

Meeting with the Party's trade union leadership, I said I would sign the affidavits as they were urging me to do, but I wanted it clearly understood that I would no longer be a party member. I could visualize nothing worse than being tried as a perjurer. They did not agree and insisted I was over-reacting. They promised to take the utmost care to assure my security, but I stuck with Glickstein's advice. "No," I said. "The party secretary will receive a return-receipt letter telling you to remove my name from the membership list and any other places it might appear."

As I write this almost fifty years later, I have grave difficulty imagining that the Party's leaders could have been so stupid or naive as to think that they were eluding FBI surveillance. The contents of my FBI file convinces me that virtually every telephone conversation, every meeting was bugged. There was nothing from the most casual telephone call to the presumably secret Central Committee meetings that the FBI wasn't in on. Could the party officials really not have known? Or was the Party so shot through with FBI moles that they were in fact setting things up, as I suspected they did in the case of the Plymouth Hotel meetings?

A few weeks after my resignation, the chairman of the New York State Central Committee of the Party asked me to meet him for a drink. In a Third Avenue bar, after some general talk about the state of the world, he told me the Party was unhappy with my attitude toward resigning. I explained that I would continue to work for the same things I had supported for most of my life but that my resignation should be taken as fact. If I decided to talk to the enemy, he warned, I would pay a big price.

That made me furious. "Are you threatening me? Resigning doesn't mean going over to the enemy!" I took the threat seriously, though, and tried to explain that I couldn't go on digging myself deeper into this dual existence: "I'm a working-class leader, not a spy, and I don't for the love of me understand why I need to go on living a dual life."

Resigning from the Party was the easy part. Getting out of the orbit of friends who were primarily lefties was more difficult. All my social connections and several of the people I worked with in the union were communists. I knew the other side would never accept my resignation if I did not prove myself by naming other reds, but I absolutely would not do that.

I had grown up believing that it was truly possible to create a utopia of universal love through socialism, though there was nothing in my everyday experience to reinforce that belief. On the contrary, everyday life was telling me it would never work. But, like all true believers before and since, I wanted a Garden of Eden so badly that I hung onto my precious dream. I was terribly ambivalent about cutting the cord that tied me to that lifelong dream, and the Party was the means to make the dream a reality. And it was far more than just the dream I would forsake by leaving the Party. It was also my friends, my extended family, the world I had known for most of my life. So I ended up disagreeing with the Party on many issues but unable to cut all ties. Although no longer a member, I continued to associate with those party members in the labor movement with whom I shared a strong bond of friendship. As the winds of the Cold War put us under ceaseless attack, we continued to be each others' most reliable support system.

My work in the labor movement proved to be a good way to avoid dealing with my doubts about the Party. The day-to-day struggle of the union remained the mainstay of my very existence. My ability to continue to function in the union was under the protection of court injunctions. For a short time after I resigned from the Party and signed the affidavit, life in the union returned to the normal routines of organizing, negotiating, and handling grievances.

In preparation for the IAM national convention scheduled for 1948, the state council sent me out on the road to drum up support for what we called a program for a "Militant Fighting Union Convention." The council's objective was to get the IAM to launch an all-out response to employers 'antiunion attacks. Our themes for getting the union back into a fighting mode were summed up in the slogans "Full Employment, Jobs for All," "Repeal Taft-Hartley," and "Secure World Peace through support of the United Nations."

The farther I traveled from the East Coast, the less support for the peace issue I found. Officers of local unions, as well as rank-and-file members, pleaded with me to "forget the world shit." A local president in St. Louis told me, "If you stick to the everyday bread-and-butter stuff you'll be okay. We can't back you on anything that has even a distant smell of support for the Iron Curtain countries."

"I don't give a damn about Eastern Europe," I responded, "but what if we're drifting toward another war that could be nuclear? How do we just say nothing?"

He thought for a long time. "Look," he said, "me and my local, as well as many others around here, are strong supporters of your fight with the International union bureaucrats. Right?" I agreed. He went on: "When it comes to foreign affairs, American workers will never go against their own government. If you don't understand that, you're not really as smart as I think you are."

The Marxist view of imperialist war absolutely required socialist revolutionaries to fight their own governments. This position was based primarily on the experience of getting the Russian military to side with the Bolsheviks in 1917. In World War II, communists opposed the war as an imperialist affair until the Nazis attacked the Soviet Union. After that, it was a war to defend socialism. Whenever I was out on the road listening to workers, particularly in the heart of the country, it became clear to me that unless the Party dropped its preoccupation with Soviet foreign policy, it was doomed to isolation and a continued loss of influence. Earl Browder, who understood that, had lost his leadership position to Bill Foster, who turned out to be little more than a mouthpiece for Stalin.

There was pressure on the attorney general's office to prove perjury when I signed the noncommunist affidavit. According to my FBI file, at about that time Assistant Attorney General Vincent Quinn asked J. Edgar for information about me to help the Justice Department's investigation of my affidavit. Quinn cited allegations of my communist activities from within the labor movement and suggested that the FBI interview union leaders who might shed light on my politics. Hoover pointed out that part 111, page 74 of the *FBI Handbook* prohibits the FBI from interviewing labor leaders without special permission from the attorney general.

The file shows that Quinn then asked where the Chicago Chamber of Commerce got its information on my communist activities. The FBI's hunt for the source of the Chamber's information turned up no good evidence. The FBI couldn't even identify the person who wrote the C of C report, because so many aliases were used. The bureau had to admit to Quinn that neither they nor the Chamber had any firsthand evidence of Schrank's party membership. In a trial, neither the Chamber nor the

FBI's own so-called reliable source would make a creditable witness. Asked why the reports of my meetings with known Communist party leaders wouldn't be sufficient proof, Hoover advised the assistant attorney general that just meeting with someone does not prove anything under the rules of evidence.

The IAM leaders must have been going nuts trying to get the Justice Department to issue an indictment before the 1948 convention. That would have been Harvey Brown's coup de grace. J. Edgar, for some strange reason, was not cooperating.

While out on the road preparing for the International's convention, I was scheduled to speak in Denver. Sandra had moved to Colorado, married, and had a child, and I very much wanted to see her. Over the six years since our trip to Aberdeen, we had kept up a surreptitious correspondence. After affirming our love, we would write about matters of mutual interest and exchange articles from newspapers and magazines. I wasn't sure whether she would want to see me now that she was a married woman, but I made the call. She was delighted and proposed that we spend a day together in the mountains.

It was early spring. We walked in the high aspen country and hurriedly tried to tell about all the things that had happened since we were last together. She had packed a picnic lunch, and we set it out in a beautiful high meadow. Lying in the grass, she rolled over and kissed me.

It was a wondrous day of lovemaking. Now that we were both married, she said, it was okay. Our loving could only enrich our marriages: "Love can only make things better, and our love will do that. We are taking nothing from others, but we will give back some of our great love." That day and night in Colorado I had what would be my first of many lessons from Sandra on the beauty and wonder of the human body. Underneath all that "freedom" and "body beautiful" talk I had grown up with, there remained a Victorian prudishness that made the body seem a shameful thing. Sandra soon dispelled all that. She was proud and happy in her nakedness, and she helped me find the same delight in our bodies.

For twelve years thereafter we arranged many such happy meetings. About twice a year we would go off somewhere to explore nature and ourselves in the mountains of Utah, Canyon de Chelly in Arizona, the desert, and a series of strange cities. I became addicted to a distant romantic love that called for none of the drudgery of ordinary everyday love. Just the thought of our next meeting would bring me a sense of great anticipation and joy. And, of course, it was very flattering. I was a working-class dropout loved by a successful, warm, intellectual doctor. There was, I believed, no greater blessing.

15

Schrank *vs.* Brown

My 1948 road trip to local unions around the country was considered very successful. We had found strong membership support for a militant defense against the antilabor attacks of employers and Congress and were heartened by our court victories over the International. In September I and the other four delegates from New York Local 402 arrived at the IAM convention in Grand Rapids in high spirits, ready to lead the fight for jobs and repeal of Taft-Hartley. We had no suspicion of what would happen on the opening day.

The first order of business was the Credentials Committee report, which determines whether locals meet the criteria for participation in the convention. Most credential challenges have to do with failure to pay per capita tax to the International union or a dispute over how much per capita is paid relative to the number of delegates. The committee report found Local Union 402 ineligible to be seated on the basis of a long litany of crimes against the IAM and President Harvey Brown. Before yielding the chair to Vice President Al Hayes, Brown, fuming with indignation, charged me and the local with supporting communist causes, criticizing the International's actions, and "impugning the motives of the president of this union."

"How dare they?" rang out from his every sentence. "They even dared send out letters to every local union criticizing our signing of the Taft-Hartley affidavits. They besmirched my good name," he railed. "How dare they?" Brown told the convention that our local had committed the supreme heresy of going to court to stop the International from putting it into trusteeship. He predicted that Justice Null, who was hearing the case in the New York Supreme Court, would drop the proceedings against the International when he learned of the convention's action. Puffing himself up for his pièce de résistance, Brown proclaimed, "We have this day advised Local 402 in New York, as well as the court, that we are dropping the charges against the local and will not appeal the New York Court order. We are confident that the action taken in this convention will be sufficient to clear the air once and for all."

Things then began moving so fast that we five delegates couldn't figure out what was going on. At the recommendation of the executive council, the convention voted to constitute itself as a trial committee. Imagine, a jury of six hundred people, with the local's delegates—and me, its president—sitting in the prisoner's dock! I made desperate efforts to get the floor to protest these absurd procedures and respond to the charges, but it was no use. Brown was finishing out his career as president of the IAM, and this convention was his last hurrah. Al Hayes, who had been anointed by the leadership to succeed Brown, was in the chair.

Years before, Hayes had commented that the only way to beat Schrank was to silence his "silver tongue" and promised he would do just that at the first opportunity. His chance had come. There was absolutely no way he was going to let me speak. Repeatedly, he slammed down his gavel and yelled, "You are not a delegate to this convention, sit down." With the floor microphone turned off, I could not be heard, so I tried hollering in my best street-corner voice. It was hopeless. In gatherings of this sort, the real power of the chair is not the gavel but the microphone control switch on the podium.

Talking with many delegates who were old friends, I heard a lot of sincere talk about the dangers of communism and the need for the country to be on guard. Too many delegates were saying that although they supported much of what I stood for, they could not go along with me on the "commie stuff." A terrible fear of communism and the Soviet Union was engulfing the country. My gut told me that the fight was over and that the convention would throw us out.

After Brown spent forty-five minutes charging me and Local 402, a few friendly delegates made brave efforts to get me equal time to reply, but Hayes would not budge. Appeals to his decisions based on Roberts' Rules were lost in rapid voice votes. It was becoming clear that the executive council had rigged the convention in advance. The convention adjourned temporarily; the trial would begin a few days later.

My hotel room was crowded with delegates friendly to our cause and eager to give us advice. The New York State Council brothers wanted me to stand trial and "really tell these bastards off." There was a unanimous agreement that I was being singled out, not for support of communist causes as alleged, but because I had taken a militant stand on the Taft-Hartley affidavits and had criticized IAM's leaders for signing them. In Joe Cronin's opinion, they were "more worried about pleasing the Chicago Chamber of Commerce than about fighting the employers."

After a while I asked everyone to leave so I could have a few moments to think. I had a vision of myself standing tall in the witness box defying the bastards. I would describe how the labor movement, as a result of the red scare, was losing its will to fight for its members. How labor leaders' growing desire to become respectable in the eyes of the Chamber of Commerce was exemplified by their rush to sign the noncommunist affidavits, a rush that was robbing the movement of its ideological fervor and leading to its slow death from atrophy of the heart. Now more than ever, when we needed the unity of the movement to defend FDR's New Deal heritage, the fight had gone out of it. I would make one last dramatic appeal to save that heritage through union democracy. I could almost see my Wagner-loving Papa applauding his son's gallant defense of his beliefs in the grand tradition of Luther or Debs. How proud he would be, even if I lost and exited like Siegfried in a blaze of glory.

A big part of me preferred the Siegfried scenario to appealing again to the "bourgeois court system" to defend us against a "workers' union." How far we had drifted from our trust in the working class! The convention reminded me of my fears of being exposed as a perjurer. The other delegates from the local union were insisting that we talk with our lawyers in New York before deciding what to do, but I was reluctant to make the call. I knew full well what they would say.

When I finally gave Hy Glickstein an update on the goings-on at the convention, he let out one of his silly little laughs. He found it hard to believe that the International's leaders could be so dumb but allowed that bureaucrats in power for a long time tended to develop illusions of invincibility.

He was silent for a moment, then said: "You know Bob, the older I get the more I believe that Lord Acton was right: 'Power corrupts and absolute power corrupts absolutely.'" He made me promise to do nothing for the next fifteen or twenty minutes while he talked with other members of the firm about strategy. "On its face," he said, "it appears to be a totally illegal action on the part of the International union and its president. Do nothing. Just go to lunch, and remember, above all, to leave J. Edgar Hoover alone. In the end, we'll teach those union bureaucrats that members have rights protected by the First Amendment, no matter what a union constitution says." He paused. "It may cost you, but think of the higher cause." Before I could respond, he said good-bye and hung up. My growing sense of doom now had some real fuel. What the hell did, "it may cost you" mean?

The atmosphere around the convention hotels had become so nasty that we didn't dare go anywhere alone. One of our delegates was slugged in the lobby by "goons" who yelled "Go back to Russia, you commie bastard." We tried to make the most of the incident by sending our brother off to the hospital and getting the police to press assault charges. The attackers turned out to be delegates from an aerospace local. These workers from one of the newest Machinists' locals were among those most infected with the red scare.

When Glickstein called back, he instructed me not to participate in any way with what he called "an absolutely illegal kangaroo court. If you take part, you legitimize the proceedings."

"Can't we even make a statement about why we won't participate?" I pleaded.

"Absolutely not. Any statement you make on the convention floor could be construed as taking part. We're not going to do that. You get it?"

"Yes, I get it. But we gotta do something. We can't just pack up and leave. Why can't we issue a statement to the delegates explaining why we refuse to participate in our own lynching?" Reluctantly, he agreed, but insisted that I read the statement to him before distributing it.

When the convention resumed as a trial committee, Brown charged the local with supporting communist causes and criticizing the International union for its leaders' haste in signing the noncommunist affidavits. He asserted that my support of John Santo was absolute proof of my Communist party ties. The convention spent a long time listening to Brown's various charges. The few delegates who pled valiantly to let me speak in my own defense were booed and called out of order.

Since our conversation at the Hotel Pennsylvania when Brown claimed he had the evidence to prove my communist connections, it had dawned on me that the FBI was feeding him information. There was no other way he could know the details of things I said—in private as well as public— whom I met with, talked with, or wrote to. Brown, like Hoover and the deputy U.S. attorney general, seemed frustrated by his inability to reveal the sources of what he called "this damning information." We were all locked into an ongoing game: the FBI cat accused, and the red mouse denied.

We hung around the hotel for a few days while the trial was going on, getting periodic reports of the utter confusion in the convention hall. There was no precedent for such a weird proceeding, and no one had the slightest idea what, if any, rules applied. Roberts' Rules of Order, the procedural bible for union meetings, contained absolutely no provision for conducting a trial. Although the union's constitution did include such a procedure, it assumed that a trial would originate at the local union level, not at a convention. In fact, the convention was the last court of appeal for members tried by a lower body. It was as if the Supreme Court were to act as a local prosecutor. It was a dumb, dumb idea and was sure to backfire.

For the second time, I was expelled from the union; the vote was 760 to 98. The International once again moved to put Local 402 under supervision. By the time we arrived back in New York, our lawyers had filed papers asking the New York Supreme Court to enjoin the International from carrying out the convention's decision. Within a few days, Justice Null issued a restraining order barring the International union from taking over the local and reaffirming our right to criticize the leadership. I was again reinstated as president of Local 402 and of the Machinists' State Council. My supporters in these organizations were jubilant, but I wasn't. We were winning the legal battles but not the hearts and minds of our union brothers. I had an inner sense that without strong support from the membership, our cause was lost.

These were the years leading up to the McCarthy witch hunts. The House Committee on Un-American Activities (HUAC) accused five government employees of spying for the Soviet Union during the war. The committee's sensationalized hearings on the communist infiltration of Hollywood, Broadway, and the unions were scaring people into turning on their friends. As a result of HUAC hearings, fifteen thousand federal employees were either fired or forced to resign their jobs. HUAC also turned over to private employers the names of sixty thousand people they deemed potential security risks. Most of these people were not party members and, in all probability, were doing nothing more sinister than supporting liberal causes.

HUAC also wanted to supoena me to testify, but, the FBI file indicates, Hoover refused to supply information, because at the time the attorney general was seeking to prosecute me for violation of the Taft-Hartley Act. The administration clearly did not want me hung out in public while it was hoping to build a case against me.

In July of 1948 twelve leaders of the Party, including Foster, were indicted for conspiracy; in October of the next year eleven of them were convicted and sentenced to jail.* A month before, in September of 1949, the Soviet Union had exploded its first atomic bomb, scaring the bejesus out of the whole country and breathing a far more fearful dimension into the red scare. The nightmare of an atomic war brought "duck and cover" air raid drills to schools and induced some families to build bomb shelters in their backyards. A cloud of right-wing extremism created a ghastly pall of fear and suspicion.

Even the CIO, that militant arm of the labor movement that had used so many communists to help organize the country's basic industries, responded to the hysteria. The influence of the Catholic Church was clearly present between 1948 and 1950 when the CIO expelled first the United Electrical Workers, then eleven more unions for being "communist dominated." CIO head Philip Murray, a devout Catholic, was a good friend of the Bishop of Pittsburgh. Everywhere in the labor movement, unions were turning on themselves as members became suspicious of each other.

*The indictment against Foster was severed from the others on account of his health and was never carried out.

Many of my longtime union friends were slowly but surely becoming distant.

People who knew me were visited by FBI agents looking for information about me and my associates. I and several friends received threatening telephone calls in the middle of the night warning about "hanging out with commie spies."

Members of the Machinists' union were well represented amongst those suffering from the red-menace phobia. Paul, who had been my closest union buddy for seven years, was having trouble looking me in the eye when he said things like, "Bob, I got a wife and two kids to worry about. I'm not like you. I don't give a fuck about the Soviet Union and all that shit you are constantly bringing up. And neither do the members of this union. It's too bad that you can't get that through your head."

"Paul, my primary concern is the same as yours, but unless the Soviet Union and the United States can find a way to peaceful coexistence the world is gonna go up in atomic smoke and all the great achievements of the union will be meaningless." Over the next year Paul and I had this conversation many times. I think now that he was warning me about what he would eventually feel forced to do.

Although HUAC and, later, the McCarthy Committee, were primarily looking to bag big fish like Foster and Alger Hiss, there was a second tier of witch hunters eager to entrap anyone they could paint as a red, pinko, or fellow traveler. The latter accusation had become such a broad brush that it sometimes included people who had a Van Gogh print on their living room wall or read *The Nation.*

Although I had heard all the stories of unexpected visitors, tapped telephones, intercepted mail, wives telling on husbands and vice versa, I was still knocked for a loop when my sister Alice called to say that Papa had had a talk with the FBI. "I don't believe this!" I screamed at her. "Who told you?"

She hadn't believed it either, but Papa himself had told her that "two nice men" who identified themselves as FBI agents had come to see him about his children's political activities. When she expressed shock that he had agreed to talk with them, Papa insisted that, unlike us, he had nothing to hide. Besides, he said, they were two perfectly reasonable people and they'd had a nice talk. Alice could just imagine him trying to convince the FBI agents of the evils of capitalism and the wonders of a free and open society.

According to the FBI file, Papa said "he had tried his best to convince them (his children) that their support of Stalin and his henchmen was wrong and they should give it up." Then poor Papa tried to persuade the FBI agents that Alice and I were "good kids and they mean well and they got carried away in their desire to make this a better world. I'm sure you can understand this." The agents assured him that they did, thanked him for his help, and said they might be back to talk with him again. Papa replied that he had enjoyed the conversation.

I think Alice was right. Knowing Papa, I can just see him trying to help these FBI men understand how capitalism turns nice kids into radical revolutionaries. Nonetheless, the information on Papa's "informing" was devastating to me. Eventually I realized that he was simply refusing to deny what he believed in, regardless of the consequences. He would not hide behind a curtain of lies. Papa would have been terribly hurt by the suggestion that he was informing on his own children and would have insisted that he was only telling the truth about his own political views. Could anyone construe that as informing?*

I was depressed and suffered from increasingly severe headaches. My only escape from the stress of that period was spending time with my delightful eight-year-old daughter Elizabeth. We were embraced in the classic father-daughter love affair. Sunday morning was our time together at the Bronx Zoo—one of those rare places I could return to as an adult with my own child and find it exactly the same as when I was a child. Holding my hand as I had held Papa's, Lizzie would say, "Your hand feels just like a hard-boiled egg, and I really like it." She loved the animals and knew many of them by name. Knowing that they were about to get "treats," as Lizzie called our stale bread, they would come running up to the fence at the sight of her. What fun it was to watch her trying valiantly to distribute her gifts equally among a herd of wild antelopes. Those visits were my Sunday morning blessing.

---

*Papa and J. Edgar were right, in their own way. Pressed between its clandestine connections to the Soviet government and our government's policy of harassment, the Party *had* became a conspiratorial outfit.

Otherwise, my life was becoming a more and more divided affair. I had always inhabited two separate worlds. In one I hung out with the guys in the union and in the other with a community of people with similar beliefs. We had known most of the latter as communists and did not ask whether they were still members—cautious behavior that grew out of a new fear of stool pigeons that, like cockroaches in a fire, came pouring out of the woodwork. In face of the growing conservatism of the country, people on the Left began to think that fascism was a real possibility in the United States. Among ourselves we began to talk about how we could survive in this increasingly dangerous environment. Several old friends talked of leaving the country for Mexico or Europe, and some actually did.

In the labor movement, the red scare almost entirely eliminated any substantive ideological discussion about the future. Adopting a policy of survival meant de-emphasizing anything that smacked of class struggle. With the exception of a few CIO unions, the "business trade unionism" of Sam Gompers became the accepted ideology. It said, in essence, that corporations should manage their business and unions should seek specific improvements in pay and working conditions. As one major employer told me, "Unions need to be in the dues business, not trying to change society. We do not want to deal with ideologues like you." The National Association of Manufacturers and the U.S. Chamber of Commerce wanted more than anything to return to the pre–New Deal days of labor relations.

I was more fearful of the political Right than I was of the Party's obsession with the Soviet Union. I no longer doubted that the Party's links to Moscow were financial as well as ideological, but I still thought the greatest danger came from the Right. The Party was evidently making plans for an underground network to carry on its revolutionary activity if and when it was outlawed. It was another example of accepting a model created in Moscow. I thought it was pretty wacky for a movement based on the need for mass support to think it could operate from the underground. It sure was not an American political model.

This was the atmosphere in which Schrank (the plaintiff) *vs.* Brown (the defendant) would be tried in the State Supreme Court. "Are we nuts for thinking we can win this case with all this 'red menace' talk going around?" I asked Glickstein.

"Listen, even if we lose, our resistance will make it easier for other rank-and-file members to be secure in their right to criticize their leaders. This fight," he said, "may well determine the future. We're going to teach the fat cats a lesson in democracy." He paused, thought for a while, then said, "even if it's the last thing I do." Ours was one of the last politically sensitive cases Glickstein handled before he went off to become a race-track millionaire.

At issue in the trial was the legality of the International's second suspension from membership of myself and the local, as well as the convention's trial procedure. Joe Cronin, president of the New England Council, as well as a number of local union officers and members who were at the convention, agreed to testify on our behalf. Cronin would also testify that the International had put his New England Council into trusteeship for simply passing a resolution criticizing my expulsion.

Glickstein rehearsed us for the trial as if we were opening on Broadway. He left nothing to chance, going over every possible line of questioning until he was satisfied that we had it right and would not be intimidated by the ornate old courtroom and officious atmosphere.

Rehearsing one of the brothers, Glickstein paced up and asked, "Now George, could you describe for the court the atmosphere at the convention during this so-called trial?" When George started to answer, Glickstein interrupted. "You're answering too quickly. I want you to pause as though you're thinking hard." George, who was starting to enjoy this acting business, described the general chaos of the "trial" in Grand Rapids. Then, after a pause, he said, "Your Honor, in a word, it was sheer pandemonium." We burst into applause.

"Perfect," said Glickstein. "Let's just run through that a few more times until we're absolutely we sure have it on cue."

In the last week of rehearsals I was put through the mill, and Louie Boudin came to help us deal with the communist questions. The lawyers were very concerned that I might be set up for a perjury conviction. Glickstein mentioned the Alger Hiss case, which was going on at the time, as an example of the kind of trouble perjury can get you into.

The four lawyers agonized over how we should deal with tough political questions about my past party membership. They finally decided that I should to refuse to answer questions about my personal political beliefs, as was my right under the first and fifth amendments to the Constitution. To questions about membership in the Communist party, I should respond that I had signed the noncommunist affidavit under the Taft-Hartley law and say nothing more.

This whole line of response was very troubling to me. I said, "Shit, if I sit there and waltz around and take the Fifth the way the party leaders do, the average guy in the union is gonna say, 'The fucker won't answer. He's gotta be guilty as sin. The hell with him.' I'm telling you that won't fly. It just won't."

Boudin said, "Bob, I understand exactly how you feel. You would like your destiny to be inside the labor movement. But if they get you on perjury, what happens to your position in the union? Our first job as lawyers is to protect you from prosecution, which in the present atmosphere won't be easy. We're going to do whatever we have to do to keep you out of jail. We have no other options."

We took a quick lunch break and came back. Glickstein wanted to go over George's testimony again. How was the vote actually taken at the convention? Who counted the ballots? What happened in the lobby of the hotel when one of the local's delegates was set upon by a bunch of goons? The grilling continued for many hours. Afterward I felt so confident I told Glickstein I was almost looking forward to strutting our stuff in the courtroom.

He replied, "Well, don't, because there are too many unknowns in this business." He let out his little giggle, "We'll be fine if the judge believes us and doesn't take the red herring." On the way out the door, Glickstein's final word was, "And Bob, out of respect to his honor, wear a shirt and tie to court instead of that dude sport shirt you've got on."

The morning of the trial Lizzie and I had our regular breakfast together and listened to Bob and Ray and the radio soap opera "Mary Noble, Backstage Wife, the story of America's favorite family of the footlights and their fight for security and happiness against the concrete heart of Broadway."

Lizzie wanted to know why I was all dressed up, but I told her very little. How could I explain what was going on to an eight year old? In fact, I shared very little information about the union's political wars with my family. Only now do I realize how troubled I was by my dual identity. How could I tell Lizzie not to talk to anyone about her father for fear he could be sent to jail? And although Edith certainly followed the events, they occurred in a very different world from the one she lived in, and I really never tried to make her a partner in my struggles.

At the appointed hour we appeared before Judge Benvenga of the New York State Supreme Court. Lawyers for both sides submitted their briefs, and the International union began presenting its case. Brown was their primary witness. Under cross-examination he conceded that never before in the history of the union had anyone been tried at an IAM convention. But, he insisted, in view of the court's rulings, he had had no alternative. Other witnesses testified about our local's support of communist causes. So far it was not nearly as bad as I had anticipated in the sleepless, fear-filled nights before the trial. The International had presented its case, and we had cross-examined their witnesses. After a short break it would be our turn.

During the break both Jerry Sturm, one of the attorneys for the International union, and I were late getting to the men's room. I knew Sturm from working with him on union cases before the NLRB as well as on the Yale & Towne strike. Standing at the adjoining urinal, he glanced over at me.

"You're pretty worried about the red stuff, aren't you?" he asked.

I was so surprised I almost peed in my pants. "What the hell are you talking about?"

He laughed. "Look," he said, "you won't be indicted by either Justice or the Un-Americans."

I couldn't believe this conversation. "How the hell do you know all this?"

"Never mind how I know," he said. "Trust me, I know. You see, they don't want your membership on the Democratic National Labor Committee in forty-four to be made public. That would be an enormous embarrassment to both the Democratic administration and the International union. Remember it was Harvey Brown who appointed you to that committee. Besides, they think you know all about the financial shenanigans that went on there. Sure as hell, with your big mouth, they figure you would tell all. So don't worry." Before I could say "Hail Mary" he was gone. What the hell was I to make of that?

The trial continued all that afternoon while I was preoccupied with the toilet conversation. We were getting to the end of our witness list, and I was waiting to be called. George made his impressive "and pandemonium reigned" speech. It went over so well that the judge asked him to repeat his description of the convention atmosphere in which the trial took place.

When George finished and stepped down, Glickstein said, "Your Honor, that is our case." Myer, one of our other lawyers, was grinning from ear to ear. He came over to tell me that they had decided there was no reason to put me on the stand. I heard one of the International's lawyers asking, "Isn't Mr. Schrank to be called as a witness?" While the judge was conferring with the lawyers at the bench, Myer explained that the other side could call me as their witness, but then they wouldn't be able to impugn the testimony of their own witness. "They won't do it," he predicted. And they didn't.

I was both pleased and disappointed. I'd hoped for the opportunity to show my courtroom stuff. I wanted so badly to make the dramatic appeal that would turn the antilabor politics around and save the day for the good guys. On the other hand, I was relieved not to have to deal with the communist issue.

I asked Glickstein, "What the hell is going on here? What was all that rehearsal for anyway?"

He laughed. "Well, as you see, it went so well we just didn't need you. Maybe you feel deprived, but for us the danger of perjury was just too great. We weren't about to let them get you to perjure yourself. That's all there was to it." I tried to tell him what I had learned in the men's room, but he was in a big hurry and rushed off.

After some time, the judge ruled in our favor that the convention had absolutely no authority to try either me or the local union. Once again we celebrated. Once again the little guys had defeated the fat cats in Washington. For the moment, we were the heroes of all the rank-and-file union fighters. Yet in spite of our victory, there was no resurgence of union militancy in the country. It was as though our success was a fluke. It probably was.

The International union was in a bind. Harvey Brown, on his way out of office, had left his successor a mess. Hayes, however, would turn out to be a far more diabolical strategist than Brown was. He decided to appeal the decision to the New York State Court of Appeals, the state's highest court. Around this time, according to the FBI file, Hoover received another letter from John Steelman, Truman's economic adviser, requesting information about me; and once again Hoover told Steelman to make his request through the attorney general. My guess is that after our second court victory, the Washington Machinists leaders were furious and, hoping to get information to discredit me, went to Steelman.

In the meantime, Local 402 got back to its normal routines. The money was put back into the regular accounts, and files were returned to the office. We decided to launch another petition drive, this time calling for repeal of Taft-Hartley. Through the state council, we initiated a campaign to gather a million signatures to present to the president. When a delegation of union leaders took the petitions to the White House, we were received by none other than John Steelman, who assured us of the president's continued opposition to the legislation.

Several FBI-looking characters in fedoras and trench coats who identified themselves as representatives of the International began hanging around the local's office. According to an anonymous telephone call from California, one of them, Brother Truax, was an ex-FBI man Hayes had sent to keep an eye us. Truax sauntered around the office whistling tunes like "Bury Me Not On the Lone Prairie," which was supposed to scare me; being a fan of cowboy songs, I just sang right along. When I asked him what his real purpose was in being there, he admitted he'd been sent to watch me, adding, "You won the battle, but you're gonna lose the war. You know why?"

"No, I don't," I said. "Besides, don't be so sure we will lose."

"Schrank, we got the resources to bury you a hundred times over long after you guys are running on empty. So in the end we will win, and you'll be out on your little commie ass."

I was furious. I knew if we ended up fighting, he would probably beat the shit out of me. So I picked up my hat and coat and announced to the secretary in a voice loud enough to be overheard that I was going over to the ASPCA to talk with some dogs I could trust.

Instead I went to our lawyers' office. They were busy preparing our case for the five-judge Court of Appeals. I was greatly relieved to learn that there would be no trial, just briefs. Glickstein and the others were working over our "brief on appeal" even more carefully than they had prepared the trial case. He explained that our case had to be very carefully presented, because it just might end up in the U.S. Supreme Court. I listened to long arguments about whether a comma or semicolon belonged at a certain point, and Glickstein drove everyone in the office crazy insisting on checking, rechecking, and checking again. All this was important, he explained, because "judges depend on people like us to write a brief that does not leave them looking stupid. Besides, our opponents will use a microscope to find an error, an oversight, or a wrong interpretation of a citation—anything that might create a doubt in the minds of those five judges that maybe, just maybe, we don't know what the hell we're talking about."

Slowly I became aware that our fight for First Amendment rights had ended up being based primarily on technicalities. Most of the brief described the process for bringing charges against a member or a local and argued that the International had violated those procedures. The point I hoped the case would make—that union members had the absolute right of free speech—was in the brief, but it wasn't the central argument. Glickstein told me that the court would make its decision on the basis of a law that sets forth what can or can't be done in such circumstances. In our case, because the International had in fact violated its own procedures, it was much easier to indict them for that than to get into a philosophical discussion regarding the First Amendment. "But," he added, "the right to criticize the union's leaders orally or in writing is inherent in this case. If they decide to go to the U.S. Supreme Court, we will argue the case on the First Amendment." Noticing my apparent disappointment, some of the other lawyers pointed out that in view of the political atmosphere in the country "we are doing pretty damn good."

They were right. The International under President Hayes withdrew the case, leaving the lower court decision to stand. Unable to beat me on the state and national level, Hayes was going to prove his respectability as a red hunter with a very different strategy.

In the Machinists' hierarchy of organizations, the district councils were midway between the local and the state levels. Council 15, which included representatives from all the Machinists locals in the New York City area, held monthly meetings and employed several business agents to provide services to members and locals. The delegates to the district council from my local, like several others, tended to be lefties. In many organizations, the lefties had far more influence than their numbers warranted, simply because others were not interested in attending meetings. Two or three delegates from each of the eight or nine locals went to the district meetings, which usually dealt with such miscellaneous business as expiring contracts, information sent by the International, and other generally boring matters. They tended to be pretty low-key affairs.

At the May meeting in 1950, some of us were standing around outside the meeting hall reluctant to go inside. It began to dawn on me that something was brewing. There was none of the usual kidding around that usually accompanied our get-togethers. Men I had known and worked with over the years not only avoided looking at me, they said "Hi" and hurried by without stopping. Paul, my oldest union buddy, in his haste to get into the meeting, threw out something like, "I hope you don't make an ass of yourself again tonight." Before I could say "hey," he had disappeared into the room. Could this be just another routine council meeting?

After going through the regular agenda items—minutes, old business, new business, reports on the welfare of the organization, and so on—we usually adjourned. That night, there was one last item on the agenda. One of the business agents announced, "We're gonna put out some traps to catch red rats." Shades of the convention!

Jimmy, a member from our local who had never even attended a union meeting before, took the floor to introduce a resolution "to see where this union stands in support of our country." He read a carefully phrased document he couldn't have written if his life depended on it. It called for "full and unconditional support of our government in the Korean War effort."

Like Pavlov's dogs responding to the sound of the bell, the delegates from my local were immediately on their feet offering amendments in support of the United Nations' efforts at mediation. The horror of Hiroshima still very fresh in our minds, we believed the war was a dangerous threat to world peace. Not just party comrades but liberals in general were scared to death that if the Korean War escalated, the Soviets might become involved and World War III could be on its way.

The resolution was a trap and I knew it, but I no longer cared. It was passed by acclamation, with only me, Sam, and Carter voting against it. That had never, ever happened before. As I left the meeting I knew my career in the union was over. My gut told me these working-class guys would give unquestioning support to the United States government in the war. All the Marxist-Leninist intellectual faith in working-class international brotherhood made less and less sense every time I thought about it. Workers would fight the police, the National Guard, or the Army in their own economic interest, but that was all. Period. Outside that context, it was "my government right or wrong."

It was past three in the morning at the Old Heidelberg Restaurant when the bartender finally announced it was closing time. Paul and I were having what would be our last extended conversation. We had come into the union together and gone through some of its toughest negotiations, strikes, internal fights, organizing campaigns, and legal battles. For seven years we had shared our thoughts, doubts, victories, and defeats. We were as close as two union brothers could be. As we drank the night away, he tried obstinately to save me from what he called, "your fuckin' stupid, suicidal support for these god-damn commie causes." He wanted so badly to convince me. Over and over he said, "Please, please give up this craziness. You know, sure as we're sittin' here, they're gonna hang you by your nuts. If you think the membership of this union will support you, you're living in a dream world."

I tried to convince him that my integrity was more important to me than pleasing the mob. As the words slipped from my mouth, I realized that Papa had just spoken through me. Full of sadness, we shook hands and parted. Paul knew what was ahead, but he wouldn't say. His parting shot was, "If you stand pat, you're dead in the water. This time the courts won't be able to save you. I'm really sorry for you. Good-bye."

Jimmy showed up again a few weeks later at our regular local meeting. This time he presented charges against Sam, Carter, and me. I had to relinquish the chair, but I didn't care. The fire had gone out. In some way the thought that it would be over soon was a relief, as though the burden of a double life might finally be lifted. I said to Sam, "I'm tired and bored with the whole business." As Jimmy read the charges, everyone in the room knew he had not written a single word of them; they were the work of some smart lawyer. I was confident that the new International president, Al Hayes, was poor Jimmy's ghostwriter.

We were charged with "supporting communist causes in violation of the union constitution and its stated policies." A trial committee was quickly appointed, and a trial date was set. The chair of the trial committee was Fred Muller, another old friend. He explained to me that he had a wife and kids and that loyalty to the country came before his friendship to me or anyone else. "You're a great guy," he said. "You could be the president of this union forever if you would only give up that commie shit. You know nobody in this union gives a good goddamn about Romania, Russia, or those yellow, slanty-eyed, sneaky Koreans. But you think you can represent us anyway. Well, you can't. So why don't you do us and yourself a favor and just go away." Fred paused. This was really hard for him. More than anything, he wanted me to just walk away. After a while he went on: "Bob, this is all planned. You're dead. Believe me. Give it up."

I told him not to worry about it. "We all do what we have to. Only time will tell who, if anyone, is right. The leaders of this union, like most of the others, are only interested in being accepted as respectable by the power structure. There is only one threat to labor in this country, and it comes from employers, not from people like me. By burning my ass they're gonna show that they're good loyal subjects of the ruling class. It's far more important to Hayes to be respectable in Washington circles and with the Chicago Chamber of Commerce than to do a real job for his members. They just want to kiss the employers' asses to show how unthreatening they are. This will be a sad labor movement when they throw out all the people who are the real champions of the working class."

Our argument over, we shook hands. As we parted, I heard Fred saying to himself, "Damn, I hate this." I argued with Fred and Paul and lots of others. What had gone out of my responses was the conviction I had had as a fire-and-brimstone street corner speaker when I was an unflinching believer in the absolute rightness of our cause. Now, as the gospel song says, "I was drifting too far from the shore." Many of my beliefs were slipping away, and I did not see any alternative to letting things take their course.

My conversations with Glickstein now took on a very different tone. He listened intently to my description of what had happened and carefully read over the charges. "Who do you think wrote this?" he asked.

"I'm sure it was Hayes's office or the International's attorneys. Hell, the guys who brought the charges can just about write their own names." Glickstein was obviously pessimistic and looking for something to hang onto. "You may be right, but can you prove it?" Of course I couldn't, not then. Glickstein, perhaps reflecting his own growing disenchantment with the Left, told me I should think seriously about doing something else for a living.

About this time, another letter sent to the FBI and the U.S. attorney general complained that "nothing is being done about Schrank." The copy in the FBI file has both the letterhead and the writer's names blacked out. I suspect that after our court victory, the leaders of the AFL and the Machinists were frustrated with the FBI's inaction. Attorneys for the AFL, I learned later, had convinced the Machinists not to appeal *Schrank vs. Brown*, for fear that it would end up in the U.S. Supreme Court and be upheld.

As I left the lawyers' offices and walked along 57th Street, I was pretty sure it was only a matter of time before the fight was over. The endless rounds of meetings, traveling, writing speeches, and just trying to convince workers that I was not in league with the devil was sapping my life energy. I was burning out. Being rejected by my very own love, the working class, was taking all the romance out of the good fight.

The local meeting at which the trial committee was to submit its findings to the membership was moved to a larger hall to accommodate the expected big turnout. Normally if 2 or 3 percent of the members attended a regular union meeting it was considered pretty good.

Outside the hall before the meeting, several men assured me of their continued support, while others—including old friends—quickly ran by or took detours to avoid looking me in the eye. Victor Rosario kept his promise to repay my favor. "Hey, Mister Presidente, I got every Puerto Rican in this union here to vote for you. I tell you you got a friend for life." I appreciated the support but wished there were more of them.

After rapidly dispensing with routine business, the trial committee presented the evening's main attraction, the report on the charges against me. This was why workers showed up who had never been to a union meeting before and probably never would again. They were impatient to do their dirty work and get it over with so they could go have a beer.

The report made much of my refusal to participate in the committee's deliberations. What they did not say was that my repeated requests for a bill of particulars specifying how and when we had violated the union's constitution or its policies had been ignored. When I tried to get the floor to respond to the report, I was gaveled out of order by the chair, my old friend Fred Muller. I learned later that Al Hayes had advised them not to let me speak under any circumstances. It was particularly painful being shouted down by members of my own local, even though I knew they had been recruited for this purpose. Muller kept repeating that "the rules allow no discussion of a trial committee report." After a while I quit trying. The vote was taken, and we were found guilty as charged.

A second vote to expel us from the union failed to get the needed two-thirds majority. Instead, we were suspended from holding office for ten years and fined fifty dollars each. I was out of office but still in the union. It was a small victory, and a brief one. When the local's penalty decision was appealed to the International, Hayes and his executive council reversed it and expelled all three of us from the union. They even added a proviso that if I ever reapplied for membership my application would have to be unanimously approved by the International executive council. My career in the Machinists' union was over.

I had set a record as the only person in the history of the AFL to be expelled from a union three times. Even so, Schrank *vs.* Brown (New York State Supreme Court, 1948, 1950) had established new legal grounds for protecting the right of rank-and-file union members to criticize their leaders. The decision reasserted that the U.S. Constitution's guaranteed right of free speech cannot be denied by any organization's constitution or rules. For many years after the expulsion, I received requests for copies of the court briefs from local unions as well as groups of members trying to exert their democratic rights. The fight we made in the IAM created a ray of hope for union members struggling to gain some control over their organizations.

In *The Machinists,* Mark Perlman writes that "Brown believed that there was danger in letting state or interstate political units grow any stronger. Schrank threatened to promote another source of power. Whether the Schrank dispute was caused by radicalism, charges of prevarication, or something else, the fight served the grand lodge's purpose of asserting its suzerainty."*

Almost a year after the trial, I unexpectedly received a sworn affidavit from Fred Muller, chairman of the trial committee. What motivated him, other than conscience, I cannot say. The affidavit describes how the plot to dump me had been hatched by Al Hayes and members of his staff. According to the affidavit, at meetings held in the Nelson House Hotel in Poughkeepsie, Hayes told Muller not to worry about the details. "All the local lodge needs to do is try Schrank," he reputedly said. "If they don't find him guilty or expel him, the Grand Lodge will take care of it on appeal." The chief mover in the local was the vice president, who wanted my job. Muller reported that everyone involved was taken care of with either cash or a job. (In red-baiting everything was considered fair.) Fred realized belatedly that the International had simply used him by appealing to his "patriotic duty."

Once out of the union, I retreated more and more from politics. The arts, in particular the theater, became part of a new search for meaning. I found I needed to see Lawrence Olivier's film of *Hamlet* again and again. What was my fascination? Did the prince of Denmark's struggle with his demons remind me of my inability to come to terms with my father's condemnation of my politics? Was my fascination and identification with Hamlet a clue to my own indecisiveness in giving up ideals I no longer really believed in? Slowly, over the years, my doubts about the dictatorship of the proletariat had grown. I no longer believed that the workers I knew could or would put my socialist ideals into practice. Through the labor movement, workers had achieved substantial economic and social gains and, what was perhaps more important, a new

*Cambridge: Harvard University Press, 1962, p. 129.

level of dignity. They had even achieved a degree of interracial unity within the sphere of common economic interests. When it came to who their kids went to school with, that was another matter. That was, I believed, as far as we could go in the United States.

On a Monday morning following the trial I was back at work punching a clock in the old shop I had helped organize so many years before. I was set to work making drill jigs for lubrication equipment. After all the postwar lay-offs, there were still a few hundred jobs in the shop and my seniority was still in force. A big sign hung in the toolroom on the morning of my return: "Welcome Back—From the Old Tool Room Gang—All Twelve Of Us." Some goodwill was left from those happy earlier days.

The union made no effort to force me out of my job. They could have got rid of me legally as it was a union shop and I was no longer a member. I was pretty sure it wouldn't have worked anyway, because the men in the shop saw me as a victim of the union fat cats and wanted me back in their little community.

After a few months, though, the work routines became dull. I was also bored listening to the endless talk of sports and pussy. Fighting for these guys when I saw them as the victims of capitalist exploitation was one thing; in that glorified frame of reference I probably never saw them as they really were. Living with them day after day was another matter.

16

Life After the Machinists

In 1949, with the Cold War heating up, some of the media were reporting secret government plans to set up "concentration camps" to house political dissidents. It was a very bad time for liberals, lefties, and fellow travelers and hell on earth for party members. Around this time, the FBI file indicates, J. Edgar issued an order that I was to be immediately interned "in case of a national emergency."

My own life and sense of purpose were in some confusion. I had left the Party and, inevitably, began to have doubts about the beliefs that had sustained me for almost two decades. Of course, the shifts in my thinking didn't happen all at once. I still believed that capitalism was evil and that the class struggle was the key to improving the lives of workers. My union experience had convinced me that we could win meaningful concessions from the ruling class. I had lost confidence in the Party but not in my belief that we could create a better world

That summer, while the decision of the State Supreme Court was pending, I decided to take the family on an extended vacation in the Adirondacks. I was depressed and desperately needed to escape from the tensions of the red scare and the trouble with the International.

The excitement began as soon as I unearthed the Coleman stove and lantern and started giving them their pre-camping overhaul. Early one Saturday morning we loaded up the tents, cots, blankets, pots, pans, clothes, and our well-used Hudson Bay ax. The aroma of our twelve-by-twenty canvas army tent brought back welcome memories of other family camping trips. Each time one of us headed for the four-door Dodge with a load, Betsy, our spaniel, would dash out of the house and jump into the front seat, ready to go. Camping was life in the woods, and the woods were clearly Betsy's turf.

After the usual delays, we headed up the Taconic Parkway, the car packed to the hilt. Lizzie, then about eight years old, had brought along her friend Joe to keep her company. During the drive she explained to Joe what would happen when we arrived. "First we have to go the ranger station to get our camping permit, then load all our stuff in a boat, because we'll be camping on an island." She informed him emphatically that Frank Bruno, the park ranger, was in charge of the lake. "If you break any rules, you know what? He can tell you to go home. Isn't that right Bob?" Lizzie always called me Bob. We thought "Daddy" was a bourgeois term.

Driving up Route 9, you ascend a very gradual rise until suddenly, tucked between two mountain ranges, Lake George appears, revealing why the Indians called it "the lake that shuts itself in." The town of Lake George at the southern tip, suffers from the Coney Island syndrome; developers are forever trying to build yet another motel or tacky penny arcade. Once north of town, however, the pine forest surrounded us again. Lamb's Boatyard in Bolton Landing lies at the midpoint of the long, narrow thirty-five-mile lake that runs north and south from Lake Champlain to Glens Falls. At its widest point Lake George is only three miles across; it is dotted with two hundred little pine-covered islands. To a nature-loving New Yorker like me, it is paradise.

By the time I had carefully backed the car down a steep hill to the boatyard, Betsy was howling with excitement and Lizzie and Joe were confident they could hear the "call of the wild" emanating from the surrounding forest. The yard was stacked with scores of the Old Town wooden canoes we had used many times before, but Mr. Lamb wanted me to try out a new large Grumman aluminum canoe with a "nice three-horsepower engine." It was supposed to be very safe and easy to paddle. I figured that with Joe along we could use the extra space in the larger boat and the increased mobility a motor would provide. Mr. Lamb was a mountain man of few words: "Grumman guarantees she's unsinkable. Plenty of flotation right under the seats, bow and stern. Yup, that's what Grumman says." Besides, the aluminum canoe was a peacetime conversion product. How could I refuse it?

Before heading for our campsite on Big Burnt Island, we stopped up the lake at Glenn Island to check in with Frank. Before shoving off, I asked one of the Lamb boys what the weather looked like. "Well, you never can tell about weather hereabouts. Best be ready, that's all we can tell anyone." I knew from my own experience that even on a beautiful clear sunny day clouds can suddenly roll in from the mountaintops with little or no warning. The sky darkens, and the wind starts to howl out of the north. The lake, peaceful and calm just a few moments before, becomes a storm-blown sea of rolling white caps. I once heard a local yokel refer to these squalls as "our own God-given roller coasters." They may last only a short time, but while they do it takes all your skill and strength to keep a canoe from being swamped.

A few hours after setting up camp on the island, we were in our bathing suits and I was stretched out on a large expanse of rock worn smooth by a couple of million years of glacial action. Across the lake was Tongue Mountain, known for its rattlesnakes and copperheads. Edith, Joe, Lizzie, and Betsy were splashing about in crystal water clean enough to drink. As I relaxed in the pine-scented noonday sun, I was overcome with the simple joy of the place.

Things were wonderfully quiet during our first week on Big Burnt. We swam, ate, read, hiked and absorbed the beauty around us. In the evening we sat on our rock and watched the glorious sunsets over Tongue Mountain. After dinner we joined other campers around the campfire for singing, square dancing, and toasting the perfect marshmallow—"just a little bit of brown all around the outside and soft and mushy in the middle," as Joe said. Edith's talents as a folksinger brought us plenty of campfire invitations. At the time, most Lake George campers were liberals or radicals; you could almost identify people's political leanings from the songs they knew. We sang union and protest songs and traditional folk tunes with the gusto of a Southern Baptist revival meeting, belting out "The Erie Canal," "Cockles and Muscles," "Hold the Fort," and "The Preacher and the Slave," accompanied by a chorus of crickets and cicadas. There were even a few people who knew all the words to some Red Army songs; I assumed they were on the far Left politically, but nobody asked. As the evening wore on and the fire burnt down, the songs became quieter as we city folk were overwhelmed with the beauty of the star-filled Adirondack sky. We were certain we had attained nirvana.

One memorable night I was deeply asleep, lulled by the sweet smell of pine and the hum of insects, when I was awakened by the sounds of canoes paddling and exclamations of "aah" and "ooh." I peered out through the tent flap and had a ghostly vision of the lake covered by hundreds of canoes filled with people gazing up at the northern sky. I woke everyone. Quickly pulling on some clothes, we climbed into our boat to see one of the greatest shows of all—the northern lights. As the night wore on, the beams of light and color shot higher and higher into the sky and were greeted with a chorus of applause. Many of us stayed out on the lake all through the night. As dawn broke, we saluted each other with a shared sense of having had an encounter with the gods.

Most mornings we got up early and went swimming. After breakfast, we would take a hike up Black or Shelving Rock Mountain where you could shower under a spring-fed waterfall. On the top of Black Mountain lived a grumpy old firewatcher. From his perch on the tower, he would yell, "Wanna cup of Kool Aid for a dime?" In 1949 we thought that outrageously expensive, but we were hot, tired, and thirsty. We figured, "What the hell! We're on vacation."

One afternoon after a hike up Tongue Mountain to listen for rattlesnakes, we decided to go for ice cream at Bolton Landing. As I headed the canoe into Northwest Bay, it occurred to me that I had not thought too much about the weather. The bay, one of the widest points on the lake, was opposite the place where the tongue of the mountain sloped steeply down to the water. The confluence of the mountain and the bay could create some of the most treacherous winds on the lake. Without warning, the sky began to darken, the wind began to whistle, and the lake started to boil. "Now listen everyone," I yelled from the stern of the canoe, "I will keep this boat headed into the wind at a nice easy pace as well as I can. Remember, if we are swamped, the boat will not sink. Above all, do not attempt to swim for shore. It's farther than it looks."

I tried to think fast about the next thing to do. Looking down at my heavy hiking boots, I thought I must be nuts to be in an oversized canoe wearing these goddamned sinkers. With one hand on the motor control, I tried desperately with the other to untie the laces. Suddenly we were hit by a huge wave and in an instant we were in the water. The stern of the boat fell right out from under us; only the tip of the bow stayed afloat. Edith was sitting in the bow holding on with one hand and calling to Lizzie and Joe. Without a conscious thought, I focused on getting the two kids to the bow. Joe was already there, and I pushed Lizzie along toward Edith's outstretched hand. All my strength was being consumed, and I began to feel the heavy boots dragging me down.

As I struggled with the laces I could see my family hanging onto the bow of the boat. I fought desperately to keep from sinking, but slowly but surely I was going down. I knew there was nothing more I could do. Looking up through the water, I saw the shape of a large hull approaching. I had no air left and began to breathe in water. All around me it was growing very peaceful, and my mother appeared smiling and beckoning. This was the first time since her death twenty-five years before that her face had appeared to me. Then I was with the my little dog Kaiyoodle meeting Papa at the train station. Some of the most serene, loving moments of life passed before me. The dark shape of the boat overhead gave me a good feeling, for I knew Edith, Lizzie, and Joe were safe. My body felt depleted, emptied of its life energy. I was resigned.

Suddenly someone or something dove down next to me, grabbed my legs, and gave me a powerful push toward the surface, shoving me again and again until I came up at the side of a launch. A boat hook grabbed me by the back of my pants and a couple of men hauled me into the boat. They laid me down with my head over the side and pushed rhythmically on my back, in and out. Water seemed to be pouring out of all my openings.

Very slowly, as I was puking my guts out, it began to dawn on me that someone had saved my life. With my stomach pressed over a gas tank and my head over the side, Betsy was enthusiastically licking my ear. I heard Edith say, "She just kept swimming around and around until help came."

The words "Someone has saved my life" kept ringing in my ears. When I was finally able to lift my head I saw in the distance a lone man rowing away in a small boat. I gurgled out, "Who is that man? He saved my life. I gotta thank him." I was groggy and still felt like a fountain spewing water. I heard muffled voices saying, "Don't worry about him, he's a fisherman. He's okay. We gotta get the water out of your lungs, get you warmed up and dried out, and see if you're okay. We'll find your fisherman later." As the launch headed back to our camp with the motorized canoe in tow, the sun reappeared as though nothing had happened. The storm was over; it was a beautiful summer day.

I can see it now as clearly as I did fifty years ago. Off on a distant horizon, seemingly locked in time, is a little rowboat with a solitary man and his fishing pole. I could not get over my deep yearning to grasp his hand and say . . . What? "Thank you for saving my life?" God, it sounded so empty.

On the trip back to the island, Edith, Lizzie, and Joe were rejoicing over our rescue. "You could all have drowned," one of the boatmen said. "This is a mighty treacherous lake when she cuts up. Never believe what anybody tells you about an unsinkable boat. There ain't no such thing. Next time wear lifejackets." When the boat docked at Big Burnt, the two guys on the launch dropped us off and departed in a shower of thanks, taking our boat with them. I didn't even remember to ask their names.

At neighboring campsites people who had already heard about the near-drowning congratulated us on our "miraculous escape." I didn't tell anyone how it felt to die. Come to think of it, no one asked me. I wasn't interested in suing Lamb's or Grumman as some of them suggested. I was just happy to be alive. It was my first intimate glimpse of the fragility of life. After that I spent a lot of time thinking about the random nature of our existence.

The day after the sinking I went to the boatyard and raised all kinds of hell about "this fucking boat you dumb bastards rented us that almost drowned my whole family!" Mr. Lamb was deeply offended by my rough street talk and told his son to give me all my money back and get me out of there.

I took the money and went up the street to Smith's Boatyard. Smith, a stocky, leather-faced lake man, allowed as how it wasn't very smart to send folks out on the lake without life preservers. "Besides, I don't think much of aluminum boats anyhow." He found us an Old Town runabout with a twelve-horsepower engine. "When you're out on the lake, especially with kids, remember—life preservers and no boots. Wind blowing through these mountains can turn a sunny vacation into a very sad funeral. You were lucky."

Big Burnt Island returned to normal, except for me. The vision of that man who had saved my life and then just rowed off into the horizon simply wouldn't go away. It became an obsession. Who was he? Where did he come from? How did he know I was under the boat? Why did he leave so quickly? I asked the men on the launch if they had seen him coming and if they had told him I was down there. No, they had not. They advised me to "just forget about it," but I couldn't.

And what about my dying? At that moment, exhausted, my energy spent, I had just given up. I never thought I would do such a thing. Life has always been too precious to me. Is the flame of life like a candle that can be blown out by a puff of wind? The questions going round and round in my head were driving me nuts.

About a week later, on a sunny August afternoon, the four of us were walking along Main Street in Bolton Landing contentedly licking our ice cream cones. As we moseyed along, a man in shorts and a plain white T-shirt passed us. I spun around, caught up with him, and took his arm. "Excuse me," I said, "aren't you the man who saved me from drowning?" He said nothing. "It was about a week ago during one of those afternoon squalls." He was a plain, almost-ordinary looking man, clean-shaven, about my height, with a muscular build. He looked at me as if he was trying to think of something to say, and I was struck by the kindness in his eyes. He still said nothing, but gave a little nod.

I was overwhelmed. If the meeting had not occurred in the middle of the busy tourist area I would have gone down on my knees before him. Instead I just kept repeating, "How do I thank you for saving my life?" He continued to stare at me with a puzzled expression as I rattled on excitedly. "If you give me your name and address, I promise I will make a superhuman effort to find a way to say thank you." As soon as I said it, I began to feel better. Perhaps I really could find an adequate way to repay such a favor.

He took a deep breath and paused, as if waiting for me to calm down. Finally he said, "Mister, I don't know if you're a religious man or not, but no matter. Go to any church along here, get down on your knees, and thank God, Allah, Buddha, or whoever for saving your life." He hesitated, seeming to have difficulty getting out the words. "You see," he said "I was out there fishing when the lake went dark and the squall came out of the mountains. As it began to blow like crazy, I heard a voice saying, 'Look over there. A boat is pulling some people out of the water. There's a man underneath the boat drowning. Nobody knows he's down there. Hurry and save him.'" As he spoke he looked me straight in the eye. "I am a Christian. When I hear a spirit voice, I don't question it, I obey it. That's all there was to it."

I was completely taken aback by his explanation. Going into church to give thanks was, to say the very least, not within the repertoire of my behaviors. I went back to pressing him for his name and address, but it was no use. He simply repeated, "Go to any church in town. Thank God. Or," he added, "Peter the fisherman. I didn't save you, they did. Don't ever forget it." With that he nodded to me and walked off into the afternoon tourist crowd. Badly shaken by my encounter with my life saver, I was glad that the kids and Edith were anxious to get back to the island.

That evening as the sun was setting, I sat alone on our rock by the lake trying to sift through my confusion. What could I make of the man's words? I was an orthodox atheist, a scientific materialist whose life had been saved by a spirit voice spoken to a lone fisherman. He told me to thank whatever spirit I believed in, but for an atheist materialist that presented a hell of a dilemma. As the sun went down over Tongue Mountain, I felt that a new journey lay ahead. Could there be spiritual influences over our lives that have no scientific explanation? My question was the first baby step of a pilgrimage that would continue for the rest of my days. Starting ever so slowly, with only a flicker of interest, I was drawn to the power of religion to reveal the unknown, the spiritual, and the healing powers of myth. As I passed churches, I had a new and different curiosity about what went on inside. Prior to my near-drowning, I saw them as agents of the oppressors working to keep the masses docile. Now I began to suspect that there might be more to it than that.

A few years later I began my journey through the religions. My new respect for the spiritual led me to an interest in extrasensory perception (ESP) and out-of-body experiences. As a child, hearing the music of Gluck's *Orfeo ed Euridice* had brought tears to my eyes. Ashamed, I would run away and hide. Many years later, learning about shamanism in the desert of Mexico gave me a new way of appreciating the art of the Louvre and Mozart. I realized that art was all about the spiritual.

Before my spiritual quest, I assumed that nothing existed if it could not be hit with a hammer, felt, heard, smelled, or counted. What we in the Party had been trying to understand through the "science" of historical materialism, religions had been attempting to explain for a much longer time. I came to believe that people need their religion as a reason for being, a way to order their lives. This understanding gave my life a new dimension, a new way of seeing.

When I reluctantly returned from the lake to deal with my last fight in the union, I had changed. The experience in the lake made me less concerned about the ongoing clamor. I suddenly thought, "This union battle is not a life-or-death situation." I had acquired a tiny glimmer of wisdom.

During those tense years of the early 1950s I had other experiences that, little by little, led me to think of myself and other people in ways quite unexpectedly opposed to my earlier beliefs.

At the time, Edith and I, Lizzie, and our dog Betsy had the luxury of a seven-room apartment in the North Bronx, a block away from Montefiore Hospital. The hospital, which was expanding its services and increasing its staff of physicians, appealed to community residents to make their extra rooms available for lodging. Thinking that the extra income would come in handy, we agreed to rent our hall room to a doctor.

A short time later a well-dressed couple showed up at our door. He was a clean-shaven man of medium height with a round face, very sad hazel eyes, and a pronounced European accent. She was a thin, heavily made up woman, who seemed to be in constant motion. They introduced themselves as Peter and Levea Horath, radiologists from Budapest, Hungary, and asked to see the room. Levea apologized profusely for their poor English. "Oh, no," we assured them, "it's just fine."

Our classical music station was playing something they recognized, and as they looked around at our prints and books, they nodded to each other in eager approval.

"Yes, please," Peter said, "we would very much like to be boarder, is that how you say?" They moved in the next day.

Some months into their stay, Peter and I arrived home to a sleeping house about the same time. In a voice a little above a whisper, he invited me to join him in a beer and "some nice blutvorst." I fried up the sausage according to Peter's instructions and brought out the beer and the booze. We sat at the kitchen table and talked for a long time, enjoying each other's company. I began to look forward to our beer-and-blutwurst talks. I always appreciated male conversation and, being out of the union, missed schmoozing with the guys. I always had an underlying sense that only another male could truly appreciate the finer nuances of my experience.

During our late-night conversations, I began to learn about their history. Peter was a medical student from an upper-middle-class Jewish family when he met Levea, who was then a ballet student. He paused: "She so beautiful." I assured him she still was. "Yes, but you should see her before concentration camp." I was shocked. It was hard to identify two such lovely looking people with the photographs I had seen of emaciated Nazi victims.

In subsequent talks I heard the full story of their prewar lives and Holocaust experiences. Whenever the subject of our conversations came close to the Nazi takeover of Budapest, Peter would begin to perspire heavily, as if he had a kind of internal shower to cool him down. On those occasions I tried to change the subject, but the more we conversed the more he seemed to want to talk about the nightmare.

Experiencing the crimes of the fascists from newsreels and pictures in magazines was very different from sitting at my kitchen table hearing a survivor describe what had happened to him. In a matter-of-fact voice, Peter described how the Hungarian fascists had come during the night, without warning, to take them away. "Nobody say it, but we know we go to camps."

Peter and Levea were sent to separate camps. Peter was set to work roadbuilding and taking care of animals, and Levea and the other younger women at her camp dug graves for the older prisoners, who were killed immediately. "Levea not like to talk about camps." Peter said. "She won't."

Near the end of the war, Levea's camp was liberated by the Red Army as the Nazi guards tried desperately to murder their remaining prisoners and bury the evidence of their crimes. "All peoples in camps along eastern front saved by Russian Army. For us in death camps, Russians angels from heaven," Peter said. "They bring us food, blankets, clothes. We go to rehabilitation center. After time, go back to Budapest, but nothing is same. Levea and I complete our studies and make many applications to come here for to finish interning."

"My God you were lucky."

He pointed to the sweat running down his face. "Well, you see, not so lucky. Is hard to live with memory. But wait, whole story not over yet. You hear yesterday, I have big fight with Levea?" I nodded. "Levea get letter from relative in Budapest who tell that her family cannot get their apartment house back. It was taken away by government. They say is benefit of all people. All private property taken." He went on. "I don't care, but Levea is so mad. She curses 'damn Russians' for taking family properties. I say to Levea, 'They save your life. If not for Russian army, you dead.' You not believe what she say: 'I don't care about that. They have not to make us poor. Don't we suffer enough?'"

Peter was very troubled by Levea's feelings and trying to make sense of them. "This is lesson I learn I give to you. Property, wealth, things maybe very important, is precious, right?" I nodded. "More precious than the life? You believe this?" I shook my head. "Now, you think Levea is nice woman, never forget Russian soldiers who shoot Nazis and save her life? No, she angry at Russians because in Budapest her family apartment is taken away. No matter how much I argue she get more mad all time.

It was after 2:00 A.M. when Peter finished his story. I went to bed, leaving him sitting at the kitchen table with a sad, puzzled expression.

Peter's story haunted me. The idea that property is more important than life itself—that it is what drives society—seemed all wrong. As I sit here writing, I can look out my window at the wide expanse of Long Island Sound. I am very possessive and protective of my property. Like my neighbors, I spend an enormous amount of effort caring for it. Would I do that, I ask myself, if I didn't own it? The answer is no.

Nonetheless, our conversations about the liberation of the concentration camps and the Russians' role in it helped me feel a bit more positive about the Soviet social experiment I was having such grave doubts about. For a time they kept alive a flicker of hope that socialism might yet work there.

In the United States, though, the preoccupation with hunting down communists and fellow travelers made my talks with Peter all the more scary. Roy Cohn was beginning to look a lot like Goebbels. I was receiving more and more FBI visits. Many mornings they waylaid me on my way to the garage. Flashing a badge, they would say, "We're from the FBI. Like to ask you a few questions. Only take a minute."

"No," I would yell, "I'm late for work, no time. Good-bye." A lot of us had to learn to avoid any conversation, because even the most innocent response to a question could become a hook to get one involved. They were very persistent. The FBI file indicates that at the time an informant designated TK-5 informed them that I had extensive contacts with communist activists in Latin American labor unions. I haven't the slightest idea what they were talking about. I had met a couple of Latin American union officials on their visits to the United States, but that was about all.

The constant FBI visits made me fearful of the effect the red-hunting might have on Peter and Levea. Edith and I discussed whether their visitor status could be jeopardized by association with known "enemies of the State." Although we enjoyed their presence in our home, we finally agreed—much as we hated to give in to the bastards—that they would have to leave, for their safety and our own peace of mind.

I tried to explain to Peter my fears about their safety and the rise of fascism in America, but he shook his head in disbelief. "No, no," he said, "It will never be like Europe here. You have too many different nations and cultures here." Looking me firmly in the eye, he declared, "Bob, I through running. From now on I stay where I want and I run no more. But if you wish, we will find other place." A few weeks later, Levea and Peter were gone. I learned later that they had separated and he had subsequently died of a heart attack.

Remember all those union meetings? To my surprise and dismay, they all went on without me. I now lived a very private existence; the only telephone calls I received came from rank-and-file union members looking for information on fighting their internationals.

The daily eight-to-five factory routine offered a lot of time for reflection. Without the power and influence of union office, the aura of importance I had been wrapped in was gone. Feeling like a nobody can bring you face to face with some really tough questions. "Who am I and why am I here?" used to have an easy answer. My life's work was bettering the lives of working people, with the eventual goal of abolishing capitalism and establishing socialism. But my vision of the latter goal had been slowly fading for some time, and the prolonged struggles in the Machinists' union certainly helped the process along.

What I saw as I looked at my personal life was not promising either. The marriage was running on empty. This is not to say that Edith and I did not have lots of good times together, but I think neither of us had a clue about what it meant to love another human being. She had been abandoned by a father at a young age. I had lost a very loving mother at a similar time in life. We were both extremely needy, yearning for love but unable to give it.

During the years I was an "important" union leader it didn't matter. Like all crusaders, I placed my cause at the center of my existence. I was totally engrossed in helping my first love, the working class, while somewhere off in the clouds I fantasized about sharing true love with Sandra. She was the only person with whom I experienced a sense of being loved. Once I asked her where she had received that gift. She described what it was like to grow up in a home with two parents who loved each other while she basked in the glow of their love. I began to realize that I was completely ignorant of what is meant by love and that the ability to love—Hallmark cards not withstanding—was quite rare.

Some years later, when I was working in New York's antipoverty program at the time of the Great Society, I was still struggling to understand love. Periodically I used to sneak into Trinity Church on Broadway near Wall Street to escape the craziness of bureaucratic politics. There on the cross was Jesus in his deep suffering. Why did he suffer so? What made him such a unique human being? More than anything, I saw, it was his God-given ability to love, unconditionally. People have been worshipping that love for a couple of thousand years. Clearly love is not easy to achieve, or it would not be enshrined in the spiritual. We need it so badly, yet it is one of the toughest things to attain. Love, I realized as I left the church one day, is the ability to get yourself out of the way in order to give to others.

I believe as a last-ditch effort to save our marriage, Edith and I decided to have another child. When our son Frederick was born in 1952, I tried to be more of a father, starting with being with Edith in labor and helping her yell "oh shit" as the doctor kept saying "That's right, that's what you want to do."

At about six weeks into his life, baby Freddie had to face his first crisis. Edith went to the hospital for what was supposed to be a routine check of a small swelling in her abdomen. Instead, they rushed her to the operating room to remove a seriously inflamed gall bladder, leaving Lizzie and I at home with a screaming baby. A friendly neighbor suggested giving him a nice warm bath to calm him down. Calm him down! His entire little body turned flaming red with fury. He would not take a bottle, he would not even drink water, he just screamed. It was scary. Fortunately, a friend told us about a woman who took care of babies, and, by the grace of God, she arrived the very next morning.

Miss MacIntyre was a large black woman who immediately reminded Liz and me of what white people in those days considered a nice picture of Aunt Jemima. She was greeted by baby Freddie crying his heart out, just as he had done for the last twenty-four hours. She picked him up, checked his diaper, and in few moments had him cleaned up and tucked peacefully under her arm while she made up his formula.

Greatly relieved, Liz and I skipped out the door, she to school and I to stop at the hospital before going to work. Edith's infection had spread, and the doctors advised a six-week stay at a convalescent home to regain her strength.

The next morning, and every morning for the next few weeks, marvelous breakfast smells of bacon and biscuits filled the house. Miss MacIntyre was up at five o'clock, cleaning up Fred and cooking up a storm. I was always eager to get home to Miss MacIntyre and her wonderful dinners. Both Lizzie and I experienced the kind of comforting love our family hungered for.

She taught me a lesson about love I had to learn again years later at Trinity Church. "The good Lord put me here to do what I do best," she declared. "I don't wanna disappoint my Lord, so I enjoy my work for him. Givin' love is the most precious gift of all. That's what the Lord taught me." And, I thought, that's what you have been teaching me, not by what you say but by the way you live here with us.

When Edith came home Miss MacIntyre insisted on leaving right away, because "You can't have two women tryin' to run a house." Sadly, Lizzie and I said good-bye, but we never forgot Miss MacIntyre's love.

Still, I couldn't seem to put what she had taught us to work with Edith. Over time, my doubts about our marriage kept growing; often I felt as if I was living in a lie. I found myself asking, "What is there between us? Why are we together?" Once he was past babyhood, I enjoyed Freddie. He and Liz were the mainstays of my life at home, and they held me in the marriage for many more years.

My romantic life, however, revolved around daydreams of Sandra. We were writing more and longer letters, and I started suggesting that we should seriously consider living together instead of holding periodic clandestine love feasts. Arranging our rendezvous had become more difficult, because working in a factory did not provide opportunities for travel. Once in the early fifties we managed to meet in Atlantic City while she was attending a medical convention. We had both saved tidbits of information and questions to share with each other. I would tell her about the losses and gains in the labor movement, and she would relate new observations about the human condition and her discoveries of what she called "everyday geniuses"—people who performed the mundane tasks of society in a way that made you feel proud of the human race. She had a real knack for finding these folks. It was her way of offsetting the daily run of grim news.

The miles of boardwalk afforded us space to just walk and talk. For the first time, she expressed concern about being seen together in public. Her worry scared me, but I said nothing. With my power in the union gone, I was desperate for greater security in my intimate life. I began to harp on the subject of being together all the time, happy and in love as we were then.

"It wouldn't work," she said. "We would leave two very unhappy adults and three miserable children in our wake. The guilt would eat away at us until we were consumed by it."

"Is it better that we continue to live a lie? Neither of us has a very high regard for our spouse. Why should we just go on being noble and thinking someone is being fooled? I don't think they are."

"No, our arrangement is far better. After all, neither of our partners are bad people. They are not inspired, true, but they are not bad souls. How could we justify hurting them? It would only create deep scars that would begin to fester. Eventually the infection would overtake and kill our love."

I found myself pleading and slowly becoming angry at her refusal to consider my proposal, but she was steadfast. She pointed out that our periodic holidays were the stuff of great romantic novels, without any of the very unromantic drudgery of paying rent or taxes, buying groceries, and taking care of kids who need a hell of a lot of attention.

"Besides," she went on, overriding my protest that I would love to share those things with her, "we would lose this delicious freedom we enjoy so much when we are together. We don't need to share our love with anyone else. Who but the most blessed have such a gift? Let's try not to spoil it with talk of permanence and forever stuff that fills old musty-smelling attic trunks." Delighted with the phrase, she laughed and threw her arms around me for a big kiss. "Don't you see? It's our freedom I don't want to give up for mortgage payments and such. Please try not to shit on what we have with your fantasy of a perfect marriage in some nice suburb where we'd both be bored to death."

Feeling the pain of rejection, I became sullen and refused to say any more. I had never let the pain show before. I was not about to start then. We parted, she to Colorado and I back to the Bronx. Our correspondence became increasingly urgent.

17

Mine Mill

The settled routine of life in the tool room was giving me an acute case of restlessness. The challenge was gone from the work. I had made enough tools to be convinced that, given good blueprints and the right machines, I could make anything. Marxist intellectuals notwithstanding, working in a factory—even as a skilled craftsman—is tedious and boring.

In late 1952 when some old friends from the Party told me about a job in the Mine, Mill, and Smelter Workers' Union, I was eager to find out about it. Being technically in or out of the Party no longer mattered much to the dedicated leftists still working in the unions. I had met Al Pezzati, the union's regional director for the Northeast, and Herb Lerner, the New Jersey director, during our anti–Taft-Hartley campaign. Pezzatti was a skinny Italian who wore horn-rimmed glasses and a Borsolino fedora and behaved as if he had seen too many Bogart movies. He had a good, dirty sense of humor, and we enjoyed each other's company. His office was in a seedy old building on Columbus Circle (now long gone to make room for the Coliseum, which will shortly be long gone to make room for something else).

Mine Mill, as the union was known, was one of the unions expelled from the CIO for being communist-dominated. It grew out of the old IWW Western Federation of Miners and had a long radical history. In the opening years of this century some of the labor movement's most memorable heroes fought the union's violent battles with mine owners and repressive state governments in Idaho, Colorado, Montana, and Arizona. Big Bill Haywood, Joe Hill, and Frank Little were legendary names I first heard sitting on Papa's knee.*

After my ouster from the Machinists, I had been certain my union career was over. There was no way I would turn down this opportunity to get out of the factory if they offered it to me. Besides, how could I resist a job in Bill Haywood's and Joe Hill's old union? Wouldn't Papa be proud?

Mine Mill represented miners of the major nonferrous metals—copper, lead, zinc, gold, silver, molybdenum, and the plutonium used to manufacture nuclear weapons—as well as workers in the smelters and refineries that processed the ores into usable metals. Pezzatti explained that they needed a union representative for three "properties"—as they referred to the affiliated mines and mills—to negotiate contracts with the companies, represent the union in grievance procedures, and generally assist members in their dealings with management.

He assumed that I had signed the Taft-Hartley noncommunist affidavit and knew about my long fight with the Machinists' International. From the way he joked about the signing, I suspected he thought I had not taken it seriously. I told him firmly that I meant it and would not want to be part of whatever party organization there was in the union. He laughed and gave me the party line: "There's no such thing anyway." There was, of course; I even attended a couple of their meetings.

Pezzatti introduced me to Herb Lerner, who supervised the position. Herb was a tall man whose straight-up posture made him look even taller. He had a pockmarked face, a ready smile, and a very pleasant disposition. As I learned in the following months, he was a stubborn Marxist. He explained that if I got the job, I would be solely responsible for locals at the American Smelting and Refining plant in Baltimore, which had about twelve hundred members, and Nassau Smelting and Refining on Staten Island, which had about six hundred. Nassau was owned by the Bell System and reprocessed all the telephone company's used copper and other metals. I would also be called on to handle grievances at the

*The IWW, which was founded in 1905, deplored the traditional AFL craft union separations and wanted to organize all workers into "one big industrial union." For its entire history, the IWW was the most persecuted, prosecuted, hounded, terrorized, framed, and spied-upon organization in the history of the labor movement.

American Metals copper smelter in Carteret, New Jersey. I would travel to the plants regularly from an office in Perth Amboy, New Jersey. There would also be some organizing assignments—which, Lerner explained wryly, meant fending off membership raids from other unions.

"Since our expulsion from the CIO, we're fair game for the picking," Herb explained. He shook his head sadly: "It's the employers' dream come true. They can just sit back and watch the spectacle of unions tearing each other apart over the communist issue. Unions spend their energies raiding each other instead of organizing the unorganized." He paused. "This witch hunt is a major tragedy for the American labor movement, and the workers will pay dearly for it."

Because the job of representative was an appointed staff position, it didn't require an election or members' approval. Being a hired hand was just fine with me; as I explained to Lerner, my experience in the Machinists had left me somewhat cynical about the unions and the working class. He thought my attitude was healthy and would keep me from having unrealistic expectations of Mine Mill.

A few days later he called to say the job was mine if I wanted it.

I liked Herb. He and his wife became two of my closest friends. Ruth was the first woman to win election to the executive board of a union international, the Fur and Leather Workers. (Its president, Ben Gold was probably the country's best-known communist labor leader.) My friendship with Herb grew gradually out of years of challenging conversations, even though our ways of thinking were very different. Herb was an avid mathematician and an excellent bridge and chess player. He sometimes spent days in the library working out the solution to a complicated mathematical theorem. His thinking was rational, systematic, and based only on provable concepts. He believed that Marxism was a scientific way of thinking about economic and social problems.

I, by contrast, had long since ceased to see Marxism as a science. When I confronted him with my theory about the guardian angel that had saved my life in Lake George, he pronounced it impossible. "That Saint Peter of yours," he said, "was just a religious zealot trying to convert you. It looks like he partly succeeded."

"Not quite," I laughed. "I was only converted to the idea that, at least for now and the foreseeable future, there's a hell of a lot about the world I don't know anything about." I was going to look into some things I had always dismissed as bourgeois nonsense. At this point he would laughingly insist that the answer was probably in some unsolved math problem, and I would suggest it might lie in understanding Shakespeare rather than Marx.

Herb's systematic, rational brain and my scatological, scrambled-egg thinking made us a good conversational team. I questioned his firmly held Marxist views, while he was out to prove I had no place else to go. "There is no other analysis that can answer the questions of our time like Marxism." He loved to prove the evils of capitalist greed by citing the history of the mineral-extraction companies. There's no doubt that the industry we were dealing with gave him plenty of ammunition to demonstrate the ruthless nature of the existing system.

He got very annoyed, though, when I asked him whether the nasty jobs in the smelter would be any better under a socialist system. I argued that "some jobs essential to society are terrible, no matter what you do." When he pointed out that miners in the Soviet Union were among that country's highest-paid workers, I reminded him of John L. Lewis's response to the introduction of mining machines: "No human being should ever have to go into the bowels of the earth to be gassed, burned, crippled and crushed in the pursuit of black coal." Knowing that Herb, an optometrist by training, had no personal experience of factory work, I would ask him if he would like to try working in a mine or a smelter. No, he admitted, he wouldn't.

Herb's math ability once came in very handy during negotiations with American Metals. Twelve or thirteen union committeemen and half a dozen company representatives were sitting around a long conference table negotiating the pension-benefits package. Herb leaned toward me: "Listen, you take up the next issue about reclassification. I'm going to the library to figure out this pension stuff. I have a sneaking suspicion the insurance company is screwing both us and the company. I'll see you back here in the morning."

The next morning Herb arrived smiling like the proverbial cat. He asked for a flip chart, stood at one end of the long table, and in a few minutes had the room mesmerized with his numbers. He proved that the actuarial tables used by Metropolitan Life were faulty and that the result was a windfall for the insurance company and a shortfall for the company and workers. Through this same research, Herb was also one of the first people to show that the standard actuarial tables discriminated against women. I had a real chuckle when the man from the insurance company referred to Herb as the "union's actuary."

Another time, after one of his library sojourns, he arrived at the office wound up like an eight-day clock. He had just completed a comparative study of the wages paid worldwide in the copper-mining industry. "You want to hear about imperialist superprofits even Karl Marx never dreamed of?" Lighting up a cigarette and smiling in utter delight, he went to a flip chart and showed me his carefully thought-out comparative analysis of the copper industry. He demonstrated how the imperialists made enormous profits from the lowest-paid miners in the British colonies. Then, with great pride, he shared his latest discovery: our very own Carteret smelter was a major stockholder in a group of copper mines in Northern Rhodesia (now Zambia)—the American Metals Company–Rhodesian Selection Trust group.

"Can you believe that African miners working right next to whites get one-tenth their pay?" he asked indignantly. As members came into the office, they were arrested by his excited voice and stopped to listen. "And in Mexico, right over the border," he said, "Mexican miners are working the very same vein of ore that our members are digging in Arizona." He paused and sort of reared up for the punch line: "The Mexican miners get paid for a day what our members make in an hour. What else is that but superprofits derived from superexploitation?"

One of the members asked, "So, Herb, what can we do about it?"

He stopped to think. "We have to find a way to help our brothers in Peru, Mexico, Africa, and Australia to start raising hell and get themselves organized so we can confront these international cartels as one voice. Look, if you divide up just the superprofits based on our own pay scales, the average Rhodesian black miner could be making two thousand dollars a year instead of six hundred. That would give him a standard of living equal to ours, and we would not be subject to competition we simply can't afford to beat." As he finished, the guys in the office applauded. He blushed and apologized for making a speech.

A short time later Herb, who was the union's principal negotiator for American Metals, wrote an article for the Mine Mill union paper about the shameful superprofits the company was earning in Northern Rhodesia. He subsequently received a strange telephone call from an assistant to Harold Hochschild, chairman of the board of American Metals. Herb had never seen or spoken to Hochschild, who was one of Wall Street's typical elusive millionaires. The chairman never had even an indirect contact with a union member; company attorneys took care of dealing with "them." The assistant said Hochschild wanted to meet with Herb to straighten out some of the "misstatements of fact" that appeared in the union newspaper.

Herb was uncertain about how the membership would view this meeting. Would they think he was making some sort of deal with the company? He finally decided to tell the local union officers about Hochschild's request. If they had any reservations about the meeting, he would forget it. Nobody did, so Herb accepted and asked me to go along.

American Metals' imposing corporate headquarters fit perfectly the stereotype of a Wall Street imperialist exploiter. When we arrived on the forty-fifth floor, we were handed from one secretary to another through a lengthy series of ornately carved, wood-paneled rooms. Finally we were led into an enormous office; couches and antique credenzas lined the sides of the room, and a huge desk stood in the center. The escort suggested we take two chairs in front of the desk that had obviously been placed there in anticipation of our visit. We sat, waiting expectantly for long enough to impress us that the person we were meeting with was very important.

Then a wall panel behind the desk opened, and a young man held the door for a middle-aged executive to precede him into the office. We were introduced, shook hands, and sat down. Mr. Hochschild, a very cool-looking man of medium height, wore rimless glasses with earpieces made of thin wire. Everything about him was impeccable; he was the quintessential Brooks Brothers man. The manner in which he carried himself, sat down, stood up, and looked over at his assistant conveyed the impression of a professional mime who was able control his realm completely without speaking. He had the bearing of a man whose entire life was lived according to an exact plan and schedule. The pasty color of his skin suggested that he had never seen the afternoon sun. His desk, like that of many high-ranking executives I met later, was devoid of even a scrap of paper. Nothing in the office gave a clue to what went on there.

Hochschild's assistant, after establishing exactly who we were and what our union responsibilities were, handed his boss a little stack of index cards. Before starting to read from the cards, Hochschild straightened us out on the companies involved in the Rhodesian copper business: American Metals in New York, Selection Trust based in London, and Rhodesian Selection Trust based in Northern Rhodesia. Then, in a very precise manner, he proceeded to read from the cards.

"In your article you claimed that African miners receive the equivalent of one dollar and a quarter a day." He paused, looked up, and, as though making an important revelation, said, "In fact they receive the equivalent of two dollars and a quarter a day." He hastened to add that it was absolutely wrong to compare American and Rhodesian wage scales, because differences in living standards made the comparison impossible. He said that with complete finality. I could almost feel Herb's hackles rising.

Herb then committed what appeared to be a cardinal sin. "Mr. Hochschild," he asked, "what living standard would *you* say is reasonable?"

The assistant, who had been standing near the paneled door, stepped forward quickly. "Mr. Lerner, would you please not interrupt Mr. Hochschild's presentation. When he has concluded his remarks you will have ample time to ask questions." The scene was taking on a certain absurd quality, and I inadvertently let out a little snicker. The assistant tartly reminded me that this was "a serious matter."

Hochschild continued to make "corrections of fact" about wage scales, hours of work, and working conditions. He then came to what he considered the real problem: "American Metals," he said, "is a majority stockholder in the Northern Rhodesian copper operations, but we do not make policy as far as wages, hours, or most important, how supervision is determined." He surprised us by saying that he agreed with many of the points Herb had raised in his article, "even if some of your facts were inaccurate." What Herb had failed to understand was that policies relating to the mining operations in Northern Rhodesia were established not by the stockholders but by the British Colonial Office. "The colonial administration," he explained, "is more interested in taking care of the Britons who live in the colonies than in running an intelligent, efficient business." This was unexpected information. The meeting was beginning to get interesting. Hochschild was down to his last card, and it was almost time for the question period.

At this point, the assistant interrupted to say that there was an urgent call for Mr. Hochschild. He excused himself politely and assured us he would return shortly. When they were both out of the room, I turned to Herb: "Do you think he has ever been to the Carteret Smelter tank house?"

Herb looked at me: "Schrank, are you nuts? I doubt if he even knows where Carteret is."

"Herb I have a great idea. Why don't we invite him to one of our Carteret local union parties? You know, the ones where after a lot of boozing and pussy talk there's a cock-measuring contest." The picture was getting to him. He was laughing. I was encouraged and kept going: "He could watch his employees work themselves to a full erection. We could ask him to predict from the flaccid state who would take the prize."

Joining in with a silly grin on his face, Herb said, "You're forgetting about the guys who have to have some dirty pictures in order to get into the competition. Are we going to let that stand?"

"Absolutely. Unless Hochschild himself disqualifies it as outside interference. Then as they line up the half dollars on their hardened dicks, he could make the final call. You remember how that goes, don't you?"

"No. Remind me."

"They lay the half dollars on their dicks and the one who can line up and hold the most wins. Wasn't it the twelve-half-dollar man who won last time around?"

"Schrank," he said, "Can't you get the details right? Our best man can do fourteen and, he claims, balance them with no hands."

The contrast between the Carteret Smelter union parties and the elegant room we were sitting in had us both as giddy as a couple of adolescents at their first peep show. We could hear Hochschild returning.

Herb, concerned that my merriment was getting out of hand, tried to shush me: "Forget the whole idea. This is serious. I have to deal with this company on an ongoing basis."

"Herb, please, just a little bit about the cock-measuring?"

As Hochschild walked into the room, Herb said, "Schrank, cut it out."

Hochschild wanted to know if there was a problem. Herb assured him there was not, and the meeting continued.

After more discussion of the factual differences, Herb asked what American Metals would do in the Rhodesian mines if it could exercise its majority interest by managing operations. Hochschild adjusted his rimless glasses, took a sip of water, and said: "First, we'd send all those Brits who live like potentates back to dear old England, where they would be clerks in the customs office—at best. The only exceptions would be some absolutely essential engineering and technical personnel, who would be replaced with locals as soon as we could train them." He paused to let that sink in. We were taken by surprise.

Herb asked him to explain the reasoning behind his thinking. Hochschild replied that bringing a lot of foreign colonials into a country encourages them to live way beyond the means of the local folks, sowing the seeds of resentment and, eventually, social unrest. It does not require a brilliant mind to understand why the natives resent the outsiders' luxurious life style. "And they are outsiders, even if they all sing 'God save the Queen' and 'Britannia Rules the Waves' together."

While Hochschild listened, I remarked to Herb that what the chairman was describing was a natural conflict between imperialist powers over control of raw materials. But, I pointed out, it also supported Herb's arguments for a living wage for the Rhodesians, suggesting that all imperialists are not the same. Herb then asked Hochschild to describe American Metals' way of managing foreign mines. Somewhat disdainfully, Hochschild cited the American Metals tin-mining operations in Bolivia. There, he said, "we have fewer than a dozen or so outsiders. We not only train local people to do the work, we make them the supervisors. And we do not have conflicts among Negroes, Latinos, and gringos. Of course, Bolivia is not a colony. The traditional colonizing policy is a dying notion." As he explained his views of colonialism, this extremely reserved man showed real emotion. I realized that there were genuine differences among "imperialist exploiters" in their views of workers. It was not, after all, so black and white.

By now Hochschild was enjoying the discussion and began describing his recent trip to South Africa: "I saw a white man on a scaffold painting the outside of one of our field headquarters. Next to him was a black helper. You won't believe this." He paused. "The black helper dips the paintbrush into the paint can, wipes it, and hands it to the white painter.

The white man makes a few strokes with the brush and gives it to the black helper to dip into the paint again. They repeat this over and over for the entire workday. Can you believe such absurdity? Of course, it's the epitome of inefficiency, but it is worst than that. It is a terrible indignity. If it doesn't change soon, Africa will be ablaze in revolt within a few decades." He seemed at least as mad as we were about what was going on there.

As he stood up to leave, he commented: "And the same thing is true in the Rhodesian mines. We don't need or want all those high-priced British colonials. We would be happy to pay the black miners a comparable African wage. If you keep in mind that image of the black helper handing the brush to the white painter, you will understand what I'm talking about." He left through the paneled door, and Herb and I were politely but firmly shown the way out.

Naturally, the Hochschild meeting gave us material for many months of argument. For Herb it confirmed what he called the classic conflict between imperialist powers and affirmed his belief that a colonial working class was beginning to develop. For me it supported the suspicion that the traditional Marxist good guys–bad guys notion was a gross oversimplification of reality. Herb was shocked when I said that I would certainly support Hochschild over the British Colonial Office. He said I was beginning to embrace some very strange bedfellows. He was probably right.*

When I made my first trip to American Smelting and Refining in Baltimore to look into a grievance, I had several big surprises. The smelter men in the union were one helluva tough bunch: much rougher, nastier, and, probably, more violent than machinists. About that time I began to think that the kind of work men do has a great influence on their personalities and behavior. It seemed to me that the more men work primarily with their bodies, the more physically aggressive they become.

---

*Years later, when Harold Hochschild died, he left his estate in the Adirondacks to a writers' colony. His son Adam, who wrote a wonderful book about his father, was a founder of the radical magazine *Mother Jones*. Imperialist wealth ends up in some very strange places.

The Baltimore local had about twelve hundred members, the majority of them—the production workers—black. The minority of about two hundred and fifty skilled workers were white, or to be more accurate, Southern redneck. During that first visit, I was shocked to see signs over the locker room doors: "Whites Only" and "Colored Only." The same signs appeared in the cafeterias, rest rooms, and at the drinking fountains. The whole place was completely segregated. "What the hell is going on here anyway?" I exclaimed loudly.

The local president, a black man named Roscoe Brown, urged me to "take it easy, man. You're in the South. We walk a pretty fine line here just to make sure we all keep gettin' along. That's what union means for us."

When we got to the tank house I was sure I had stepped into a new version of hell and damnation. First off, I could hardly breathe because of the fine mist of acid from the electrolytic copper-refining process. My eyes watering and my skin prickling, I asked incredulously, "People really work in this place all day?"

"They sure does, and that's the grievance," Roscoe answered. "We want the company to just do somethin' about improvin' the ventilation in here. All of us is goin' blind or our lungs are bein' eaten up with acids." He looked at me and chuckled: "Hey Swank, how would you like a job here?" He slapped me on the back and let out a big laugh, enjoying his little joke.

The tank house floor was about the size of a football field and covered with steel tanks maybe three feet wide, twenty-five feet long, and four feet deep. They were filled with sulfuric acid. Two electrodes discharging thousands of volts of electricity were connected to each tank. Copper plates weighing two hundred pounds each were refined by lowering them into the tanks. The plates arrived from the ore smelter 96 percent pure and emerged from the tank house 100 percent pure, ready to be made into copper wire, pipes, and so on. The men who worked in the tank house placed the plates in the tanks and removed them, checked the acidity, and made sure that the electrodes were discharging the correct amount of current.

As my eyes burned and my skin smarted from the ever-present acid, I recalled my own short stint in a foundry. Between the blistering heat of summer, the cold of winter, the fumes of the molten metal, and the dust of the molds, I was convinced the foundry was hell on earth—until I came into this tank house. "How the hell does anyone survive in here?" I asked Roscoe indignantly. "Why do they to put up with it?"

He looked at me and shook his head tolerantly, as if speaking to a child. "You got no idea of what black folks does just to have a job." Before I could apologize, he went on: "Man, look around this tank house. Do you see any of your white brethren here? No you don't, and you won't. This here is nigger work. Nigger work, and don't you forget it. And most of us figure we're the lucky ones." I got the point. I was also sure that the men who worked in those smelters would enjoy a very short fishing season in their old age.

By the time we finished our investigation of the grievance, it was lunch time. I suggested to Roscoe that I might join him for lunch, but he didn't think it was a good idea for me to eat in the "colored place." "It won't sit good with those white boys. Beside, you needs to let them get to know you. I take care of the black boys. You go get the white ones. Okay?"

I asked him how a progressive union like Mine Mill could permit this segregation. "Christ," I said "This union got thrown out of the CIO for being communist-dominated. How the hell can it tolerate this shit?"

Roscoe Brown gave me another lesson in race relations: "Baltimore is a Southern city. If you don't remember this, you're gonna gets us in a hornet's nest of troubles." I protested that Mine Mill had one of the oldest traditions of being against any kind of discrimination, but Roscoe just laughed. "Man," he said, "don't you know what we declare in union resolutions and them policy statements and what goes on in the real world at mines and smelters is two different fish? Two different fish. You just gotta know the difference." He went on, "You see, one is just a bunch of folks sittin' around in a big fancy hotel room and bull-shittin'. Now what we're dealin' with here is the real world. Like my old Granny use to say, 'Roscoe you gots to learn to deal with the facts of life. They is what counts. Not some dreamed-up stuff we is wishin' for, but the real world.'" I couldn't help but be reminded of Frederick Douglass's distinction between the ideal, the real, and the actual. I was beginning to understand that the facts of life in this local were a great example of the actual.

The white guys were the skilled workers—the electricians, pipe fitters, machinists, and foremen. The blacks, at the bottom of the ladder, were the production workers. The black majority could vote to end segregation any time they wanted; but, Roscoe explained, they would do so at the cost of unity and could easily lose the union altogether. He thought the white workers would listen to me because I was a machinist. "You go convince the white boys they don't need to come to our house or we to theirs, but we all get more out of the company if we support each other. Remember, we gotta live together here long after you catch the evening train to New York." He was right. I was an outsider.

Herb was surprised when I told him about the segregation. He figured everyone accepted the status quo because they didn't know how to change it without tearing the local apart. Probably the overwhelming majority of Mine Mill's locals were just as conservative. The union got itself thrown out of the CIO because of a very small cadre of party people—maybe a dozen in all, most of them in staff positions. Otherwise, in spite of the union's militant history in the Rocky Mountain hard rock mines, local leaders and members were not very different from those in other unions. Obviously, the membership did not support the leftist positions of the leadership, and the anticommunist fears being stirred up by McCarthy's witch hunts were a threat to the union's very existence.

I asked Herb how long he thought the leadership could hang onto its leftist stance before the continuous defection of locals to other unions caused it to disintegrate. "Not long," he conceded. "We'll have to merge with another union relatively soon or we'll be picked to pieces. And to get a decent merger, we need to hold on to what we've got. That's our overall survival strategy."

We agreed nonetheless to take a stab at winning over some of the white Baltimore shop stewards to the idea of ending segregation in plant facilities. So began many months of very patient meetings with the "white boys." Their initial responses were something like, "Hell, leave good enough alone. We know our place and they know theirs. What's wrong with that?" As the discussions went on, the responses got closer to the bone: "Next thing you know the niggers will be wantin' to go out with our daughters. One thing will lead to another and before you-all know it they'll be wantin' our jobs." The political gulf between leaders and members of the union was exemplified by the white man who asked, "Who sent you down here to stir up the niggers against us? Those commie union leaders? We got along good until people like you come stickin' your god-damn nose in our business."

We learned that the company had been supplying the white skilled workers with information about my expulsion from the Machinists' union. Fortunately my status as a competent machinist seemed more important to them than the expulsion.

Herb, who had spent a lot of time with the local's leaders as part of Mine Mill's national negotiating team, decided to join me in Baltimore for a nonstop round of meetings to pitch desegregation to the skilled workers. We based our argument solely on the economic advantages of increased unity. After endless arguments, cajoling, coaxing, threatening, and sweet-talking, we asked Roscoe if we could bring up the desegregation proposal at the next local meeting. After checking with his "key boys," he decided that the idea had enough support to prevent it from tearing the union apart.

The night before the vote, Herb and I argued late into the night over what I called "the murderous prejudices of our white working-class brothers." Convinced that my disillusionment was solely the result of the troubles in the IAM, Herb argued that I had lost sight of the fact that it was bourgeois influence that produced the prejudice and hatred.

"Herb, I know you believe this is all the fault of capitalism. So did I once, but after years of living with workers I no longer think that all the rotten, shitty things they do grow out of the culture of capitalism. Even if they do, what makes you think that will all just disappear in a socialist society? Nothing in human history suggests we can live together in the vision of the brotherhood we sang about in the Party."

The next day's meeting in a dark, dingy room over a local tavern had an unusually large turnout. The desegregation proposal won by a pretty good majority. The next step was to petition management to end the separate facilities. The plant manager was not at all happy with the idea; he was sure it would lead to trouble. The local committeemen, most of them black, assured him that they would keep the peace, and Roscoe surprised us by saying, "If we're gonna have a confrontation, I'll reverse the decision." It was finally agreed to take down all the signs within a week. I felt good. We had won a small victory for freedom.

In the weeks and months that followed, I made regular visits to check on the progress of desegregation. Nothing much happened. Not when the signs came down and not for years afterward. As Roscoe said, "All the black boys is still eatin', dressin', and washin' with themselves. Same with the white boys. We get along okay 'cause we need them and they need us, and they know that. But that's okay. We gonna leave it that way." I began to wonder if there were some very fundamental cultural differences that permit unity on economic issues but will not bridge the social gap.

Next, Herb wanted me to work on getting blacks promoted into skilled jobs, but Roscoe was against the idea. Again Herb and I argued about how far leaders of a union can go when they're not supported by the membership. Reminding him of my experience with the Romanian issue, I pointed out that what he wanted these men to agree to was much closer to home. Although the Party had been trying to win support among black workers for ages by championing equal rights, it just hadn't worked. I believed that black workers, like white workers, were more interested in being part of the existing economic system than in over-throwing society. After much discussion, we agreed to launch a program of education about the need for unity among all workers, regardless of race. In the Party, "educate 'em" was always an excuse for doing noth-ing, because nobody had any better ideas.

The more Herb and I argued, the clearer it became that I was aban-doning socialism. He accused me of becoming more and more conserva-tive, and I *was* coming to believe that without an incentive or fear of unemployment, most workers simply wouldn't put out. "We see it every single day on the factory floor, Herb. Why would they change under a system with a different name that makes the same demands?" Our argu-ments frequently ended with yet another review of his experience at the St. Joe lead smelter.

The smokestacks of the lead smelters the union was trying to organize were belching poisonous lead fumes into their surrounding communities. At the smelter in St. Joe Lead, Herb had raised the issue of the effect of lead fumes on the workers' children. He was convinced the family health issue would catch on, but it never did.

Herb couldn't understand the company's indifference either. It was dumping hundreds of tons of lead into the air every year. He completely lost his cool over the issue; talking about it, he got madder by the minute:"This goddamned place ought to be shut down," he thundered. "I'll bet you half this town is suffering from some form of lead poisoning." I had never seen Herb so angry; he was usually a very calm, rational guy. "Do you realize children can suffer permanent brain damage from overexposure to lead at a early age?" No, I didn't. "You don't know what raw, uncaring exploitation is about until you've dealt with these bastards in the mining and smelting business." He paused and looked at me as if I were a naive innocent. "The guys that run these places are the last of the robber barons. I bet you never experienced this kind of exploitation in your nice civilized machine shops, now did you?" He was mad at everyone, including me.

I responded with a pretty lame comparison to my foundry experience, but he didn't accept it. He thought the materials the foundrymen worked with were not nearly as toxic as the chemicals used in the smelter. Besides, he said, the steel companies were far more modern in their labor relations than the old line mineral-extraction industries. A lot of what Herb said was true, but I still couldn't understand the intensity of his anger. At some point, I began to get an idea. "Did you ever work in any of these places?" I asked him.

"What difference does that make?"

"Well, I'll tell you." When I first went to work in the foundry, I explained, I couldn't believe anyone could work in a place like that and survive. Then I learned something. Some of the men who had spent their entire work life in the foundry told me that they liked it. How could that possibly be? After a while I realized that in the midst of those god-awful physical conditions they had built bonds of friendship and support that made them a community. "You could compare them," I told Herb, "to the soldiers at the Anzio beachhead when you were there. Work, especially dangerous work, forms a bond and a mutual trust they are proud of. It makes it possible for them to endure what seems to outsiders like a living hell. Because we're sure we could never, ever work in a place like that, we can't understand them." I thought that was also why intellectuals who are genuinely concerned about the working class don't have a clue to what these people are about. "In this country at least, workers are primarily interested in how they can make it in the existing system." Herb didn't agree with a word I said. He said it sounded to him like a lot of bourgeois sociology.

One night driving back to New York from Baltimore, I asked Herb about his wartime experiences at Anzio. I knew he didn't like to talk about it, but—not having gone to war myself—I was interested. Besides, Ruth, his wife, had suggested I ask him about the Patton episode.

Before his career in the labor movement, Herb was a professional optician. When he was drafted during World War II, he was sent to the medical corps of the Sixth Army, then under the command of General George Patton. Herb described landing on the beach at Anzio in southern Italy under intense German shelling. They were pinned down on the beach for many months while the Germans occupying the heights above fired away at their leisure. Naturally casualties were heavy. Because of the constant shelling, they had a lot of guys on the injured list and no way to evacuate them, and Herb had to make a hell of a lot of new eyeglasses.

In his usual understated way, he told me that he was a correspondent for *Stars and Stripes*. He laughed, "I was sort of the rank-and-file voice of the army." I asked if he had tried to recruit for the Party while in the army. "No," he said. "This time we were fighting on the right side. We just needed to win." He did manage, however, to make contact with the local party organization, and he became their source for cigarettes, chocolate, and booze from the PX. That surprised me. Wasn't he concerned with the political implications of that contact? In those days, for that short period of history, he explained, the party people in places like Italy were allies against the fascists. Lots of them were in the Resistance. He remembered it as a wonderful time.

Among the troops, though, it was a terrible time. "A lot of the guys felt trapped. They were sure they would never get out of there alive. Believe me, we had morale problems up to our ears." Because there was no evacuation route, the injured were overflowing the medical tents.

When the brass became concerned about troop morale, they decided that a field visit from the general—together with the presentation of purple hearts for the wounded—would raise the men's spirits. Together with lots of other medical corpsmen, Herb accompanied General Patton on his tour around the hospital tents. He described Patton as the archtypical tough, mean, hard-nosed, no-nonsense general.

As they moved through the tents, whenever Patton spotted a soldier with an obvious limb missing or an eye knocked out, he congratulated him on his bravery and pinned a medal on his chest. Herb paused. "You won't believe what happened next. A GI with no apparent physical injury was sitting on his bed. The general came by, stopped, and turned to the company commander. 'What's the matter with him?' The medic in charge explained that the soldier was suffering from shell shock." At this point, Herb said, Patton grabbed the soldier, pulled him out of bed, and said: "I'm not going to tolerate this yellow-bellied behavior in front of all these brave men." With that, he slapped the poor confused GI across the face and told him to get back to his company and do his duty as a soldier. The medic tried to tell him that the man was genuinely ill, but Patton waved him off. 'You've got your orders.'"

Afterward, Herb said, he sat in his tent fuming, wondering what he could do. I said, "You were about to become a shop steward."

"Yes, in a way. A few hours later I was at the typewriter writing an indignant letter to *Stars and Stripes*." He laughed, "I never, ever thought they would print it. But not long after, there it was, a headline in *Stars and Stripes*: 'Patton slaps sick GI.'" That was the beginning of the end for Patton. Eisenhower gave him a dressing-down over the incident and, Herb believed, realized for the first time that he had a rogue elephant in command of the Sixth Army.

I was laughing. "What do you think would have happened if it had come out that the GI who blew the whistle on Patton was a member of the Communist party?"

"I don't think it would have made any difference," he responded. "Those were the days of political milk and honey." Still, I was sorry Patton never knew that it was a nice Jewish communist boy from Newark, New Jersey, who did him in.

There was a pronounced split between Mine Mill's national leadership and the locals. Not by any stretch of the imagination did either local officers or members of Mine Mill consider themselves part of a communist-dominated union. The ideology-driven Marxists in Mine Mill's national leadership, for their part, assumed that workers who did not respond to their own "correct position" had been influenced, brainwashed, propagandized, or frightened by the employers.

As 1953 drew to a close, attacks on Mine Mill leaders were coming in from all sides. These assaults, especially in the small town press, were very embarrassing for local union officers. Herb Lerner was one of the Newark *Star-Ledger*'s favorite targets. Hardly a week went by without some charge being leveled against him. These attacks and the quickening pace of membership raids from CIO unions forced Herb and the other party people in Mine Mill to spend a big portion of their time running from local to local putting out constantly reignited fires of revolt. Only the members' great respect for Herb's negotiating skills kept them from running him out of the union.

You sure can pick 'em, I thought to myself. Here I was once again involved in a political fight—though this time just as a foot soldier, more of an observer than a participant. That observer status didn't last very long. Events out in the Rocky Mountains soon pulled me into the front trenches of a new fight.

18

Trouble in the West

It was one of the coldest nights in January of 1954. Edith and I had gone to bed early and were propped up on a pile of pillows finishing our ritual reading of the Sunday *New York Times*. Around eleven o'clock the telephone rang. It was Herb.

"I got a call from Denver a short time ago. The union in Montana is in one hell of a crisis. The leaders of Mine Mill Local 1 in Butte have announced that it and all the locals in the state are quitting Mine Mill to join the Steelworkers' union."

I couldn't believe my ears. "I thought Local 1 was the very heart of Mine Mill? How the hell did this happen? Didn't anybody in the Denver headquarters know what was brewing?" What he told me was incredible. Apparently the secession had been in the works since the previous fall, but for some unexplained reason the national union leaders didn't take the threat seriously. "That's a long story," Herb sighed. "But if we lose the state, it's the end of Mine Mill—and of any hopes for militant unionism in this country." He paused. "Bob, This is going to be a bitter fight. We've got to save this union."

"Herb, are you asking me to go to Montana? You must be kidding. If I'm all this union has to call up in an emergency, it's in fuckin' deep trouble. What the hell do I know about Rocky Mountain hard-rock miners? Nothing!"

"Bob, you're a good organizer. That's what they need there. Besides, you're a new face, and you still have some of the old organizing fire in you. It may be enough to make the difference."

"Okay Herb, thanks for the flattery. But this union better have more than that. So how did it happen?"

"As I said, that's a long story. The Anaconda Copper Company wants Mine Mill outa Montana. Since the CIO tagged us as communist-dominated and expelled us, the company has been scheming against us relentlessly." He paused. I was thinking about Butte Local 1's origins as a Western Federation of Miners union and its incorporation into the Industrial Workers of the World (IWW). During its early years, it epitomized the militant determination of hard-rock miners to gain some control over their working lives. Forgetting my growing cynicism for a few seconds in the call to battle, I fantasized that the immediate crisis was about preserving the last-remaining militant working-class tradition.

Then I had a worrisome thought. "Christ, Herb, isn't that where the Pinkertons or some other fuckin' company vigilantes hung Frank Little (the Wobbly organizer) from a railroad trestle?"

Poor Herb was in agony over asking me to do this. "Bob, they don't hang union organizers any more."

"You're right," I said, "Now they just shoot 'em in the ass. This is sure some great assignment. Okay Herb, what do you want me to do?"

"Denver wants you to pack and leave for Butte tonight if you can. Once you're there you can make an evaluation of what needs to be done."

"Have any of the local leaders stuck with us? Christ, I have to have someone to contact when I get there."

Herb was trying to give me the bad news in small doses. "I'm afraid there's no one." He told me that in Butte, as well as in the smeltermen's local in Anaconda, the Mine Mill leaders headed by Bill Mason had taken everyone to the Steelworkers. They took possession of the union halls, the books, records, membership lists, everything. After a long pause, he said: "Listen, I know what I am about to say is going to sound awful. I hate to say it, but what can I do? What we have to do is get enough signed authorization cards to petition the NLRB for an election. Then there'll be a campaign between us and the Steelworkers. That's our only chance of winning the whole thing back."

"Herb that has got to be the dumbest fuckin' thing I ever heard of." I couldn't believe such an unrealistic strategy had any chance of working. I went back to pleading for a contact. "Herb, please, just give me one name, somebody. Somebody to tell me where the mines are. Anything." To Herb, my questions were a terrible embarrassment.

"No, I really can't. You'll have to start from scratch. Tackle it as though it's a new organizing campaign. And remember, every move you make will have the combined opposition of the Anaconda Company and the steel union. It's going to be very tough. As you know, these guys don't fool around. Keep your back to the wall. No dinners, lunches, or breakfasts with anybody you're not sure of. Watch where you stay. Make sure any room you're in has at least two exits. Good luck to you."

"Gee thanks, Herb. That was a real confidence-building send-off. What am I supposed to do now besides piss in my pants?" What the hell was I getting into? He had scared me half to death, and I began to look for a way out. "What about my usual work? And the lousy weather?" We were having a blizzard and the airport was probably closed.

"Bob, if you can't get a plane, take the train. The quicker you get there the better. Don't worry about the other stuff. We'll figure out what has to be done here."

I hung up the telephone and lay there thinking for a while. I turned to Edith, "What do you think?"

"What do I think? You know you don't care what I think. You'll go— and you'll love it. You always do."

She was right. I didn't much care what she thought. And even after my bitter experience with the Machinists, there was enough of the true believer left in me to be challenged by this assignment. Christ, Butte was old Wobbly stomping ground! I still couldn't resist the siren's song of the working class.

My anxiety level, though, was sky high. Unable to sleep, I called the airlines. Storms in the Rocky Mountains had closed the Butte airport. They had no idea when it would reopen. Herb had said to be ready for thirty degrees below zero, so I dug out all my old hunting clothes—boots, woolen socks, hunting caps, and mackinaw, all the cold weather clothing I owned—to take to the frontier. I looked up Montana in the encyclopedia. It's huge geographically, twice the size of New York, with only one-thirtieth its population: half a million people, thirty thousand of them living in Butte. I couldn't visualize myself in Butte. I would be a complete outsider, a total stranger from—where else?—New York City. Sure as hell, they would run me out of town in the first twenty-four hours.

I ended up taking a train. As I huddled in my sleeping compartment on a Milwaukee Road pullman out of Chicago, I thought it had to be the coldest January night in history. The four blankets did nothing to warm my icy feet. At one stop during the night I scraped a small opening in the thick glaze of ice on the window. I could vaguely see strange-looking figures, their heads covered with large fur hats pulled down so that only their eyes showed. Like creatures from another planet, they kept beating their arms against their chests and stomping their feet. The station sign read, "Bismarck, North Dakota.

Unable to sleep, I got up and made my way through the train to be at the dining car as soon as it opened. The conductor had said something about dropping off most of the passenger cars well before Butte, and I thought I might meet the two FBI men who had been following me since I left New York. If so, I would suggest we have breakfast together. Spotting them on the platform in Chicago when I changed trains, I had asked them on a sudden impulse, "Since we're all going to Butte, how about we pass the time with a nice, friendly game of three-handed pinochle?" Surprised, they spluttered something and denied knowing what I was talking about.

"Of course, you do. You guys have got to be FBI agents. You've been following me since New York." When they continued to stutter and stammer their denials, I laughed. "Okay, just let me know if you change your minds about the game."

On the run from Bismarck to Butte the question "What the hell am I doing here?" kept repeating inside my head like a broken record. Throughout the day, as the train stopped periodically while the tracks were cleared of snowdrifts, it got further and further behind schedule. I now had a new fear: that I would arrive in Butte at some ungodly freezing hour of the morning to find the station abandoned.

We finally pulled into Butte well after midnight. The conductor shook his head ruefully: "This is it, boy. Good luck. I sure hope someone's here to meet you. It's gotta be twenty below out there."

Dragging my heavy suitcase, I climbed down off the train. All I could see was a snow-covered landscape and a lonely old station. Standing on that platform in the bitter cold, I was overwhelmed with the sheer beauty of the pale blue snow reflecting the navy sky. Not a living soul was present: no taxis, no automobiles, nothing but snow and a brilliant starlit heaven.

I began to panic. I was even sorry the FBI guys weren't there. When I took a deep breath, the air froze on my tongue and my nostrils burned. Remembering stories of people whose lungs had frozen from breathing-in subzero air, I quickly wound a scarf around my face.

For a moment, as the train pulled slowly out of the station, I thought of running to get back on. Who cared where it was going; anyplace was better than being left there to freeze to death alone. I was sitting on my suitcase with tears freezing on my cheeks as I watched the two rear lanterns of the caboose fade from sight. If I didn't do something quickly, one union organizer would end as an inglorious frozen cadaver on the Butte railroad platform.

Walking around the station I found a telephone and prayed to God it was working. I had never imagined that the sound of an ordinary dial tone could sound so welcome. The information operator had trouble understanding my outpouring of gratitude until I explained my predicament; then she hastened to give me the number of a cab company. The guy who answered sounded half-asleep. "What the hell are you doing at the railroad station? I haven't made a pickup there this late in at least twenty years."

I was apologetic: "The train was late. It got in just a few minutes ago. I'm going freeze to death out here if you don't come and get me."

"I'll be down as quick as I can."

As I waited, I ran back and forth pounding my arms against my chest as I had seen people doing in Bismarck. Finally I saw a welcome pair of headlights. As I got into the cab, the driver kept shaking his head. "I can't believe it. Don't you know anyone here? Suppose I hadn't come in the middle of the night?" He was also a bit curious: "What on earth is so important that you had to get here by train at this hour?"

My caution flag went up. I had better not say. "I absolutely had to be here to take care of some important business tomorrow."

My reply increased his curiosity. "Do you work for the company?"

"What company?"

His voice full of scorn, he asked, "Don't you know anything about Montana? Mister, there's only one company here, the Anaconda Copper

Mining Company. They own this state. They control the governor, senators, congressmen, mayors, banks, newspapers, whorehouses, country clubs, hospitals, dogcatchers, and goddamn nearly anyplace you sit down. They own it, if not on top of the ground, then what's under it. That's called mineral rights. Lots a folks here in Butte get dumped outa bed at night when they're blasting underground. Mineral rights, mister. Mineral rights made a lot of millionaires. Are you here for the company on special assignment?"

"You could say I'm on special assignment, but not for the company." We pulled up to the Hotel Finley. The wind on my cheeks cut like a knife as I got out. The neon signs in the crystal cold night twinkled like distant stars. There was not a living soul on the street.

The lobby of the Finley was ornamented in the art deco style of the great movie palaces of the thirties. I thought the night clerk looked at me with suspicion. I was getting paranoid. Who but a murderer or a messenger from God would arrive after midnight on a night like this? "Do you have a single?" I asked.

"How many nights?"

"I don't know."

"What company are you with?"

"I'm on private business." Now he would surely be suspicious.

As he hit the desktop bell, he said, "Okay, sign here and let me have your credit card." A bellhop appeared out of nowhere. As we walked toward the elevator, I asked him who stayed at the hotel.

"Mostly company officials. Their headquarters is up the block."

The room was small, but after my last two nights on the trains the bed looked wonderfully comfortable. Though I hadn't taken a tub bath for years, I climbed into a steaming hot bath to warm my icy feet before going to bed. As long as I was in Butte, the hot bath was my nightly ritual.

The next morning I was up early, had breakfast, and bundled myself up for a walk. I wanted to get the feel of the place; see where the miners lived, check out the churches, clubs, stores, restaurants, bars, and cemeteries. The sound of the snow cracking underfoot made me feel that I was walking on broken glass. In the clear, cold air the vapor from the mineshaft ventilators seemed to rise straight up to heaven.

I had promised myself a visit to the grave of Frank Little. He was a Wobbly organizer who, in the view of the copper companies, was one of the most dangerous men in the Rocky Mountains. Little was half Indian and had only one good eye. He arrived in Butte in July of 1917 to help organize a strike in support of a six-dollar-a-day wage for copper miners. A short time earlier, during a strike in Bisbee, Arizona, he had been badly beaten by company goons. The copper companies there had driven the Bisbee strikers from the state, and Montana's Jeannette Rankin, the first woman member of the U.S. House of Representatives and a great humanist, was concerned that the same thing might happen in Butte. Since the state government was simply an extension of Anaconda Copper, she was trying desperately to involve the federal government in stopping the terror in the copper camps.

Before she could make any arrangements, a terrible outrage occurred in Butte. In the early morning hours of July 31, six masked vigilantes dragged Frank Little, clothed only in his nightshirt, from his rooming house. They drove him to a Milwaukee Road railroad trestle, tied one end of a rope around his neck and the other to the trestle, and threw him off. His dead body was found hours later with a note pinned to his nightshirt: "3-7-77"—the vigilante code for a grave three feet wide, seven feet long, and seventy-seven inches deep. A reward was offered, but no one was ever charged with his murder. His funeral procession was the longest in the history of Butte.

In my father's pantheon of heroes, Frank Little held an honored place. There was no way I could fail to pay my respects. As I stood at his headstone and read "Murdered by Company Vigilantes 1917," I knew Papa would be very proud of me.

The city of Butte sits on top of a six-thousand-foot prominence once referred to as the richest hill on earth. Except for the saloons on every block, Main Street in Butte was very much like that in other small industrial towns. On a corner in the center of town stood the traditional three-story, redbrick bank building. Surrounding the business district were the miners' homes—small wooden A-shaped houses, each with a little porch, a sharply peaked roof, and, usually, a pickup truck out front.

Having no contacts to orient me, I was trying to get to know the place by walking around the streets. The map I picked up in the hotel showed the location of all the major mineshafts. I was fascinated by the huge gallowslike frames that acted as hoists to haul up the ore as well as to take the miners down into the mines and up again. The bone-chilling cold prevented me from standing around outdoors for any length of time; so I spent most of those first few days walking around, reading the *Montana Standard*, drinking coffee, and listening to "Your Cheatin' Heart" on the radio. I still wondered what the hell I was doing there.

After several days walking and studying the map, one afternoon I ventured into the M&M bar on Main Street. The warm air of the room was dense with cigarette smoke and the smell of beer and booze. Hank Williams was singing "Jambolaya." It was a great relief to get in from the frigid weather. During my stay in Butte, I became a big Hank Williams fan. After a while, some of the miners started calling me "Hank Schrank."

The bar at the M&M was easily the length of a bowling alley, and a full-length mirror behind it made it easy to see who was in the joint. A highly polished brass rail ran in front of the bar, and shining brass spittoons were spotted along it at exactly equal distances. At one end of the bar a red-curtained doorway led, as I learned later, to a gambling room. The place was a perfect setting for a Hollywood western.

It was full of miners who had come off shift and stopped in for a couple of beers on the way home. Most of the men wore heavy workboots, mackinaws, and fur hats with ear flaps. Looking for an empty stool, I walked to the end of the bar. Every eye in the joint followed me. I could only hope that my uneasiness wasn't showing. I climbed on a stool, unbuttoned my coat, and took off my hat. When I looked up it seemed as though half a mile of men sitting on bar stools were silently staring at me. A little voice inside said, "Just be cool, and it will be okay."

The bartender, a big friendly guy, came toward me: "What'll you have stranger?"

I looked around to see what others were drinking: mostly whiskey and beer or whiskey with a water chaser. "Whiskey and water."

"A ditch?"

"Yes, of course." I didn't know what the hell that was.

"Been here long?"

"Just a few days." The bar was a warm, cozy place. The miners hailed each other with joking comments on their clothes, their drinking, their car, their girlfriends. They seemed like a friendly bunch. There was a lot of traffic in and out of the back room. Men who came out smiling sometimes bought a round; other guys came out and borrowed a quarter for a drink.

After my second drink, the bartender came down to my end of the bar. "Welcome to Butte. Welcome to the M&M." He introduced himself as Sturd, "as in Sturdavitch," and placed another glass of whiskey and water in front of me: "On the house." I began to talk with the guy next to me, and pretty soon we bought each other a drink. My third and fourth ditch were staring me in the face and I was still drinking my second one.

Over the sound of the jukebox twanging away about who broke whose heart, I was trying to pick up any bits or pieces of conversation about the job or the company. Most of the talk was about who was screwing whom, the mines, and sports. The mine talk focused on good working spots and complaints about "blasting on shift." I asked the guy next to me why were they so pissed about blasting on shift?

"You're not a miner, are you?"

"No, but I'm trying to understand what they're talking about."

"They're fuckin' mad about the dust that rolls through the mine when some hungry asshole blasts while the shift is still in the mine. It's against the law, and everyone knows it, but no one does shit about it." If we ever have a campaign, I thought, this might be a good issue. I thanked my companion and decided it was time for me to find my way back to the Finley before I fell off the bar stool. Once outside, the blast of cold air sobered me up fast. I slept well that night, mostly from the booze, but I never was able to get warm.

After that, the M&M became my nightly hangout. I had been in town almost a week and still had not spoken with anyone about what I was doing there. The bartender and a few of the regulars now knew me by name, but I hadn't really learned anything. I resolved to keep my drinking down, but it didn't work. As someone at the bar said, "What the fuck else is there to do in this godforsaken place?"

One night I was on—damn, I forget—my second or third ditch and pretty well pickled. I was rationalizing that my drinking problem was the result of the mile-high altitude and lack of oxygen when a pretty young woman came into the joint. Her breasts almost bursting out of her blouse, she asked if she could sit on the stool next to me. Things were looking up. If my brain, instead of the bourbon and my groin, had been in charge I might have noticed that she was only one of two women in the joint. She was in her early twenties and wearing lots of make up and enough perfume to overwhelm the smell of booze and miners' sweat. A close look at her blond hair revealed that the bleach had not made it down to her brunette roots. Ordinarily I would have quickly figured out what her trade was, but here in Butte I was ready to play the role of the stranger in town. Giving me a big smile, she sat down next to me and pressed her leg against mine. She ordered a whiskey sour and inquired, "Are you new here?" A blind woman could have smelled that I wasn't from Butte. So what was I doing in town? I answered that I was just poking around. Where was I staying? I told her the Finley. Her curiosity began to concern me, but the room was spinning around and I had my hand on her leg.

She told me her name was Helen and that she lived down at the bottom of Butte hill where the new town was being built. "The old town here sits right on top of the mines. The blasting can keep you up half the night. When I was a little girl growing up up here on Maple Street, the dishes would rattle in the kitchen and we'd say, 'That's Daddy down there blastin.'" She guessed from my accent that I was from New York and said with a sweet smile, "I would sure love to go there."

I was trying hard to believe that she was a hard-rock miner's innocent daughter, a poor victim of a brutal life, but even in my bourbon haze I began to wonder about her. I was thinking about inviting her to the hotel for dinner, but when I tried to catch the bartender's eye to pay for the drinks, he retreated to the other end of the bar and motioned for me to come down there.

She seemed annoyed when I excused myself. I had to catch myself from sliding down onto the sawdust floor as I slipped off the bar stool.

Giving me a big all-knowing smile, the bartender asked, "Are you the new union organizer?"

I was surprised, "How'd you know?"

"Oh, bartenders know everything." Nodding toward Helen, he asked, "Do you know who she is?"

"Who? Her? Helen? I just met her."

He shook his head. "Listen boy, every guy in this bar except you knows Helen. She's a high-class hooker. Most of her clientele comes through the company. You know, out-of-town executives who want a little nooky while away from home. If you want to be any use around this town, be goddamn careful of anything she suggests. Now forget what I told you. But just remember that the bartenders in this town know everything. I mean everything. And we're 100 percent union."

I felt like a first-class jackass. Curious to see what Helen would suggest, I didn't say anything. Her sweet-talking voice was gone. In response to her question about the bartender, I said he was reminding me of a poker game he had set up for later.

After another drink she suggested that "we get out of his dump and go up to the Club. It's a nice place where we can eat, drink. Afterwards we can have a nightcap at my place." Then, teasingly: "Who knows? Maybe we can have breakfast too." I told her there was no way I could back out of the poker game. Figuring I had been tipped off, she was really pissed.

"What's the matter, you got no balls? I heard New Yorkers were hot stuff. Why not show it?" I excused myself and stumbled up to my new-found friend, the bartender. I asked him about the "Club," and he told the miners standing around him. They were all whacking each other on the back and laughing themselves sick. Clearly, I was boob of the year. Helen walked past, looked at this spectacle, and threw out a "Fuck you and them too!" as she flounced out the door.

When the group stopped laughing, Sturd said, "The Country Club is the hangout of the Anaconda executives. Now, you guys, listen and make sure I get this right." He looked at me: "You go to the Club, chances are here's what happens. The two of you will be all nifty and cozy together. Probably as you exit arm in arm, or are maybe having a nice kiss under the Anaconda Country Club sign, guess what? There just happens to be a photographer waiting to take your picture. At the right time in your organizing effort, there it will be on the front page of the *Montana Standard*, our local rag, controlled by—guess who?" All the miners agreed that's about the way it would happen. I apologized for my stupidity and thanked them all for saving me.

I was in a pretty foggy condition as I leaned over the bar and asked the bartender in confidence: "How'd you know I was from Mine Mill?"

"I told you the bartenders in Butte know everything. We learned about you from the taxi driver who picked you up the in the middle of the night at the train station."

"How'd he know I was a union organizer?"

"I don't know. He probably figured no one else would be coming here on a train in the middle of a freezing cold night." It turned out that Sturd had been a member of the Western Federation of Miners and had lived in Butte all his life. In his opinion "all those local baboons who went over to the steel union ought be run out of town. They sold out to Anaconda. They're just a bunch of crooks working for the company. Anything I can do to bring back a real miners' union, by God, I'll do it."

He told me that just about everyone who works in Butte belongs to some union. There were more than sixty bars in the towns of Butte and Anaconda, one for every five hundred adults. "Now you know where folks here spend their time, so bartenders have a pretty good idea who's who out there, and they're all for Mine Mill. You come to our next union meetin', and we'll get the bartenders to help you identify Mine Mill supporters so you can pull them together. Before you know it, we'll get the old union back." He laughed, "Nothin' to it, eh?"

He also told me to see the bartenders' business agent, who worked at a bar in Meaderville, a small town right next to Butte. "Tell him I sent you. He'll fill you in on every bar in town, where it is, and what bunch hangs out there—like Swedes, Finns, Irish, Spicks, Guineas, Krauts, Uncle Jacks, and Indians—and where they stand on the unions." Another guy in the bar that night, after repeated assurances that the company would never know, told me he was eager to "get a real fightin' union in here to teach this fuckin' company a lesson." In his anger at Anaconda and his fear of losing his job or a good work site, he typified the classic dilemma of the worker asked to sign up for the union. Getting signatures of supporters was always a slow process.

I had been calling Herb regularly, mostly complaining about being here. Now I had some progress to report. He was pleased and, I think, surprised, and said he'd keep Denver headquarters informed.

A few days later I took a cab to the Meaderville bar and was welcomed by Hank Snow twanging out "It Makes No Difference Now" on the jukebox. Behind the bar was a mural-sized Budweiser poster of "The Battle of Little Big Horn—Custer's Last Stand," a familiar landmark in Montana bars. There was Custer in all his glory, mounted on his black stallion and leading the charge against the Indians. In 1954 the myth of Custer was still a real booster for Budweiser drinkers.

The bartender was another ex-miner. He had the most smashed-in face I had ever seen. He had no nose, just two nostril openings in the middle of his face. There was a deep indentation in his forehead as though the top of his skull had been knocked in. My first reaction was revulsion—until I met his very kind eyes. My shock must have shown. Anxious to put me at ease and speaking softly and confidentially, he said, "I was in a mine explosion five years ago. Now I'm a bartender."

"Sturd at the M&M sent me."

He nodded. He already knew who I was. "First, whata ya drinkin'?"

"Whiskey and a ditch." I had my map of Butte spread out on the bar. He told me to sit down at the end by the cash register. In between customers he would show me where all the bars were and tell me which of the miners who hung out in them might be Mine Mill supporters. A few drinks and a burger later, I was once again pretty well pickled, but I had a map pinpointing every saloon in Butte.

"Smashed"—that's what the miners called him—had marked on my map the Irish, Slovak, Crow Indian, Chicano, and Guinea bars. The Chicanos hung out in three or four bars, depending on where they were from in Mexico, and the Irish had two or three. Then there were the Uncle Jacks. "Most of the Uncle Jacks," Smashed explained, were Welsh mine foremen and supervisors. They were called that because "it seemed like every damn one of them brought over from Wales an uncle named Jack."

He suggested that I concentrate my efforts on places where the "real men" of Butte hung out and began to give me their names. As he saw me write the names in my little book, he got nervous. "Look, these names I'm giving you are the best men around here. If you lose that book or it gets into the wrong hands, these guys will be fucked but good. So sleep with it under your pillow."

As I made my way back to the hotel, the icy wind cut at my face, but inside I was feeling warm—probably because of the bourbon and the hopeful signs of organizing potential. I had some names. The bartenders were my friends: one had saved me from a setup with a company hooker and another had given me all kinds of useful information. Not bad for someone who a couple of weeks earlier had been sitting at the station in tears.

It was time to let the union's national headquarters in Denver know what was happening. The Denver officials were terribly embarrassed about losing the Butte local, as indeed they should have been. Their confidence shaken, they held a dim view of the union's future in Montana. The national secretary seemed pleased, although somewhat surprised, by my optimistic report. A few days later he called to say that Dan Noonan, the union's public relations man, would arrive in Butte the next day. He suggested emphatically that I meet Dan at the airport to get updated since we couldn't talk on the telephone. "We have to assume that all the phones in Butte are tapped and that the company will hear anything we say."

It was a cold, clear, sunny day at the airport when Noonan bounded down the landing stairs. He was a short bald man with a long face. Behind his dark-rimmed glasses his merry brown eyes darted about in a constant state of alert. Noonan had been a reporter for the Chicago *Daily News*. With his fedora pushed back on his head and his ever-present cigarette hanging out of the side of his mouth, he looked like a police reporter straight from Central Casting. His nervous, high-speed speech created a sense of urgency, and he had a funny little giggle. I liked him instantly. As we walked to the car with our breath steaming in the frigid air, he mumbled, "What the hell are we doing in this godforsaken, fuckin' dump? I left a nice warm home and family for this? I must be nuts. Is there any decent place to eat? Is there anything here besides ice?"

"Sure," I said. "There's a movie house that's open two days a week. And I have it on good authority that Blond Emma's whorehouse, in the best Wild West tradition, has red velvet curtains and leather upholstered chairs."

"Schrank, are you horny already?" he giggled. "Christ, you just got here! What you gonna do in a couple of months? You better find somebody to keep you calm."

We decided to set up our home away from home somewhere away from the Finley Hotel, where our every move could be easily observed from Anaconda headquarters across the street. Not knowing how long the campaign would last, it seemed like a good idea to find a place with a kitchen so we could make a cup of coffee and warm up some soup. We moved into the Mount Royal Motel down on the flat and before long were fussing over the thermostat setting every night like an old married couple. Dan needed the heat up, and I wanted it down.

Dan admitted that it had taken the leadership far too long to wake up to the consequences of the Montana mutiny. Still, once they had recovered from the shock and received my encouraging report, they had decided to go all out to win. Otherwise, they knew, it was curtains for Mine Mill. Worried about future merger possibilities, they had come up with a real budget for us to work with.

"If we lose in Montana, who the fuck will want to marry this outfit?" Dan snickered. "Maybe the barrel or harnessmakers' union. Or maybe we can all go back to selling apples or Electroluxes."

The next day we rented a couple of cars and an office for Dan's PR campaign of leaflets, press releases, radio and television announcements, and what he called "attention-getting capers." I continued my recruitment efforts at the bars, reasoning that if I got five signatures at every bar, by the end of a month we would have three hundred miners signed up. I also needed to start recruiting efforts among the smeltermen in Anaconda, a town about sixty miles west.

Dan said, "You're making a damned good start, if you don't end up a fuckin' drunk. But if you do, we'll put you in AA, and you can recruit some other drunks from there."

For some reason, the VFW hall was the watering hole for the most disgruntled, dissatisfied, and disappointed miners. They hated, first, the company; second, the operating superintendent, a Mr. West; and third, the old local's leaders, who, they said, had "sold out to the Steelworkers 'cause that's what the company wanted."

It was at the VFW hall that I met a most unusual man, Bob Ellenberg, who became my Butte mentor. Big Bob was a good six feet four and looked more like eight feet. Almost as wide across as he was tall, he was awesome. He had huge shoulders, muscular arms, and a big round head like a giant. Like many miners, he had learned to speak with his lips closed to keep the rich tobacco juice in his mouth from becoming an unwelcome shower for his listener.

There were shining brass spittoons everywhere in Butte to accommodate the legions of tobacco chewers. Upon arriving at a bar, a chewer would seat himself within safe firing distance of one of them. As he talked, he chewed. Suddenly there would be a loud *Ssppfffttt*, and before the eye could see the ear would hear a ping as it hit. I never saw Big Bob miss. Strangely enough, he was also the only man I met in Butte who never cussed. He said it was out of respect for his wife's religious beliefs.

Big Bob had grown up in Butte. "I was muckin' when I was sixteen. There was not one of them twenty thousand miners I couldn't lick, boy." He took to calling me "boy" or "son." I found it reassuring. He went on, "This town was wide open then. There were thousands of whores, gamblers, pimps, and suckholes of every description. You *had* to know how to fight. Otherwise, some silly son of a gun would whip you good. The only real honest union we ever had here was the IWW. I don't know how you see it, son, but I figure the company that shot those poor Wobblies and hung Frank Little from a railroad trestle is still right down the street. Butte is a mean, tough place." He paused to spit. Then, looking around as if checking to see who might be listening, he asked, "Now boy, do you know how to be tough?"

"Well, I'm not sure how you mean it, but I think so."

"If you can't be tough, don't waste your time hanging around this town. Just get out. And remember, miners don't like any diddly-shoot, double-talk stuff. You got to talk simple and straight to these guys." He bit off a new hunk of tobacco. "Nobody here gives a damn about the company, or the union, or any of that stuff. 'Cause their work is dangerous. Miners got to care about themselves. If they don't, they're gonna be dead or dusted. The union that cares most about the miners is the one that's gonna win this election." He paused and looking at me quizzically asked quietly: "By the way, boy, are we going to have an election here or is that just more bull?"

"No, I think we'll have an election. We have to sign up enough authorization cards to petition the NLRB, and then we'll have to wait for them to authorize it."

"Well, the *Montana Standard* already said it doesn't think there's a need for an election because the Steelworkers clearly represent a majority. Read the *Standard* like it was the company bulletin board. That old

Mine Mill local leadership was just runnin' a company union. All the miners know that."

I was now feeling defensive. "I assure you, we'll petition the NLRB for an election as soon as we get enough cards signed."

Big Bob dismissed my assurance impatiently. "Now boy, that's what I mean by bull. You got too much confidence in that NLRB and all those government agencies. What you got to understand is that this here is a company state. When somethin' bothers the company, all they do is pick up the phone and the folks in all those agencies run around saying 'yowzir' while kissin' Anaconda's behind. You better have a plan to get around those agencies."

In his quiet way, Big Bob was scary. His confidential manner seemed to elevate every problem to a crisis level. When I asked him what issues would get the miners fired up enough to organize a real union, he thought for awhile. "Pay no attention to the Steelworkers. Ignore them. Don't even mention their name. Miners don't give a bead of goat turds about one union fightin' another. If you want to win this election, fight the company. The old local's leaders never did. Just remember, the enemy is the company, not the other union."

He paused and let go a spit. "Okay. The big thing the miners worry about is dust. See this big man standin' right here in front of you? I can't mow my own little lawn. I got a quarter of a lung left. The rest is gone to silicosis. Dusted is what I am. I'm a watchman now. I walk around lookin' for bad timbers or fallen roofs. So I gotta be careful. If they find out that I'm active in the union, I'll be out of a job, and there's no other way I can support the wife."

Before he left, Bob invited me to his house for a home-cooked meal. "And then I'm going to give you some things you're gonna need for this campaign." While we were talking, the bartender had set up three shot glasses of whiskey on the bar in front of Bob. One after another, he picked them up and, whipping his head back, tossed the whiskey down his throat. He nodded to the fellows at the bar, gave me a powerful handshake, and was gone.

The men at the bar told me that in his time Big Bob was one of the toughest, meanest, best men that ever worked on the hill.

"He could lick any two men in Butte."

"One of the best damn miners this town ever saw."

"Everybody in this town respects and loves him."

"If he's your friend, then consider yourself damn lucky."

The miners who had been standing around listening to Big Bob now began to sign cards. That night I waved the signed cards at Dan and told him about meeting Big Bob. We actually had some signed cards. Hooray! He was delighted and insisted on celebrating our great beginning.

About a week later I drove down to Big Bob's house on the flat. The evening sky boasted one of those brilliant Montana sunsets that make everything sparkle like crystal. As I lifted the gate latch and made my way up a path bordered by snowdrifts, the ground crackled under my feet.

The door was answered by a small, shiny-faced old woman. "You must be the union organizer," she smiled. Bob's told me all about you. He thinks you're a wonderful man. Do come on in out of the cold, and I'll fix you a good strong drink. Dinner will be ready in a bit."

Their house, like most miners' houses I visited, had tiny rooms. There was just enough space in the living room to move between the couch and the coffee table. Little lace doilies had been carefully placed on the arms of the two overstuffed chairs, and the floor was covered with dark-green linoleum.

Big Bob came in and sat in the chair that was clearly reserved for him; it was the one with the spittoon alongside. Mrs. Ellenberg disappeared into the kitchen and did not appear again until it was time to eat. The meal of pea soup, pork chops, potatoes, string beans, beet salad, beer, coffee, and rice pudding was the best one I had while I was in Butte.

Mrs. Ellenberg worked in a hospital. A woman in her early sixties, her bright eyes gleamed with sympathy, but also with pleasure, when she talked about caring for the sick. A wonderful sweetness shone from her as she described the suffering of the men in the hospital. Even when she described the terrible effects of the company's neglect, it was hard for her to be angry. I thought how lucky she was to love her work. She was a remarkable woman who gave off a wonderful feeling of love. Big Bob sat there beaming with pride.

Suddenly Big Bob got up from the table and excused himself. "I'm gonna go and get something." I could hear a lot of clattering in the garage; he returned with something long wrapped up in a sheet. As he slowly unwound it, he muttered, "It's important to be ready for trouble, ready for trouble." It was a big old double-barreled shotgun. There was also a long-barreled Smith and Wesson revolver. Goddamn, I thought, this is definitely the Wild West. What the hell am I doin' here? He picked up the handgun. "Do you know how to use these, son?"

I said uncertainly: "Well, I've used a double-barrel hunting. I've shot a revolver occasionally on a range, but frankly I'm not much good at it."

"Well, you're gonna need both of them."

"Won't they just fetch me more trouble from other guys with revolvers and shotguns?"

"No, they won't. They'll just let 'em know that you're not gonna let some company fink or bums run you outa town, that's all." I was getting nervous. "Well, what about permits?"

"You ain't in New York now. You don't need no permits in Montana. This is wide-open country. Around here everybody carries a shooter. Here's what I want you to do with these irons. Keep the shotgun across the front seat of your car so that the double-barrel sticks up in the window. The six-shooter you keep in the glove compartment for protection. I don't give a damn if you never use it, but folks have to know you got it. Then they'll know you ain't no sittin' duck in a shootin' gallery."

In the many organizing campaigns I had worked in, I had always followed the advice of old-timers never to go armed. If you do, they said, the union busters were likely to get scared and start shooting. For a few seconds, I did entertain the fantasy of Papa's pride at my union hero's burial in Butte next to Frank Little. Fortunately, that dream of instant immortality never got the best of me.

I tried to convince Big Bob that the shotgun seemed all right, but the six-shooter made me uneasy.

He insisted. "Keep it in the glove compartment, that's all." Although Big Bob was making me nervous, I decided that if we wanted to get anywhere in this campaign we would have to listen to his advice. I took the guns.

To change the subject, I asked Mrs. Ellenberg about the miners who were dusted. "They can't breathe and can't work, so they end up going on welfare," she said. "You know, there is no compensation for silicosis. None of the miners have been able to prove they got it in the mines."

I couldn't understand what she was saying. "You mean doctors here won't certify that silicosis comes from working in the mines?"

"No, not in the state of Montana. Oh, they say the miners have emphysema, they smoke too much, or they have pleurisy or pneumonia, or it's the high altitude. Or they're just old and can't breathe anymore. The word *silicosis* is never mentioned. There's not a doctor in this state who would diagnose their symptoms as silicosis. If he did, he would not be practicing here for long. The company would see to it. We've been fighting for years to get the state legislature to make silicosis a compensable disease. That would at least give these men something better than welfare."

She glanced sideways at her husband. "Bob doesn't like me to get too militant, you know," she went on. "He'll say, 'Now Ma, don't get yourself worked up over these things. You know how you are. You will get yourself all upset and feel bad 'cause you can't do nothin' about it. '" She didn't seem overexcited to me, but Big Bob obviously thought this was "men's business talk," and she took the hint to leave the room.

An exclusive men's conversation was about to take place. Big Bob laid a map out on the table. It showed the Butte hill, with each of the about a dozen mines pinpointed and identified by name: Little Orphan Annie, Leonard, Mountain Con, Lexington, Anselmo, and the new long-wall mine, the Kelly. He described each mine on the hill, how deep the main shaft went, whether it was cold or hot. Some were "just a deep freeze"; others were "hotter than hell"; still others were wet, "like it's rainin' all the time." That was the worst kind, because of the constant drip of copper-oxide water: "If it gets on your skin, it will burn a hole in you. But if you cover yourself, it's like livin' inside a man-sized condom full of sweat, grime, and dust all rubbed into your soaking wet skin. You can't get dry 'til you're outa there."

One of the mines, the Leonard, was over a mile deep. "That's far down into hell, boy, and don't you forget it. It took good shaft miners to dig that hole. They're a dying breed. Now we got college-trained engineers who got a lot of book learnin' but don't know the feel and smell of the rock like those old-timers did."

He described the miles of underground railroad tracks that haul the copper ore out of the hill. The entire ten-mile radius of that richest hill on earth was honeycombed with tunnels and tracks from a hundred feet all the way down to five thousand feet. Big Bob also explained that a "stope" was a steplike excavation for mining successive layers of ore. The men would build up timbers around each new layer they were going to work. Then with the big multiple drill they would make a series of holes for the dynamite caps that were supposed to be blasted at the end of the shift so the dust could settle before the next shift.

Bob went on for a long time, reviewing conditions in each mine. He gave me the name of each foreman and kept asking, "Are you taking this down in your little book?" I assured him I was. He promised he would arrange to get me into a mine so I could see what it was all about.

Finally, as he folded up the map, Big Bob turned to stare at me. "Do you know why I'm telling you all this?" He shot a wad at the spittoon; it pinged, and he grinned briefly. Before I could answer, he went on: "Remember this, boy. Every union in this town sooner or later becomes a company union. There ain't nobody who can resist the temptations of the Anaconda snake." (The reference was to the company logo.) "Someday remind me to tell you the story of this communist guy, Bill Dunne. He lived here. I knew him pretty good. His weakness was booze. He couldn't afford to buy it, but every week a case of bourbon would show up at his door."

I had heard of the legendary Dunne brothers and had trouble believing this whiskey story. "Didn't Dunne know where the booze was coming from?" I asked. "Christ, he must of guessed."

"He didn't want to ask. It might stop coming."

It was getting late. As I was walking out to the car, he said, "Hold it just a minute, boy." He went into the house and came out with a sleeping bag. "Never travel outside of Butte without this in the car. If you ever get stuck somewhere, don't get outa the car, get inside this bag or you'll freeze to death." He threw it on the back seat.

I thanked him for everything and asked him to thank his wife for me. I wanted to give him a big hug, but after all the tough talk it just didn't fit.

The handgun went into the glove compartment of my rented Mercury, and the shotgun went across the front seat. I had gotten an earful. I couldn't help thinking what a strange place this was. Were these people just playing out the plots of western movies or was it for real? I kept glancing at the shotgun. It looked more like an old rusty pipe. Things were getting scary.

A few weeks later a local publication referred to me as, "Double-Barrel Schrank." The miners loved it. Big Bob was right. I was at least looking tough.

When I got back to the motel, Dan was waiting impatiently, smoking and pacing back and forth. "What happened? Where you been? We've got a lot of planning to do." Before I could reply, he was off on what was becoming his favorite topic. "Were you out getting laid again? For Christ sake, you were sent here to do a job, not fuck your head off." It was obviously more on his mind than mine.

When I told him about the meeting with Ellenberg, he was pleased but worried about the guns. I could always tell when Dan was getting nervous. He would rub his hand over his shiny bald head. "Christ, Schrank," he said, "they got more guns than we do. We're gonna get our nuts shot off. We shouldn't do it."

"Ellenberg knows this town. We ought to listen very carefully to what he thinks. I say the double-barrel stays on the front seat."

"Okay. I don't give a fuck about you and your guns." He kept walking back and forth, puffing on his cigarette. "What are we going to do tomorrow? How do we get an election, so we can get the hell out of here? That's what I'm interested in." We had a cup of coffee and agreed to continue visiting the bars. In the past couple of weeks we had gathered about seventy signatures that way. We might as well keep up our saloon recruitment until, as Dan said, "we either have enough cards or we're both fuckin' alcoholics, which ever comes first."

We were getting up every morning at six to check the temperature. If it was lower than ten below, we plugged in the electric car-block heaters, then previewed the day's activities over breakfast at the motel or the coffee shop on Main Street.

As the days rolled by, both Dan and I were feeling lonesome. We would periodically call home—he more often than I. Edith used to say that with me it was "out of sight, out of mind," and she was right. My work had always been all-consuming. Dan, though, was really suffering. Before going to sleep, he would pace, drink, smoke, and yell things like

"This barracks life stinks. I did it in the war, and man, that was enough. Goddamn it, I have a family in Denver, a nice home, a dog, a hi-fi. I'm not like you. I'm a homebody. I don't know how to fuck anyone but my wife. I just forgot that shit, and I don't want to get started with it again. Now you, I think you would fuck anything."

"Hey, Dan," I protested, "it's all in your mind. I like girls, sure, but so far I've just looked at 'em."

A few days later just before we turned out the lights, he said, "Oh, by the way, I hired a secretary. When you see her, try to keep your hands off your fly."

As he pulled up the covers and turned on his side, Dan said, "Holy Christ, what we don't do for the movement."

Dan's reports to the Denver office were getting more optimistic about our chances. Big Bob was bringing people to meet me. He must have briefed them ahead of time, because they all had a prerecorded way of saying that they wanted to see a reconstructed, militant Mine Mill union back in Butte. Compared to the bleakness of the earlier weeks, things were looking up.

We hit another cold snap, with the thermometer dipping to 35 and 38 degrees below at night. On one of those freezing mornings, Dan said, "Give yourself a treat today. After your leaflet distribution at the Kelly mine, come by the office if you haven't frozen to death. I'll show you something that'll warm you up." He giggled.

Distributing leaflets at the various mineheads was a regular early morning activity. We huddled around an oil-drum fire trying desperately to get miners to accept a leaflet on their way to the mine. It was so god-damn cold they didn't want to take their hands out of their pockets. If they looked at all friendly, I would offer to stick it in the pocket for them. Sometimes we would sneak into the "drys"—that's the miners' locker room—to put leaflets in the overalls hanging from the ceiling on ropes and pulleys. If the guards spotted us, we were quickly shown the exit. The leaflet distributions were real survival tests, and they won me a lot of oil-drum fire pals.

The office Dan rented was in the old three-story, redbrick Metals Bank building on Main Street. The date on the stone lintel said 1902. The building featured an open-cage elevator and etched glass on all the office doors. Sam Spade, Private Detective, must have had an office there. I opened the door to Noonan's office, and there she was. Dan introduced me with one of his little giggles: "Laurie, meet Bob. Watch out for him, he's a horny fellow." Laurie was a five-foot-five Chicana. Her snug-fitting pink sweater showed off her warm caramel-colored skin and her alluring breasts. I thought she had to be the most beautiful young woman in the state of Montana. She had a shy look about her, a luscious mouth, and dreamy brown eyes that gave her an air of longing. I looked over at Noonan and whispered: "What have you done? Is this some kind of supreme biblical test of my will or a joke?" After our tentative handshake, I asked her, "What are you doing Saturday night?" In a low, throaty voice she said, "Nothing." I suggested that we go out somewhere to eat, dance, whatever, and she said, "Great." That's all, just "Great." Hungry for female company, the thought of a date with Laurie warmed me all over.

Dan looked over at me. "Just make sure it's 'Not tonight, Josephine.' The big guns are coming from Denver today. And try to remember that her brother's a miner. You'd better be careful or he'll shoot your nuts off!"

She told me to call her anytime—"tonight, tomorrow, whenever. There ain't much to do in Butte." Without waiting for me to ask, she gave me her address and telephone number.

That afternoon several of the top union officers arrived from Denver to review the organizing campaign. The president of the union, who been a hard-rock miner, was happy that everything was going well. He was a nonpolitical guy who had no taste for a fight. He wanted everything to be nice and friendly. Other officials, including some of the Marxists, wanted to hear all the details of our organizing and plied us with questions: "How are you planning to reestablish the union local?" "What will be the main issues in the campaign against Steel?" "Have the Steelworkers' goons beat up on anyone yet?"

One of the officials' major concerns was how we should handle the inevitable red-baiting. McCarthyism was still very much abroad in the land, and the fierce employer and congressional attacks on labor were continuing. Within the labor movement, unions were split between those who wanted to "get more militant and give them a real fight" and those who argued that it was "a time for accommodation." Mine Mill, in spite of its radical past, was split the same way as the other unions.

The few radicals or communists in the national Mine Mill leadership had never managed to radicalize the membership. The miners, like the men I worked with back East, cared nothing about the class struggle. It was the mundane, day-to-day problems of most industrial workers— wages, hours, job security, working conditions, safety, health, speed-ups, and so on—that concerned them. People in Butte weren't much interested in the red-baiting going on in Washington either. It was another world out there, and I liked it that way.

Noonan and I insisted that we stick very close to local issues and just ignore the red-baiting. That was Big Bob's advice. Some of the party people from Denver, though, wanted us to take on the issue to prove to the Steel union that we were *not* communist-dominated. It dawned on me then that while we were fighting the Steelworkers in Montana, there were folks in Denver trying to figure out how to join them. It made me want to catch the next plane out, but Noonan convinced me it was all bullshit.

As a result of the division of opinion, we were given no clear direction and ended up making decisions on the basis of the real situation—a pragmatic and far more reliable strategy than some grand scheme out of headquarters. They returned to Denver. We went back to the saloons and the oil drums.

Fortunately, these formerly pessimistic Denver officials had been infected by Noonan's and my naive optimism. They decided that Mine Mill might possibly win the Montana election and gave us a sizable budget increase. Besides providing for more radio and television advertising, the extra money let us bring in additional organizers.

Not long after this, we decided that we had enough names. It was time to call a meeting.

19

Rebirth of a Union

It was time to call a meeting to set up a Mine Mill organizing committee. If anyone showed up, step two would be organizing an operating local union and electing a president, secretary, vice presidents, executive committee, shop stewards. and so on. At this point in the campaign, everything we did related to the organizing meeting. We had not yet generated much publicity in town, and the company had not reacted to our presence; there was only a passing mention of organizing activities in the *Montana Standard*. Although from time to time we spotted two guys in a car parked outside our motel with their engine running, Dan and I agreed that "they" were not taking us seriously yet. After the organizing meeting and the launch of our major public relations campaign, the situation would change drastically.

A few days after the Denver officers' visit, the union's national secretary called to ask Dan if he thought the union's ex-president, Harry Walters, would be useful to the campaign. Walters was born and brought up in Butte and had worked in the Anaconda mines for many years. His family's name was legend in the state, because his mother was an early crusader for the right to organize and known to every old-time miner. Besides, he had actually been a miner himself, a distinction neither Dan nor I could claim. Denver thought that was important, but Dan didn't.

I did. I had heard an equal number of stories about Walters's glorious deeds and monumental faults. In one account he was an inspired leader, unafraid of the company. In another he was a drunk and a gambler who used any money he could get his hands on, including Anaconda's. Whatever his faults, he had guts, he was a miner, and he had grown up in Butte. His name spelled tradition. I thought it was worth giving him a try.

Dan was not so certain. He knew Walters and had worked with him. "Goddamn him! Sure, he'll be great if he stays sober, but if he goes off on a fuckin' drunk, it could cost us the election." I thought Walters might have changed. After all, for the past few years he had been working steadily as a longshoreman in San Francisco. There was a murky side to every legend that left room for doubt. I was curious about this old legend and willing to run the risk.

Dan said, "You're a damn fool. This guy may turn out to be such a pain in the butt you'll be sorry you ever heard his name." He paused. "All right, you want him? Let him come. We can use all the help we can get. But," he muttered, "I wish I was sure this guy's gonna help."

As the day of the organizing meeting drew near, my anxieties grew. Would anyone show up? Did we make enough reminder calls? Was the room we rented too small? Dan greeted the last worry with his nervous giggle: "Schrank, you're dreaming again."

The meeting was scheduled to start at seven in the evening. We arrived at six-thirty and were surprised to find the room empty. We kept telling each other, "Oh well, it's early. Yeah, it's still early." We sat at a table down in front. We had set out about thirty chairs.

Soon Dan, his fedora pushed back on his head, got up and started pacing up and down the room, puffing away on a cigarette and growling out ideas: "Blasting on shift. That's it. Let's make that our theme." He grumbled, cursed, and mumbled about the "sons of bitches out there trying to do us in. We'll show *them*, Schrank. You watch."

As the hour of truth approached, we were saved by the arrival of a couple of miners bundled up in big woolen jackets. Embarrassed at being the first, they did a lot of stomping and coughing: "Gee, are we the first ones here?" We introduced ourselves. One said, "Where's the booze and the girls? You guys gonna serve booze tonight? I hope this is gonna be a party. Where's the crowd?" I said it was still early and that we expected more people to show up real soon.

At the appointed hour, miners began to arrive. On the lookout for potential new leaders, we began questioning them about mine problems. What are the big beefs? Over and over we heard it: "Dust! These guys blasting on shift. It's killing us." One guy said, "In Orphan Annie I counted a dozen fuckin' blasts, just today. Nobody seems to give a damn anymore. The shit is rollin' through there like a dust storm. You can't take a breath without gettin' dusted."

I decided to start the meeting. When everyone was seated I announced, "We propose to reestablish Local Number 1 of Mine Mill with a whole new leadership. Please begin thinking about a president, vice president, executive board, and so on. But first, tell us what should be the issues in the upcoming campaign." By then the room was crowded. Big Bob was standing in the back by the door, smiling away and nodding his approval.

A heated discussion developed over blasting on shift. One miner argued that it wasn't the fault of the miners: "Don't go layin' it on them. The company just keeps pressing for more." Another man interrupted, "You're fuckin' well right it's the miners' fault. Some of them money-hungry bastards down there would blast in their own kitchen if they thought it would get more tonnage." A third voice piped up: "Some of the foremen figure if they can get a few blasts off during the shift, hell, they're way ahead of schedule."

Apparently another key issue was safety. "Guys are being seriously hurt in these mines every day. I betcha you don't know that there's a man a week killed down there. There was fifty-two last year." "You're right," broke in another: "For a real miner, safety is life or death. On my shift today, two guys were caught between a train and a wall. The Mine Safety Book says there's got to be enough room in between so if a man's caught there he don't get his legs crushed, but the company don't give a shit about it. These two guys got their knees mashed. Hell, they'll be out for months. Maybe they'll never be right. And what do they get? They get workmen's comp, a lousy couple of bucks. Safety. Safety's the big issue."

The meeting was going great guns. Everybody wanted to say something. This was the first opportunity these miners had had to be heard in a long time, and I was having a hard time as chairman getting them to speak one at a time.

Favoritism in work assignments was another issue that had a lot of men on their feet. "I'm sick and fuckin' tired of kissin' ass to get a decent work area. I've been stuck in a dripping-wet hole for months just because I told some suckhole foreman to kiss my ass." Everyone agreed that somehow the company had to be forced to respect the seniority list. In recent years, they said, it had been totally ignored.

Finally, there were some serious charges against the "old Mine Mill crowd." A belligerent Finnish miner pointed out that "Mine Mill, your union, was here for many years, and it didn't do shit about safety. Hey, it was supposed to be a militant, lefty union. How come the local officers was in bed with the company?"

"You want to know what it was like in old Mine Mill? I'll tell you. Everybody around here was lax, and the contract was just a hunk of paper you could wipe your ass with."

"No, never," someone yelled, "It wasn't even good for that. It was too stiff."

"The main reason those guys could take the locals into the Steelworkers was that nobody around here gave a shit about this union anymore. Once the union collects our dues, it don't matter if the office is in Denver, Pittsburgh, Washington, wherever. Hell, they don't never come out here anyhow."

My doubts about turning this around were growing. I was beginning to understand why Big Bob said tough action and not a lot of talk was the only way to get miners' support. I heard a Slovak named Malivich mumbling something that sounded like, "We drive the fuckin' Steel finks outa Butte." When I gave him the floor, he started off slowly, unsure of the language: "Too long this talk. We must to act. Take few sticks blastin' powder. Go to Steel office in union hall. Boom, they outa here. Too much talk." He got a big hand.

I tried to laugh off his suggestion, then realized some of the miners were taking him seriously. There was a ten-minute discussion of the pros and cons of "blasting the sons of bitches outa here." Working with dynamite every day influences how people think about solving problems, as the violent history of life in the coal fields shows. Dan and I were vastly relieved when cooler heads prevailed: "It's just not a good idea, at least not at this early stage of the campaign," someone said. Although the idea was tabled, it never altogether disappeared. From time to time, when the frustration level rose, the "let's blow 'em outa here" solution would reemerge.

The feeling that they might actually get their union back brought up a whole new topic: possession of the miners' union hall. When the local's leaders deserted to the Steelworkers, they took the building, together with all the local union's legal paraphernalia, with them. Big Bob had never mentioned the hall to me, but now he was insistent. He argued that the hall was a symbol of the organization's strength and unity. "That's why we gotta get it back if we wanna win this election."*

Several miners mentioned "the safe." Big Bob said we not only needed to get the building back but that possession of the items in the safe was "absolutely essential to reestablish the legitimacy of this union." Well, what could we do? There was a lot of intense discussion of schemes for taking back the building and the safe. The things in that safe seemed to be imbued with the powers of a sacred tribal bundle. Whoever possessed them was in control of the union.

Near the end of the meeting, Fred Zorn, a highly respected shaft miner, took it upon himself to summarize the discussion. "Okay, here's what we have to do to win this election. Go after the company on safety. Stop the killing and maiming of miners. Get the union hall back. Stop the favoritism in work assignments. Stop blasting on shift. If we do those things, we'll win." There was a big round of applause. We planned a series of poster-size leaflets focusing on these issues to distribute at all the mineheads. We would also make a series of radio and television programs and spot announcements to talk about these problems. Influenced primarily by Big Bob and the other miners, we decided to ignore the Steelworkers and take aim solely at the Anaconda Copper Mining Company.

Finally, an organizing committee of twelve was chosen to reestablish the local union. A second general meeting in a larger room would be held in a week. Everyone present agreed to bring at least two of his buddies. There would be refreshments, but no dancing girls.

As the miners drifted out, Dan and I, realizing we were alone, let out a "Wahoo!" and started jumping up and down hugging each other. The meeting had succeeded beyond our wildest expectations. We had a core group—something to build on—and could begin an intensive card-signing effort.

A few days after Dan reported our successful meeting to the Denver office, Harry Walters arrived in Butte. "He's all yours, buddy," Dan

---

*In 1917 the hall was blown out of existence by the hired Pinkertons, and the union went with it. The present miners' hall was the old Silver Bow Country Club, which the employers' association built in the 1920s. It was bought by the union in the heyday of the 1940s.

announced, "You better keep an eye on him." At the airport I saw a tall husky man with a large square face and fair complexion. As he walked toward the terminal carrying his topcoat, I was struck by his well-tailored suit, which contrasted sharply with the casual western-style dress I had become accustomed to. Walters smiled and looked around at the bright winter day as if it was his very own welcoming committee. As we shook hands he said, "God, it's good to be home. I grew up in Butte, and I'm sure glad to help save this union."

He explained in a deep, resonant voice that he was staying with his mother: "She's quite old, but she's still alert to the problems of the miners." I could see why he was considered a remarkable speaker, but I was unable to figure out his immaculate attire. In his starched white shirt, carefully knotted silk tie, and carefully pressed blue-serge business suit, he could have passed for a company executive. I dropped him off at his mother's house. That night Dan regaled me with stories of Walters's shenanigans that were a combination of dramatic heroics and colossal personal blunders.

During the next few weeks, with Walters's help, the campaign really began to pay off. We spent most of our time in routine organizing work—holding meetings with the organizing committee, handing out leaflets, and making new contacts and getting authorization cards signed. Every morning we would target a different mine. Knowing nothing of the radical world I grew up in, the miners had a lot of trouble figuring out why I would come all the way from New York to stand around an oil-drum fire stamping and shivering in twenty-below weather.

Early one Saturday night Laurie and I were sitting at the bar of the Meaderville saloon talking to Smashed. I'd had a couple of bourbons and was beginning to have a nice warm feeling about the sweet evening ahead when I heard a commotion from the gambling room behind the bar. I walked back there and saw a woman leaning over the gaming table crying, exposing everything she had down to her belly button. A big miner had just whacked her across the face. "Look buddy," I protested, "you shouldn't hit this nice girl. She's just trying to make a living like the rest of us."

"She's nothin' but a fuckin', sneakin', cheatin' cunt, and I'm gonna get my chips back if I have to kill her. She's just a cheap whore." Without thinking of what I was doing, I stepped between the two of them. He looked at me in total surprise. "Boy, I don't know who the fuck you are, but you better back off or I'm gonna drop you." I was as startled as he was. What in hell was I doing? Luckily for me, Laurie brought over a couple of husky guys. They took hold of the miner and coaxed him away, saving me from severe embarrassment, not to mention pain. I could only attribute my bizarre gallantry to the bourbon and the altitude.

Back at the bar, Smashed told me I had made a good friend. "Evelyn is a pal to every hooker in this town. Next to bartenders, hookers know everything goin' on in Butte."

Laurie was very impressed with me for stopping "that stupid asshole from beating up on a hard-working girl." She explained that in Butte a woman grows up to be a miner's wife, a waitress, or a hooker. "Those are the choices in this dump."

As the evening wore on, Laurie grew more pensive. Her dark eyes stared at me as though she was trying to tell me something. As we were slow dancing to "the Tennessee Waltz," she started to whisper in my ear: "Listen, what I'm gonna tell you, if you ever let out that I told, I'll be killed by my own family. Promise me, on your life, you'll never tell anybody. Promise?"

In my wildest imagination, I couldn't think what secret Laurie could possibly know that would threaten her life. "Okay, I promise. No one will ever know." As Patty Page crooned "my friend stole my sweetheart from me," I kept saying "What? What?"—not because I didn't hear, but because I couldn't believe what she was saying.

"My brother, who is on the organizing committee and is being proposed for the local's executive board, is working for the FBI."

"Are you sure? How do you know?"

Almost inaudibly, she whispered: "They met at the house and I was in the kitchen listening to them. He's supposed to get invited to secret party meetings and tell them who was there and what they said."

I tried hard to enjoy the rest of the evening, but it didn't work. I was too upset. I took Laurie home and promised her we would go out some other night.

Shortly thereafter, I received an anonymous telephone call. It warned me that a guy named Charles Field, an official in the Laborers' Union, was on his way to Butte to set up a sting operation for the Justice Department under the Smith Act. According to the caller, Anaconda had a direct line to U.S. Attorney General Herbert Brownell and was pressing him to do something about "that bunch of commies in Butte." *Click*, the telephone call was over. On several occasions, Field did invite me to his house to talk things over with "a group of us." I declined.*

I couldn't tell Dan about Laurie's brother, but I could tell him about the phone call. He wasn't surprised. "What do you think, we're playing tiddlywinks here? This fuckin' company is dead serious about whipping our ass any goddamn way they can. They aren't going to play by the Marquess of Queensberry rules either. You don't seem to get it. You got to be on twenty-four hour guard against a setup." I was convinced.

Another piece of evidence came at breakfast in the coffee shop a short time later. Evelyn and three of her friends informed us that the company had plans to "do us in." Evelyn laughed scornfully: "Guys like to talk when they're with us—to show off, impress us with how important they are."

"So what's their plan?" I asked.

All four of them started talking at once. One woman said, "The company is going to stall the election with objections until you guys go broke, and that'll be the end of Mine Mill." Others added tidbits like "They're goin' to put out a lot of stuff about you guys bein' a bunch of commies and shit like that." I thanked them for their help and paid for their breakfasts. Evelyn reminded me she owed me: "Anything I can do for you, let me know."

Things seemed to be getting worse and worse. How the hell would we ever get an election with all this going on? At one of the planning meetings when I tried to raise an objection to putting Laurie's brother on the executive board, Dan thought I was crazy. "Damn it, Schrank, he's the best Chicano we got. Why the hell are you against him?" What could I say? Nothing. He ended up on the executive committee. A couple of

---

*My FBI file seems to support this story. Hoover received a number of inquiries—at least one of them from the attorney general—about my presence in Butte, my prior activities, when I signed the Taft-Hartley affidavits, and so on. Hoover obliged, but the file blacks out the information on exactly what he gave to Brownell.

years later he was a major witness for the government's case against the Mine Mill leadership.

At every opportunity, the organizing committee was badgering us about getting the union hall back. They were insistent that it was the only way for Mine Mill to regain its standing with the miners. We spent hours devising repossession strategies. Walters thought we should break in at night and that I, being an ex-machinist, could change the locks; the next day the building would be ours. Dan figured that would just get us thrown in jail for breaking and entering.

One of the most important things Walters contributed to the campaign was a local lawyer named Arthur Hennessey. Hennessey was something of an Old West character who sat at a rolltop desk and wore suspenders over his Buddha-like paunch. He told us to forget about going to the courts to get the building back. "They'll do whatever the company tells 'em to." He paused. "I'll tell you what I'd do. I'd round up a couple hundred miners and just walk in and take it. Then put enough guys in there to keep it. Christ, who's gonna try throwing 'em out? Not the local cops. They'd shit themselves just thinkin' about it. It would take the National Guard, and you can bet your ass this governor ain't gonna do that. I'd just stop talking and take it."

Wow, what an idea! Walters agreed with Hennessey, but Dan and I were nervous. Could we mobilize enough miners to do it?

We put it to the transitional executive committee. Fred Zorn had agreed to act as president until the election. They retreated to a corner of the office to discuss the idea while Dan, Walters, and I waited impatiently. After a few minutes, the miners' backfield huddle returned with a resounding "Yes." Zorn said: "We figure we can get five hundred to a thousand miners to a meeting at the high school. When the subject of the union hall comes up, somebody will make motion to 'stop all this bullshit and just go take our hall back from the company stooges and resume this meeting in our own building.' That's how we see it. What do you guys say?" Walters and I were for it instantly; Dan wanted to check with Denver. Remembering Big Bob's advice about being tough, I told him we shouldn't second-guess the miners. "If we fink out when it comes to a real fight, they'll think we're chicken." Dan agreed. Another of Walters's local contacts paid off when he had a little chat with the police chief to make sure there would be no surprises.

In the five days before the Saturday morning meeting at the high school we distributed leaflets to every house, made announcements on radio and television, and placed ads in the *Montana Standard*. As the newspaper stepped up its red-baiting of Mine Mill, reporters from the national press services realized that something was afoot and began showing up in Butte. Among them was a *Life* photographer who asked me if he could follow me around and take some pictures. I told him it was a free country and I couldn't stop him even if I wanted to. The truth is I was flattered and enjoyed the idea of my approaching notoriety.

On Saturday morning we were startled by the results of our work. Over a thousand miners packed the high school auditorium. Zorn chaired the meeting and without warning invited me to speak. The mood of that meeting reminded me of the Bronx street corner gatherings so many years before. I told the miners that we were there to give the union back to "the Butte miners—you men here in this hall." The place broke into whistling applause. For a street corner rabble-rouser that crowd was a dream. It greeted the stream of hell fire and damnation I poured on Anaconda's mistreatment of the miners with whistles, clapping, and stomps of approval.

Walters spoke next. Everything I had heard about his spellbinding talent was true. He was a master. He knew the miners, the company, and Montana. By the time he was done, a resolution to go and tear down company headquarters would have carried easily.

When he finished and the applause subsided, there was a few moments of silence. Expectation seemed to grip the crowd. Then a miner, Al Kalifatch, stood up. "Brother Chairman, I make a motion that we go and take our own union hall back from that goddamned bunch of company stooges." A pandemonium of cheers and shouts of "let's go" broke out. Zorn said, "All those in favor, start filing out in parade formation as we go up Main Street." He took down the American flag hanging by the stage, handed it to a miner, and the parade got under way.

As Dan and I walked out with the crowd I had a moment of panic. "Oh my God, we forgot the key and the locksmith! We don't want any damage."

"Relax," Dan said, "Walters took care of that last night. While you were out working the bars, he took a locksmith buddy of his up to the hall to make keys. Now they'll change all the locks."

"You see? I told you Walters is okay."

"So far, so good," he answered.

God was on our side. The bright, warm sunny day was brought by a wind the folks there call a Chinook, which can send the temperature up to forty degrees, even in February. People walked along Main Street in a festive mood smiling and greeting each other. The police, rather than trying to halt the parade, acted as its guardians, controlling traffic and making sure there was no interference. No one in his right mind would have thought of trying to stop this determined tide of hard-rock miners.

People out doing their weekend shopping hailed the marchers as though they were heroes. One woman yelled over and over, "Go get 'em fellas. Throw that bunch of company suckholes out. Do it once and for all!" The miners shouted back: "It's our union now. We're gonna send the finks back to Pittsburgh!" To the miners, it felt like a victory right out of unionism's legendary past. Most of them probably realized it wouldn't last, but they didn't care. Whatever came later, they were determined to enjoy the wonderful feeling of power over their own lives. The jubilant atmosphere reminded me of the Yale and Towne general strike.

The marchers halted momentarily at the broad steps in front of a grand old building. Then the lead group walked up the stairs and unlocked the two large doors as a cheer went up from the crowd. Bursting with pride, the miners filed into the building to repossess what Fred Zorn called, "the symbol of our strength and self-respect." As they walked from room to room, the men were like newlyweds happily touring their first home. Finally I understood why the hall was so important to them.

The recessed meeting resumed in the miners' own union hall to elect round-the-clock patrol committees to secure the building. The Steelworkers had apparently been tipped off, for they had removed all the files and records that were not in the safe. Besides the man from *Life*—who told me he had taken at least two hundred and fifty pictures—there were a lot of photographers and newsmen who had somehow learned about the march. I believe the company executives, expecting a confrontation with the police, had tipped off the press.

Anaconda had badly overestimated the effect of the red-baiting on the workers. (So, I believe, did we.) It simply did not do the kind of damage out there that it did in New York or Baltimore. These westerners were even less political than the workers back East. The company had also underestimated the anger and resentment of the miners. I'm certain they were as surprised by the turnout as we were. A few days later, Evelyn told me that the company figured very few miners would show up and that the police would attempt to stop the march, causing the kind of riot they had in the days of the Western Federation of Miners. That, they were sure, would be the end of Mine Mill.

Big Bob was carefully watching our progress. Now, he said, we had to retrieve the local union charter. Dan said, "Holy Christ, first we gotta get the building back. Now it's some fuckin' old piece of paper. What do you think will be next, Schrank? Some old bear teeth and eagle tailfeathers?!" There was a great scene at the union hall when a large roomful of miners silently watched as the local locksmith, his ear pressed hard against the safe door, turned the combination wheel ever so slowly. After a lengthy period of turning and listening, turning and listening, he pressed down the door lever. As the safe door swung open, the hushed crowd broke into whoops of victory. The local secretary reached in, took out a parchment scroll, and announced, "Here is the charter of Local Number 1 of Mine Mill. We are back in business." Dan could not contain a snigger: "These poor guys don't have a fuckin' clue that if we don't win this election, he can wipe his ass with that charter."

The successful march to repossess the union hall created a burst of national press coverage of the "union wars" in Butte. The April 12, 1954, issue of *Life* ran twelve pictures of the campaign and the parade. The headline on page 47 read, "Party Members March to Take Back a Union." In Montana too, the organizing drive was receiving far more attention than we needed. The *Standard* had contracted a severe case of commie pinko fever. Their characterization of me as an organizer "from the hotbeds of New York" caused some good laughs. Miners passing me on the street yelled comments like, "Hey Schrank, how's the pussy in those hotbeds?" The Steelworkers' union gleefully joined in the red-baiting, repeatedly citing Mine Mill's expulsion from the CIO as proof of "control by reds."

A split on strategy occurred over our response to the McCarthy-like attacks. Denver kept bugging us to deal with the red-baiting by making a big issue of the First Amendment right of free speech and all that legal-ideological stuff. But our on-the-scene experience was telling us that Big Bob was right: "Don't pay no attention to that red stuff. What the miners care about is dust, tonnage, safety, paychecks, and avoiding Dugan" (the local coroner and undertaker). "Stick with those issues and you'll be okay."

As the campaign heated up, I had to travel to Anaconda properties outside of Butte. The company's main smelter was about sixty miles away in the town of Anaconda. One night, when attending a local meeting there, a major new issue emerged: the definition of the bargaining unit. The company wanted each of its half dozen properties in the state to be a separate bargaining unit, and a group within the smeltermen's local was supporting the idea. We assumed the company had put them up to it. Dividing the union would weaken the bargaining position and fragment feelings of solidarity. Besides, it was becoming apparent that Mine Mill's support outside Butte was not strong. We figured on winning with a big enough majority there to carry the Anaconda properties in the rest of Montana.

On my way back to Butte from the meeting where this issue came up, I got caught in a blinding snowstorm. Suddenly I saw headlights coming at me, and the next thing I knew I was sideswiped by a pickup truck. I ended up in the ditch buried in a snowdrift. 'Okay,' I figured, 'this is it, the bastards want to kill me. I'm gonna freeze to death out here alone.' Then I remembered Big Bob's advice and the sleeping bag on the back seat. Luckily, it was right where he had thrown it.

Bundled inside the bag wondering whether I'd get out alive, I asked myself if it was all worth it. What would be gained here? What will happen when Dan, Walters, and I leave? Where the hell was the damn snowplow? I was getting cold and remembering stories I'd read about people freezing to death when they fell asleep. I tried to keep wiggling around inside the sleeping bag to keep myself awake. I thought about Lake George. Where was my fisherman now?

The snow had completely covered the car windows, and I was getting drowsy when I felt a thump on the car. I tried to open the doors, but they were blocked by the snow. I blew the horn, praying someone out there would hear it. There was a clanking sound, and the car began to move onto the road surface. I was saved! I managed to squirm out of the sleeping bag and open the door to thank the snowplow driver for saving my life.

"It's nothing," he said, "It's part of my job to know when folks get stuck in these drifts. Part of the job, that's all." Here I was again, thanking my guardian angel for saving my life.

When I told Dan what had happened, he agreed that the campaign was getting mean. The Steelworkers had brought in some goons, and we figured it was their pickup that had put me in the snowdrift. After that, we took precautions. We avoided traveling alone; if we had to, we scheduled our time on the road and called when we arrived at our destination. If one of us didn't hear within the prescribed time, the other was to alert the authorities.

A new local leadership was emerging. Our best find, a young miner named Barney Rask—a former high school basketball star—was the new local president. I spent many evenings at Raymond's Bar teaching him Roberts' Rules of Order. Barney, a big handsome guy who loved women, had one hell of a temper. He would say things like, "Just let me flatten one of those son-of-a-bitch steel union reps." Over and over I had to explain that that's what the company wanted, so they could stall the election by claiming union violence.

With thousands of authorization cards in hand, it was time to get the new local leadership functioning as a union. We organized Mine Mill committees in each of the eleven mines on the hill, ending up with an active core of sixty-five miners to act as union representatives. Dan, Walters and I, knowing there would be serious challenges to our petition, agreed that when we had a few hundred more cards it would be safe to appeal to the NLRB for an election.

I told them what Evelyn and her friends had said about the company never agreeing to a vote. Dan protested about taking advice from the "whores' committee," but Walters agreed with them: "Why should the company agree to anything we want to do?" I was convinced that we couldn't sustain the enthusiasm for too much longer—maybe another month or six weeks at the outside. Dan too thought that when the march euphoria wore off we'd be in trouble. We agreed to a tight timetable for a radio, television, and leaflet blitz to get enough cards to petition the NLRB.

Walters did the first radio broadcast. In his deep bass voice he spoke sincerely of "my home town. The shame of the health and safety hazards in these mines is beyond my worst nightmares. It's all going to change with our new local leadership, who will truly represent the miners of this community."

As Dan and I listened, we were practically in tears. I asked him, "Isn't he just about the best thing we've got going for us?"

He shook his head doubtfully: "I just hope he stays this way. I love him when he's like this."

That week we also broadcast the first of our twice-a-week, fifteen-minute television programs. We bought the time right after the "NBC Evening News." Dan had written a speech for me. I didn't like the idea of reading a speech, but the station insisted and agreed I could do a little ad-libbing here and there. Although I had done many radio broadcasts, this was my first time on television.

The studio was about ten by fifteen feet, with a camera at one end and a yellow circle on the floor at the other. One man in a glassed-in area at the side served as engineer, announcer, and prop manager. I had to stay within the circle. "If you step outside it, you're off the air. I'll signal you through the glass when to start and give you a two-minute countdown to sign-off."

Waiting for his signal, I felt the same tension I always experienced before speaking. I started strong, going hell bent after the company, slamming them for their indifference to the health and safety of the miners—their absolute disregard for the rules of safety laid down by the U.S. Bureau of Mines and their failure to stop the blasting on shift. I was going great guns, but the engineer kept shaking his head in disapproval. I plowed on, raising hell over favoritism in workplace assignments and, finally, blaming the old corrupt local leaders for the bad state of things and promising that the new officers would change all that.

I couldn't wait to rip into the engineer when it was over. "Why the hell were you shaking your fuckin' head like a Puerto Rican toy duck when I was trying to make a speech?"

"Hold it a minute, I gotta shift some programming, and then I'll tell you. Don't get me wrong." he said, "I'm one hundred percent for the union.

After he switched his programs around and got us coffee, he asked me if I'd ever been on television before. I hadn't. "That's your problem. You think you're in a union hall or on a street corner haranguing a crowd. But on television you're in someone's living room, bedroom, or kitchen. If you start hollering at them like you're mad, you know what? They're gonna click you off. Would you want to be hollered at in your own living room?"

He was right. We took the engineer's advice to heart. Our next television programs included interviews with miners, their children, and their wives. We even created the Miners' Union Quartet and sang lyrics about the company, the Steelworkers, and the foremen to the tunes of country and folk songs. I supplied the guitar accompaniment, though we had to pay the musicians' union a stand-in fee. The engineer loved it, and so did Butte. We were having fun laughing at our antagonists, and almost everyone in town was laughing with us. *Life* magazine ran a picture of the quartet. Whenever I walked into the M&M bar, I was greeted by miners singing one of our television ditties:

Oh, don't you remember
Sweet Willie from Butte
Stole the Miners' Union treasury and thought he was cute . . .

With a lot of local folks on our program, we easily won the top rating between the two existing channels. I became an instant celebrity. When I walked down Main Street, people would stop and talk to me as though we were old friends. It was a bit scary. I found myself longing for radio, where folks could listen to you but had no idea what you looked like.

When we had more than enough cards to request an immediate election, Dan flew to Denver to file the petition with the regional labor board. The card count for Butte was far heavier than for the rest of the state, but we were filing for a single bargaining unit for all Anaconda properties in Montana. After all, the overwhelming majority of the company's employees worked in the Butte mines.

With the new Mine Mill local leadership and shop-steward system in place, we were anxious to be seen as a functioning organization. Our first formal request for a meeting with the company got a flat "No." The vice president for operations refused to meet with us until the issue of the legitimate bargaining agent was resolved. That night Walters, the police chief, lawyer Hennessey, and I were sitting in Raymond's talking about what to do. (In a bar Walter always carefully pointed out that he was drinking ginger ale.) Hennessey thought we needed to do something to convince the company we were in control. He suggested cutting the tonnage a bit. The word went out at the next shop stewards' meeting, and, lo and behold, the vice president called a week later to schedule "an informal session on immediate grievances." Mine Mill was back in business.

While Dan was in Denver filing our petition, Walters came with me to a meeting of the smeltermen's local in Anaconda. The local leaders there were still insisting on being a separate bargaining unit. Walters, at the microphone, was supposed to be making a pitch for Mine Mill unity. Suddenly I could not believe what I was hearing. In his most resonant tones, Walters said he could see no reason why the smeltermen should not have their own bargaining unit. "After all, they're very distinct from miners and should be independent." The crowd, of course, loved it and, as if on cue, started whistling and stomping.

I jumped up and grabbed the mike from Walters. I glared at him. "What the hell do you think you're doing?"

He looked at me in puzzlement, then said, "Fuck you, you're no miner" and walked out the door.

Convincing the audience of why we couldn't agree to separate bargaining units was an uphill battle, practically impossible. I argued as long and as well as I could, but it was getting late and people were tired. The meeting just petered out. I was angry and felt stupid for having trusted Walters. What could have made him do that?

I was ready to drive back to Butte, but no one seemed to know where Walters was. One man said he saw him heading for McMurty's bar, but when I got there the bartender said he'd had a couple of drinks and left.

This was what Dan had warned me about. He was furious when I called him in Denver and told him what had happened.

"Goddamn it, I warned you. You gotta find him before he really fucks us up."

"What could he do?" I asked.

"Oh, he can borrow money from the company. He can sign away the union hall. Christ, I don't know what he'll do. Just find him and strap him to a bed or ship him the hell out of there."

My hunt for Walters took me from bar to bar, but he always seemed to be thirty or forty minutes ahead of me. Days passed, and I began to hear stories of where he had been and how drunk he was.

On the evening of the third day, back in Butte, I was in the M&M when I heard an uproar in the gambling room. Pushing aside the red-velvet curtains, I saw miners standing on chairs watching a dirty, unshaven man playing four hands of Twenty-one against the house. I hardly recognized him. It was like Jekyll and Hyde; Walters had been turned into a monster by booze. When he won, which seemed to be often, he turned to the crowd and yelled, "The drinks are on me, fellas. Go get 'em!" The miners screamed with delight.

"What do I do now?" I asked my bartender friend Sturd.

He shook his head. "There's nothing you can do until he drinks himself down. He'll wind up in the hospital ward with the DTs, and they'll dry him out."

A few nights later the police picked him out of the gutter and called to tell me he was in the hospital. Dan was still in Denver dealing with our election problems. He had bad news about our request for a quick election: "The company and the steel union have raised more goddamn objections than Carters got little liver pills." He advised me to get Walters on a plane out of Montana. "He's a sick man, and we ain't runnin' no clinic." When Walters came out of the hospital he was again Dr. Jekyll, immaculately dressed in his starched white shirt and carefully pressed blue suit and acting as though nothing had happened. I advised him of our decision that it was "best if he left." He seemed puzzled. Then I made the mistake of telling him I knew someone at the Institute for Living in New Haven, Connecticut, where he could go for help. In a flash, he was all over me. With fury in his eyes, he hissed: "How dare you? Who do you think you're talking to? If you ever say anything like that again I will never speak to you again." And on and on.

The next day he was on a plane out of Butte. Nobody in town seemed to care. Big Bob said, "Okay, you guys tried. Don't waste time worrying about it. Miners understand. Just get on with the election."

When I got back to the motel that night I had a message from a *Montana Standard* reporter. He wanted to meet at Raymond's in half an hour to show me something very important. I was nervous, and suspicious. We sat in a booth. After hemming and hawing for a while, he took out some eight-by-ten glossies and placed them in front of me. I wasn't surprised to see Laurie and me coming out of a motel in Helena, Laurie looking her usual sweet innocent self. I was in a panic, but I sure wasn't going to let him know it. "So what?" I said.

He looked very serious. "Look, we know a lot about you. The very first thing you did when you got here was to pay homage at Frank Little's grave. We knew right off you had to be a red pinko." Goddamn it, I thought, do I need to explain to this knucklehead that Frank Little was not a communist? He went on: "I don't want to run these pictures, but if you're not out of here by tomorrow night, that's what the *Standard* will do."

"Isn't this called blackmail?"

"Oh, no. It's just reporting the news." Unsure of what to do and concerned about Laurie, I asked him to let me think about it and promised to call him in the morning.

He got up to leave. "I'll expect to hear you're leaving tomorrow. Sorry buddy, it's my job."

After Dan's phone in Denver rang and rang, a sleepy voice finally answered: "Now what the fuck do you want? Why don't you go get laid or something. Stop bothering me."

"Listen, I got a real big problem here. Are you listening?"

He shot back, "Hurry up. I'm trying to get some sleep." Somewhat ashamed, mostly at getting caught, I told him the whole story. Then I heard his nervous little giggle. "Is that what you woke me up for? Now listen, you tell that blackmailing dumb son-of-a-bitch to run that picture in full rotogravure across the whole front page."

"What do you mean?" I said. "Her family will kill me."

"Listen, asshole, they'll never run it. There's an unwritten law in the news business. You don't run pictures or stories of guys having a little hanky-panky. Christ, if they did, the papers would be full of nothing else. Everyone—politicians, judges from the Supreme Court on down, police chiefs, mayors—all of them are out there fucking around with girls. You fool around with a boy, you're dead. Girls don't mean shit. Tell that blackmailing bastard to stuff those glossies up his ass. Good-night." The next day I made the call. Dan knew what he was talking about. They never ran the pictures.

A couple of days later Dan came back from Denver with no hope for an early election. "We may be sentenced to this fuckin' Siberian hellhole for years. You can stay here, Schrank, but come June I'm goin' home, no matter what."

Dan told me there was a new movie about a strike at a Mine Mill local in Arizona and New Mexico. The Denver office thought showing *Salt of the Earth* in Butte would boost the campaign, so we rented it for a free Wednesday-night showing at the local movie house. We advertised in the paper and on radio and television and got a full house.

I was sitting with several members of the union's recently elected executive committee. As the story of the Morenci strike against Phelps Dodge unfolded, the film showed Hispanic women taking over the picket line from the men. On my left, our new local president whispered in my ear, "I told you Schrank, you can never trust a fuckin' Spic. Look at those chicken fuckers sending their women out to picket. No red-blooded American would do that." On my right big, Harry Murphy, our new vice-president, said loudly, "Schrank, what Irishman would send his woman out to do his fighting for him?" When I tried to explain that the movie was about women being part of the struggle, they laughed at me.

Dan was plenty mad. "The Chicanos got up and left," he told me after the showing. "Goddamn fuckin' left-wing Hollywood intellectuals, they don't know anything about these people out here.* Damn it, let's just

---

*Dan was right. A group of blackballed Hollywood writers, producers, and actors (including several members of the Hollywood 10 who had been jailed for refusing to name names to HUAC) decided to make a movie about a union. So what did they pick? A very unusual situation in which women play a major role in picketing. It was their agenda, but it was not at all relevant to the struggle of the western mining unions.

hope our new executive committee doesn't throw out all the Chicanos it's taken us weeks to recruit."

I said, "There's one I wish they would expel."

"What the hell you talking about?" he said.

"Oh forget it, forget it. I don't know what I'm talking about."

The new Mine Mill local was handling its routine functions well, but without an election the issue of which union was the real bargaining agent remained suspended. Sometime in early May we were in Hennessey's office talking about some legal problems involving Walters's bar debts. Somebody mentioned our need for an election. Hennessey leaned back, put his feet up on the rolltop desk, and announced with mock solemnity that "this town has taken all the disruption it can tolerate from union fighting." He thought we should petition the senior Silver Bow County judge to hold an election, "solely for the purpose of reestablishing peace and tranquillity in Butte, mind you."

Dan and I looked at each other in disbelief. "Counselor," I said, "with all due respect, the jurisdiction of these representation elections is the federal government. How can a local judge possibly order one?"

He looked at me contemptuously: "This is Montana, boy, and judges can do things here you never heard of in New York. Mind you, this wouldn't be a union representation election. It would simply be a vote of preference asking the miners for their opinion, just to return the community to peace and tranquillity *pending*—you got that?—*pending* a regular NLRB election. In the meantime, whoever wins the poll can represent the miners until the NLRB vote is taken. It's perfectly legal. If you authorize it, I'll get ready to petition the judge."

Dan and I believed Hennessey was off his rocker, but the local's officers thought it was a helluva an idea. Anyway, as Dan said, "We got nothing to lose except the two hundred bucks he wants for drawing up the petition."

Hennessey went before the judge a couple of days later, after speaking to him privately to "warm him up to the idea." The hearing in Judge McLernan's courtroom was set for the following week. The *Standard* ran a blistering editorial castigating the county judge for interceding in what was clearly a federal matter. At the courthouse, we were very surprised to see half a dozen NLRB lawyers come rushing in in their uniform pinstriped suits. They were practically still opening their briefcases at the lawyers' table when they started shouting objections.

Judge McLernan looked over his horn-rimmed spectacles: "Is this all you people have to do? Spend the taxpayers' money flying around the country? Do you figure it's gonna take five of you to convince me of whatever it is you want?" To their objections, Judge McLernan replied that he had only one concern, "the peace and tranquillity of this community. I don't care about all your Washington rules and regulations." Every time one of the Washington lawyers objected that he didn't have the authority to hold an election, you could feel the judge's determination growing.

Finally, Hennessey broke what seemed like a hopeless impasse. "I'll tell you what," he said to the NLRB lawyers, "you give us an election in the next week and we'll withdraw our petition to the judge." He paused to ask Dan and I if this was okay. We nodded enthusiastically. It was clear that the NLRB didn't want the precedent of local judges holding representation elections, informal or otherwise. The Washington lawyers huddled, came back, and said a week was out of the question.

After a lot of back and forth with Hennessey and the judge, the lawyers finally agreed to holding an NLRB election within a month, "unless something unforeseen prevents us."

"If that happens," the judge said, "I will order the elections, or a poll of choice if you want to call it that."

That night we held another celebration at Raymond's and began planning our strategy for the last month. In the morning when I stopped at the coffee shop for breakfast Evelyn and couple of her working partners were there. I told them about the election agreement. "Yeah," Evelyn said gloomily, "We know."

I stopped, "What do you know?"

They looked at each other. Then Elaine said, "The company now figures that Mine Mill will win, so they're already working on the local's new leaders. They figure if they can get outsiders like you and Dan outa here, they'll get the union back under control. And you know what? They will. They always do."

I felt very sad, primarily because I believed them. How do you live in a place like that and somehow avoid the overpowering influence and control of the company?

Still, we had to make the final push as though it mattered. The Denver office decided to send in as many organizers as we could use for the last weeks of the campaign. Because we were weak with the Chicano miners, they sent up Maclovio Barraza from Tucson. His strategy to gain Chicano support was to have cookouts in the desert. "My Chicano brothers will come, and we can talk union with them. We'll roast half a pig on a spit and get a barrel of beer. Roberto, you bring the guitar, and we'll sing all night. That will help win the election." I remember most an awful lot of miners, mostly but not all Chicanos, wanting to sing just one more song until my fingers bled and the guitar was smeared with mustard and barbecue sauce. Maclovio was a rare union organizer. In spite of his years fighting with the big mining companies in the Rocky Mountains, he had lost none of his humanity.

The Steelworkers' union also brought additional forces into Butte. We now had to be careful to avoid any actions that could lead to charges of "unfair labor practices," which could stall the election. We instructed everyone, include our visiting organizers, that no matter what the provocation, fights or violence of any kind were out. This was hardest for our fiery young local president, who still wanted to "flatten one of these guys" every time he saw a "Pittsburgh man." Dan and I kept telling people to "Cool it, cool it," and they did.

I was in my office at the union hall when I heard the accident whistle blowing at one of the mineheads. They went off fairly regularly, but this one was more insistent. One of the miners said, "Somebody probably got Duganed" (killed). A couple of them left to check it out.

An average of twenty to thirty miners were killed in the Butte mines every year, and there were hundreds of accidents, many leaving men severely injured for life. Federal and state mine safety laws, although numerous, went largely unenforced. Among miners—and so many other blue-collar workers—fatalism is an underlying cause of accidents; it leads to passivity and acceptance of otherwise unacceptable conditions. Maybe living with death as part of everyday life makes it seem normal. Nobody even got indignant or mad about it. The worst of it was, the more we looked into these accidents, the more they turned out to be preventable.

This time a miner named Martin Johnson had been sent into a section that had not been worked for some time. He set the multiple drilling machine into a battery of existing holes. The drill hit some old unexploded dynamite, and, said my reporter, "the blast just blew his head off." I was shocked by what happened, but more so by the matter-of-fact way it was told to me.

The most respected shaft miners in Butte explained that sending a man into a section that had been shut down for over thirty days without inspecting existing blast holes was an gross violation of the mine safety code. We had a long discussion with the local executive board about what we could do to make sure it didn't happen again.

Dugan, the coroner, certified that it was a "death by accident." When questioned about it, he said, "That's how I always sign 'em."

Dan and I huddled until late that night, then proposed that the union set up a committee of highly skilled miners to investigate the accident and report their findings to a meeting of the local. The miners thought it was a great idea and, expecting a large turnout, held the meeting in the high school auditorium. The executive board invited both the coroner and representatives of the company to the meeting, so they could respond to the investigating committee's report.

Dan was concerned that the committee might decide it was just another accident. "Then what?" The most I hoped for was that the coroner would change the cause of death to "negligence," which would open the company to a lawsuit by the victim's widow. "I believe the only way this company is gonna give a damn about safety is if they have to pay," I said. "Otherwise, forget it, nothing will happen."

The committee, headed by Fred Zorn, decided to conduct the meeting as a hearing. After presenting the evidence they had gathered, they would ask the members in attendance to vote on the cause of Johnson's death: "accident" or "negligence." If the latter, they would ask the coroner, right then and there, to change the death certificate.

One night before the meeting Big Bob caught up with me at Raymond's. "Boy, you guys are doing wonders for this town," he congratulated me. "The company hates you and the folks love you 'cause the place has come to life. That coroner's sure gonna sweat. You know he gets elected to that job, and the union has him on the hot seat." That was the last time I saw Big Bob. His breathing got worse, and his wife had to get him out of the "dust of Butte."

Not everyone was so pleased with me. The afternoon before the meeting the union president in Denver called to cuss me out. "What the hell do you guys think you're doing staging this mock hearing on some poor miner's tragic death?" I started to say we just want to make the company liable but never got it out. "Do you know our legal counsel received a call from the U.S. attorney general quoting you as saying you were going to 'pull out the maintenance men and flood the damn mines?' Are you crazy?"

I tried to explain. "That's not quite right. What I said was we *might* have to consider the idea if the company didn't do something about safety. Besides," I said, "it was just a threat. No one here expects us to do it." It didn't help. I realized that my career in the union was coming to an end. The union leaders in Denver badly wanted to win but were afraid of looking too militant.

The night of the hearing the high school auditorium was packed, with the overflow crowd listening to a loudspeaker outside the building. The committee did a very professional job. They had interviewed everyone who had anything to do with the accident and kept detailed notes. The accident site had been carefully drawn on flip charts showing in a dozen pages the exact sequence of events step by step. Fred Zorn presented the findings: "The area in question had not been worked for over eight months. The company had made a visual inspection of the roof and had actually placed some new support timbers." He paused, looked out at the crowd, and said: "There is no record of anyone checking the blast holes." A rustle of disbelief rolled through the auditorium.

The company's safety man described the company's safety policies but never mentioned inspection of blast holes. The miners asked many detailed questions about the rescue teams. The Butte miners took enormous pride in their rescue teams. Like volunteer fire departments, they conducted regular competitions for speed and efficiency in rescue work.

At the end of the hearing, Barney Rask, the local president, asked for a motion to change the official cause of death from accident to negligence. It passed easily. Dan and I, watching from the sidelines, began to sympathize with the coroner. Dugan looked and moved like a beaten dog.

Hopelessly trapped between the old lax tradition and this new-found militancy, he was a tragic figure. When he agreed to change the cause of death, cheers filled the auditorium and the street outside. The miners had won an important victory against the company. Still, some seemed to know, as one miner put it, that it "was just a small battle in a big war. In the end, they'll win the war."

As we left the meeting, I told Dan about the telephone call from Denver. He shook his head sadly. "This campaign is an aberration. The whole industry is changing. These shaft mines are dead anyway. They'll all be open pit in a few years, and that'll be the end of these miners." As for the Denver leaders, they were just concerned about looking respectable. The charge of communist domination had created a strong desire to avoid militant action. "That's why they're not here. So they can blame the 'overzealousness' on you and me. More than anything else they want to get back into the mainstream of the labor movement." It was the Machinists all over again.

In a few weeks the election was held and, except for a few minor incidents of pushing and shoving, went off smoothly. Mine Mill won an overwhelming victory, beating the Steelworkers' union by a better than two-to-one margin. Noonan was in ecstasy, primarily because he was going home. I was ambivalent. A part of me loved the kind of fight we had made in Butte, but deep down I knew this was the end of the brawling union battles. As Dan said, these workplaces would soon be gone, taken over by monster machines.

That night the miners' hall was packed to celebrate "the miracle of the spring of '54." Local folks told us how much they would miss "the fun you guys brought to this otherwise dull town." Besides," someone else said, "for once we showed the company we could stand up to them." That, I believe, was the most heartfelt expression of what happened that spring. Workers dream of a day when they can get some retribution for employers' disregard of them as human beings.

The next day, Dan and I packed up and drove to a Mine Mill convention in Denver where, together with Butte's new officers, we received a hero's welcome. The major issue on the agenda was the fate of the union. There was general acknowledgment that Mine Mill could not survive as an independent organization and would never again mount the kind of campaign we had won in Montana.

I spoke to the convention about the campaign and the ingredients of our victory and urged the delegates to consider merging with the United Mine Workers. At the time, the UMW was controlled by its president, Tony Boyle, who was notorious for his gangster methods of operation. In spite of that, I believed a Mine Mill–UMW merger would create a powerful, nationwide miners' union. Hardly anyone agreed with me.

Strange at it seemed after the bitter fight in Montana, the Denver leaders of Mine Mill favored merger with the Steelworkers. Not long after, they carried the day. Why the Steelworkers? I believe the leaders simply wanted to safeguard their own pensions. After the merger, it was sad to watch the leaders of the steel union treat their counterparts from Mine Mill with contempt. Once their locals were integrated into the Steelworkers, the leaders of Mine Mill were shunted aside and ignored. The noble traditions of the old hard-rock Western Federation of Miners and its successor just withered away.

20

Untangling the Web

With some severance and accumulated vacation pay from Mine Mill, I had time to think about where I was and how I got there. It was depressing. I was thirty-seven years old, and the two worlds that had constituted my fundamental existence, the Communist party and the labor movement, were gone from my life. I had given up on the Party because of its slavish adherence to Moscow's policies and its failure to understand the American working class. Even before the Mine Mill experience, I had been disillusioned with the labor movement as well.

In the beginning, the people in the labor movement, as well as most members of the Communist party in America, focused on improving the life of the workers. Tremendous injustices existed, and we were out to rally the oppressed against the oppressors. In my first union, the newly formed United Auto Workers at Packard, I took part in a workers' campaign against the Big Three automobile companies that was part of something even bigger. As a result of the Wagner Act, a union crusade was then sweeping across the country, organizing the mass-production industries. We marched, we picketed, we staged sit-ins, and we sang "Solidarity Forever" with gusto. We had a clear, heartfelt sense of purpose and a tremendous camaraderie.

We created a better world. Once the tough organizing work was done, the higher living standards of unionized workers became very tangible. They had a new dignity at their workplaces. They became proud homeowners and new-car buyers. Many of them said, "Now I can send my kids to school so they never have to work in a factory." The labor movement had achieved much of what it set out to do. The standard of living of the organized American worker was the highest in the world. It was an historic achievement, and it is a blessing to have been part of it.

So what happened? When the primary exploiters of labor—the basic extraction and manufacturing industries—were organized and mechanisms to start correcting the injustices were in place, the unions' primary goals were accomplished. During the Cold War and the anticommunist fever of McCarthyism, union leaders redirected their efforts toward attaining respectability. That shift undermined the unions' fundamental purpose, which was to equalize the balance of power in the workplace. With its vision thus eroded, labor was no longer a "movement." We stopped singing, and our goals gradually became unclear. The leadership got old and tired and isolated from the rank and file. There was no system to encourage the development of new leaders. In time, that deficiency resulted in an organization that existed primarily for the benefit of tired old bureaucrats living on memories of their glory days. The ideologues were driven from the movement, and the number of corrupt union officials living the life of the nouveau riche on the backs of the members increased.

My own union career reflected that process. I was an elected officer of a conservative craft union, the IAM; later I worked as a paid staff member in a supposedly leftist industrial union, Mine Mill. But how different were the two unions? Not very.

In the IAM, I and my fellow true believers became the enemy. Why? Because we challenged the authority of the national leadership. Of course, they didn't like my politics. Still, if I had done nothing to question their authority, would they have cared? I doubt it. The Communist party was a handy excuse.

In Mine Mill, as long as Bill Mason, the head of the Montana locals, went along with the left-wing leadership in Denver, the national leaders weren't concerned about the kind of representation the miners and smeltermen were receiving. But when Mason decided to take the membership into the Steelworkers' union, he became public enemy number one.

What the Machinists and Mine Mill had in common was their national officers' need to maintain absolute control. That control assured them that their authority—and their job security and pensions—would stay intact. Politically left, right, or center—all organizations are hierarchical. Those who make it to the top of the power structure want to stay there.

This observation became fundamental to my understanding of why socialism failed too. At some point, it began to dawn on me that what the executive council of the AFL-CIO and the Central Committee of the Russian Communist party had in common was the "royalty syndrome"—the absolute need to maintain their power and authority for life.

As for Marxism itself, my loss of faith was mostly brought on by observing the everyday life of the working class. It was a slow process, but finally I could no longer believe that changing the ownership of the means of production would be a catalyst for the emergence of socialist brotherhood. It appeared to me that Karl Marx had spent too much of his life in the library and too little, if any, with the workers. If he had gone into their factories and homes he might have noticed that all the sins of greed, selfishness, aggression, and desire for power he attributed exclusively to the ruling class were equally shared by the working class. The argument that once the profit system was abolished all those sins would vanish was not supported by my day-to-day experience.

I concluded that Marx knew a hell of a lot about the economics of capitalism but little or nothing about human nature. What this meant to me was that I needed to learn more about real human beings, rather than seeing them as pawns in an economic chess game. Economics is very important, but it does not explain everything.

By early 1954 I had been out of the Party for years, although the FBI file indicates that the bureau continued its surveillance, because I refused to name other party members. The file also vaguely suggests that, as some of my friends were probably still party members, I might be part of an underground apparatus. Hoover was not yet prepared to let me go.

A short time after my return from Butte I began to feel an urgent need to talk to Papa about my confusion over the Party and the unions. Throughout his entire life Papa had continued to live in the Tanzer household. During the 1950s I visited him there from time to time, and we would spend hours talking of the world, politics, and art. The paintings he had started as a pastime to help him escape from the painful reality of fascism and of socialism gone wrong had become professional, and he was selling them. He had begun by restoring old paintings he picked up at book auctions, then slowly progressed to repainting whole canvases with his own pictures. Nature was his subject, and he took great care to depict it accurately. Sometimes when I dropped in on him I found him so deeply engrossed in his work that it was difficult to get his attention. I was happy he had found a way to express the emotions that used to go into his passion for radicalism.

In early 1952 Papa had been diagnosed with bladder cancer and had an operation. After a brief convalescence he went back to painting, taking orders from interior decorators for landscapes in "colors to match the decor." Papa laughed as he said that: "Imagine! They are paying me for doing work that is fun." The world Papa had grown up in believed work could never be anything but a form of suffering. *Arbeiten* was not fun but a duty. Even for an old anarchist, work was a form of penance, a purifying activity. If there was no drudgery, could it be real work? Painting pictures and being paid for it was fun, not work.

By 1954 his cancer had come back, and I wasn't sure having an emotional discussion about my political doubts would be good for him. But before he left "this potato" (as he called planet earth), I wanted to clear things up between us.

He greatly enjoyed my Butte stories and wanted to know whether any Wobbly tradition had survived there. "No, not in the union," I said, "but in individual miners' fierce sense of militant independence I saw something of the old Wobbly spirit." I described Big Bob and the retaking of the miners' hall as examples of that old fire.

It was recalling the visit to Frank Little's grave that led me to ask, "Papa, in my lifetime, underneath all the rhetoric and propaganda—from the Russian Revolution through Hitler and Stalin—you seemed to know in your gut what was really going on. How come?" He was silent. "Papa, how did you know when your hopes and dreams for the 1917 revolution were turning into a terrible nightmare?" His eyes welled with tears. I felt sorry for upsetting him and apologized: "Maybe this isn't such a good idea."

No, he wanted to talk about it. "All of us," he said, "have inner guideposts. I like to think of it as a philosophical compass that keeps you on the right road headed for your destination."

"Well, Pop, I had a compass—the overthrow of capitalism and the establishment of socialism. What was wrong with that?"

"That's not a road to travel by. That's a destination, and you got lost on a way called the 'means of getting there.' The difference is in the word *philosophy*. My compass, my guide, contains a whole set of beliefs that cannot be violated or set aside for the 'means of getting there.' If a person begins to make little, convenient compromises in those beliefs, they gradually diminish and the way is lost. When that happens, you are Faust making bargains with the devil. Once that starts, as it did in Stalin's purges and the forced collectivization, the ideals of socialism are destroyed on the road to getting there."

"At the time I thought those actions were absolutely necessary to protect the revolution from its enemies."

"Humbug!" The word came quickly with Papa's old certainty. He loved that word. "Once you start violating your fundamental philosophical values as a means to an end, the end has been lost. You are on the road to hell. Once you're on that path, you can justify anything to attain some distant place that actually no longer exists—because you have lost your way."

"How did you come to understand that?"

"Oh, I had many good teachers. Goethe taught me the importance of knowing what you believe and, more important, practicing it in everyday life. There can be no temporary, expedient deals with the devil. Freud taught me the dangers of running with a mob, even if it appears to be moving in a direction I approve of." He paused to roll one of his little wrinkled cigarettes and light it. As always, it dangled from the corner of his mouth.

He hesitated a long time over what he was about to say. "Bobby, I think you had a great need to belong, so you ran with a crowd that was supposed to be on the road to a utopian dream of socialism. What you didn't know, or didn't want to see, was that the leaders at the head of your mob had already made their pact with the devil. Stalin would keep them in power only as long as they conformed to his dictates and, above all, suppressed any notion of freedom of expression or opinion."

I was in tears, but he laughed at me: "Now don't assume that everything you did was terrible. Nothing like that. What you and so many others like you were doing—organizing workers, building unions—that was just fine. The question you needed to ask yourself was 'Did I practice my philosophy, my beliefs, in my everyday activities?' That's all one can be held responsible for. That's where your integrity lies. In the end, maybe all we have is our integrity."

"But Papa, I defended the bargains with the devil."

He thought for a while. "Yes, you did, and that was wrong. But do not assume responsibility for the actions of people you never met and did not even know. Don't play God. No human being is strong enough to do that."

Papa was trying to console me, but I still felt shamed. I asked the question that had been bothering me for a long time: "All the time I was in the Party I sang the praises of the Soviet Union. Why am I less guilty of Stalin's crimes than the ordinary Germans were of Hitler's? Is claiming that I didn't know a good enough excuse?"

"You could more honestly say you didn't know what was happening in Russia than Germans could who were living in the country where Jews were being rounded up in front of their eyes. Your observation that it was the pictures of the concentration camps that horrified the world was right. Too bad there were no pictures of Stalin's massacres. They would have put Hitler in second place as a mass murderer. The end can never justify the means. If we can only remember that, we will make fewer mistakes."

Papa was tired. It was time for me to go. He gave me a painting he had done of what he called, "his dream cottage high in the Swiss Alps." We said good-bye. As the cancer continued to spread during the next few months, Papa was in and out of hospitals. The next time we met he would be there for the last time.

Papa's being sick had created new tensions in the Tanzer house. Tanta Belle was still his best friend. Siegfried, on the other hand, was increasingly resentful of his presence. I never understood why Papa stayed in that house so long. Being independent and making your own way was the basic message he had always given me. Yet, I now realize, he was unable to apply it to himself. For thirty-five years he had lived in two small musty rooms on the second floor of someone else's house.

When I left him after our conversation I walked the few blocks to the street where we lived when Mutter died. Looking at the house, I realized that Papa had a persistent longing to regain a hidden loss. The Germans I grew up with all seemed to have an obsessive longing for something— romance, heroism, beauty, joy, utopia. I was sure that quality of yearning was deeply embedded somewhere in the German character or in their collective unconscious. In his guilt over what had happened so many years earlier, Papa longed for forgiveness by staying two blocks from where his great tragedy had occurred.

It made me very sad.

After a spell of hanging around on severance pay and unemployment insurance, I was pressed to think about a new career. I wanted to do something entirely different. Having shed at least some, if not all, of my past, I spent a year trying to answer questions like 'Who am I?' and 'How do I support my family?' The necessity of making a living postponed the first question, but the road leading to a mid-life crisis was beginning.

During this year I considered many harebrained ideas. The one that excited both Lizzie and me the most was running a boarding farm for racehorses. Lizzie was the classic horse-crazy young girl. The idea of the horse business was first seriously suggested to me by the union lawyer, Glickstein. He became the controlling shareholder in two racetracks and encouraged me to familiarize myself with their operations. "Learn how they work and then we'll see where you might fit in." A boarding farm was one of the "fit-in" possibilities.

Lizzie and I spent months looking at properties, mostly in southern New Jersey. Some were small farms with a capacity of twenty or thirty horses; others could accommodate fifty or more horses and had indoor riding rings. They cost a lot of money, as much as half a million dollars; but when we calculated the potential income, they seemed like pretty good business deals. Glickstein said if I lined up enough boarding commitments beforehand, he would arrange financing for me.

However, it was not Glickstein but our Puerto Rican landlady, Lydia, who gave me my practical introduction to horseracing. She and her husband owned a small butcher shop in East Harlem and had bought a couple of horses at claiming races in Rockingham Park. They had a crazy Cuban horse trainer who swore he would make them and their friends rich.

Lydia sometimes asked me to join them at the track when one of their horses was running. My role was to place their bets. She was convinced that if she showed up at the betting window everyone would know they expected to win and the odds would go down. At a memorable race at

Monmouth Park, the Cuban trainer convinced the couple that their horse, Xalapa Streak, would win. I bet their two thousand bucks for them. The horse didn't even come in in the money. My landlady fainted, and the Cuban explained that Xalapa couldn't win, because one of the mares in the race was in heat: "Xalapa wanted to fuck her, so the jockey couldn't get him to pass her." My thoughts of a horse career came to an end with Xalapa Streak, who finally not only won a race but set a track record. He fell down at the end of that race, broke his leg, and had to be shot in his moment of glory.

My marriage, like my occupational life, seemed to be deteriorating, but I didn't know what to do about it. I thought more and more about making a life with Sandra. Edith was successfully working at several private nursery schools as a part-time music teacher, Fred was in nursery school, and Lizzie was in the tenth grade at P.S. 88. I was wandering around in an emotional fog trying to figure out the rest of my life. Sitting in a closet was my oak toolbox. It was my security blanket. In the darkest days of the union fights I had reassured myself that I could always go back to being a machinist. There was something comforting in the orderliness of the box's series of neat little drawers; it seemed to have the same appeal for me as piling bricks in the basement after Mutter died. Was I creating order on the outside to still my anxiety about the disorder on the inside?

One Sunday I saw a *New York Times* advertisement for diesetters at the Ford Assembly Plant in Mahwah, New Jersey. As Ford had been organized by the UAW, I could ask for reinstatement of my membership from the days I worked at Packard. Besides, the UAW was still one of the most progressive unions in the country. I decided to apply.

The next day I took the forty-five-minute drive to the Mahwah plant and filled out the application form. They had advertised for diesetters, and that's what I said I was. As a toolmaker I had *made* dies, which is far more difficult than setting them. On the application I had, with the permission of the owner's Marxist son, substituted machine-shop experience at the Commodore Machine Company for all the years I had spent as a union official.

They gave me a variety of tests, which I passed easily. The personnel interviewer, a young energetic cheerleader, was enthusiastic about my application. He had found an urgently needed experienced diesetter who could start work immediately! "Welcome to the Ford Motor Company family," he declared warmly. "Can you show up for the second shift tomorrow?" Of course I could.

On my drive home I was one happy fellow. I had a job with good pay and great benefits, and I started tomorrow! Betsy the spaniel, who sensed my triumphant mood, gave me an extra-happy greeting when I arrived home. That night after dinner I carefully went over the toolbox, checking each of the ten drawers and trying to remember what the hell all those tools were for. I wouldn't use most of them for diesetting, but I was proud of my tool collection. They would all come along.

The next day the security guard at the main gate directed me to report to the personnel office. The receptionist gave me a funny look. "Have a seat. Mr. Talbot will see you shortly." I asked if I should get my toolbox from the car, but she shook her head: "I was told you were to wait and speak with Mister Talbot."

I began to smell a rat. Something must have gone wrong. I was supposed to start work in five minutes. Instead I was cooling my heels in the waiting room. Finally the receptionist showed me into Talbot's office. It was a size up from the interviewer's little cubbyhole. He glanced at me with a bewildered expression and picked out a folder from a pile on his desk. After he read it, he looked up and shook his head in disbelief: "What the hell did you ever do? Your application lit up all the red tilt lights on the machine. There isn't a word," he emphasized, "a *word* of truth in that application. Why did you think you could get away with it?" I was about to answer, but he went on: "You've been a radical union organizer most, if not all, of your working life." He paused, then looked at me, "You are Robert Schrank, aren't you?"

"Yes, I am." I tried a little a slip-and-slide: "Look, I might have made some mistakes in my dates and places. Heck, we all do that when we're filling out one of these forms."

Talbot cut me short with a laugh: "Listen fella, whoever you are, you're probably on the FBI's most-wanted list for all I know. Would you like my advice?"

"Yes, please."

"Forget the Ford Motor Company, or any major corporation. They all have clearinghouses that can hook a fish like you out of the water in a matter of minutes. Don't waste your time." He paused. "Find a little company somewhere that won't care what you did in New York, Chicago, Elmira, and Butte, Montana. Christ, what the hell were you doing in Montana? No, forget it. It's none of my business." He seemed really pleased that the system to keep out radicals had worked. "Good-bye and better luck next time," he said cheerfully.

In contrast to the day before, I was in a panic on the drive home. What the hell do I do now? Would I be haunted by my past for the rest of my life? Was there some way to get off a blacklist? This time I arrived home angry, and Betsy knew it. She took one look at me and dove under the couch. I said nothing to Edith. I just went into the bedroom, shut the door, and poured out my heart in a letter to Sandra.

Why didn't I talk about what had happened with Edith? Only now do I realize that I felt unable to ask for her help or support. I was sure she was too needy herself and lacked the emotional energy to aid me. Not wanting to make her anxious, I hid my haunting fears of being out of work, unemployed, and poor, just as Papa had. I thought that sharing my problems with Edith would disclose a vulnerability that would sharply reduce my control over the family and add to her own obsessive fears of poverty and abandonment. But by not telling Edith about my concerns, I was reinforcing those same fears and increasing the distance between us.

Papa's illness returned in the late summer of 1954. This time he was sent to a special cancer hospital connected to Columbia Presbyterian. My sister Alice and various friends were making regular visits to the hospital as Papa's life slowly ebbed away. I learned from one of the nurses that Anita, his lifelong mistress, came to see him when none of us were there. Once we passed each other in the lobby, but she quickly looked the other way. I was sure she had never forgiven me for the "dirty little story" Goldstein the bootlegger had told twenty-seven years earlier. For Papa and his lover, this last illness was an extension of their secret way of life. It continued until death did them part.

The inability to acknowledge their love for each other was another one of the mysteries about Papa. The only reason for it I could imagine was Papa's Wagnerian sense of doing penance for his dead wife. Would refusing to profess his love for another woman be sufficient atonement for the guilt he felt over the way Mutter died? Neither of them seemed able to forgive: Papa could not forgive himself, and Anita could not forgive the little boy she assumed disapproved of her. Nothing could have been further from the truth.

On October the eighteenth, the day before my birthday, Papa and I were alone in his hospital room. Fluorescent lighting and the stark white tile walls gave the room an eerie resemblance to a public toilet converted into a hospital room. An overwhelming smell of chemical disinfectants filled the air. What little life was left in Papa was being sustained by an array of rubber tubing that resembled a giant spider: he had tubes coming out of his nose, his arms, his penis, and his chest. I did not want to remember him like this. I sat next to the bed holding this hand. It brought back sharply the reassuring feeling it always gave me as a small boy to hold tightly to that big warm hand.

Every once in a while he would mumble a few words. It was mostly his eyes and a slight motion of his head that spoke to me that last time. They seemed to ask me to come closer, as if he had something to tell me. I leaned down, my ear close to his mouth. A thin little voice said, "I did not kill your mother. I knew nothing about it. Do you believe me?"

I was shocked. "Oh, Papa, of course I believe you! No one has ever suggested that her death was in any way your fault. Please, please believe me." I sat there for some time, crying silently and clutching his hand. He seemed to smile, oh so little. Then he looked up at the plug in the wall.

I asked, "Should I take it out?" Again he seemed to try to smile and nodded. I held my hand on the plug. "Papa are you sure?" He nodded again. I pulled it out.

I sat there for a time, and he seemed to go to sleep. A nurse came by, looked around, said nothing, and left. She came back a few minutes later with another nurse. They checked Papa's pulse and heartbeat, and one of them said, "He's sleeping peacefully now and won't wake up. Why don't you leave? We have work to do here." It was about nine o'clock when I left the hospital. No matter how hard I breathed I could not get the antiseptic smell of death out of my nostrils. I walked, ran, and cried from 163rd Street in Manhattan to 231st Street in the Bronx. I was crying for my poor Papa. How could he have carried this terrible guilt about the abortion to the edge of his grave? How could it be that this intelligent, liberated anarchist, a reader of Freud, could not overcome his guilt. When I reached home there was a telegram waiting for me. Papa had died. He missed my birthday by an hour.

In Papa's philosophy there was little or no room for what he derided as "stupid ritualistic behavior." He believed that holiday celebrations were created as tools for conformity and supported by Macy's to ensure that people bought all kinds of unneeded junk for Christmas, Mother's Day, and funerals. So Papa's funeral was very simple. At the short service, some old socialist friends spoke of his absolute devotion to truth and justice, and a recording of the last movement of Beethoven's Ninth Symphony was played. He was laid to rest next to our long-departed mother in a cemetery in Queens.

Sometime during his illness he had said to me with a laugh, "There is nothing to fight over or worry about when I die. You see, I came into this world with a bare behind, and that's how I am leaving it. Nothing to worry about." After the funeral I hurried to the Tanzer house to clean out the rooms he had lived in for most of his life. Piled in a heap, the little things he had collected in a lifetime looked inconsequential and sad.

Alice asked some of her artist friends about his many paintings. The artist Harry Shulberg told her Papa was very talented: "It's too bad he started so late in life. He didn't have time to develop as a painter." Many of his pictures went up on the walls of friends. Some of them are there still.

To me, Papa remains a mystery. He was a completely self-educated Renaissance man who landed in America as an illegal immigrant and managed to become a leader in the local anarcho-syndicalist movement. He had taught himself history, science, philosophy, and literature; he had read every writer from Aristotle to Galileo, Racine, Goethe, Shakespeare, Darwin, and Dewey. He knew the stories of all the major operas and all about the lives and musical styles of the leading classical composers. He could speak four European languages. Over a cup of coffee, he could explain the Peloponnesian War or the reasons for Napoleon's defeat at Waterloo.

Papa had a close lifelong friendship with the famous psychologist Abraham Maslow, who taught at Brandeis University. Papa regularly visited him, his wife Bertha, and her sister Anna in Boston. Years later I had occasion to visit Abe Maslow, who described Papa as his inspiration for the self-actualized man. Yes, in his intellectual pursuits, I thought, that was certainly true. But in his personal life he seemed wholly unable to break free of old entanglements in order to "self-actualize." I so much wanted to remember him as all-powerful. I never told Maslow about Papa's inability to resolve the dilemmas of his personal life.

Somehow in the months that followed, Papa's death became all mixed up in my mind with Mutter's. I was unable to control the sudden tears that were triggered by anything that reminded me of Papa. I spent days hiding out in museums and parks, trying to deal with my grief.

By mid-1955 my unemployment insurance was running out. Simple necessity forced me to focus once more on earning a living. This time I was lucky. The *New York Times* ad read: "Wanted, Machine Shop Superintendent. Down-to-earth knowledge of running a toolroom and plant-maintenance shop." The job sounded right. I applied for it and got it.

The A. Kimball Company had a small specialty printing and die-cutting plant not far from the Commodore Machine Company in what is now SoHo, as well as plants in Xenia, Ohio, and Toronto, Canada. The New York operation employed a couple of hundred people spread over five floors in two adjoining buildings. Kimball was an old family firm that was sinking as a result of a stubborn tradition of, "this is the way we do things here." The mess I found there was very encouraging, because there was no place to go but up.

I established a good working relationship with the dozen men in the machine shop by the simple act of getting the oil off the floors and cleaning the place up. When I came there was no preventive maintenance program. In close consultation with the men I set up a regular schedule of machine maintenance. Together we decided to purchase some badly needed new equipment that would provide a quick pay-off by reducing the time machines were down for repairs. Finding the blueprint files hopelessly out of date, I hired a temporary draftsman to update them. In a relatively short time we made substantial improvements in the plant's efficiency.

Although it was my first experience with being called by that terrible four-letter word, *boss*, the company was satisfied. And I was enjoying the work. After the initial shock of being a boss instead of a shop steward, I realized that the two jobs were not that different. Better still, nobody seemed to hate me.

At the time, a series of new computer-linked inventory-control systems for retailers was being developed. They utilized miniature punch cards that—attached to garments and many other items—could be used to control inventory at the point of sale as well as to record sales. (The bar code eventually made punch cards obsolete.) However, adapting printing presses to both print and very accurately punch these cards presented a number of technical problems.

When Kimball decided to try to solve them, our machine shop got the job. One of the first problems we encountered was the paper used to make the punch cards, which IBM supplied. Solving it required me to develop relationships with paper suppliers and learn something about their production processes. In our shop, I came to rely on the foreman, Teddy, a self-taught mechanical genius, to develop a machine that performed as it was supposed to. Oddly enough, my own experience in wartime aircraft engine work also helped us create a specialty printing press with considerably closer mechanical tolerances than those previously used to make punch cards. I was learning a lot about engineering and manufacturing and found the work very exciting.

The machine-development work also entailed some travel to Kimball's other plants in Ohio and Toronto and created occasional opportunities for Sandra and I to meet for a few days of romance and talk. Our rendezvous were becoming somewhat stressful. Hanging up my shield as a crusader for the working class seemed somehow to increase my personal needs, and I was pressing Sandra to find a way for us to be together. She ducked the whole thing by saying she thought my new work with innovative machinery was replacing my old political enthusiasm. "That's probably the answer for you," she said. "You need a challenge to keep from sinking into the self-pity stuff." She was probably right.

Even the FBI thought I was on a new road. When two agents showed up at the plant one day, I had no idea how the company would react.

This time I couldn't simply brush them off and jeopardize my job. The file says the agents came away "encouraged," because for the first time "the subject" seemed willing to talk. They reported that I had switched my interest from politics to machinery and hunting. I showed them a captured Japanese sniper rife I and some of the hunters in the shop were converting to a sporting gun. When they asked about my past affiliations and wanted me to supply information about others, I pointed out that any information I had would be hopelessly out of date. Besides they knew it all already. According to the file, they found this comment encouraging and were told to "continue the contact."

In those years of the Eisenhower presidency, business was prospering and unemployment was low. We were singing "Hernando's Hideaway" and young men were identifying with James Dean in *Rebel Without a Cause*. In about 1956 the Kimball Company was bought out by the United Shoe Machinery Corporation (USMC), an old Boston firm with a worldwide monopoly on shoe-manufacturing machinery. The company did not sell its machines but leased them and received a royalty on each pair of shoes produced. (IBM did the same thing with its equipment until the Supreme Court ruled that the practice constituted an illegal constraint of trade.) Forced to sell its machines, USMC reaped windfall profits and used them to buy various companies.

USMC made Kimball a part of their new data processing division and invested in a new plant in Brooklyn. I was promoted to chief engineer and given major responsibility for development of punch-card manufacturing machines.

Over the years, as my disillusionment with the old world of left-wing politics deepened, I had drifted away from many old party friends. Designing and testing high-speed machinery absorbed more and more of my attention. Sandra was right. Making a better machine had become a challenging substitute for creating the brotherhood of man.

Even so, I was never able to completely block out the world outside. Having spent the first third of my adult life in the radical Left, I kept one eye peeled on that quarter. Party members, lefties, fellow travelers and assorted liberals, and ex-party members were about to be treated to a mind- and soul-shaking trauma. Even for those, like myself, who had given up on the Party, the news from the Soviet Union was like the proverbial whack on the head with a two-by-four to get the mule's attention.

In the middle of the frigid Moscow winter of 1956 at the party congress in the Kremlin, Joseph Stalin's successor, First Secretary Nikita Khrushchev, delivered a "secret report." It was not secret for long. Khrushchev described in excruciating detail all the crimes of the Stalin regime: the killing of millions of peasants as a result of forced collectivization, the frame-ups and murders of the old Bolsheviks, the labor camps for dissidents, the secret-police intimidation—all the vicious excesses of Stalin's rule.

We had, of course, heard rumors of some of these horrors; and we knew about others but refused to acknowledge them, even to ourselves. Still, the harrowing details were worse than we could ever have imagined. As I read and reread the nightmare accounts, not sure that I wasn't having a terrible dream, Papa's face seemed to appear before me, tears in his eyes, asking his young son how he could be so gullible: "A blind man can see that Joseph Stalin is a direct descendant of Ivan the Terrible. You're looking through the Party's rose-colored propaganda glasses seeing nothing but your wishful fantasies." Once again I was being reminded of how the precious dream of socialism had turned into a nightmare of torture and imprisonment and murder not unlike that of Nazi Germany.

Worldwide, Communist parties were struck dumb. Many of Europe's best-known intellectuals, lifelong supporters of the Soviet Union like Jean-Paul Sartre, suddenly fell silent. For decades, people had dismissed the charges against Stalin as nothing but "capitalist propaganda." Then, out of the blue, all of the so-called lies became facts acknowledged, not by some ill-treated dissident writer, but by the first secretary of the Soviet Communist party. A few party leaders continued to deny the stories, claiming that the new capitalist devil was Khrushchev himself. Or they hastened to declare that the old undemocratic past had been swept away and the Soviet people could now begin to build a truly socialist society.

I called my old friend Herb Lerner. He and his wife Ruth, both long out of the labor movement, were running an employment agency in Newark. We had dinner and spent the evening, like a lot of other ex-lefties, trying to figure out what happened while we thought we were building a society based on the brotherhood of man. I remembered our long arguments about the politics of human rights and Herb's story of General Patton. "How we could have been so concerned about a soldier being slapped when we hadn't responded at all to the rumors of terror and abuse in the Soviet Union?" I wondered. Perhaps, Herb thought, if we had experienced that abuse at first hand the way he had witnessed the Patton incident, we might have responded. I reminded Herb of the effect pictures of the Nazi concentration camps had had on us, and he acknowledged that pictures of Stalin's crimes might have made a difference. But, he added doubtfully, we still might not have believed them, because we didn't want to.

We agreed that our bitter experience of dealing with capitalist exploitation and greed on a daily basis had created a simplistic view of society: all evil stemmed from the capitalist class and all good came from the working class. It was simplistic, yes, but not wholly wrong either. The contributions we had made to the unions and the fight for American social and economic justice needed no apology. The improved lives of the workers and their families stood as a tribute to those efforts. Perhaps without our slavish defense of socialism the American labor movement would not have been so successful. That was fine as far as Herb and I went. In the silence of my room, however, it did little or nothing to lessen my shame.

Suppose I *had* seen actual photographs of the Stalin holocaust? I thought. Would it have made any difference? I had heard and read reports of Stalin's murders, if from no one else certainly from Papa. Had I believed them then? Long after my gnawing doubts had started, I remained silent, in a kind of paralysis, unable to give up a dream that was in reality a nightmare. Had I, like the Germans shown the mounds of bodies in the death camps, in effect shrugged and said, "I never knew that was happening"? Could I claim absolution on the grounds that I had walked in front of the German Embassy to protest Hitler, though I never carried signs about the Siberian camps to the gates of the Soviet Embassy?

After the fall of Berlin, many Germans, confronted with vivid pictures of Nazi atrocities, could only respond with silence. Our response to Stalin's crimes was very much the same, silence in the face of an inexplicable evil. Could it be that when shame is too overwhelming our only recourse is to a paralyzed silence? How else do we explain the stillness of so many pro-Soviet intellectuals and radicals after the Khrushchev revelations? Surely it was time then for us to say, "Yes, there were excesses on the part of McCarthy, Hoover, the House Un-American Activities Committee, and the rest of the extreme Right. But the Khrushchev bombshell also shows that we on the Left supported what turned out to be a fascist state." To have uttered such thoughts aloud might have driven us into the madhouse. The alternative was silence, and that's what we chose.

I was very troubled and needed to rethink everything that had happened in light of these cataclysmic revelations. Although their full impact was postponed, they contributed to a severe personal crisis I suffered a few years later. In 1956, fortunately, I had to concentrate on building high-speed printing presses, and the sound of the machines helped drown out the cries from Stalin's concentration camps.

Like me, a lot of former comrades had to find ways to put their lives back together. Many continued their work for social and economic causes from comfortable homes in Westchester, Westbury, or Westport —instead of the Bronx or the Lower East Side. A lot of them, no longer restrained by a devotion to socialism, decided it was okay to make money and went into business or embarked on new professional careers. Besides Glickstein, with his racetrack investments, I knew leftists, ex-union officials, and liberals who ran successful businesses selling junk, writing millions of dollars worth of business liability and retirement insurance, and running a chain of supermarkets, to name a few. At the time I thought their successes were a great tribute to their abilities and to the free market system.

I began to wonder too whether revolutionary zeal came in part from a phenomenon I called "soreheadism." It meant "change the society in which I am an outsider to one where I can be an insider." Once former communists found that they could be insiders in the capitalist world, it didn't seem to be so bad after all.

Ever since my days as the Machinists' State Council president, I had been fascinated with the hunting rituals of my brother union members. In upstate New York, so many workers took off work on the opening days of the deer-hunting and trout-fishing seasons that some plants had to shut for lack of manpower. Even though Karl Marx had suggested that in an ideal world workers would have time to hunt and fish, I was always too busy with the all-important work of changing the world to participate in these blue-collar rituals. They had seemed to me just another trivial escape from reality.

No longer involved in a crusade, I now wanted to experience a hunting trip with my working-class brothers. Several avid hunters in the Kimball machine shop, after helping me modify a Japanese sniper rifle for hunting, invited me to join them for a week-long deer hunt at East Carry Pond in the wilds of Maine. Their tradition was to take off for a week in the woods right after Thanksgiving dinner.

Edith couldn't understand why on earth I wanted to spend a week in the Maine woods with a bunch of nuts, while Liz was troubled at the thought of my shooting a poor innocent animal. Fred was still too young to have an opinion but was excited by the shoot 'em-up feel of the expedition.

The six of us—Adjuda, Fritz, George, Eddy, Tony, and myself—climbed into Eddy's station wagon with our duffel bags and what seemed like enough guns and ammunition to start a war. Full of turkey dinner and booze, I slept my way to Maine.

Eagle Eye Smith was one of the last of the great Maine trappers. His East Carry Pond Lodge was at the end of a long, rocky jeep trail that followed an old creek bed. The camp sat on a sloping field that led down to the pond. The large main lodge was ringed by a number of log cabins of various sizes. A rowboat and the seaplane Eagle Eye used to run his trap lines were tethered at the boat landing.

Ours was the largest cabin. It had two rooms: a kitchen and a sleeping room with six barracks-style steel beds. In the center of each room was a woodburning stove. From my first whiff of burning maple and oak I felt I was in a place I wouldn't mind calling home.

One night over coffee and apple pie, I decided to try and head off the sex and sports talk. Still trying to understand the workers as I wrestled my old Marxist ghosts, I asked the guys what they thought were the best and the worst things about the country. They laughed: "You mean up here in the woods?"

"No, silly, I mean the good old USA."

Eddy answered my question earnestly: "I went to war for this country and lost half my head doing it. And I'd do it again tomorrow, 'cause I love it. I grew up in Staten Island in a poor family with five brothers. We all worked real hard, and we all made it. Sure, life ain't perfect, but that's not the fault of the country. That's because, like every place, we got some assholes who are gonna fuck things up no matter what." The uninjured side of his face laughed. Then he added, "Just like we got right here." People looked at each other, wondering who he was talking about.

Trying to keep the discussion on track, I asked Adjuda what he thought. His parents were immigrants who spoke very little English. "I was a prize fuck-up as a kid," he answered after some hesitation. "I didn't really get wise until the war. Then when I got a defense job I figured, hey, I could really make it. Now I own my own home, have a couple of kids and a car, and, Christ, can take a week off to come up here and hang out with this bunch of knuckleheads. You can't beat that now, can you?"

"What about the rich?" I asked, "Aren't they rippin' the country off?"

George said, "Sure. We all are. What the hell are we doin' in the plant rebuilding your gun, overhauling Eddy's outboard, rebuilding car engines? Hell, ain't that a rip-off? Sure it is, and everyone does it however they can. It's only when it gets done real big that anyone notices. This is a great country if you wanna put out. If you wanna sit on your ass and do nothin' that's okay too, but, Christ, don't complain about it."

Fritz was by far the most emphatic. He had come from Germany during Hitler's time and as a small child had experienced the poverty and inflation of the twenties. "You guys got no idea what is to be hungry. That's the trouble with this country. People's got it too good. You need some real starving, then you'll appreciate what you got here."

They pressed me to say what I thought. I told them I agreed with a lot of what they said but thought that too many people got left out of the goodies. "That's always seemed unfair to me." The consensus was that it was their own fault and that "welfare people are just too fuckin' lazy to work."

Like most of the working-class men I had encountered in the unions, these men had worked hard and learned a trade. In the prosperous years after the war, they bought cars, married, purchased homes, had children, dressed well, and went to the drive-in on Saturday night. They considered themselves successful. In the context of their lives, the old Marxist notion of "nothing to lose but their chains" sounded, to say the least, ludicrous. There didn't seem to be any connection between the everyday experience of these workers and the theory I had lived by.

The men went back to their poker game, and I went out into the clear, cold northern night to take a walk and think. I was still doggedly trying to understand how for all those years I had confused the simple mission of making life better for the workers with a nutty, grandiose notion of the dictatorship of the proletariat.

In his early manuscripts, Karl Marx talked about how workers under communism could be hunters, fishermen, poets, musicians, and lovers of the arts. Thanks to the contributions of the unions, I was beginning to see, part of Marx's idealistic dream was being lived in the United States— but under capitalism. The Trotskyites and other anti-reform leftists were probably right: without wanting to do so, the Left had contributed to the survival of capitalism. It is even possible to suggest that the Left, especially those in the unions, saved capitalism from the consequences of its own worst abuses. The Marxist ideal required us to reject the possibility that without a revolution workers could achieve the kind of lives those men described to me in the Maine woods. Yet the Kimball workers and others like them were enjoying the fruits of their labors—not to the extent that they would have liked perhaps, but enough to give them the feeling that they were living the good life. That was the actual.

When I got back to the cabin, the guys were slapping the cards down on the table with energetic good humor. I went off to read my book. I loved these guys for their earthiness, but when it came to my need for intelligent conversation I was at a dead end with them.

21

Corporate Life

One afternoon while I was discussing a machine problem with one of the maintenance crew, the loudspeaker blared out, "An important call from Boston for Mister Schrank." It was Dana Woodward, USMC's vice president for manufacturing. The company needed a quick evaluation of a new high-speed keypunch machine manufactured in Stockholm. How soon could I go to Europe? Eager to leave right away, I suddenly remembered the passport problem. The application asked very specific questions about past or present membership in organizations on the attorney general's subversives list. If I answered yes I could forget the passport (and maybe my job); if I answered no I was risking a perjury indictment. Catch 22! Thinking fast, I said, "I would be happy to go, Dana, but it will take at least a couple of weeks to get a passport." He assured me that the company's travel office would handle everything. "Just tell us when you can leave. The sooner the better. If this machine is any good, we don't want our competitors to beat us out. We're trusting your judgment on this one." I said I would leave as soon as the passport was available.

He laughed, "Oh, incidentally, for purposes of this trip you have a new title. You're the director of engineering. Europeans don't have much respect for anybody below director."

A few days later a messenger arrived with a passport issued by the special corporate business office of the U.S. State Department. USMC had simply ignored the questions about subversive memberships and said my trip was for essential business and had to be made as soon as possible. Liberated to travel outside the United States for the first time, I felt the world suddenly opening up.

I flew first class to Europe. I found it easy to shed my old blue-collar image and recline like a potentate in the wide leather seats. At my first stop, Düsseldorf—where I was to be briefed on the equipment by USMC's European engineers—I was quickly cleared through customs and addressed, with a slight bow, as Herr Director. The company executive who met me directed me to the second of two black Mercedes limousines; the first one, I was told, was an escort. I laughed. Dana wasn't kidding about the director title!

At the USMC office, the European engineering group received me with enough fanfare for a Nobel medal winner. The twelve men who participated in the review session were all fluent in English. Thus I had no opportunity to practice my rusty German, which I had tried, with the help of a Berlitz manual, to brush up during the flight. After the machinery review and lots of *Danke schön*s, *Bitte schön*s, and *Auf Wiedersehen*s, I was driven to what had to be the best hotel in Düsseldorf.

One evening after I had shaken off my German hosts, I strolled around the streets looking at the damage that remained from the wartime bombing. Hearing people speaking German brought back some of my most tender and terrifying childhood moments. People's faces, expressions, and little snippets of overheard conversation seemed all too familiar. Even the architecture and the smell of the air came together as a place I had known before. Was I just remembering the culture of my childhood, or was Papa's history somehow packed into my genes? This comfortable familiarity came as a big surprise to me. I had been certain that my knowledge of the death camps would overwhelm any friendly feelings I harbored toward Germany. It did not. I was very happy there. I felt as if I had come home.

It was late when I returned to the hotel. I sat in the bar having a nightcap, wondering about the engineers and company executives I had met. They all seemed like perfectly nice folks. Could this be the country of both my dear father and the murderous Nazis? I struck up a sort of conversation in my halting German with a lovely blonde woman who seemed anxious to meet the American. She spoke not a word of English, but it didn't matter. It was a very old story: I was a stranger, a little lonely, and far from home, and she was a lovely blue-eyed Mädchen in a very sexy low-cut blouse. We sort of introduced each other. Her name sounded like Helga.

Fooling myself that we might somehow have a thoughtful discussion, I asked in my terribly limited German about the war and its aftermath. She laughed and, as best as I could tell, didn't seem interested in serious conversation. Or was it my German that was making her laugh? Whatever I said—even when we were in bed—she just giggled. It began to make me nervous.

Suddenly the universal male fear came over me. Was she laughing because it's too small, too skinny, too short, because its foreskin is missing or it comes too quickly? I pointed at my penis, trying to say, "*Ist es zu klein?*"

"*Nein, nein,*" she said, "*Es ist ganz gut.*"

I managed somehow in my meager German to ask, "*Meine Freunde, warum lachst du mich alle Zeit?*" (My dear friend why are you laughing at me all the time?)

"*Du bist ein gross Mensch aber du Deutsch wie einen kleinen Kind sprichst*" ("You're a big handsome fellow, but you speak German like a little child"). When I managed to figure out what she was saying, it hit me. My mother spoke German to me until I was six years old; then she disappeared from my life and I never again tried to speak the language. Now here I was, speaking German like a six-year-old. No wonder the Düsseldorf Mädchen thought I was hilarious. What she didn't know was that I was, and still am, haunted by the sound of a woman speaking German.

When I arrived in Stockholm I learned that in February the sun doesn't rise there until ten in the morning, and it is gone by three in the afternoon. With all this darkness, I thought, it's no wonder so many Swedes commit suicide.

Svenn, head of USMC operations in the Scandinavian countries, briefed me about the new machine's operation at a plant near Uppsala, a smaller city northwest of Stockholm. To conduct my evaluation I would I need to commute to the plant by train. The trip became a daily joy ride. The trains were clean, on time, and operated by polite civil servants. This, I thought, is the way socialism is supposed to work.

As the plant operated around the clock, I asked permission to visit at any time. I wanted to go in and out mostly with the second shift, when few, if any, managers were around. The people in Uppsala were very eager to sell USMC the machine, and I preferred to talk to the operators and maintenance mechanics when the bosses weren't around.

After I had hung out in Uppsala for a few days, Svenn suggested that we go for dinner to one of Stockholm's grand old restaurants, the Gildena Frieden. It was located at a medieval castle in the old city. You could almost smell the presence of the heroic knights in armor who spent their nights here drinking out of tankards and slapping full-bosomed wenches on their behinds. I was interested in the history hidden behind the castle's stone walls, but Svenn wanted to know what I thought about the keypunch machine. Was it as good as the manufacturer said it was? Although I had some doubts, I replied that it was too soon to tell. I wanted to spend a few more nights at the plant. He didn't understand why I was going there at night, and I didn't enlighten him.

As we talked, I noticed waitresses dressed in old-fashioned Swedish peasant costumes carrying trays laden with food and drink up a flight of the castle's curved stone stairs. Svenn asked the maître d' what was going on. He informed us that the yearly meeting of the Bellmann Society was being held in the tower. "Yes, of course," I said, "I know of Karl Bellmann. He wrote songs, poems, and ballads in praise of nature, freedom, and drink. It was some time in the eighteenth century, I think." Was there, I asked, any chance we could attend? Svenn and the maître d' were very taken aback. On the one hand, they were extremely surprised that an American would knew about Bellmann. (I had learned of him that summer in Aspen when Edith was studying with Richard Dyer Bennett.) On the other hand, I had apparently exhibited an outrageously American brashness by asking to attend the occasion. The maître d' was completely flustered.

Svenn explained rapidly that the Bellmann Society was the most exclusive club in Sweden, having only fifty members. Only those who had made a very substantial contribution to business, the arts, science, or service to the country were admitted to membership. In addition, members had to show mastery of some art form, be it music, poetry, or painting. New members were chosen only after someone retired or died.

After we completed our meal with the usual after-dinner aquavit, I was feeling expansive. The maître d' had explained that at their meeting each member of the Bellmann Society was called upon to demonstrate his particular talent. "Do you think," I asked the maître d', "that it would be possible for us to sit in and just listen to the presentations?" The poor fellow turned pale. I handed him my "Herr Director" business card and requested him to give it to the president of the society and advise him that I knew of Bellmann's work and would be honored if my friend and I could just sit and listen. He took the card, shaking his head in what I interpreted as a patronizing response to an overbearing Yank.

After a long while the maître d' returned, smiling brightly. "Since you are a visiting American who knows of Bellmann's work, the president says you may come up and sit outside the room and listen to the presentations." Svenn was utterly astounded, but elated by the chance to see the famous club in action.

As we climbed the winding stairway to the tower, I wondered how many millions of pairs of boots had worn the deep impressions in those stone steps. Approaching the top, we breathed in the pungent fragrance of a pine forest—the entrance to the Great Hall was spread with fresh pine boughs. Through the open double doors we could see a large horseshoe-shaped table that circled half the room. It was covered with every conceivable kind of food: pheasant, little pigs with apples in the mouth, salmon, wursts, all kind of salads, and creamy pastries of every description. It looked like King Arthur's round table. We were invited to sit just outside the room on two chairs that had been placed there for us.

One of the members was reciting a Bellmann poem in Swedish. The ninety-some-year-old man was Sweden's leading astronomer, and he read with deep emotion. Whenever he faltered, the men around the table simply continued for him. He finished to a round of applause. The president then introduced Svenn and "his friend from America," noting that it was the first time the society had ever permitted visitors. However, as I knew about Bellmann, he felt sure that "that is what our beloved poet would want." Given glasses of aquavit, we participated in the toasts.

The next performer, the owner and editor of Sweden's leading publishing house, sang a Bellmann song, accompanying himself on a lute. By the last chorus the whole room was enthusiastically singing with him. And so it went, each man at the table taking his turn. Some played piano accompaniments to a song, others recited poems written by Bellmann or by themselves. They were a unique group of people—leaders in business, industry, and academia who were also professionally accomplished artists and performers. They were men who in my previous life I would have considered part of the evil ruling class. In the United States, I thought, this kind of thing could never happen.

Well after midnight, Svenn and I were invited inside the hall to eat and drink at the horseshoe table. I had had no warning when the president tapped on his glass, looked over at me, and announced, "Now I am sure our guest from America would like to perform something for us."

I couldn't believe it. Svenn was laughing uproariously: "Well, you asked for it. You can't back out now."

I was at least three sheets to the wind from all the toasting. What the hell could I do? Some one suggested that I sing something.

"Oh, I would love to, if only I had my guitar here."

"Guitar?" laughed the president. "We have plenty of them in the instrument room." I picked out a beautiful classical guitar, but for the life of me I couldn't tune it. The chief of the Swedish Air Force came to my rescue. He handed me a tuned guitar and escorted me to the center of the horseshoe to a round of applause.

I sang "It Takes a Worried Man to Sing a Worried Song." It was perfect for the occasion.

It takes a worried man to sing a worried song.
I'm worried now, but I won't be worried long.

I was singing and playing on automatic pilot, and they loved it. They gave me a big round of applause and shouted, "More, more." And so a long, merry night of singing began. Most of the songs I knew had Swedish versions, so the whole room could join in. We ate, drank, sang, and compared songs well into breakfast time. In the morning the president invited me to come back next year. "You did your country proud," he assured me.

I spent the next few days finishing my evaluation of the keypunch machine, arriving at the plant for a full day or night shift along with the operators, maintenance mechanics, and designers. I found that the machine had a fundamental flaw: its punching system did not leave clean holes in the paper. Far too many fibers remained in the punched holes for the electronic scanners to get accurate readings. The loose fibers, as I told Vice President Woodward on the telephone and in my memorandum, would produce false data. He was delighted with my report, which saved the company a good deal of time and money. As I had concluded the evaluation well ahead of schedule, he raised no objection to my spending a week in Paris.

Paris was Papa's favorite city. It was not at all like Düsseldorf, yet it too felt familiar to me. So much of the culture I had grown up on was there. I went up in the Eiffel Tower, climbed among the gargoyles on the roof of Notre Dame, and spent hours in Papa's favorite place, the Louvre. I walked the streets and read the bronze markers on the homes of the masters whose names were familiar from my childhood: the writers Hugo, Zola, Rousseau, Balzac; the painters Matisse, Courbet, Pissarro. It was like visiting old friends.

There was no way I could leave Paris without calling on my old machinist friend, Marcel Camus. He was delighted to hear from me and quickly brought together a room full of the brothers who had benefited from our IAM local's donations in the grim period after the war. They could not understand why I was no longer in the union and, worse yet, how I could work for a major corporation. No matter how many times I explained that the union had expelled me not once but three times, Camus and the French machinists couldn't believe that a workers' union would do such a thing. They were a nice bunch of guys, but it was clear to me that we no longer had much in common.

A short time after I returned from Europe, Vice President Woodward asked me to come up to Boston at my convenience to discuss a "personal matter." The words had an ominous sound. There were a lot of things about my past that had not been included on my original job application, for obvious reasons.

We scheduled a visit for the following week. I would have dinner with Dana, stay over at the Parker House Hotel, and spend the next morning at the company's research lab in Beverly. The latter appointment eased some of my anxiety. If I was going to be fired, why would he ask me to consult on mechanical problems at the research lab?

When we met in the lobby of the Parker House, Dana seemed perfectly friendly and at ease. We dined at a Boston landmark, Locke-Ober's, a very elegant Old Boston restaurant with black waiters in white jackets that matched the snowy tablecloths. Our talk was primarily about the equipment I had evaluated in Sweden. Why, he wanted to know, were the European engineers so wrong in their judgment of the machine? I thought it was probably their lack of experience with point-of-sale miniature punchcards and the problems of using high-speed IBM readers. He laughed appreciatively when I told him about my performance at the castle in Stockholm.

Somewhere between dessert and coffee, he said he wanted me to know something. It was his reason for asking me to come to Boston and was not the kind of thing he liked to say over the telephone. "The FBI came to see us about you," he said. I thought, I knew it! Those dirty bastards! Dana continued: "They told us that you had been a notorious communist in the past and had caused considerable problems in the unions." He paused. "They did say that was all some years ago. Now they think you could be helpful to the government by supplying information about other subversives." He stopped again, looking at me with amusement. "Were you really such a hell-raiser?" He didn't wait for an answer. "They wanted to know if the company would be supportive of their efforts." He gestured to the waiter for more coffee.

When the waiter had left, he said, "You need to know what we told them. First we discussed the situation with the personnel department at headquarters. We had to acknowledge that you had, for obvious reasons, made some mistakes in your job application." He laughed, and this time he slapped me jovially on the back. He was obviously trying to make things easier for me, but I thought it was all a nice warm-up to prepare me for the sad ending. What he said next made me certain I was hearing things.

"We informed the FBI that as far as USMC is concerned if you have broken a law you should be arrested, brought before a grand jury, and indicted. Then you should receive a fair trial and if, he paused and emphasized again, "*if* you are found guilty, the company would consider its course of action. Until then, we will do absolutely nothing. Furthermore, we would appreciate it if the FBI did not harass our employees at the workplace."

I was shaking my head in disbelief and was close to tears. Dana explained that the company was doing nothing special in my case. "This company firmly believes in the American system of justice. We don't want to be part of any games some people might want to play with it." I thanked him and said how much I appreciated their confidence; I hoped I would never disappoint them.

"Oh, incidentally," he said, as we got up to leave. "We never realized you didn't finish high school. No," he reassured me as I started to protest, "your application didn't say you had a high school diploma." It seemed that people in the personnel department thought I would have good potential for moving up in the company if I had a college degree. They wanted me to go through an evaluation and testing process to see where I would come out. "Then," he finished, "we could think about how the company might help you obtain your degree."

Sitting in my room a few minutes later I tried to make sense out of this conversation. My mind was spinning webs of joy and confusion. Not that long ago "imperialist" companies like USMC were my supreme enemy, and the working class and the unions were, I thought, my allies, my friends. Now it was all upside down. Now the bosses were defending my constitutional rights, telling the FBI they didn't give a hoot about my politics. What a contrast to the union leaders who pled with Hoover to do something to get "this notorious red" out of their hair. Which side was I on anyway? As I write this now, it seems ludicrous that I had the world so neatly divided between good guys (workers) and bad guys (bosses). I had grown up believing, in the words of the IWW Constitution, that "the working class and the employing class have nothing in common." I was still trying to get it through my head that it wasn't like that at all. Some corporate people were as humane and kind as any I worked with in the labor movement. Of course, some were bastards too, like some of those in the unions. The real world was turning out to be far more complex than the naive class definitions of good and evil I had absorbed at home and in the Party.

At the suggestion of the company I went to New York University's Educational Testing Center to evaluate my potential for college. I took a battery of tests spaced out over a four- to six-day period so I would not become "tested out." I showed up at the center the first day with an anxiety overload, sure it was my doomsday. The smell of the chalk and dust in the school building triggered reminders of some memorable failures at P.S. 34.

The session started with a short oral interview and write-up of my life history. The pleasant young woman counselor told me she was glad to have an opportunity to interview an, "older person"—no, she meant "a more mature man." The testing then began with a general knowledge or "extended intelligence test," to establish my level of acquired knowledge and help them develop an individual test plan. Supportive staff members went out of their way to put me at my ease, and I began to relax as I moved from one test room to another.

On the second day, I was given a series of spatial relations tests in which I had to piece together little blocks in a limited time. It was fun. For an old machinist accustomed to fitting together complicated assemblies of nuts and bolts, the tasks were ludicrously simple. Near the end of the second day, I was given an oral test of general knowledge. The questions began with simple ones like "Who is known as the father of our country?" then became increasingly difficult (Who was Galileo? What was he noted for? And so on).

The music identification test followed the same pattern, starting off with a few opening bars of "Stars and Stripes Forever," progressing to the Beethoven Fifth, the march from *Aïda,* and finally, Gregorian chants. The music counselor was interested in how I had learned so much about music. Living with Edith obviously played a role. But much further back, I explained, I grew up in a house full of music lovers. Papa loved opera, and we had many of the early records of Caruso, McCormack, Schumann-Heink, and Galli-Curci, as well as of the great symphony orchestras.

It was the same story with the art, books, plays, and ideas they asked me to identify. I probably learned about them all from the dinner-table converstions I sat through as a child. Hardly an evening went by without an argument over the day's events, politics, a new book, an art exhibit, and so on. Then there were the regular visits to museums and, when we could afford it, to the theater. I explained that Papa was a perpetual teacher for whom every situation was a learning opportunity.

Even an ordinary subway ride could turn into a lengthy discussion of the cultural backgrounds of the ethnic groups that inhabited the city. Apparently my brain was a sponge that absorbed whatever information was orbiting around it.

The test of my abilities in arithmetic, math, algebra, and geometry went better than I had feared. I was not pleased, however, to be asked to report to the director's office the next day! I was almost forty years old and was once again being sent to the principal's office. But it wasn't anything like P.S. 34; the director and his assistant went out of their way to be friendly. They were puzzled though. They asked to see the worksheets for the geometry problems, and I searched frantically through my briefcase until I found the crumpled yellow sheets at the very bottom.

The two of them huddled over the diagrams I had drawn. "Could you show us how you did this?" Using my compass, I demonstrated the various ways to square a circle, create triangles and parallelograms, and measure various distances and angles with the help of *Pi*. I had learned these methods, I explained, in the machine shop so I could lay out a job or operate various tools. They were pleasantly surprised with my novel way of learning by doing.

The last item of my evaluation was a projective test in which I was shown pictures and had to describe what I thought was going on. Maybe if they had given me a Rorschach test they would have discovered how troubled I was.

At the end of the testing the director and his assistant gave me their evaluation of my career potential and recommendations regarding college. The director described my test results in a matter-of-fact voice: "You scored in the top two percentile of all college graduates," he summarized. "Why do you think you need to go to college?" The percentile number simply didn't register with me right away; it was part of the academic jargon that intimidated me so much. I told him that my employers believed having a college degree would improve my potential as an executive. Besides, I knew there were major gaps in my education that I would like to fill in. "Like what for instance?" the assistant wanted to know.

"I know little or nothing of psychology, literature, religions. Besides Marxism, which I know too much about, I need to learn something about economic theory. The same can be said of sociology, history, and science."

The assistant explained that my creativity score was very impressive and that he believed college might do me more harm than good. The director, however, didn't agree and thought I was old enough not to be influenced by the conformity demanded by the university system.

"Me, conform?" I laughed, "That's rich! Almost the first thing Papa taught us was that we had to stand alone and not conform. In my childhood home, our heroes were the rebels of history: Spartacus, Tom Paine, Emile Zola, Emma Goldman, Sacco and Vanzetti, and any other nonconformists you can think of. Our child heroine was the little girl in the fairy tale who pointed out that the emperor had no clothes."

We all laughed, and the director suggested that I should come back to the center for retesting of my creativity after I finished college. They recommended that I look into a new accelerated degree program at Brooklyn College. It permitted adults to take exemption examinations to demonstrate competence in subjects learned through life experience; that would probably cut my class time in half.

Before I left, the director gave me a written summary of my test results. It was a warm sunny day, and I sat down in Washington Square Park to sort out the turbulent feelings the new information had unleashed inside me. Although I had learned long ago that I was not as dumb as I was judged back at P.S. 34, I had always doubted that any academic intelligence test would register the fact. It should then have come as wonderful news to learn that I had a high IQ and had scored in the top two percent of all college graduates in general knowledge. Instead I sat in the park in tears, the new information just adding to my growing depression. The report noted, among other things, that I was a person of "extreme mood swings," and I was beginning to learn how true that was. One of the winos who regularly inhabited the park invited me to take a sip of his Thunderbird. "Make you feel better, buddy. That's why I drink it. Makes me feel better."

"No, no thank you." I felt an overwhelming sense of shame for my years of stupid, blind, communist conformity. All the many excuses for being a failure that had taken me a lifetime to construct were demolished in those few days at the NYU Testing Center: "I was no good in school.

I never had a chance to go to high school. I'm just a dumb blue-collar worker, not like the intellectuals in the Party," and so on.

I tried to think. Where should I go from there? What should I do? In the weeks and months ahead I became increasingly depressed. I had a constantly growing sense that I was slipping toward an abyss. I needed to immerse myself in a new project, perhaps learn something about people and society and why they behave as they do. I might even learn something about myself.

22

Starting Over

With a glowing letter of recommendation from the NYU Testing Center, I was easily accepted into the new adult degree program at Brooklyn College. The company was pleased with my decision and were very cooperative about accommodating my class schedule. Four days a week I left the plant around five, grabbed a bite at Wolfie's Delicatessen, and was in class by six-thirty. Leaving school at ten-forty after a short schmooze with other adult students, I arrived home some time around midnight. I was up the next morning at six to eat breakfast with the kids and drive to the plant.

The adult degree program began with a series of seminars in the humanities, starting with the history of western civilization as seen through the eyes and ears of the writers, painters, composers, architects, scientists, philosophers, and—lastly—historians. Ruth K., the seminar coordinator, thought that the least effective way to learn about culture and tradition was by reading history books. "If you want to know who we are and where we came from, read the essayists and novelists of the time," she told us. So we read Homer, Aeschylus, Plato, Socrates, Thucydides, Racine, Austen, Mann, Wharton, Hemingway, and dozens of others.

A whole new world was opening up for me. But in order to make room for some fresh new ideas, I had to clear out all the tired, pat responses based solely on the class struggle. That was very hard. I began to realize that I had to get out of my own way. The old communist dogmas were like unwanted weeds in a newly planted garden; they constantly came creeping back into my thinking to supply fast, simplistic answers. It required constant vigilance to keep my mind clear of them. To make it ready for new growth, I developed the technique of visualizing my mind as a blackboard; before entering a classroom I would mentally wash it clean.

There was, however, a painful side effect of this cleaning. In the process of erasing what was left of all I had once believed in, I removed defenses I had built up over half a lifetime. I became far more vulnerable to the ghosts that had been safely hidden away in childhood closets. It was a treacherous process. Each time I opened myself to new learning, I became less and less able to avoid the shades of the past.

In Psychology 101, for example, I learned that the first step on the road to maturity was accepting responsibility for one's own behavior. That simple realization struck home hard. I had never taken responsibility for the conditions of my own life. No matter what had happened, it was always, "the system" that was to blame; there had to be an external cause for my problems. For me, it was eye-opening to read Carlyle's observation that the alpha and omega of all wisdom was to know whether to change oneself or the situation. I had always understood the necessity for doing the latter, but never the former. The class struggle had provided a wonderful escape from individual responsibility.

Of course, it sometimes *is* true—as it was during the Great Depression—that problems are primarily beyond the control of the individual. Yet even under those circumstances, there is always more to the story. In the sixties when I worked with teenagers from the Lower East Side ghettoes, I wished fervently that they had something equivalent to a Young Communist League to explain to them why the situation they faced was not wholly of their own making. Even a minor focus on the objective conditions would have helped them understand that they were not to blame for their poverty and its resulting misery. The Black Muslims were the only organization I saw that enabled some black kids to develop enough self-esteem to escape the trap of self-destructive ghetto culture and start assuming responsibility in a healthy way.

The psychology department at Brooklyn College was influenced by Abe Maslow, who had taught there some years earlier. The faculty members were not impersonal academics but compassionate human beings struggling to understand the effects of tough social and economic problems on human development. They helped me begin to understand the relationship between what goes on inside an individual and the world outside, and to see that people do have some control over at least parts of their destiny. It sounds pretty trite now, but at the time it was a sparkling new insight for me. It helped me understand that the Party and Marxist-Leninst theory, with their exclusive focus on the state, had no concern for the individual. If the inexorable forces of history determine everything, the individual simply does not count. Only the "masses" matter. In the early decades of this century, the Party dismissed the ideas of psychology that were then blossoming as pabulum for the masses, an excuse for bourgeois exploitation. It was that denigration of the individual that permitted leftist radicals to find excuses for Stalin's crimes.

One day in 1958 we were informed that the data processing division of USMC, including the old Kimball division, had been sold to Litton Industries. I had become quite comfortable working for USMC and had no idea what the sale would mean. USMC was a sleepy, kindhearted old monopoly that had, as I mentioned before, lost the right to lease their machines exclusively. Loss of the monopoly started the company down the road to being gobbled up by a conglomerate.

As in every takeover before and since, Litton assured the employees that everything would remain as it was under USMC management, except that the home office would be in Santa Monica instead of Boston. Just about everything did change, however. Litton was bottom-line obsessed. They were also politically very conservative. To my growing depression, I added a heightened paranoia about my communist past. A mere telephone call from the FBI, I was certain, would send me flying out the door on my ass.

For a while my work at the plant continued without much dislocation. In any case, my life was almost completely bound up in my college courses. Eventually, though, Litton became a very difficult place to work. The primary interest of the executives in Santa Monica was the almost-daily profit-and-loss accounting of our division. They wanted a regular profit margin of at least 15 percent. When we tried to explain the seasonal nature of our business, they were uninterested.

At USMC I had met a young entrepreneur who was developing a machine for making metal-encased plastic high heels for women's shoes. He was a liberal-lefty sort of guy, and we hit it off pretty well. He convinced me to help him with his heel project; if it was successful, we could both become rich. At this point of total confusion in my personal life, it was a nice detour and allowed me to bury myself deeper into work and school.

Although my college courses were my retreat, a monastery in which I could bury myself in learning, I still sometimes lapsed into my old persona. One night in Ruth K's humanities seminar, a student was reading from Dylan Thomas's play *Under Milkwood*. I was sitting at the back of the room, and I guess Ruth thought I wasn't paying attention. She asked me what I thought of Dylan Thomas. Without thinking, I replied that he had made some good free associations but didn't write very good poetry. As the last word came out of my mouth, I regretted being such a wise guy. Damn! I thought, will I never change?

She didn't give me a chance to apologize. Everyone in the class was silent, listening for what would happen next. After thinking for a few moments, Ruth said, "Mister Schrank, your assignment for this semester is to write a four-page, double-spaced poem in the style of Dylan Thomas. All right class, now let's have a real discussion of *Under Milkwood*."

That night as I drove home along the Hudson, I was overcome with a terrible hopelessness. I was sure I would never get the nasty, sarcastic side of myself under control. In spite of many resolutions, the old behaviors seemed to have a tight grip on me. Just past the George Washington Bridge I pulled the car over into the breakdown lane. As I gazed in tears at the bridge and the dark waters beneath it, I heard for the first time an soft inner voice telling me how very simple it would be: "Just walk up on the bridge, climb over the rail, and all your troubles are over."

The next night in the college bookstore I bought everything they had by and about Dylan Thomas. I spent every spare moment reading his poems and stories—*Adventures in the Skin Trade*, "A Prospect of the Sea" and, especially, "Do Not Go Gentle into That Good Night," which brought back aching memories of Papa's death. I learned that much of Thomas's intensity—and much of his appeal for me—came from his preoccupation with death. At the sad end of his days, he sat in the White Horse Tavern in Greenwich Village, drinking his life away. I never understood how his many admirers could think themselves kind for plying him with booze. In those last years, Thomas seemed to be running away from his own doom. Now, to me, he became a new-found friend who was opening up another world. Through him, I discovered the joys of reading poetry.

Writing it was another matter. I began tentatively, embarrassed at how personal it felt when I read my efforts to Edith and Lizzie. It was as though I were revealing the most secret parts of myself, parts I never knew existed. It didn't matter whether my verses were good or bad. I was only surprised that I could write them at all.

Around a month after she gave me the assignment, I unobtrusively laid my poem on Professor Ruth's desk before class. She said nothing, just picked it up and put it in her briefcase. After leaving me in a state of anxiety for several weeks, she finally asked me to stay for a few minutes after class. As she was shuffling through her briefcase, I kept up a nervous prattle about a movie I had seen, sure I had failed the assignment. She was a short, stocky, bright-eyed woman endowed with large breasts that made her look more maternal than sexy. What was most impressive about her was her intense devotion to her cultural mission. Her commitment to the humanities reminded me of myself as a Marxist.

"Oh, here it is," she said as she unearthed my paper. She smiled up at me with an expression of approval: "Is this your first effort at poetry?" I nodded. She questioned me about how I felt while writing the poem. Did I enjoy doing it? I confessed that at first I was scared to death and very sorry I had opened my big mouth. But once I got into the writing it became fun—at least when I was not stuck. Then it was terribly frustrating not being able to get the words to say what I wanted them to. She laughed, "You and every other human being who has ever tried to write a poem. You have a real knack for combining fine old English with 'turdy-turd' street New Yorkese. Wherever did you learn to write a line like, "it behooved the crook to consider the consequences?"

"I don't know. It just comes out that way."

For the rest of the semester she encouraged me to write more poems and spent out-of-class time going over them with me. Poetry became an important wedge for opening the dark closets where my childhood ghosts were hiding. For many years afterward, I always carried a little pocket notebook to jot down ideas and poems. I've written poems on subways, trains, planes, buses, park benches, and even in business meetings.

Between classes I was busy preparing for exemption exams. After all those years of debunking capitalist economics, I found the theories of markets, wage-price relationships, inflation, unemployment, and all their possible interactions relatively easy to grasp. The speech courses also turned out to be a waltz. The professor told us to pick a subject from a blackboard list and take ten minutes to prepare a fifteen-minute talk. I chose the Algerian struggle for independence.

At least one part of my past life proved very useful. "Where on earth did you learn to do that?" the speech professor asked when I finished.

"On Tremont and Prospect." He looked bewildered. Was there a speech school there that taught extemporaneous public speaking? I said, "There sure as hell was, right there on a street corner in the Bronx."

I did well in American history, government, and a variety of other subjects. I thought I knew some German, but that was just a laugh to the professor, who told me to forget it. Take Spanish, it's easier." I did. In all I accumulated fifty-four credits in exemption exams.

My mid-life college experience was like letting a poor child loose in an FAO Schwarz toy store to explore and choose from among all the goodies. There were intriguing new ideas to examine, and I was discarding old prejudices and dogmas. My courses in the arts and humanities opened the door to the spiritual and artistic sides of our natures and helped me comprehend, in some measure, the guardian angel fisherman on Lake George. He would periodically visit me and whisper in my ear to be tolerant of spiritual things I could not count, measure, or weigh.

My science courses gave me an opportunity to examine critically the claims that Marxism-Leninism was a science. I thought a lot about why communists needed to wrap themselves in the mantle of science. Because for modern men and women science is seen as dealing fundamentally with "facts"—and not with morality—speaking in the name of science permitted Marxist leaders to dehumanize the movement while simultaneously claiming that they were creating a "brotherhood of man." The so-called science of historical materialism and the "inevitability" of the workers' eventual triumph made anything done along the way excusable.

Studying the physical sciences helped me understand something of what is meant by the "scientific method of inquiry." My physics professor,

Homer Jacobson, taught us two of the fundamental organizing concepts of science: the periodic table of elements and the electromagnetic spectrum. Although before taking the course I had had some vague notion of these two concepts, I never really understood how the forces behind them affected literally everything in our lives.

A few years later, when I was teaching in the graduate program at New York University, I remembered the lessons in teaching I learned in Professor Jacobson's college physics course at Brooklyn College. It was just after the second semester midterm exam, and I was really struggling. He asked me to stay after class. He was a small, balding man with a kindly but somewhat distant expression. When he asked me if I had ever gone to high school, I told him that I had only taken a few night school courses. The problem was, he explained, that I didn't know enough algebra to work out the problems. Conceptually, he could see, I understood which formulas should be applied, but I got hopelessly lost in the math. I knew where to go but didn't know how to get there. I was embarrassed, feeling that I shouldn't have signed up for the course until I had taken some algebra.

As there were quite a few other adults in the course who lacked a math background, Professor Jacobson suggested an experiment. We should continue in the course but, in the tests, simply plug in the appropriate formulas without trying to work through the math. That would suffice to show whether or not we understood the solution to the problem. I thanked him and ended up doing okay in Physics 103.

On another occasion, Jacobson was lecturing on Boyle's law: the volume of a given quantity of gas varies inversely with the pressure exerted on it. He asked for a volunteer to describe the process. I raised my hand and made what I was certain was a crystal-clear explanation and sat down. Jacobson paused for a long moment, looked over at me, and said, "Absolutely wrong. But you said it with such certainty that I really wished you were right." The class laughed, and I realized ruefully that I was still operating in my old dogmatic mode.

Homer then went on to demonstrate the law with the help of a calculus proof of the formula $V = K1/P$. Starting at the blackboard in front of the room, he worked through the formula, keeping up a running commentary on what he was doing. Deeply immersed in his calculations, he covered a second blackboard wall with numbers. Finally, he stopped, turned to the class, and asked, "How many of you understand what I am doing?" Slowly moving from left to right, our heads signified a reluctant, "No"—reluctant because we loved Homer.

For a time he stood in quiet thought. Then he said, "Why doesn't the class go home or for a walk while the teacher goes to the library to see if he can figure out how to teach this course so his students will know what on earth he is talking about." The class stood and applauded him. I have never forgotten the lessons of that remarkable man. He became my lifelong model of a good teacher.

A few weeks before I was due to graduate in 1965 I received a message to come to the dean's office. What did I do now? I wondered, but Dean Gaeter was very friendly. "First, let me tell you that you've made Dean's List."

Not knowing what that was, I said, "How did I manage that, whatever it is?" Throughout my college career I had avoided receiving my grades, figuring that if I passed my courses that was good enough. He then told me that I would probably graduate magna cum laude. All this was very pleasant, but I was pretty sure it wasn't why he'd called me to his office.

I was right. The poor man could hardly get himself to say it. "We have just realized that you did not graduate from high school."

"That's right. I never said I did."

Now came the hard part for him. "No, you didn't. But because of that, we should never have admitted you." I thought to myself, Well that's your problem, not mine

He was clearly embarrassed. "Oh God, how can I say this? I know you'll think this is absolutely crazy, and it is. First I tell you will graduate with honors and then I ask you to take a GED examination to fulfill your high school requirements. There it is. I said it."

Stunned by the flattery of being an honors graduate and by the simultaneous humiliation of being told to take a high school equivalency exam, I lost my cool. "You know, Dean, I'm not going to take that chance.

Suppose I fail? How will the college look then? You can stick your honors and degree up your ass. I'll transfer to that nice Catholic college, St. Johns. They'll be happy to graduate me with the same honors." Out the door I went, slamming it behind me.

I was sitting in the cafeteria, close to tears and wondering what to do next. My classmates were sympathetic, but a bit amused. One friend, Michael, was, as always, philosophical: "It's just the system telling you to run once more around the track to satisfy some idiotic rule. By now nobody even knows why they made it." Someone else said, "Christ, Schrank, go take the test. It's just a couple of hours, and it'll be duck soup. Don't jeopardize what you've been working for these last years."

In the end, I decided they were right, but I can still remember the indignity I felt that Saturday morning slinking into Stuyvesant High School to take the GED with a bunch of scared, raggedy-looking kids. The Dean was pleasantly surprised when I handed him the GED diploma. He said he was sure I would go on to earn a Ph.D. and do the school proud. Having taken the GED later proved useful; when I was working with kids on the Lower East Side I was able to convince them to take the exam by using myself as an example. I also had a pretty good idea what they needed to know to pass it.

While all this was going on, my internal life was unraveling, and I was writing urgent letters to Sandra. "I need you now more than ever," I pleaded. "Please think of some way for us to be together." It was a cry for help, but she did not give me much encouragement. In my failure to convince her, I was becoming angry and frustrated. Having recently read Simone de Beauvoir's *The Mandarins,* I accused her of being one. In reply I received a treasured, and devastating, letter.

I am not at all concerned about the "eyes of society upon us" or on preserving a financial security for myself or my children. . . . I am concerned with the integrity of my relationship to myself—to you—the people I have a daily relation to are a test of my own identity, are a part of what I am and will be to you. I am in love with the world. I have a conviction that if we are honest we can live in it and fulfill ourselves. . . . I have not submitted, as you suggest, to the old codes or social pressures. I have done only what I felt was uncompromisingly true for me and you. . . . I think we can have whatever we want—if we know what we want. . . .

I refuse any but the most superficial of your analogy to "The Mandarins." . . . You can be mad at me for not being with you when you need me—as Harry is when I am with you. As I am when you punish me for the ways of the world. If we were with each other—we would not be together at all times—least of all if situations had transpired which you thought I would not have the grits to participate in. How about yourself in this situation of our own making? Do you have the grits to see it through with integrity? . . .

Right now it is you that are living in symbols not I. You are looking for a place in a fixed frame that has a mountain made of rocks and a sky that is only up and romantic simple people. If I cannot regain your trust and if you cannot learn it through your love of me, you will have to live out this nostalgic dream and then come back to me. I understand why you are stuck on this snag. It is not me. It is your world of machines and large numbers of faceless people. . . . I could be a retreat from it. A temporary retreat. In the end we would have to find out how to relate to your world of machines and faceless people. And that we can do now—not IF circumstances were different. . . .

I learned, much later, how right she was. *I* was the problem.

Probably as a result of my pressuring her, Sandra became increasingly distant. I got, finally, the letter that shattered me: "I looked in the mirror this morning and decided I am old," it said. She wanted to keep our wonderful relationship just as it had been, rather than subject it to the degeneration of aging, which was not the stuff of passionate romance. Again I felt an overwhelming hurt and rejection.

For years I had hoped that somehow she would find a way for us to be together forever. Out there in Colorado was the solution to all my wishes, the living myth, the embodiment of all my dreams of happiness. But the letter convinced me that we would never be together. After sitting in bars night after night listening to sad country songs and crying in my beer, I saw that I could end up on Skid Row. Difficult as it was, I had to bury myself in my courses instead of on "the lone prairie."

Sometime before, on the excuse that my school work kept me up late at night, I had moved into the room we had rented to the doctors from Hungary. Edith and I shared nothing but our common interest in Fred and Lizzie. Gradually I moved in my clothes, bought a small television set, and installed a coffee machine. Edith said I had become a boarder. She was right. The realization that Sandra and I would never be together had destroyed something inside me. Except for school, my life was on automatic pilot.

One day I put the Japanese sniper rifle into the trunk of the car. I wasn't sure why. A few days later, with Fred and Edith watching in a complete state of shock, I loaded my desk on top of the car, took my clothes and books, and moved into an uninhabited house in Forest Hills. It belonged to my sister Alice and her husband, but they didn't plan to live in it for some time. It became my monastery. I lived there in one small room with a bed, a desk, and some books in apple crates.

There was a garage behind the house. One night I drove in, left the engine running, and shut the door. Sitting in the car in a nice half dreamy state, I saw in my imagination my sister coming into the garage and finding me. She let out a god-awful scream that woke me with a start. I turned off the engine, staggered to the door, and opened it.

Across the street from the house was the Flushing Meadow Pond. I sat on the shore watching as the planes came in to land at La Guardia Airport, scattering the ducks. A few days later I wrote in a notebook.

Steel legged caterpillars Eat at the mallards' home.
Gorging the earth Giant metallic wings Bed with a shattering roar.
The wind whistles In winter's naked trees. Hear the fury of flapping wings
Where can they sleep?

Alice was concerned about me and insisted I get help, "before it's too late for all of us. Remember, if you do what I think you're contemplating, it's the ultimate act of hostility. Who are you trying to get even with?"

"Alice, what good is a life with absolutely no bodily feeling? Except for a small part of my brain, I am the embodiment of the walking dead. I really believe if you stick me with a knife I will neither feel it or bleed. I feel nothing, and I don't want to live this way." She persisted, insisting that there was help out there, but only if I wanted to go and get it.

After interviews with several different therapists, I met Ralph. He started his working life as a coal miner and had once been a psychology professor at the University of Washington. During the dark days of McCarthy, he refused to say "uncle" and was fired. He then became a practicing therapist. I was very lucky to have found him. He became a strong arm to lean on and a devoted friend.

The most painful part of the separation was my relationship with Fred, who was just eight years old. He would get on the telephone, crying and pleading, "Dad when are you coming home?" I tried to get together with him at least once, sometimes twice a week, but I saw that he was becoming a very sad-looking child. After one of our visits, I dreamed of him standing at a window, looking out and calling someone's name and crying. It tore my heart out. I went back to live with Edith and Fred, swearing to make it all different. My guilt and the projection of my own childhood trauma onto Fred caused me to remain in the marriage for another ten years. I doubt if it did any of us any good.

By the time I moved back home I was seeing Ralph twice a week. What we were dredging up was basically the story I have told in this memoir. How much crying can one person do? Or how many tears can be shed over traumas thought to be long gone? How many times do I have to relive the terror of those cat shadows dancing on the cellar walls? At each of our sessions I would start by talking matter of factly about something that had happened. Then from out of nowhere would come what Ralph called a "gotcha." Describing my visit to Frank Little's grave had me weeping uncontrollably, unable to speak. Very quietly, he asked, "Whose grave are you visiting?" It was Mutter's of course. Everything that related to death aroused the memory of that unresolved loss.

What saved me from sinking into a hopeless state of ceaseless crying was, I think, Ralph's wry midwestern humor. Like almost all men, much of my self-image was identified with my dick. When I complained to him that it's only use now was as a pisspipe, he said he didn't believe all the Freudian and Reichian notions that our whole being is embedded in the libido. Most of our troubles don't start there. Impotence is just a symptom, because we can't separate our sexuality from the rest of us. He suggested that I forget about sex for a while. Once I began to feel alive again, my friend down there would know it. "Just trust me. Once the erectile tissue gets reconnected, it will know exactly what to do."

A few days later I arrived at his office fuming and roaring that he didn't know what he was talking about. "The damn thing won't work. You said I'd be okay if I took it easy or something like that. Well, you know what, it's a total bust? I wish I was a Penitent. Then maybe I could get rid of those old ghosts with some good hard flagellation or a hair shirt or something." Ralph was laughing, wiping tears from his face. "What the hell is so funny? My tears are from crying and yours are from laughing. This is some weird kind of therapy. You ought to be paying me."

Wiping his glasses, Ralph said he couldn't help it. All of his life he had been looking for examples to prove his hypothesis that many men have far more brains in their penises than in their heads. I had finally given him substantial proof. "From the top of your head to the bottom of your feet, you say, you feel like the walking dead. Is that right?"

"Yes, that's true."

"Really now, how can you expect that thing between your legs to be its old perky self? Try to get it through your head that it's just part of the rest of you. The day you begin to feel like your old rambunctious self, so will it."

As the therapy proceeded, I found "gotchas" in the most unlikely places. My new job took me into an old industrial section of Brooklyn where there was a stable for horse-and-wagon peddlers. Often the best part of my day was stopping to pat the horses, smell the barns, and talk with the old Italian peddlers while they readied their wagons for the day's business. They said, "Nobody wanna do this no more. Kids, they just wanna hang around, do nothin'. Make much trouble. You see, we like the horses here. Like this old horse, we all die soon. That the end. No more peddlers ever. Is too bad, no?" It *was* too bad. I remembered how as a child I had listened for the friendly early-morning clip clop of the milkman's horse and ridden proudly on Miter Howe's wagon.

One morning as I passed the barn, I saw a dead puppy lying in the gutter with one eye open. It seemed to be staring at me with an accusing look I tried to close the eye. The peddlers advised me that the dog had been dead too long: "You no can close now." As I walked away, I started crying uncontrollably. For the rest of that day, I had to hide my tears behind the excuse of a terrible head cold. I couldn't get rid of that vision of the accusing eye.

When I told Ralph, he asked, "Who else's death are you responsible for?" In an instant I was gripped by violent sobs, unable to speak. He came to sit next to me on the couch. "Let it all out. It's okay. This is all the crying you didn't do when she died." He explained that all the secrecy and the story that Mutter had gone away were bound to make a small boy think he was somehow responsible for what happened to her. "Now this same small boy grown into a man feels in some strange way that he is responsible for the death of a poor little puppy dog on a Brooklyn street."

Occupied with my job, my school work, and intensive therapy, I had little or no emotional energy left for family life. Little by little, with no great drama, the family was breaking up. Hoping that a fresh start would bring me some measure of peace and happiness, I left the house for the second time after Lizzie left for Laos to work for the International Voluntary Service. Fred was in college escaping the draft and feeling mad as hell at his daddy for abandoning him. Years later while we were out sailing, he let me have it in an explosive burst of anger that cleared the air for us to begin building a new relationship.

For several years Edith's friends had been nagging her to go back to school and get "a life of her own." She finally decided to do just that and became a certified preschool music teacher with a full-time job.

Not long after she left for Laos, Lizzie, with the almost complete lack of ceremony typical of our family, sent us a postcard saying she was getting married. Growing up in a world of anarchists, I had gained no sense of the meaning of ritual in everyday life. Papa imbued us with a hostile attitude toward religious and patriotic celebrations and taught us to see them as "straitjackets of the mind." As a result, I knew nothing about how rituals create occasions for bringing and holding families together, and my kids missed out on that.

I now believe that as my political world unraveled so did my personal life. The beach in front of the house I live in now is visited every fall by horseshoe crabs shedding their old shells. I have often watched the long struggle as they fight their way out of the shell in order to grow a new one. If they don't, they die. Fighting off old dogmas was much like that; it required an enormous effort. The process of questioning all aspects of my life left me with a numbing depression.

Epilogue

The Brooklyn Museum of Art was a short distance from the heel plant, and I often went there to eat my lunch. It was an oasis of beauty in a desert of urban decay. In its galleries I was learning to see, through the eyes of the artists, that demons live in all of us and that mine were not unique. I was discovering the spiritual nature of art, which spoke to the very emotions I was trying to understand.

On a beautiful spring day in May of 1962 I finished my lunch under the watchful eyes of Gaston Lachaise's big-breasted fertility women, then drove to a machine shop in Long Island to pick up some molding dies. The convertible top was down, and Mozart's *Magic Flute* was playing on the radio. When I got near the plant the weather suddenly changed. Dark clouds were rolling in fast as I parked the car and closed up the roof.

The plant was some distance from the parking area. The path to the front entrance was surrounded with a glorious burst of spring color from masses of azalea bushes. They were the same color as those at the cemetery where Papa and Mutter are buried. As I paused to admire their splendor, the heavens suddenly opened up and the rain began to pour down. I was wearing a short-sleeved cotton shirt, and I could feel each individual raindrop as it pelted my arms. Every drop made my skin sing. I stood there laughing joyfully, my face tilted toward the sky. From the windows people inside the office were peering out at me. I had an urge to rip off my clothes so I could feel the raindrops on my whole body. I am better, I thought. I can feel again. It's a miracle. I need to thank my guardian angels, the museum, Alice, Ralph. I need to call him right away.

I was soaking wet and still laughing by the time I made it to the office. The folks there thought I was nuts. The boss was shaking his head: "I've heard of people who didn't know enough to come in out of the rain. You're the first one I ever saw just stand out there loving it."

"Yes, yes," I said, "I do it all the time. I'm just a freak when it comes to spring rain." He wanted to know if I had any dry clothes to change into? "No, it's alright," I said. "I just need to use your phone."

Some weeks later a former vice president of Litton Industries, Frank Ricciardi, called to tell me he was taking a job at the Linde Corporation and wanted me to come with him as a plant manager. It was a good-paying job within commuting distance of the city. I said I'd have to think about it. Somehow I had a strong feeling that this was not my path. Serving time in the corporate world had been a great learning experience, but it was time for something different.

A few days later Professor Harold Prochansky from Brooklyn College called to tell me about another job opportunity. The attorney general of the United States, Robert Kennedy, was concerned about rising rates of juvenile delinquency in the cities and was putting together a program to tackle the problem. Training for work was to be an important component. He suggested I talk with Jim McCarthy and some of the people at Columbia University who were planning the program. The idea, which became the Mobilization for Youth, was an ambitious effort to help ghetto youth gain the skills they needed to rise out of poverty.

On my way to the interview, I drove through the streets of boarded-up buildings, empty stores, and rubbish-strewn lots of the Lower East Side. I thought I must be nuts for even thinking of working there. The interview went well. With my experience in "the real world of work," the planners thought I would be a great asset to the program. There was one problem: the pay was about half of what Linde Air Products was offering. I said I would have to think about it.

Driving home along the East River, though, I knew I was going to take the job, low pay and all. It was a real challenge, in some ways similar to my work in the unions. This could be a new movement, a cause. It wasn't a far-off dream like establishing a socialist workers' paradise but an attempt to fix a hard social and economic problem in the here and now. That's what the unions did so well, and what I did so well.

The job was a start on a whole new life journey, a discovery of a world hidden from my old, narrowly focused conception of the class struggle. I had been looking through the wrong end of the telescope. Once I turned it around I saw that the world abounded in an endless chain of connections and ambiguities. There were no simple answers, just limitless opportunities to explore the time-honored questions: Who are we? How did we get to where we are? Why are we here? Learning how our predecessors had asked and answered these questions would give me plenty of challenges for the rest of the twentieth century. My rebirth was proving to be a remarkable experience.

Index